WOMEN SHALL P

CELEBRATING 125 YEARS OF ORDAINED WOMEN IN MINISTRY IN THE CUMBERLAND PRESBYTERIAN CHURCH

THE HISTORICAL FOUNDATION
OF THE CUMBERLAND PRESBYTERIAN CHURCH
& THE CUMBERLAND PRESBYTERIAN CHURCH IN AMERICA

MEMPHIS, TENNESSEE
2014

Women Shall Preach: Celebrating 125 Years of Ordained Women in Ministry in the Cumberland Presbyterian Church. Compiled by Susan Knight Gore. Digital preparation and formatting by Matthew H. Gore for the Historical Foundation of the Cumberland Presbyterian Church and the Cumberland Presbyterian Church in America. Entire contents ©2014 by the Historical Foundation. Individual contributions remain the intellectual property of the writers who are entirely responsible for their content. Inclusion does not imply endorsement by the Historical Foundation nor any other team, board, agency or institution of the Cumberland Presbyterian Denomination.

First printing, May 2014.

ISBN10:   0692221433
ISBN13:   978-0692221433

Historical Foundation of the Cumberland Presbyterian Church and the Cumberland Presbyterian Church in America

8207 Traditional Place
Cordova (Memphis) Tennessee 38016-7414

WOMEN SHALL PREACH

CELEBRATING 125 YEARS OF
ORDAINED WOMEN IN MINISTRY
IN THE CUMBERLAND PRESBYTERIAN CHURCH

Introduction

Matthew H. Gore

What went through the minds of those members of Nolin Presbytery as, on Tuesday, November 5, 1889, they set apart diminutive Louisa Mariah Layman Woosley as an ordained minister of the Gospel? Were they aware of the monumental step they were taking? Did they realize the significance it would have in the Cumberland Presbyterian denomination and, indeed, in the reformed family of churches?

Louisa Woosley was, like *True Grit's* Mattie Ross, "a Cumberland Presbyterian and proud of it." In a ministry that touched seven decades, Louisa never left the Cumberland fold. In 1906, when a large portion of Cumberland Presbyterian clergy left for the Presbyterian Church, Louisa remained to watch her detractors depart.

With her ordination in 1889 came a battle on the synodic and denominational level over the ordination of women and the place of women in God's plan. It was not until after the so called liberal clergy departed in droves in 1906 that opposition to her ordination withered and not until 1920 that women were denominationally recognized as fit to be ordained.

It seems so obvious today. Simply, our God is not limited by our prejudices over who is, or who is not, needed to serve the Kingdom! Still, over six generations later, there are still those in Christendom, even in Presbyterianism, that deny the power of God to use women to spread the gospel as ordained clergy.

This is not the case in the communion called Cumberland Presbyterian. While women may still struggle with salary equality and may sometimes have a harder time finding a church to pastor, there is not a presbytery in either Cumberland Presbyterian denomination which would deny the right of Cumberland Presbyterian women to be ordained.

On the occasion of the 125th anniversary of Louisa Woosley's ordination, this volume celebrates Cumberland Presbyterian clergy women. It includes the heartfelt preaching voice of women across the spectrum of Cumberland Presbyterianism, 69 sermons in four languages from three continents. There can be no doubting the sincerity of that voice.

Certificate of Ordination

of

REV. *Mrs. Louisa M. Woosley*

This Certifies that *Mrs. Louisa M. Woosley*
the bearer, is a regularly ordained minister in the
Nolin-Leitchfield presbytery of the Cumberland
Presbyterian Church, having been ordained by
Nolin presbytery of said church on 5th
day of *November* in the year *1889*.

SIGNED:
Rev. Henry C. Hook ———— Moderator
Elder W. M. Kelly ———— Stated Clerk
OF *Nolin* PRESBYTERY
THIS THE 5th DAY OF *Nov.* IN THE YEAR *1889*.

Ordination Sermon by Rev. J. S. Ward. Text: Mark 16:15.
Rev. W. E. Wortham presided and gave the charge.

vi

Mothers Who Stand Alone

Louisa Woosley

To be unequally yoked together as husband and wife, father and mother, in the home is one of the saddest pictures upon which it has ever been my lot to look. At best this is a hard old world for women. Now as from the beginning, man in his fallen state, because of the depravity of his nature, continues to rule over her. Witness the degradation of the women of China and India where the light of the gospel of Christ has not shone.

Many mothers are forced to walk the way of life alone. Their sons are not with them. They must see the world, are busy here and there, sowing their wild oats regardless a mother's tears and prayers. While the place at her side, where father and husband should sit, is vacant. Some of these mothers have waited long, with heavy hearts and aching heads, the ushering in of a brighter day. They feel deeply the absence of their loved ones from the place of prayer and song.

This feeling of moral and spiritual separation, as they tread alone the narrow way, is one of the sharpest pains that ever thoughtless cruel son or husband thrust into the heart of wife or mother. O the sorrow, the agony, she suffers, forced, as she is, to leave behind in her onward march those she loves best. Many mothers today are wholly responsible for all the spiritual training their children will ever get. In the home she is the one signboard and guiding star. In spite of the handicaps of a father's indifference, many Godless lives, Christless examples and, mayhap, teaching, she may succeed in bringing her children into the kingdom and inspire them to noble lives and heroic deeds; to the dedication of their time and talents to the Master.

I once read in an old book of one who came with her two sons in spite of the fact when they were in the place of worship the father was always conspicuous for his absence. These can, in course of time, be numbered with the twelve and serve as a monument to her fidelity and training, a witness to a mother's power, and the influence of her love in overcoming opposing conditions to mold the young manhood of the world. Dare any of you criticize or condemn this noble woman because of seeming ambition and place seeking when she came to Christ with the earnest plea, "Grant that these my two sons may sit one on thy right hand the other on the left in thy Kingdom." Who but a mother would dare ask so much?

True to her strongest characteristic she still carries her boys on her heart. Mother-like asking for them not herself—but for them the first place. So long as the record stands that "She came with her two sons to worship him," so long shall she remain a model mother and picture of loving devotion and worthy of the sympathy and imitation of all the mothers in Christendom. God grant us a generation of such mothers!

A most pitiful sight, a Godless, Christless mother. On earth no needs Him so much as the mother, and for no other has he done so much. To me one of the most pathetic sayings in the whole Bible is that of **Matthew 22:20**, *Then came to him the mother of Zebedee's children with her sons worshiping him.* What a picture; how beautiful. And they did not forget, nor did God forget, mother and sons going together, to the place of prayer, their little hearts like wax to receive and marble to hold, are taking lessons under a mother's guidance, their first lessons in school of God. Impelled by a mother's love, she braves the storm , climbs over the difficulties, and leads the way. I see the salvation of the sons only over the shoulder of their mother who struggled bravely on in spite of the father's carelessness or indifference. All honour to such mothers. I am not surprised to find her, with a few others, moved with love and pity lingering around the cross when all masculine courage had failed, and again at the break of day at the sepulcher of the Lord on that glorious Easter morn.

I feel the world should call a halt long enough to pay a tribute of love and respect to this woman—the wife and mother—who gave to the world, to God, and to the church two such illustrious sons. To what extent her beautiful consecrated life and example inspired and influenced the lofty careers of James and John none but God can know. With their lives before us we believe as never before though she is dead she still lives and speaks, and her works do follow her. Who could possibly overestimate of the influence set in motion by this one mother? Yet her work is not done; she stands in the book of God an inspiration to motherhood an incentive to honest earnest effort, even though we stand alone without the encouragement of the husband and father. As we are unable to sound the depths of a mother's love, so we are unable to measure the power of her influence.

What a happy scene! A mother in Israel leading with her own hands two manly boys, the pride of her heart, to the Christ and with them kneeling to him in worship. Could they forget? Could you forget? Not me, while memory holds her throne. What would the world and church do today but for the mothers, who like Salome are leading by precept and example their children to Christ, to the place of prayer. Instilling into their minds and hearts the principles of a holy faith, a faith that shall abide the storm of doubt and time. But for them the church, the world would be poor indeed, many homes mantled in darkness and much of our manhood would be shorn of those lofty qualities of character that make men good and great. Mothers, be not cast down or discouraged, though for awhile you, like Salome, kneel alone. God in heaven knows how you mourn the absence of those you love. Though the father fails, you need not.

Aye; there's the rub. Here we have run upon the skeleton in the family closet. There seems to have been only four in that home. How different things might have been. But for the shadow of the husband and father this would be an ideal home. He is the one discordant note, marring an otherwise beautiful picture. He breaks, and makes a happy family circle incomplete. But little is said of him; the only distinction he has is that of being the husband of Salome and father of James and John. He seems to have lived and died in obscurity. The fame of the other members of the family emphasizes his obscurity and give ground for the supposition he was not in sympathy with them and their aim, and was indifferent to the cause they loved.

His continued absence from the family and place of worship suggests his character and manner of life. In spite of all this Salome maintained her integrity and with her faith fixed in God, a faith that will not falter, laughing at the impossible and crying it shall be done; took her sons by the hand and made her way to the place of prayer and would be satisfied with nothing short of a crown and throne for her sons. A throne and a crown! Do you see them? Are they not worth working for? They are for you and your children. With mothers like that there will not be as many empty pews in our churches, altars forsook, pulpits vacant, and spiritually orphaned children.

Only a mother's love can endure such trials, and triumph over such obstacles. Ring ye bells of heaven! Shout ye angels of God! Open wide ye gates of gold! Mother is coming, her sons with her, to receive a crown and reign in glory forever! "And I heard a voice saying Hallelujah it is done and they stood before the throne and before the Lamb, clothed with white robes, and palms in their hands, saying Amen. Blessing, and glory, and wisdom and thanksgiving and honour, and power, and might be God's forever and ever. Amen. Then one said "What are these which are arrayed in white robes, and when came they?" And I said sir, thou knowest. And he said unto me, "these are they which came up out of great tribulation and have washed their robes and made them white in the blood of the Lamb." Therefore are they before the throne of God day and night—in his temple. They shall hunger no more; neither thirst anymore; for the Lamb which is in the midst of the throne, shall feed them, and shall lead them into living fountains of waters; and God shall away all tears from their eyes, and there shall be no more night.

CONTENTS

Introduction

    Matthew H. Gore v

Mothers Who Stand Alone

    Louisa Woosley vii

The Sermons

Faith: Dead or Alive?

    Mindy Acton 1

Find Your Passion

    Marty Aden 8

The Space Between Us

    Lisa Anderson 15

Blessed Be the Tie That Binds

    Mary McCaskey Benedict 19

The Walk of Love

    Elizabeth Karen Brasher 24

The Holy Spirit Is Coming

    Elinor Swindle Brown 27

Does Prayer Make a Difference?

    Whitney Brown 32

Ditching Jesus

    Jill Davis Carr 36

180 Degrees: Jacob

    Amber Clark 39

Getting Rid of Our Excess Baggage

    Marcia Compton 46

What Is Your Name?

    Lisa Cook 50

A Call to Break Paradigms

    Maria del Socorro Delgado 56

The Transforming Love

    Esperanza Díaz 60

Misses to be Avoided

    Gloria Villa Diaz 67

The Hem of Jesus' Robe

    Virginia Espinoza 75

If Walls Could Talk

    Nancy J. Fuqua 80

New Life in Christ

    Michele Gentry 85

Putting our Baskets in the Water

    Linda Glenn 93

God is in Control: Easter Sunday

    Melissa R. Goodloe 97

Witness

    Susan Carole Guin Groce 101

*The Responsibility of the Believer is to Be
Respectfully Obedient to God, Our
Sovereign Lord*

    Luz Dary Guerrero 107

The Call
      Donna Stockberger Heflin........ 112

For We Cannot But Speak The Things Which
      We Have Seen And Heard
      Luz María Heilbron. 116

Nothing is Trivial to God
      Donna Lee Hollingshed......... 121

The Present of Christ's Presence in the Present
      Linda Smith Howell. 125

Ms Helen's Funeral Service
      Cardelia Howell-Diamond. 129

Hero of the Era
      Ella Hung. 133

Women are Always Starting "Stuff"
      Versey Jones................ 144

The Difference a Dollar Can Make
      Abby Cole Keller. 148

I Am Calling You
      Mary Kathryn Kirkpatrick....... 154

Baptism of Christ
      Sherry Whitaker Ladd. 161

God's Refination
      Jenny Lam. 165

Step out and Follow the Leader
      Paula Shepard Louder.......... 170

Wake Up!
      Tiffany Hall McClung.......... 175

The Price
      Rhonda McGowen............. 179

Sheep or Goat? Trouble Everywhere!
      Judy Madden.. 186

Earthly Treasures
      Melissa Malinoski............ 195

What Happens When Jesus Comes to Town?
      Theresa Martin. 200

Bridges
      Brittany Meeks. 205

With God on the Mountain
      Jennifer Newell. 216

Waiting on God
      Sharon M. Notley. 223

Not What But Who
      Lisa Oliver. 233

Doubt
      Susan Parker................ 239

Hunger Pangs
      Lisa Peterson.. 245

The Towel of Jesus
      Pam Phillips-Burk. 250

Gone Fishing
      Patricia J. Pickett............. 254

Father Forgive Them
      Zenobia Rivera.. 257

Love—the Most Excellent Way
      Linda Rodden. 260

In the Garden

     Missy Rose. 265

A Life That Hits the Bull's-eye

     Josefina Sánchez. 270

Arise, Shine!

     Lisa Scott. 275

Invitation to the Kingdom of God

     Nobuko Seki. 281

Untie Me and Let Me Go

     Teresa K. Shauf. 286

The Children's Table

     Sandra Shepherd. 292

There's Just Something About This Jesus

     Terra Sisco. 297

What Cha Talking About?

     Cassandra O. Thomas. 303

Rock-Faces and Trust

     Micaiah Thomas. 315

Whom Will You Serve?

     Laura Narowetz Todd. 321

Heavenly Rules You Shouldn't Forget

     Diana María Valdez. 327

Get Up!

     Fran Vickers. 331

Reign of the Shepherd

     Joy Warren. 337

The Storms in Life

     Gloria Washburn. 345

Blinded by the Light

     Diann White. 352

Let Your Light Shine in the Darkest Places

     Virginia Washington. 357

The Father's Heart

     Eliza Yau.. 362

Strangers in a Strange Land

     Betty Youngman. 366

Do Not Be Afraid

     Grace Yu. 372

The Arm of the Lord

     Susanna Yuen. 376

The Contributors. 382

Faith: Dead or Alive?

Mindy Acton

(James 2:14-26)

Acts 20:26b: "…Also, I preached that they should repent and turn to God and prove their repentance by their deeds."

We have discussed repenting and turning to God. Now we prove our repentance with our deeds.

About Faith—

We tend to see faith as sacred like grace, justification, righteousness, and redemption.

But it is not. Faith in itself is not sacred at all. It is not part of the Deity. Yet it is vital to our salvation. It is a vehicle, a tool; like our free will. Our free will cannot save us. It is vital to our salvation. We have to USE our free will to gain Christ. That is how it is with faith. We must USE our faith in order to be saved.

My hope today is to change your understanding of what faith is and is not. I will compare it to marriage throughout the sermon. Marriage changes everything in your life. You do things and do not do things based on the fact that you are married. All of your decisions are filtered through marital relationship. The same is true for your Christianity. Everything changes—what you do, what you do not do, how you do it, etc.

Faith is the *vehicle* through which you live your life in Christ. That relationship, like a marriage, changes in every way. The way you "do that change" is through the vehicle of faith.

So the term, *dead faith*, is it an oxymoron? Is it mutually exclusive? No it is not. Can a marriage die? Faith can, and sometimes does, die.

Faith—(pis-tis) persuasion, moral conviction, system of religious truth, system of beliefs.

Examples: Christianity, Atheism, Humanism, Jehovah's Witnesses, Islam, cults, pagan idols.

All of these, along with Christianity, are systems of belief. The non-Christian ones are just wrong systems of belief.

What beliefs do:

| Console | Moral Compass | integrity | ethics |
| Convictions | lifestyle | Priorities | hope |

Belief determines what truth is to the person. We see this in politics, denominations, created laws, etc.

In the case of Christianity, our faith is built on the *eternal Truth*—factually proven historically recorded death-conquering faith.

But our faith can be as dead as idol worship **IF** it is faith without corresponding actions.

This may seem strange, but we see dead faith regularly:

- Global Warming—proponents live opposite of this
- Socialized Healthcare—proponents don't want it for themselves
- Class Warfare/Socialism—not their money, others

Faith is a vehicle to be used to gain salvation. It is not the saving agent itself. What Christ did is our salvation. Christ's factually true events of birth, sinless life, death on a cross for our sins, descent into Hades and resurrection is what grants—provides

salvation for us.

Faith is the vehicle we use to receive the free gift of salvation. It is the package in which our salvation is wrapped. Like a present. We don't keep the paper and throw away the gift.

Back to Dead Faith—

People use faith for dead things all the time:
Idolatry—worship the soccer god
False religions—worship a dead prophet
Money—worship a dollar bill
Sports—football, basketball, baseball, etc.
Etc.—and on and on…

On the other side of the coin…

People also use dead faith trying to gain REAL salvation without evidentiary deeds.

Claiming Faith without Actions/Works—

- People claim salvation "by faith" (they say) But nothing changes in their lives, priorities, relationships
- People become "silent Christians" (closet believers) Ashamed of the Gospel
- People are NOT living their belief out loud (Peer pressure) What will they think?
- People are NOT sharing their faith, loving unconditionally, telling the world (ashamed of the Gospel)
- People are NOT caring for the poor, sick, widowed or imprisoned (narcissism)
- People are NOT, NOT, NOT!

BUT!!!

James 2:18 "Show me your faith without actions, and I will show you my faith by what I do."

Believing in God does us no good. It is irrelevant. Does this offend you? Remember even the demons believe in God—and shudder. That does not save them! It won't save us either. THAT kind of faith is DEAD FAITH.

James' question, "Can faith without works save you?" is rhetorical. The answer is an understood "NO!"

Faith without deeds is dead (a corpse). Like a body without a spirit is faith without works.

Matthew 7:21-23 tells us to do the woks the Father commanded in His Word. Otherwise, our faith is dead.

So, how do we make it alive? With actions!

Hebrews 4:2 "For we also have had the good news proclaimed to us, just as they did; but the message they heard was of no value to them, because they did not share the faith of those who obeyed." ("…because those who heard did not combine it with faith.")

Here we see the perfect example of the symphonic harmony of faith and works. It could not be expressed better. The ones who obeyed are the ones who had (& mixed) faith with what they heard.

In other words, what they heard impacted them so strongly, that they did what was said, and proved their faith.

What kind of actions?

- Witnessing actions—tell your story, live the joy, give the love
- Lifestyle actions—banking your life on the Truth of it (Rahab, Abe for Isaac),
- Discipleship actions—in Word, prayer, worship

- Holy Living actions—Rom. 1:1 set apart = limited by boundaries

James gives us two big examples in our passage.

Abraham with his son Isaac being offered. Abraham is considered the "Father of our Faith." He banked his heritage and family line on the Truth of his faith. Abe had already received Isaac raised from the dead. He knew God had called him to be the "Father of Nations." God also promised through Isaac it would come. His faith was considered righteousness before God. He willfully and obediently took Isaac to the sacrifice and was ready to offer Isaac on the altar.

Paul refers back to Abe's faith in Romans 4 telling how it was attributed to him as faith. The promise God gave Abe was physically impossible. Yet Abe chose not to waver in unbelief. He strengthened himself in faith…being fully persuaded that God had power to do what He had promised!

What has God promised you?! Do you still believe?

Rahab was the opposite of Abe. She was a female and a Gentile AND a prostitute. She, like Abe, was saved by her faith. The faith that she proved out in her actions. She housed, fed and protected the spies from the guards in Jericho. Then sent them home the opposite way she sent the spies. She banked her life on her faith literally. Her actions that proved her faith saved her AND placed her into the lineage of Jesus.

Have you banked your life on your belief? Does your faith prove what you believe? Have you laid it all on the line for what you believe? Lesser faiths have laid it all on the line for a lie. Can we do it for the Truth!?

Put up or die!

Other Examples—

The disciples left everything and everyone to follow Jesus.

Paul, then Saul, lost everything, suffered many abuses.

Phillip lost his life. He was the first martyr in the New Testament.

What about you? What have you lost? Has your faith cost you anything? Do people know you are a believer? (I mean the ones who don't see you in church.)

- Do you "believe aloud?"
- Do you love others unconditionally?
- Do you help the poor? Orphans? Widows?
- Do you verbalize what God has done for you?

Such works that our faith produces are the purification of our lives. In other words, my genuine faith causes me to do things that purify my life. (Just like my carnal flesh causes me to do things that destroy my life.)

- If I believe the sermon on the Mount, I will change as it commands me to.
- If I believe pure and undefiled religion is attending widows and orphans, I'll do that.
- Etc. throughout the Scriptures.

These are ways to make our faith alive. These deeds/corresponding actions prove our faith, belief in our hearts.

True faith will have actions alongside of it. Only dead faith will have no deeds. We saw this in Abraham and in Rahab. We saw it in the disciples, Paul, and Phillip.
Romans 5:1 (Read)

This passage tells us what our faith ***does for us:***

- Justification (sinlessness)
- Peace (in relation to a holy God)
- Grace (power to do what is right)

What is the other side of the coin? ***What do we do for our faith***?

Faith, we said, proves our belief and reliance on Christ. What do we do with this faith that proves such belief in Christ?

- He who wins souls is wise (Prov. 11:30)
- Looking after widows and orphans (Jas. 1:27)
- Be peacemakers (Matt 5:9)
- Giving to the destitute (poor)

And on and on. Love, learn, and live God's Word. This is how we are made able to learn and do "faith proving" actions.

We all know people who say they have faith but have no actions to prove or even indicate it. Our Scripture today tells us this faith is dead- a corpse.

It is also called other things in the Bible:

- Dead Fruit (Jesus w/fig tree)
- Living under the Law is death. It's a substitute for true works of faith
- Obedience to Jesus is how we prove our faith in Him.

Faith can and is dead sometimes. Make sure this is not true in your life.

Hebrews 6:10, 11 "God is not unjust; he will not forget your work and the love you have shown HIM as you have helped His people and continue to help them. We want each of you to show this same diligence to the very end, *so that what you hope for may be fully realized.***"**

Let us leave with James' words about faith and actions:

- Faith, by itself, if it is not accompanied by actions, is dead.
- Show me your faith without deeds. I will show you my faith by my deeds.

Find Your Passion

Marty Aden

Preached at Winter Park Presbyterian Church in Wilmington, North Carolina, by Rev. Marty Aden, March 24, 2103.[1] Following is a transcript of a recording of her sermon that Sunday.

Thank you for having me here in this capacity this morning. I think everyone here knows me, but in case you don't I'll say again, I'm Marty Aden. I'm the Director of Spiritual Care at New Hanover Regional Medical Center, which encompasses Cape Fear and Pender, and several other campuses that the hospital has made agreements with. And this is the first time publicly I get to thank you for all your prayers and support that you gave me when I had back surgery. I know you've seen me walking around here with a cane, and I've got it behind me here, as I walk down the aisle with it today. I may not need it, but I'm afraid I'm going to fall and I sure don't want to go through all that again! So I thank you for all the prayers and support you gave me through surgery and the healing process.

As I was telling the children, today is Palm Sunday. It's the beginning of Holy Week. In the gospel of Luke, Luke puts a lot of stories that may be familiar to us in the context of Holy Week. So we don't hear all the way from chapter 19 to chapter 23 this week, which is all of what Luke puts in the context of Holy Week, but we remember some of these stories. Like as soon as Jesus comes into Jerusalem, he weeps over Jerusalem, and says, "Oh, if only you would recognize me and recognize who comes to you." He goes to the Temple very quickly, and turns over the tables and "cleanses" the Temple. We talk about him cleansing the Temple. He has various debates with the Pharisees and the Scribes, one of which is about paying taxes to Caesar. They say, "Here is a coin that has Caesar's head on it, so who do we pay our taxes to? To God or to Caesar?" And Jesus says, "Give Caesar what is Caesar's and give God what is God's." With each encounter he knows that he's

---

[1] Winter Park's senior pastor retired at the end of 2012 and Marty was asked to preach a few times before the church called an interim senior pastor. Marty currently serves as the Director of Spiritual Care for New Hanover Regional Medical Center in Wilmington. She attends Winter Park Presbyterian regularly.

gaining popularity with the people, but he's also infuriating the religious leaders.

They come to the Temple one day when he's teaching, and they ask Jesus, "Where do you get the authority to teach and preach in the Temple like you're doing?" Instead of answering them, he says, "Well, where did John the Baptist get his authority from? Was it from humans, or was it from God?" So they stepped back a minute, huddled with each other, and said, "Well, if we say 'His authority came from God.' then he'll say, 'Then why didn't you believe him?' And if we say 'His authority was from people, humans' then the people are going to rebel because they believe John was a prophet." And so they said, "We don't know. We're not going to answer that." And Jesus said, "Then I'm not going to answer you either."

The week went on like that, and they never could really catch him in anything that would get him into trouble. But they just got madder and madder at him because he was gaining popularity and he was doing stuff like that, that made them feel foolish.
And so... that had been going on before he went to Jerusalem, and so I think, kind of like Martin Luther King knew before he went to Memphis, that there was a chance he was going to get assassinated, I think Jesus knew, before he went to Jerusalem, there was a good chance he was going to be killed.
So why did he go?

One reason was, it was Passover. It was a Jewish festival. It's one of the three pilgrimage festivals that Jewish people celebrate, especially - still do - but especially during that time, the place to go was Jerusalem. The Feast of the Tabernacles and the Feast of Pentecost, which will be coming up soon, and at the Feast of Passover- these were times when every good Jew went to Jerusalem, to be in Jerusalem to celebrate this holy time.

That's one reason the people were set up in the Temple selling things, because this was like a big... say the Superbowl was coming to town. And everybody's coming to town, and you got the vendors setting up, and they've got all their wares, you know, because there was a big crowd coming - people who usually weren't in Jerusalem. They were coming to town. And that's the people Jesus chased out of the Temple, saying, "You're just making this all about money. You're not making it about being faithful; you're making it about

9

making a profit." So he cleansed the Temple of those kind of people. That's why they were there.

So Jesus knows; he did go, knowing there's going to be trouble; he spent the week teaching and talking to the people in the Temple; and making the leaders so mad that by Thursday, he's got a pretty good idea that things are going badly in Jerusalem. And things are going to come to a close pretty quickly.

So at that supper, the Passover meal they were celebrating together, he tried to teach his followers, tell them one more time, and show them, what they were supposed to do when he was gone. And they didn't quite get it… until he was arrested, tried, and convicted, and finally executed on Friday. So this Holy Week remember his crucifixion on Friday. We call that his "passion." The Passion of Christ. That's what we call that event. So today is both Palm Sunday and Passion Sunday, which points toward his death on Good Friday.

The word "passion" means "suffering," or means "to suffer." We usually think of passion as meaning something about love or about sex, but an older, archaic definition of passion means "to suffer." It can also mean a strong desire for something, or an intense driving conviction, or an unflagging pursuit of a cause. So this morning I want to talk about passion.

While I was preparing the sermon, I was somewhere, in the hospital, probably doing something, and waiting on something, and there was a TV going that was showing some gymnastics. And I watched these girls who were 12 to 14 years old on this balance beam that looks like it's about 2 inches wide - it's probably about 6 inches wide - it looked about as wide as their foot - and they would jump and spring off, and do these flips in the air and come down and bam! land solid on this bar. And they just froze there.
Or they would flip and land - and land - you know, sit down on the bar, and I thought, "Gosh, that's got to hurt." You know? And then they'd dance around and make it look - whether they meant to or not - they'd make it look like, "I meant to do that," and they'd do their routine and finish it. And then the camera switched and they had these young men who look like they're about 18 to 20 years old - a little bit older - on those parallel bars. And you know they would do the same thing. They would flip and stand straight up in the air, and just stop. Then they would flip and flip and drop on their armpits, and - oh! - and then

they'd hold their legs straight out, and they'd just stop right there - spilt second stop. And I thought, "Man, that's got to hurt!" It's beautiful to watch, but I think it's got to hurt. What would make somebody practice that much? What would make somebody dedicate their life to doing this? Because you can't get that good unless you give up everything else. You give up going to the mall with your friends, and you give up going to movies and stuff, and you are dedicated to doing this one thing so you get really good at it. The people who do that, do it because they have a passion for it. Hours and hours of practice because they have a passion for it.

And at the same time I was thinking about this sermon, I started looking at this website by this guy called Scott Dinsmore. The website's called "Live Your Legend.com" He talks about "finding your passion," and how do you live that out. I was talking to one of my friends at work about that, and she said, "That sounds like Simon Sinek's book, Start with Why. He says you have to figure out why you're doing something so that you know your purpose, and when you know your purpose you can connect to your passion."

All around me, I was hearing the word Passion.

Now these two guys I was just talking about were talking about business - what you do for a living - and finding what you're really supposed to do, and why you're supposed to do it. But both are talking about passion, and saying that life is too short to be miserable. You need to have passion in your life to make life worth living. And passion is knowing that you have to do this thing - whatever your thing is - you have to do this thing, or you're just going to die. That your life will be meaningless, so you might as well die, if you don't get to do this thing.

You may not know who Louisa Woosley is. I'm a Cumberland Presbyterian minister which means I'm kind of a cousin to you PCUSA folks. She was the first woman ordained as a Cumberland Presbyterian minister, and probably the first woman Presbyterian minister of all faiths - all ilk's - ordained in 1889. She felt called to preach early on, at about 12 years old, but knew that women didn't do that kind of thing, so she fought that call. She thought, "Well... I'll marry a preacher, and that's almost as good. I'll be a good preacher's wife, and that's how I'll fulfill that calling." But her husband wouldn't answer the call either, so he wouldn't be a preacher. So she was a good wife and a good mother -had some children - and she kept wrestling with this call and running away from God. She fought it, and got so depressed, and got so sick that she was literally on her death-bed. They had candles set out for the vigil, and they had the made her coffin, and they were bringing it into the house. She was really that desperately ill, on her death-bed, and she finally said, "Woe to me if I do not preach!" At that moment, she surrendered to the call, got up out of bed, and I think started cooking for the visitors in the house. At that moment, she was like, I've got to do this thing or I'll die. And so she did. For the next 50 years or more, she lived out her passion, and brought many people to the gospel, started several churches, went on to be moderator of the presbytery which at first wouldn't recognize her ordination, and made her way and lived out her passion.

That started me thinking about this church. What's our passion as a church, as a congregation? I hope we can, and I invite us to give that some thought and prayer as we enter the search for a new pastor. I know it's too early in the process, and we Presbyterians do all things "decently and in good order" - I know it's too early in the process to do that profile of the congregation that we have to do. The Session has to put together what our strengths are, what our weaknesses are, what we'd like to do, and that kind of thing. But, I don't think it's ever too early to try to figure out what our passion is. What's the one thing that we must do, as a congregation, or we might as well just give it up and go home. What is that one thing we must do?

My passion, personally, is to help others find healing and wholeness. That's my ministry—it's my calling—and that's why I do the job that I do. I'm not just Director of the Spiritual Care Department - even though that's very important to me—I'm a Clinical Pastoral Education Supervisor. When I was going through Clinical Pastoral Education, or CPE, my Supervisors helped me heal some old wounds, and become more of a whole person and find more balance in my life. If I'd had CPE before I was a pastor, I sure would have been a better pastor. When I realized that, I thought, man, that's what I've got to do. I have got to help other ministers find healing and find wholeness so they can be better leaders, so the churches that they serve can be places of healing and wholeness for the people in the church. That's my passion. I get passionate about education and I get passionate about ministry and about people healing the wounds that they carry around with them. That's what I must do, or else I might as well just die. It's the one thing that gets me up in the morning; it's what keeps me going when I get discouraged.

So as a congregation, what's our passion? What's our Why? Why are we here? What purpose is God calling us to accomplish?

I remember when I was a youth and I went to camp, one of the things they use to do with us in small groups was tell us to pretend like your house was on fire and you've got to get two things out before the house burns down. What are those two things you grab? It was an exercise intended to help up clarify our values and what's important to us. As I remembered that story, I remembered a story about this church. One of the stories in the history of the church is that the church caught fire, and the two things that were rescued were the bible and the baptismal bowl. Right? You remember that story right? I don't remember the name of who did that, but I remember the story. So if we claim that history, if that's who we are - we people of the bible and baptism - is that where our passion is? And what does that mean? Does that mean that we're here to make disciples, like through evangelism? Is that what we should be doing? Are we here to make disciples through education, and that's our purpose? Do we want people to hear the Word of God and be baptized so that they can enter a meaningful relationship with God? And what does that mean? Are we people who take the gospel and our own baptism so seriously that it effects all the aspects of our life? And if we are, does that mean that this congregation would look different than it looks now?

Howard Thurman, the famous theologian, said this, "Don't ask yourself what the world needs. Ask yourself what makes you come alive, and then go do that. Because what the world needs is people who have come alive."

So my challenge to us today is to find our passion, and find out what makes us come alive as Winter Park Presbyterian Church. But as I issue that challenge, I have to say that there's a risk involved too. Marianne Williamson said, "Our deepest fear is not that we're inadequate. Our deepest fear is that we're powerful beyond measure." So one risk of finding our passion is that we'll find and claim our power. And the world doesn't always welcome power - especially if it upsets the status quo. Which is what Jesus found.

Elizabeth Kubler-Ross said, "It's very important that you only do what you love to do. You may be poor, you may go hungry, you may lose your car, you may have to move into a shabby place to live, but you will totally live. At the end of your days, you will bless your life because you've done what you came here to do." That's living with passion.

The risk of living your passion is that you could be laughed at, you could lose the things and the people who are important to you, you could get in trouble, or, like Jesus, you could be killed. Like Gandhi, Oscar Romero, and Martin Luther King Jr., we could be killed for living out our passion, living out our calling. What if we decide as a congregation that we're going to work for justice and equality, and that means we're going to get involved in the efforts to end racism in the Wilmington area. How would the town react? What would Presbytery say?

What if our passion is to welcome all those who are not welcome anywhere else? The homeless, the drug addicts, the homosexuals who can't find a church home? And we said, "We don't care who you are. God loves you and we're going to live that out and prove it to you. What would the neighbor's think? Would we go beyond the bounds of PCUSA somehow and ruffle some feathers? Know what? Once we connect with our passion and know that that's the one thing we have to do, it really doesn't matter anymore.

Jesus rode into Jerusalem knowing that he had to teach and preach and tell the truth - even if it cost him his life - because not to do it would mean his life was worthless. So once we connect with our passion and find that one thing that we have to do, then we'll know we are doing what we were put here to do, the thing that God is calling us to do, and in the end, nothing else really matters.

May God bless us in that journey. Amen.

The Space Between Us

Lisa Anderson

(Luke 16:19-31)

The Rich Man and Lazarus[2]

19-21 "There once was a rich man, expensively dressed in the latest fashions, wasting his days in conspicuous consumption. A poor man named Lazarus, covered with sores, had been dumped on his doorstep. All he lived for was to get a meal from scraps off the rich man's table. His best friends were the dogs who came and licked his sores.

22-24 "Then he died, this poor man, and was taken up by the angels to the lap of Abraham. The rich man also died and was buried. In hell and in torment, he looked up and saw Abraham in the distance and Lazarus in his lap. He called out, 'Father Abraham, mercy! Have mercy! Send Lazarus to dip his finger in water to cool my tongue. I'm in agony in this fire.'

25-26 "But Abraham said, 'Child, remember that in your lifetime you got the good things and Lazarus the bad things. It's not like that here. Here he's consoled and you're tormented. Besides, in all these matters there is a huge chasm set between us so that no one can go from us to you even if he wanted to, nor can anyone cross over from you to us.'

27-28 "The rich man said, 'Then let me ask you, Father: Send him to the house of my father where I have five brothers, so he can tell them the score and warn them so they won't end up here in this place of torment.'

29 "Abraham answered, 'They have Moses and the Prophets to tell them the score. Let them listen to them.'

30 "'I know, Father Abraham,' he said, 'but they're not listening. If someone came back to them from the dead, they would change their ways.'

31 "Abraham replied, 'If they won't listen to Moses and the Prophets, they're not going to be convinced by someone who rises from the dead.'"

---

[2]Luke 16:19-31 read from *The Message*

I was privileged to work as a chaplain in hospitals for 20 years of my ministry. In one of my first experiences as a companion to children who were dying at a local pediatric hospital I realized that whether I wanted it or not I was forever changed by the experience. I was keeping vigil with a family in the ICU one day. I walked to the window to glance outside of the dreadful suffering I found myself to be part of for just a moment. Out that window was a major interstate packed with automobiles and trucks on their way somewhere very quickly. I thought to myself, they have no idea what's happening in this room and I used to be them but once you know suffering exist in such graphic ways you can never stop knowing it.

In another ministry setting I met a homeless women, her name was Gwen. She was a devout Christian, a gentle soul who came to our church to experience hospitality through food, clothing, a hot shower and a safe place to sleep. As I got to know her she would share more and more about her story and most of all about her relationship with Jesus. She always had her Bible with her and told me it was the only possession of the very few she had that she cared about. Gwen stayed with us at the church once a week for 5 months. Shortly after our Room in the Inn ministry stopped Gwen was murdered downtown on the steps of a church. She had told me that she would most often sleep on the porches of churches because it made her feel safe. I can imagine the busy flow of traffic on work days and on Sundays that passed Gwen without even seeing her yet she was there, clinging to her Bible and hoping that at some point the church doors would be open to her to ease her burdens. Yet she died on the outside, just within reach of the sanctuary protected by locked doors. Once again I had an experience that would change my life because once I knew Gwen and her tragic story I could never stop knowing it.

The story Jesus told to his followers in this passage has roots in a folk tale that seems to have its roots in North Africa and through that great oral tradition found its way into Egypt and into the villages where Jesus was teaching. The church that Luke was writing to would have been familiar with at least the gist of the story.

The descriptions of the two main characters are even familiar to us today:

16

The rich man lived in a gated community and wore the regal garb of a fortune 500 company, he lived the life of a person of wealth and privilege that gave him no time for even seeing the needs around him.

The description of Lazarus is just as clear but oh my . . . we experience it more graphically. Starvation, sores soothed by the tongues of dogs . . .and now we are turning our heads away from the graphic suffering too.

These two guys never interact with each other which is the point this story makes about the enormous chasm created by their economic differences. They were separated not by their location, not by their humanity and not even by their religion. What kept them from having a relationship was their place in the economic structure of society.

Somewhere in the sharing of this Jesus teaching Lazarus gets a name and the rich man just remains nameless, which is another way of helping us to understand that for Jesus, the poor are ALWAYS more real than those who do not see them. Lazarus looked longingly at this man, seeing that he has the ability to ease his suffering. The rich man never sees Lazarus . . . which is his ultimate sinful undoing, it lands him in a painful reality of his own.

The two men die and even in death they continue to be separated by this gap that cannot be filled at this point. It is interesting to me that after they die the descriptions of the two are reversed. We get a small sketch of where Lazarus is and how things have turned out for him but we receive great detail of the suffering of the rich man. . . unquenchable thirst, torment, agony. And now we want to turn away from him.

The emphasis on the story continues to be helping us to see what it is that brings about suffering, both in our immediate life and in our spiritual condition.

Even in this after life misery the rich man cannot separate himself from worry about the very things that landed him in a pit of suffering. His wealth has isolated him in his earthly life and now even though he has a story to tell, it is for the most part still focused in a selfish way. His concern is focused in a narrow way on the members of his own family and on preserving for them a way of life that he could not give up.

Just let Lazarus go tell them, how could they not listen to a man who has come back from the dead. Well the answer is the same as it was for the rich man himself. They would never see him, in their world of wealth and privileged status Lazarus would still be invisible, eternity did not make him wealthy so his message would be no more heeded than the message of Moses and the prophets which clearly inform God's people that we are instructed by the Creator of the universe to give preference to those who have less than we have.

So here is the scandal for today: God is biased toward the poor and in a society of injustice and preference toward greed and wealth we must ignore that to continue on our way and in our life of comfort.

Who do we believe about the realities of the world around us?

We believe stories of poor people taking advantage of the system, we believe stories that it's the poor people who have made the system corrupt and broken, we believe stories that our help will only make the problem worse. We follow examples of charity that never builds relationship and structure that does not offer healing.

So maybe if someone could just come back from the dead and explain it to us. Well I don't want my friend Gwen to ever have to come back here and I believe that would be the reason for keeping Lazarus safe in the bosom of Abraham for God also. But WE are the people of that very story. The tellers of the story of a God person, Jesus of Nazareth, who showed preference to the poor, the lonely, the sick and the oppressed and yet we are still waiting for that God person to rise from the dead as an avenger and warrior. We are often as deaf to the realities as those who have not heard.

Thanks be to God we have a chance on this side of eternity to get it right and to bridge a gap between us and those who suffer because it is what God calls us to do. Amen.

Blessed Be the Tie That Binds[3]

Mary McCaskey Benedict

(Ephesians 3:14-21)

[14] For this reason I bow my knees before the Father,[a] [15] from whom every family[b] in heaven and on earth takes its name. [16] I pray that, according to the riches of his glory, he may grant that you may be strengthened in your inner being with power through his Spirit, [17] and that Christ may dwell in your hearts through faith, as you are being rooted and grounded in love. [18] I pray that you may have the power to comprehend, with all the saints, what is the breadth and length and height and depth, [19] and to know the love of Christ that surpasses knowledge, so that you may be filled with all the fullness of God. [20] Now to him who by the power at work within us is able to accomplish abundantly far more than all we can ask or imagine, [21] to him be glory in the church and in Christ Jesus to all generations, forever and ever. Amen.

Over the last couple of nights together we have approached this section of Ephesians through the lens of our relationships with God and our relationships with the church and within the church. Now that we have built a solid foundation of our most critical relationship, that with the Lord, and our history within the church, we are ready to take on the relationships that tend to shape our day-in, day-out lives—as followers of Christ and leaders in ministry—those relationships within our families.

I am always bothered by the encounter of Jesus when there is the announcement that his mother, brothers and sisters are outside the meeting place and they want to see him. Jesus seems, at times, to cast off his family, saying that the people around him are his brothers and sisters. He summarily dismisses his family with a few words . . . on the other hand, as he is dying on the cross, he looks down at his mother, he gives her over to John who is standing beside her, saying "Woman—your son, son, your mother." We learn, in this moment, He was concerned in taking care of his mother.

---

[3] The final sermon from a series of three presented at the Presbyterian Chaplain's Retreat, Montreat, North Carolina, 2013.

As you well know, One of the Ten Commandments is directly related to our family—"Honor your father and Mother". I could continue to build a case with other examples from Scripture, but surely you know that your family is important. And the Christian faith has a great deal to say about and to influence us about our families.

The writer of Ephesians says "14 For this reason I bow my knees before the Father,[a] 15 from whom every family[b] in heaven and on earth takes its name." Let's examine our family relationships.

I.   FAMILY RELATIONSHIPS ARE DIFFICULT

We could spend all night discussing details about the obvious—family relationships are often difficult, particularly given our roles within the military during a time of war, but you know that. You know that prolonged separations, constant relocations, carrying other's burdens as we serve in ministry during a great time of need for the military all lead to unique challenges within our family relationships. Being a military wife myself and seeing the challenges my own family faced as my dad served as a Chaplain, I have seen firsthand many of the challenges your families have probably faced and are possibly currently facing tonight. Given those very personal experiences and combining my time with other military wives Bible studies I've led and with other families due to my role as a Family Readiness Group Leader for my husband's command, I just want you to know that I get it. I'm sure I haven't seen it all, but it's safe to say that I've seen enough to know that Christian families, military families, and families in ministry need desperately to take a hard look at what's going on within their own walls and their own family trees. All too often we spend our time trying to take care of those outside our family and neglect those within.

But instead of dwelling on the obvious all night, let's spend our time a little more fruitfully—examining some truths from Scripture about how we can strengthen and grow these key relationships.

A.   We are called to be both forgiving and loving in all our relationships, and those within our families often provide the greatest opportunity, right? The end of Ephesians 4 teaches us to forgive each other, just as in Christ forgave us. And 1 John 4:19 reminds us to 'love because He first loved us." I was amazed, in preparation for these sermons, how many family relationships are recorded in the New Testament alone—I have already mentioned sisters Mary and Martha, cousins Elizabeth and Mary, but there are brothers Simon and Andrew, James and John, even Mothers-in-law as with Simon Peter, whose mother-in-law gets out of a sick bed to fix a meal for Jesus and the disciples—Timothy and his mother and grandmother, Barnabas and his nephew John Mark, husband and wife Priscilla and Aquila, the Jailer and his family—the list is endless . . . but perhaps the most poignant family story is one that is probably very familiar to you—of a father and two sons—one who is wild, and goes for escaping the family and living an uncontrolled and permissive life—the other son who stays with the father, doing just about everything a good son should—and when, after wasting everything he had, the youngest son comes home to seek forgiveness and reacceptance, the good son becomes self-righteous and is bitter because the father has not only accepted the young rebel but threw him a party. You can draw lots of truths from the story of the prodigal, but one that works in family relationships is that we often need to accept and forgive one another. There will be a time when someone in the family says something they shouldn't—when someone in the family forgets a special day—when someone in the family engages in activity that goes against the grain—and it will be important for the family to be both loving and forgiving. The father, in Jesus' parable is living out one of the main requirements of family relationships—forgiveness.

Not only is that important, but we need to forget —separate as far as the east is from the west. Aren't we thankful that we can approach the King of Glory with complete confidence and freedom because of the grace that has been poured out on us? It's that same radical forgiveness that we are expected to extend to our family members, not keeping any records of wrong as 1 Corinthians teaches. Perhaps love is never tested as it is in the family. But because of that and the weakness we all display there, what an incredible opportunity for God's power to be made perfect in that weakness so that He can be glorified. John 13:35 teaches something so simple and yet so powerful—"By this everyone will know that you are my disciples, if you love one another." If we're having difficulty in our ministry calling perhaps it's time to take a look at how we're loving those closest to us, trusting that the Lord will be made known by how we love one another. And perhaps, what Paul said to the Corinthians is worth remembering over and over again, if you are anything like me: "Love is patient; love is kind; love is not envious or boastful or arrogant or rude. It does not insist on its own way; it is not irritable or resentful. It does not rejoice in wrongdoing—it bears all things, hopes all things, endures all things." All of that works in the family relationships.

B.   I could probably stop there and we'd all have enough to chew on when it comes to the relationships within our families, but I want to go a little further. If we really believe that the Lord orchestrated these relationships and can use them for our good and His glory, then we should move one step beyond just forgiving, loving, and accepting one another. We should identify and celebrate each other's unique gifts.

Martha owned a house near Jerusalem—living with her were her sister Mary and brother Lazarus—they were good friends with Jesus—there are recordings of Jesus visiting this house, and Martha, working in the kitchen while Mary sat and listened to Jesus teach. Martha complains, asking Jesus to send Mary to the kitchen to help. Jesus does several things, but one thing he does do is allow for both Mary and Martha to offer their gift—Jesus doesn't tell Martha to leave the kitchen and join Mary, nor does he send Mary out of the room to work in the kitchen. Not only should we celebrate each other's gifts, we should not be jealous of the other's gift. My Mom is able to sew—to make clothes from scratch—it is not my gift—I applaud her gift. I may have gifts that she doesn't have. Together we can celebrate. Elizabeth and her cousin were both expecting at the same time—one would birth the Messiah, the other an announcer of the Messiah, a forerunner (a supporting character in the life of Christ). Together they sing songs of praise, neither saying my expected baby is more important than yours. I remember drawing some awful pictures when I was in grade school (art was not my gift), but when I brought them home, they were placed on the fridge as if they were award winning pictures. Isn't it interesting and true that the qualities that once attracted us to our spouses are the same ones that later grate on us as annoying? Perhaps that's because those are the qualities that are the weakest in us and the strongest in our spouse and God didn't do that by accident—that's an opportunity to learn and grow, as iron sharpens iron from Proverbs.

Let's celebrate the gifts of each member of the family, keeping in mind that we were all created in the Father's image so we certainly all have something uniquely beautiful worth celebrating.

II.   FAMILY PRIORITY

As we conclude this series and this time together in this incredible place, I want to leave you with something that you may have already realized during this downtime with family, or reflecting on family. We must pay more attention to our families if we expect to grow in our relationships with Christ or be effective ministers of the Gospel. To be concerned about the marriage relationships of our young troops and ignore our own marriage relationship is a travesty—to worry about the children of our service people and ignore our own children is a sin . . . as we minister to families, we must minister to our own families first. If we destroy our health trying to be so much to others that we can't reach out to the inner core of our own family, we will have done an injustice to the very calling we have. And as spiritual leaders, if we see ourselves as constantly needed and can never "unplug," then we are elevating ourselves above God because God alone is able to do immeasurably more than all we ask or imagine.

Paul urges us to live a life worthy of the calling we have received, in the beginning of Ephesians 4. He goes on to explain how to do that, starting in verse 2—"Be completely humble and gentle; be patient, bearing with one another in love. Make every effort to keep the unity of the Spirit through the bond of peace. There is one body and one Spirit—just as you were called to one hope when you were called—one Lord, one faith, one baptism; one God and Father of all, who is over all and through all and in all. But to each one of us grace has been given as Christ apportioned it." Let us remember, as we go out from this place, that His grace is sufficient for us and covers all we have done and all we do. Let's move forward, in our personal relationships with God, in our work as ministers of the Gospel, and in our relationships within our family, with a fresh realization of that grace and expectation of God's power as we seek Him in all we do.

Conversion causes us to walk the walk and talk the talk. And that brings us to a conclusion—a recognition, a celebration—that we are Children of God—joint heirs with Jesus, and having taken a look at our covenant relationships, we affirm with Paul: to him be glory in the church and in Christ Jesus to all generations, forever and ever. Amen.

Communion

Since we know we have a relationship with Christ, let's prepare to affirm that as we remember that Christ's body was broken for us . . . that his blood was shed for us . . . and that because of that, we are children of God. As we have feasted on information, on the Word of God, now let us feast on the bread and wine of the Gospel . . .

The Walk of Love

Elizabeth Karen Brasher

(2 John 4-6)

[4]"I rejoiced greatly that I have found some of your children walking in truth, as we received commandment from the Father.[5] And now I plead with you, lady, not as though I wrote a new commandment to you, but that which we have had from the beginning: that we love one another. [6] This is love, that we walk according to His commandments. This is the commandment, that as you have heard from the beginning, you should walk in it."

Our walk of love starts with our own desire to share the free gift of Jesus Christ to all the world. My example of the walk of Love for Jesus Christ is when he carried the Cross to Calvary for all of us. Can you just close your eyes a minute and try to picture Jesus walking up the hill to Calvary with the Cross on his back and the crown of thorns on his head. He loved us so much that he was willing to give his life freely so that we could accept him into our hearts and have everlasting life. This is the kind of love that we cannot give back the same way Jesus gave to us, but we can give back a different kind of love through loving one another and sharing the Gospel of Christ whenever and wherever we can.

Walking in the truth means having a relationship with God. It means learning and teaching ourselves daily how to gain a closer relationship with him and have him close to us in our hearts. To walk in God's love with a genuine heart, the relationship must be based on his Word. The only way to do that is to read and study God's word daily and talking with him on a daily basis. We should even pray that God will guide us to things like books, conferences, Bible studies and much more to learn his word every way that we can.

God's number one commandment for us was to love one another. We cannot witness to others without that love and compassion for our lost brothers and sisters in the world. When John is talking about "the elect lady" in these verses, he is talking about the Church. We are all part of the Body that makes up the Church of Jesus Christ, and that means that every one of us should do his and her best to share his Word with as many people as we can on a daily basis.

We learn, as we have read our passage today, that God's love is the basis of His own desire for our obedience and love. Jesus Christ revealed his will through his teachings in his Word. We should not only read his Word daily, but we should live his Word out loud as much as possible. A lot of people will see our faith and love for Jesus Christ through our testimony of living that Word. When we show love to one another, we are obeying God's Commandment and showing him that we love him enough to share his Word with others.

I once read a statement that has stuck with me and I think about it almost on a daily basis. That statement is "Love is an unlimited resource readily available to us, and it is tremendously effective in furthering the work of Christ." (James Merritt) Every time I read this, I am reminded that we can always give the gift of Love. Not only just in holiday season, but Love is a gift that we can give daily throughout the year. It does not cost us anything to give but it may require that we reach out to unlikely people and sometimes it may require us going or doing something that is outside of our element to do.

When we walk in Christ's commandments, we will know that God's blessings are upon us. God will supply our needs and he wants us as Christians to supply his Love to as many people as possible. I encourage you to look around when you go to the grocery store, post office, or department store and share the love of God whenever you can. When you leave the check-out line say such things as "Thank you" and "God bless you." You never know when you are planting seeds of God's love. When you see someone at the grocery store or department store that needs help reaching something, or even they may have dropped something, be kind and show love by helping them. When you leave, say "Your welcome" and "God bless you." An example of mine would be: The other day when I was leaving the grocery store their was a little older lady parked beside me and she was trying to put the groceries in the trunk of her car. I immediately stopped and began to help her. She started smiling from ear to ear and just kept saying thank you so much you are very kind. I told her she was very welcome and I hoped that she had a great blessed day. The older lady looked at me and said " May God bless you in many many ways. Sometimes it just takes a smile and a kind word to help turn around someone's day.

Showing God's love is just as important and maybe even more important, than just saying the words. When people see you live what you say, it makes a huge difference. This is exactly what God wants us to do in our lives each day. God is Love and he will guide you every single time if you just ask him to. He will guide your steps and show you his love every day. Never ignore the Holy Spirit, and always know that God will never put more on you than you can handle. Even when it seems like the load too much to bear; the Father, Son, and Holy Ghost never leaves your side.

It is important to recognize and know that the Holy Spirit is your guide. When you feel that unction to do something outside your comfort zone, know that God is with you. We know from reading the Holy Bible and even reading our own Catechism that "God is the one living, active Creator of all that is, seen and unseen. He will guide and direct your thoughts, words and actions. Our fear filled zones are the Holy Spirit's comfort zones. When we cannot, He will. When we freeze up, He flows freely.

We are all made in God's own image, and "God reveals Himself to us as Father, Son, and Holy Spirit." We know as Christians that the Holy Spirit is everywhere and the Holy Spirit connects us to God and his love. We learn that the Holy Spirit calls all of God's people to trust in Jesus Christ and to live our lives in the Covenant of his precious and Holy Grace. We cannot fully understand the power of the Holy Spirit. We can fully know in our hearts, through the Bible, by the church, and as believers that God, through his Holy Spirit, will be our Guide.

Keep in mind that all through your Christian walk you are going to fall short from time to time. The ones that fall short and learn from their failures are the ones that develop a closer relationship with him. God knows we are not going to be perfect. He does not expect that from us. God does expect us to come to him when we fall and allow him to show us the correct path for next time. I myself receive comfort as well as direction when I turn to his Holy Word for help.

In closing, I just want you to think about the walk of love that Jesus Christ took for you and me as he walked up the Hill of Calvary. Ask God to guide your walk of love and to show you his will for your life and what he desires for you to do. It may be as simple as sending a card to someone or just smiling at someone and telling them that Jesus loves them. We all need Jesus Christ in our lives. He desires for us to lead the lost to his free and unspeakable Gift. That Gift is the Gift of salvation. I encourage you to read and study his Word daily and talk to Jesus on a daily basis. Let him, and him alone, be your Guide.

We first must know Jesus Christ Who is the Son of God. Then we have to accept Jesus Christ into our hearts through the Holy Spirit. Then we can begin to walk with God the Son, Father, and Holy Spirit and know one day we will be with our Heavenly Father forever.

Thank you and God Bless you. Let us Pray.

The Holy Spirit Is Coming

Elinor Swindle Brown

I believe I have been filled with the Holy Spirit. Do you? There are specific times that I can point to and say to myself and God "The Holy Spirit was with me especially here." I have been filled with so much emotion while writing a sermon that I know the Holy Spirit had to be with me. I could have been struggling with the words left and right and suddenly the words began to flow out onto paper like I was holding one of Harry Potter's wands rather than a pencil. I have been filled with inspiration while creating a church banner. One minute there was nothing. The next minute, I am drawing, something that does not come easily to me and I am creating something that is meaningful, not only for me, but to others as well. I know this could only have come from the Holy Spirit, so much so that I cannot possibly take credit for what just happened. I once sat in the General Assembly, in Albuquerque, New Mexico, listening to the special music of the Heights Church musicians. I could not stop myself from sobbing because the music written especially for our denomination's important meeting spoke to me with such force. I knew that the Holy Spirit was with the musicians and with all of us who were worshiping there.

And then one of those eerie times when I knew the Holy Spirit was with me. A time when I did want to reach down and take my shoes off for I knew I was on holy ground.

It was several days before I was going to meet with the session of the Cumberland Presbyterian Church of Germantown, where I normally attend church, to invite them to begin a discernment process. I woke that particular morning with thoughts about a scripture I might use to begin the meeting. As I ironed my clothes that morning, I remember the scripture that kept coming to me was "By the waters of Babylon, we laid down our harps and wept. How can we sing a happy song in this foreign land..." Whoa, that doesn't sound like a good scripture to encourage a church to go through discernment. "Too depressing God. Sorry, try again." But all day long, this scripture kept coming back to me and I continued to put it out of my mind.

Davis Gray, the executive director of the General Assembly Council at the time, was down the hall from me, so I marched down to his office. "Davis, God keeps telling me that I need to use this scripture about Babylon. It's depressing and I don't want to use it. I don't even know where it is in the Bible. Do you?" Well, he didn't and that surprised me because he knows his Bible. But he didn't know where, so I told him, stubbornly, "Well, I'm just going to use our "go-to" discernment scripture, Psalm 139." 'Search me O God, discern my ways,' etc. etc." And so I marched back down to my office, flopped in my chair and flipped to Psalm 139.

Then I just "happened" to glance to the page opposite page in the Bible. What was there? "By the waters of Babylon, we laid down our harps..." to which I responded "Ok God, I hear you." And I knew I was in the midst of holy mystery and the Holy Spirit was doing the guiding. That night at the meeting, the electricity went out because of a rainstorm. Since it was dark, I couldn't do what I normally did with the other presentations. So we met around the library table with a candle lighting our faces and spoke about the hardships our church had faced in the past and we like, those captives in Babylon, were ready to be led by God into our future.

Can I put myself in the place of those disciples who were being filled with the Holy Spirit as they proclaimed the good news in many different languages? Oh yes I can! But that is not where they started. They started in a small room crowded together waiting and praying as Jesus had told them. He said in the first chapter: "You don't get to know the time. Timing is the Father's business. What you'll get is the Holy Spirit. And when the Holy Spirit comes on you, you will be able to be my witnesses in Jerusalem, all over Judea and Samaria, even to the ends of the world." They watched as he was taken up. They watched as two angels teased them about continuing to look toward heaven. Their teacher was gone and so they began waiting and praying for his promises to come true.

I admire people who are always looking for the Holy Spirit to come. I think about Louisa Woosley, our first ordained woman minister in the Cumberland Presbyterian Church and in fact the first woman ordained in the whole Presbyterian and Reformed world. She struggled with a call from God within her even to the point of being deathly ill. Once she had come to grips with her call, her synod had to come to grips with her presbytery experiencing the Holy Spirit within her preaching. Indeed her presbytery stood behind her to the point that they found a way to keep from taking away her ordination since they knew

God was on this journey with them. And certainly God was. In her lifetime, her records show that by the age of fifty, she had preached a total of 6,343 sermons, witnessed 7,664 professions from which 2,506 members had been added to church rolls, and baptized 358 persons in as many as thirteen states. She recognized that God was using her and she sought out ways to work for the kingdom. In 1908, she said "...I will not do [any] thing that I would refrain from doing if Jesus were in person standing before me or undertake anything I cannot ask Him help me do. Nor will I do anything I think it possible I may repent in the uncertain hour of my certain death. Every day shall be marked by at least one act or look of love. Wherever I do, whatever I do I will pray to God that I may commit no sin, but be the cause of some good. I will open and close the gates of day with prayer. I will sigh to God continually for the Holy Ghost to fill me and help me carry out these rules and so keep myself unspotted from the world and in all humility sit at Jesus' feet until His will shall be my meat and drink and He shall say it is enough, come up higher. So help me God with steady gaze, til then to look to Him whose heart bled and broke for me." (Louisa M. Woosley, August 1, 1908, Woosley Papers from Shall Woman Preach? Louisa Woosley and The Cumberland Presbyterian Church by Mary Lin Hudson, IV) Many people did and continue to see Louisa Woosley's life as one filled with the Holy Spirit. I do.

William Willimon, one of the great preachers of our day, says that this is what prayer is: "...the bold, even arrogant effort on the part of the community to hold God to his promise....What may appear as prayerful insolence by the Church in praying that we shall receive the Holy Spirit, the kingdom, power, and restoration is in fact the deepest humility, the church's humble realization that only God can give what the church most desperately needs." (Interpretation: A Bible Commentary for Teaching and Preaching: Acts, William H. Willimon, John Knox Press, Atlanta, 1988, p.27)

And so sit the followers of Christ in a small room waiting for the Holy Spirit. They have been through a lot-the death of Jesus like a common criminal; his Easter resurrection, his final ascension into heaven. And they were about to go through a lot more-Pentecost.

I don't know about your neighborhood, but in mine when a big branch falls or a strange loud noise booms, everyone comes out of their houses. In the same way, when the wind began to blow like it did at the earth's creation, everyone ran out to see what was going on. A strong wind, gale forces came from out of nowhere. The Holy Spirit began rushing around the room and each began speaking in a different tongue. They were creating such a ruckus that everyone came running. And what they saw and heard astounded them. In fact it confused them so much that they looked for a rational explanation to an irrational event! They started naming all of the languages they heard and they were from all of the places they knew existed. It was not rational so some even joked that they must be drunk.

But they were not drunk. They had been given the first fruit of the Spirit-the spirit of proclamation. And no one was excluded from hearing the proclamation of God's mighty acts through history. The Spirit gave them the power to witness. And look who is the first to stand. Willimon says "Peter is the first, the very first to lift up his voice and proclaim openly the word that only a few weeks before he could not speak, even to a serving woman at midnight." (Interpretation: A Bible Commentary for Teaching and Preaching: Acts, William H. Willimon, John Knox Press, Atlanta, 1988, p.31) The Holy Spirit was giving some pretty powerful gifts and not just to Peter.

Peter says "Of course they're not drunk." Can you imagine being drunk and being able to speak another language because of it? Then he explains what the prophet Joel had already foretold: "I will pour out my Spirit on every kind of people. Your sons will prophesy, also your daughters; your young men will see visions, your old men dream dreams. When the time comes, I'll pour out my Spirit on those who serve me, men and women both, and they'll prophesy." Joel was talking about the Spirit giving all people the gift of proclaiming the good news. "The Spirit, once the exotic possession of a prophetic few, is now offered to all," says Willimon. (Interpretation: A Bible Commentary for Teaching and Preaching: Acts, William H. Willimon, John Knox Press, Atlanta, 1988, p.35)

Can I empathize with the confused audience who were trying to come up with a rational explanation for what was happening? Most definitely yes! But do I know that God was in the midst of this grand and glorious act? Beyond a shadow of a doubt.
When have you seen signs of the Holy Spirit working in your lives? What should we do with them when we see them? I can't answer the first question for you. You yourselves have to come at life with the faith that the Spirit is with you and you will see the signs when they come.

And I suppose I can't even answer the second questions for you because I don't know what you will do with these signs of the Holy Spirit once you recognize them. But I can tell you what I do with these signs. I share the good news with others. The signs become part of my story that lets others know why I believe what I believe and how I know that the great message of the Gospel is my message too.

My moments with the Holy Spirit may not be holy to other people. That's ok, because my faith is my faith and the Holy Spirit speaks to me in ways that I will hear. But if my encounters with the Holy Spirit are part of my faith story and my story can encourage others to write and tell their own faith stories, we all as a community are enriched.

The Holy Spirit is coming to you, probably even this week. When the signs become apparent to you, share them with someone-use the gift of proclamation. We may come running back together next week seeing and feeling the rush of a strong wind called creation and hearing the noisy gift of proclamation.

God of wind and fire, blow through us so we will receive your gift of proclamation and use it to tell everyone the good news that Jesus Christ lived, that he died, that he was raised from the dead, that he ascended to heaven and that he sent your Holy Spirit to lead, guide and direct us all the days of our lives. Amen.

Does Prayer Make a Difference?

Whitney Brown

(1 Samuel 1:9-18, 24-28)

I want to share with you this morning a story from the book of Samuel: a story of a wife, a husband, a priest, a baby, and a God who does incredible things in the strangest ways. A story that a year ago began teaching me a lesson that has reoccurred in my mind time and time again so much so that I knew it was what I would share today.

In 1 Samuel, Chapter 1, we find a woman named Hannah and her husband Elkanah and his other wife Peninnah. Hannah is the favored wife, which is strange for their culture and society because Hannah—has no children. And although Elkanah loves Hannah and favors her, giving her double portions to sacrifice at Shiloh, Hannah still grieves for a son. This is where we pick up in our reading which is 1 Samuel 1:9-18, 24-28.

There are a lot of words in this passage to describe Hannah's mind set upon entering this time of prayer. She is brought there by pain, irritation, grief, distress, misery, bitterness, anxiety (Have you been there?)…

The title of the sermon today is a question, "Does prayer make a difference?" But I may have led you a little astray, because what I mean is—does prayer make a difference within YOU? For what do you pray? –Healing? Guidance? Comfort? Security? Church growth? Freedom? …have you prayed like Hannah? Let's look at a few MORE questions, and how we can look at this story of Hannah as a model for allowing prayer to make a difference within us.

DO YOU COME BEFORE GOD WHOLLY HONEST WITH THE STATE OF YOUR HEART?

Hannah hides nothing from the Lord, she comes before God freely…

Now, in Old Testament times people… most certainly women… did not just walk right in to the temple and present their requests to God, they depended on priests and sacrifices to help them communicate with the Lord. But, here comes this woman, close enough for Eli the priest to take notice of her, and she looks crazy. She looks drunk, and without asking for any help, without even concern for the priest sitting by the door, she lays it all out on the table before God. She's not concerned with who sees her or what they think, she's not trying to present God with a nice, well worded presentation of what she needs or wants. She's a mess, so she's a mess before God! Her heart is a wreck, so she comes to this place where God is believed to be most present, and is exactly who she is and asks God for exactly what she believes she needs. Have you been honest with God? Have you been free in your communication with Him? Have you "poured your soul before the Lord" or have you tried to hide the ugly parts? …Have you prayed like Hannah?

DO YOU CONSIDER HOW YOU WILL RETURN THE BLESSING YOU'RE ASKING GOD TO PROVIDE?

Hannah does this, and she is very specific in telling God how she will literally give God back the blessing… and this is not a barter but because Hannah understands that all things are for God's glory.

In the very breath following Hannah's request of God, she makes a promise—to return God's blessing right back to God. When God gives her a son, she will give her son to God. Let's take a minute to realize exactly what she's saying, to remember how much pain and desire has brought her to this place. This is no small promise. This child whom she wants and needs so much, the very thing that has brought her before God in such agony, she's saying she'll nurture him just long enough as is necessary, and then return him to God's service. (Samuel stays, his family goes.) I can hardly even fathom that concept… so, it was at this point that I realized that I rarely- if ever- have prayed like Hannah. We pray for ourselves and for others, for comfort and peace and guidance and such a wide range of other things, but how often do we take time to think past just why we need that thing and consider how, once we understand God's answer to our prayer—we will return the blessing SO FULLY to God's glory and service. I see it more often in my life, and I dare say I am not alone in this, that I pray, and on a good day I listen and wait for God's part of the conversation, but I'm most concerned with airing my needs, my thoughts, seeking what I need, or even seeking what God would have me to do… but not seeing the full picture, not bringing it full circle to exactly how it can be returned so fully to God. What about you?

Have you prayed like Hannah?

And then there's this…

DO YOU LEAVE PRAYER WITH A CHANGED COUNTENANCE, A MORE JOYFUL HEART, A TRUST THAT GOD KNOWS BEST? OR WILL YOU CONTINUE TO WORRY?

When Hannah leaves that space and time of prayer, verse 18 explains that her countenance was changed, she was no longer sad. This woman who comes in half crazy, so full of grief she's accused of being drunk… leaves completely changed. I attribute that to her faith, her belief and trust that God knows best and would answer her prayer as He saw fit. So, she goes, and she is changed. Then she rises in the morning and she worships.

Have you cast your cares upon God? Will you rest in the trust of His faithfulness? Or will you continue to worry? Will you worship with a changed heart? …Have you prayed like Hannah?

As you leave this place today, I hope these questions follow you as they've followed me this year. I hope they stick in your head in the most annoying of ways.

And most of you knew I wouldn't get through this sermon without asking you to DO something… You will find in the pockets of each pew index cards and pencils. Take some time to consider those things that are weighing heavy on your heart or are constantly on your mind. Write them down. And if you're ready, pray like Hannah:

Come before God wholly honest.

Consider how what you're asking of God can be returned to God's glory.

Then fold up your card. These are private, I'm not reading them; no one is looking. Following the benediction, you're invited to offer your prayers to God in a symbolic way by coming forward and placing your cards on the altar or in the offering plate…

And then leave changed.

Grab a card and a pencil, and let's pray…

God, the same God who heard Hannah centuries ago, we know you hear us still. We lift our souls to you and thank you for your presence. Help us to return your blessings. Help us to be changed. In Jesus name, Amen.

Benediction:

Seek God. Pursue Him. Openly and honestly speak to Him.
Let your prayers, your worship transform you. Be changed.
Expect God to move, and GET READY. Amen.

Ditching Jesus

Jill Davis Carr

(Mark 14:32-42)

The church I grew up in has pictures of Jesus hanging in the hallways and in classrooms. I call them "old people" pictures because they look like pictures old people have hanging in their homes, faded and enclosed in antique frames. They portray Jesus in a very solemn way, with a halo, clean and pressed clothing, groomed hair and beard, and sometimes in a metaphorical pose: Jesus with a lamb around his neck or Jesus holding a lantern knocking on a wooden door. Even as a child, these felt unnatural to me. There is one picture of Jesus praying in the Garden of Gethsemane, again looking solemn, clean, and posed—complete with a halo. There are no tears, no anguished expression, just a regular day at the office for Jesus, or so it seems.

Jesus is actually on the brink. His mission of making the reign of God present and visible on earth will not be fulfilled without his imminent arrest and death. He knows it and he has tried to tell the disciples, though much like children, they don't seem to quite get it. Jesus has spent his time in ministry revealing the new kingdom of God, or the reign of God, to a heavily oppressed people and to their oppressors, the Roman Empire as well as the Jewish leaders. Showing this world a new way of thinking and living is threatening these oppressors and is liberating the oppressed. What Jesus has started with the new reign of God is met with resistance and, at times, violence. Jesus is a witness to the new reign of God through his incomparable ability to meet challenges, threats, and violence with nonviolent resistance. All that he has taught his disciples and has shown the people is now

36

at stake; the completion of his mission and the continuation of the reign of God are at stake.

Now alone with his three closest disciples, he tells them he is "deeply grieved, even to death" and to "keep awake" while he prays. Jesus does not assume the position of this pretty and sanitized picture. He throws himself on the ground in prayer, wracked with grief, and, we can assume, explosive heartache from the knowledge of his dearest friends' human weakness and impending abandonment through betrayal and desertion.

Jesus is not a passive victim who is submissively compliant in the events about to unfold: arrest, public humiliation and dishonor, horrific torture, and death. At no point during Jesus' ministry does he defer to Roman authorities, the Jewish leaders, or anyone who does not welcome the new reign of God. Neither does he now. Jesus prays (and I envision that Jesus begs), for this "cup" to be removed, if possible, but indicates his willingness to accept God's decision. Jesus is no martyr, serenely awaiting death. He does not seek death, nor provoke it. Jesus hopes and prays for another way to fulfill his mission on earth, but he will complete it through death, if necessary, so that redemption and salvation through the new reign of God is possible for all people.

Peter, James, and John are caught sleeping three times, and this is after an initial instruction by Jesus to sit and wait. Jesus specifically calls out Peter, using his given name of Simon and referencing Peter's old life and person. Perhaps this is because Peter made two specific promises earlier in the evening: (1) he will not desert Jesus, and (2) he will not deny Jesus, even if he must die with Jesus. This is in addition to an earlier disagreement between Jesus and Peter over Jesus' passion prediction to the disciples; Peter refuses to believe that Jesus will die. (8.31-33) James and John carry some baggage too. They have previously promised Jesus that they are able to endure the same "cup" of death that Jesus will, but now they can't even stay awake and have no explanation why. (10.38-39) The three are speechless, like children who know they have done wrong, but have no excuse for their behavior. If I were Jesus, I would want to employ "three strikes and you're out." I would feel like telling them all just to go ahead and leave me now.

Jesus doesn't. He speaks sternly and tells them his betrayer is "at hand." Ironically, or perhaps divinely, the same Greek words are used when the kingdom of God is proclaimed at the beginning of Mark's Gospel. (1.15) Jesus is betrayed as quickly and in the same manner as the new kingdom, the reign of God, is inaugurated. He faces his ultimate betrayer, Judas, rather than fleeing himself, even though it seems he has ample opportunity. When "the hour has come," Jesus still has faith in the three sleepy heads. He doesn't leave them behind. He includes them, *invites* them, to come along. Jesus does not abandon those who, after his death and resurrection, will continue sharing the reign of God and spreading the good news of the gospel.

The abandonment of Jesus is complete in the subsequent verses, 43-50. Judas betrays Jesus with the kiss of friendship and all the disciples flee Jesus and the armed mob. They don't even stand by and watch him taken away; instead, they run like cowards. We embrace the weak flesh, fearful spirits, and confused minds of the disciples because it gives us "reason" to be the same. We figure if the chosen 12, and especially the "top gun" three, can let Jesus down in every way—spiritually, psychologically, and physiologically—at the gravest point in his life, then surely we "regular folk" can have a pass on doing the same. While the disciples abandon Jesus, unable to remain faithful to him and the reign of God, Jesus remains faithful to them and to his mission. The reign of God will not be stamped out with Jesus' betrayal, arrest, and death. Jesus' death becomes a sacrifice *as a result* of pursuing his mission. During the Passover meal, just prior to praying in the garden, Jesus promises the disciples he will drink of the fruit of the vine again in the new kingdom of God (14.25) and that after he is raised up, he will go before them (14.28). Jesus lets them know, and is letting us know, that the reign of God will continue. Jesus is the visible manifestation of the reign of God during his life and ministry, and in his death he makes the reign of God present in the personal lives of people—past, present, and future. Jesus not only remains faithful to the disciples who desert him, but he also *entrusts* to them the continuation of the reign of God.

On this Holy Thursday, let us fall on the ground in the garden with Jesus and confess our weaknesses that prevent us from remaining faithful to God. Let us remember and give thanks for a faithful savior who doesn't leave us behind, but invites us to share in his mission despite our lapses of denial, cowardice, and abandonment. With resolve, let us seek courage, humility, and grace to continue making present and visible the reign of God on earth, as Jesus taught us to do in his life and entrusted us to do in his death.

180 Degrees: Jacob

Amber Clark

(Genesis 32:22-31)

22 That night Jacob got up and took his two wives, his two female servants and his eleven sons and crossed the ford of the Jabbok. 23 After he had sent them across the stream, he sent over all his possessions. 24 So Jacob was left alone, and a man wrestled with him till daybreak. 25 When the man saw that he could not overpower him, he touched the socket of Jacob's hip so that his hip was wrenched as he wrestled with the man. 26

Then the man said, "Let me go, for it is daybreak."

But Jacob replied, "I will not let you go unless you bless me."

27 The man asked him, "What is your name?"

"Jacob," he answered.

28 Then the man said, "Your name will no longer be Jacob, but Israel, because you have struggled with God and with humans and have overcome."

29 Jacob said, "Please tell me your name."

But he replied, "Why do you ask my name?" Then he blessed him there.

30 So Jacob called the place Peniel, saying, "It is because I saw God face to face, and yet my life was spared."

31 The sun rose above him as he passed Peniel, and he was limping because of his hip.

Today we come to the story of Jacob in our 180 degree series. Jacob's story is not a story of conversion. His 180 degree turn is not from unbelief in God to believing in God. Jacob believes in God but that does not mean that Jacob is immune to wrestling with God.

When we come to belief in God that does not mean that our problems, questions and doubts are automatically resolved. If nothing else, we take on new problems, questions and doubts. We still wrestle. We are not perfect, we are always in need of transformation and many times we struggle through those transformations. Most people's faith lives are not clean but messy and broken. Patrick Wilson says that, "If we take [Jacob's] story seriously, we understand that God sometimes appears as our antagonist, the one with whom we must struggle—not necessarily an enemy, but one whom we must wrestle nonetheless." Sometimes we fight fiercely with God; about what has happened to us, about what God wants us to do, about anything. And as the scripture ends today Jacob limps away as the newly named Israel to face his brother Esau.

Jacob and Israel, the same person, a new name given, but a past not forgotten. In this story of Jacob we see that often in the lives of God's people there are changes, there are transformations, and there are new days. Here in Jacob's story we see that just because you become Israel doesn't mean that Jacob isn't still there. I think that if we forget our past we don't have the chance to learn from it and be changed by it. The name "Jacob" is a reminder to this new Israel of what he has been, of how far he has come and to the possibility of a new future.

So what's in a name? In one of the greatest plays of all time, Shakespeare asks this very question. As Romeo and Juliet meet and realize that they belong to two families that have a deep feud they ponder this question. "'Tis but thy name that is my enemy; Thou art thyself though, not a Montague. What's Montague? It is nor hand, nor foot, nor arm, nor face, nor any other part belonging to a man. O! Be some other name: What's in a name? That which we call a rose by any other name would smell as sweet; So Romeo would, were he not Romeo called, Retain that dear perfection which he owes without that title. Romeo, doff thy name; and for that name, which is no part of thee, take all myself." There is a lot to a name as this passage from Romeo and Juliet proves. There would be no conflict, no stress and there would be no story if it weren't for their names. Names can mean a lot. They let other people know who we are, maybe where we came from and they connect us to our families. There's lot's of history tied up with our names and that can be good or bad.

So when Michael and I found out that we were having a baby we felt this stress of choosing a name for your child. Maybe for some people it isn't that big of a deal but for me anyway, it was a big decision. I wanted to get it right because this would be the name that this child would have to carry with him for the rest of his life. There are a lot of things you have to think about when naming a child, you don't want them to get made fun of, you don't want their initials to spell something weird, you don't want them to have the same name as everyone else, but you don't want a name that is so different no one can spell it or pronounce it. Your name is important. I bet right now if I said a certain name to you, it might make your skin crawl, or you might get mad, it might bring you to tears or bring a smile to your face. Or maybe you have heard your name called, you weren't the last one picked for the team, you graduated, or you got married. Our names are our identities. So Michael and I debated and talked and thought up names and finally we came down to about three names that we really liked but we just couldn't decide. We had people mad at us because we hadn't picked a name yet, and they really wanted to know. We got asked that question so many times, but we hadn't decided. We also decided not to tell anyone what our top three were so that really drove people crazy. We told everyone that they would find out when the baby got here. But the weekend before we went into the hospital, I don't know what it was but we both looked at each other and said that the name was Eli. I don't know why or how but we both just felt that was this baby's name.

Compassion International's website says this about names, "Names are a gift from God. They contain His power. They define things. They define us. God said, "Let there be light." And there was. He named it into existence. God said, "Let there be an expanse between the waters to separate water from water." And there was. He called it sky. And He called the dry ground land. From that land, God made man. He made Adam. Then God gave the power to name to Adam. Adam named the animals. And he named Eve. And that power has been given to us. Consider the freedom that comes in naming a fear you have, or the cause of shame you hide, or the root of anger strangling you. When I own my fears, say them out loud, identify them, then I loosen the controlling grip they have over me. That's power. That's the power of a name [and the power of naming]."

There are a lot of things tied up in our names. When we ask someone the question "what is your name?" We are essentially asking "who are you?" Names can carry a lot of baggage, and well Jacob lives up to his name. Jacob's name means supplanter, one who grasps the heel. Jacob is given this name because when he was born he came out of the womb grasping the heel of his twin brother Esau. Jacob is a deceiver and a trickster. The first time he is asked the question "what is your name?" it is by his father Isaac. Jacob answers with a lie, claiming that he is his brother Esau so that he could receive the blessing that is supposed to be given to the first born son. From the time of his youth he is trying to be someone else, he wants what others have the right to and he is not afraid to lie, cheat and steal to get what he wants. Isaac is fooled and gives Jacob the blessing that has always been meant for Esau and of course Esau is angry, ready to kill, fuming and so Jacob leaves and from that moment on he is on the run. He continues his life of deception when he takes

41

refuge with Laban and marries two of his daughters. Jacob deals shrewdly and perhaps more than a little dishonestly with his father-in-law as they split up livestock and familial wealth between their households. Here we see the common get-ahead strategy of tweaking a situation to benefit one's own well-being or desires in undeserved ways. Jacob wasn't exactly lying, but he wasn't speaking or acting on the whole truth either, and eventually he has to leave their too. The only place he can go back to is the Promise Land. So he packs up his wives, children and all of his possessions and heads back to face Esau. Jacob has no where else to go, he is scared for his life, but he must face Esau, he can't manipulate his way out of that but he can try to manipulate their meeting. He plans to send a gift to Esau with the hopes of curbing is anger. He is so scared that Esau is going to kill him and all that he has that he separates his family and possessions and sends them on away from him so that they can be safe. Jacob finds himself at the side of the river Jabbok, alone.

And all of a sudden he is in the fight of his life. He doesn't see this person coming. He has no warning, he doesn't have a clue who this man is, what he looks like or why he would want to attack him, but they wrestle till daybreak. I can't imagine how tired Jacob would have been after fighting this person all night long, he is probably dirty and he probably stinks but he doesn't let go. Then his hip goes out, the man strikes it out of socket and Jacob is broken, but he has fought all night and he still doesn't let go, he begs for this man to give him a blessing. God has brought Jacob to a place of brokenness, he is not strong enough to win, and he can't win by his normal ways of being Jacob. He asks for help. He asks for a blessing.

Jacob is still trying to be Jacob. See Jacob has been aware of God, but doesn't seem to have grasped that he needs to live his life differently. This is not the first time he has had an encounter with God. As he is on the road to meet Esau before this wrestling encounter, Jacob lies down for the night. He has a dream about a ladder that goes between heaven and earth and on that ladder he sees God's angels ascending and descending. Jacob saw God standing above the ladder. God repeated the promise of support he had made to Abraham and Isaac. He told Jacob his offspring would be many, blessing all the families of the earth. God then said, "Behold, I am with you and will keep you wherever you go, and will bring you back to this land. For I will not leave you until I have done what I have promised you." When Jacob awoke, he believed that God was present in that place. He took the stone he had been using to rest his head, poured oil on it and consecrated it to God. Then Jacob named the place "house of God". Even though Jacob had had this amazing vision with God he still had to wrestle with God. It seems that God really needed to get Jacob's attention and dreams weren't going to do it. Even going into this wrestling match he is still trying to

42

manipulate the situation by trying to buy Esau off. Even though he has had a relationship with God, he has heard his promises he still hasn't lived his life differently. The same seems to go for us too. Just because we are a Christian, even when we have accepted that name gladly and we carry it; it doesn't mean that we don't wrestle with God. Not even pastors are immune to wrestling with God.

I have been through a wrestling match and I imagine that if I am truly trying to grow and learn throughout my life I will probably go through many more. When we were in Texas I went through a period of time where I wrestled with God. I was struggling for meaning and dealing with a lot of doubts. It was very painful, it hurt tremendously. In the midst of the struggle I didn't know if I was going to come out of it okay. But I hung on. I hung on for a long time. On the other side of it, I can honestly say that I can put up a good fight, but God never left. I believe that this experience has shaped me tremendously and I hope into a better, stronger person. I think that God has helped me to see new possibilities that I would never have seen before. By naming my fears and my doubts I was able to understand myself better and understand God just a little bit better. There is nothing like recognizing that God has been there the whole time even if you didn't acknowledge it. There is nothing like a new identity formed in the struggle. Patrick Wilson also says this, "We know that darkness of the night and the aloneness. We know the limping too, because no one emerges from such a wrestling match unwounded, unbloodied, untorn. We know also the blessing. In the dark, in the wrestling, we hear our true name spoken; in the dark...a new identity is wrenched from us; and before dawn breaks we are given an incomparable blessing."

God asks for Jacob's name. In his brokenness, Jacob admits who he is. Instead of lying like he has always done he owns his past and his present by giving his name, Jacob. Through giving his name, he confesses everything about who he is. I think that he knows that this is the last person that he can hide from. He has no choice, standing before this man but to be exactly who he is, Jacob and all that that name holds for him. God gives Jacob the blessing of a new name, Israel, which means "one who strives with God". In this moment, Jacob is given grace. In all his unworthiness God blesses him anyway and Jacob knows it. He knows that he has been given something that he has in no way earned. That moment would change anyone. He has been released from his past and he can go into his future with a new understanding of who and whose he is. This is the 180 degree moment. This is that moment when Jacob going in one direction, encounters a God who turns him in a new direction.

Throughout the rest of Israel's story he is at times still called Jacob. His past isn't erased you see, it just doesn't have a strangle grip on him anymore. He owns and admits that part of him is still Jacob but in taking the blessing of the name Israel, a name given by God, he is able to move forward into new ways of being, new ways that only God knows. Jacob in turn asks for the man's name and he isn't given an answer, I think because Jacob already knows who this man is. The man departs and Jacob names the place Peniel, where he has seen God face to face and lived, and then he limps away.

Jacob has been changed, he has received a blessing. But the wrestling match comes with a price and Jacob limps for the rest of his life. No one emerges from a conflict unharmed. We bear the scars of our wrestling matches whether they are with God or with someone else. But I think those scars can serve as reminders that we are broken and in need of healing no matter where we are on our journey with God. We are a wounded people but there is always hope that we are not defeated, if we hold out for that blessing and receive our true name.

So what are you wrestling with today? Are you struggling hard, are you fighting for your life, do you know your name? I think at times that we think that if we struggle as Christians then there is something wrong with us, that we don't believe enough or we don't believe in the right way. But here is a story of a man who actually, physically wrestled with God and came out of it better. I think there are some traditions and people out there on TV that preach a gospel that says that once you believe everything will be okay. You will live this wonderful life; you will have all the things that you need, that your life will be perfect and wonderful. We hear this message that Christianity is all puppies and flowers and like a sitcom everything can be resolved in 30 minutes if we just do the right things and believe the right way. This has not been my reality and I would imagine that it has probably not been yours. I think that is the reason that real stories of people's lives are what ring true to us. I think that is why campaigns like "I Am Second" and the personal stories that are told move us so. One of the stories that are featured in the book is the story of Josh Hamilton. Michael showed his story some time ago during one of his sermons one Sunday. Josh is someone, even with his success as a major league baseball player, still struggles and wrestles with his demons. He even says at the end of his story that he always will struggle, even though he is a Christian and tries to live his life like Jesus would live it, he still messes up, he is still broken and he is reminded again and again that he needs Jesus. I remember that after Michael showed his story that we found out that he had had a relapse of some sort. But his story rings with truth because we all struggle and wrestle with something.

But when we find ourselves in the midst of a wrestling match, may you have hope because the good news is, is that we do not wrestle alone. Whether it is God who you are wrestling with or you are wrestling with someone else. God is there. When it seems like you are standing alone on the side of a river bank, when you find yourself in the deepest darkest places of your soul, when you can't seem to find the light, God is there. We do not have to wrestle alone. God is waiting and wanting to transform us each and everyday, because our faith shouldn't be stagnant, it should move and grow, and when we let God work on and in us it is not usually an easy thing. God has plans for you and maybe you are like Jacob and God needs to get your attention through a wrestling match. Jacob had his 180 degree turn in the desert along a river and afterward he shaped an entire nation. While the wrestling match can be scary, again remember that you are never alone, you might even come to find out you have been wrestling with God all along. But if you can hold on, God will bless you and you might even get a new name.

Getting Rid of Our Excess Baggage

Marcia Compton

(Colossians 3:8-17)

When I began packing to go to Colombia, South America, I knew there were some things I would have to leave behind. Some of the things were not really necessary. You can only fit so many things in a suitcase. Some of the items were clothing. Some were things I used often, but did not really need. Then I began to think about some other things in my life, things that you cannot see. Things like anger and resentment and worry. These too were things I could do without. These were things I did not want to bring along. These were things I knew God wanted me to let go.

There was someone in my life that I had been harboring resentment against. Resentment is not a good thing to bring on a trip to Columbia, South America. In fact, resentment is not a good thing to bring anywhere.

In my mind, I packed an extra bag, I put anger, resentment and worry in that bag and closed it up. That bag was staying home. It was not going with me. I was going to dump that bag on my way to the airport. I really never wanted to see that bag again.

God took the bag, and I said, "thank you, you can have it. You can deal with it. I don't need it. I'm going on a trip to serve you and I don't need this excess baggage." And God answered me and said, "Yes, give it to me." I was reminded of the verse in I Peter 5:7, "Cast all your cares upon me, because I care for you." It seemed as though God was saying to me, "I love you; I want to take all of your excess baggage."

This morning, are you carrying around some excess baggage? Are you caring around some resentment against someone who has wronged you? God encourages us to love our enemies. God says to love those who harm us. God says to do good to those who persecute us. This is God's way. It is not man's way. We can only live this way as a child of God. We can only show this kind of love, filled up with the Holy Spirit. This is supernatural love. In our own strength, on our own power, we may find it very difficult to give up resentments or to give up anger.

We could carry anger around with u, and the only one we would be hurting would be ourselves. God does not want you to go around hurting. He does not want you to go through life limping. God wants you to get rid of your excess baggage. God wants to take away any anger you may have. He wants you to turn to Him to trust Him to bring justice where you have been wronged.

Maybe you are carrying around something else this morning. Your excess baggage may be pride. You may think that you do not need God. You may believe that you can handle everything. Well, think about it. Have you really been able to handle everything that came your way? Give up your pride. Turn you life over to God. He is the only one who can really handle everything.

Perhaps you are carrying around some guilt this morning. You know, He wants that too! He took care of that at Calvary. He took all of your sins, He paid the penalty. No longer did man have to sacrifice animals to alone for his sins. Jesus took care of it. He became the blood sacrifice, Jesus, the Son of the Living God. He hung on the cross for your sins. You don't have to carry them around anymore; no, not even for one moment. You can be free!

God's Word tells us that He remembers our sins no more. So why do we torment ourselves? Why do we drag around this excess baggage? Get rid of it. Give it to God once and for all. If He will not remember your sin, why should you. Follow God's example. Cast it into the deepest sea, add a brick, and get on with your life. God rid of anger, rage, bad feelings toward others, all immorality, and walk in love.

God has a plan for you, great and mighty works for you to do. Greater is He that is in you, than He who is in the world (I John 4:4). Satan doesn't stand a chance against you, once you dump your excess baggage, and live a life of servant hood. Jesus is our example. He was spit on, flogged cursed, and worse, but you never hear Him saying, "What a raw deal this is" or "How could they do this to me." No, he dusted his feet off and continued to serve the people. The people in Moroquim near Cali, Columbia have very little but I never heard anyone complain. They were serving one another. They could be bitter but they are making the best of what they have.

Are you serving people, or do you have too much excess baggage. A group of Americans went to Columbia, South America to serve, to work for God and for the people of Columbia. Every one of them had to leave some excess baggage behind. They knew there was work to do. There is much kingdom work to be done, many people to be won for Christ.

God made us to glorify and serve Him We can do that in many ways. Through prayer, reading the Bible, and serving our neighbors. We cannot do any of these things very effectively unless we have the Spirit of God living in us, unless Jesus Christ is our Lord and Savior.

Would you like to get rid of your excess baggage this morning? Don't wait. There is no need to carry it around any longer. Give it to God. He wants to take it. There is a Spanish word, *Tranquillo*, don't worry. I like that word, why should I worry, when God says, I can cast all my cares upon Him.

Once you have gotten rid of your excess baggage, there are some important things that you need to put in your bag. Colossians 3:12-16 tells us what to take with us wherever we go. We are to clothe ourselves as God's own chosen ones. Our behavior should be marked by tenderhearted pity and mercy, kind feelings, gentle ways, patience. We are to be gentle and forbearing with one another, readily forgiving one another, as the Lord has forgiven you freely. We are also called to be people of peace thankful people who love one another.

Instead of packing around resentment and anger, you are to take kind feelings, readily forgiving one another. If you walk in forgiveness and you are forgiving others then you will not have anger and resentment any longer. Kind feelings replace bad feelings. Love replaces bitter and angry feelings. God wants us to live in love and harmony with our fellow human beings.

As Colossians 3:16 says, "Let the word spoken by Christ the Messiah, have its home in your hearts and minds." Does Christ have His home in your heart this morning? Have you given Him all of your excess baggage? Turn it all over to Him—your life and your excess baggage—whatever it may be.

Give God your excess baggage and let Him fill you with His love, to the His chosen one, purified and holy. Be filled with pity, mercy, kind feelings, gentle ways, patience, with power to endure whatever comes, with good temper. Let God fill you with gentleness, forgiveness toward one another and enjoy His perfect peace.

Let us pray that God may empower you with His goodness so you can leave your excess baggage behind for good.

Dear Lord, we acknowledge that we have acted in sinful ways, ways that were not pleasing to you, forgive us of our sins. Help us to trust you each day, to depend upon you, to serve you, to give you our excess baggage. Keep us from trying to retake our excess baggage. We don't need it. You don't want us to carry it around. Empower us as God's own chosen ones. May we speak the works Christ spoke, may your Holy Spirit dwell in our hearts and minds. Thank you for saving us, thank you for redeeming us. Thank you for your Holy Spirit, that helps us to forgive others when we cannot forgive in our own strength. Thank you for all things. In Jesus name we pray. Amen.

What Is Your Name?

Lisa Cook

(Luke 8:26-39)

Opening Prayer:

Gracious God from whom all blessing flow, please allow these words to be yours and allow us to hear only that which brings you glory. AMEN.

Names are important. Names confirm our individual existence. With our name we become a recorded part of history and society. Our names are forever linked to what we do and who we become. All cultures place a high importance on names; rituals and traditions abound when names for babies are considered, selected and given. It is one of the first pieces of information we want to know, and give, when we meet others.

Our names differentiate us from each other…well except in cases like what happened when my younger brother, Bobby got married…to a woman named Lisa!…you can imagine the confusion created from having two Lisa Cook's in the family!

But you know what, when that happened, my mother adapted to the situation by once again using the power of names to tell us apart. My mother now calls me "my Lisa" and my sister-in-law is "Bobby's Lisa." Names are powerful.

And in the story we just heard from Luke's gospel, we have an example of how a name, just a name, can tell a sad, sad story all by itself. A story told in an unexpected placed to an unusual man named Jesus who cared enough to ask: *What is your name?*

Now, chapter eight of Luke's gospel is full of activity! The chapter begins with Jesus doing a lot of traveling and teaching.

Then we are told about half way through the chapter that one day Jesus got into a boat and suggested they go to the "other side." Along the way there is a storm. A really bad storm; and the disciples began to fear for their life. Jesus wakes up and calms the storm. Makes it stop just like that. Then the disciples fear Jesus, wondering, *"Who is this guy that even the water and winds obey him??"*

After this time at sea, we shift in chapter eight to an arrival in a place called Gerasenes. We are also told that Gerasenes is "opposite" Galilee. This is our first clue that we are in an unexpected place. Jesus the Jew and his Jewish friends are in Gentile territory. And if you need further proof of this, look no further than the herd of swine that are nearby.

Then it seems that as soon as they step on land they are greeted by an unexpected welcoming party of one. You heard the description of him in the reading and we will not get caught up this morning in a discussion of biblical "demons" and "exorcisms" or how they can be compared to our modern day experiences with mental illnesses.

This man in Luke's gospel is an outcast at best, and if we knew more of his history, no doubt it might reveal worse.

And what does this outcast do, he falls down and calls Jesus by name. *"Jesus, Son of the Most High God."* Then, for whatever reason he begs Jesus not to torment him; suggesting possibly that torment is what he has come to expect from others, given his situation in life.

Jesus is unlike others however, and he does not have torment on his agenda this day. Instead he asks the man a simple question: *"What is your name?"* And the heartbreaking reply that is given is simply, *"Legion."*

To know why that answer just breaks my heart, I need to talk a bit about this word, *legion*. This word commonly refers to a unit, if you will, of Roman soldiers totaling about 6,000 in number! So, knowing how powerful names are, you see how heartbreaking it is, that this man could not reply with his own name when asked, but rather he replied with a name symbolizing the fact that he has been taken over by so many "demons," that he has now lost his very identity...lost his name...and he now identifies only with a name that describes the legion of "demons" tormenting him day and night?

51

How sad to no longer know who you are, to no longer know your own name, amidst the chaos of life.

I asked before for us to be intentional this morning about not focusing on the demon/mental illness trajectory this story can take. I want to be intentional about this because I think it is here, with this discussion about a name in this story that we in this day and time can most connect with and learn from this story in Luke's gospel.

When we take the other path, it is way too easy for us to put distance between ourselves and the story. Mental illness, demons, and exorcisms are what other people deal with, not us! Not me…

But when we focus instead on the question Jesus asks, *"what is your name?"* this, my friends, is something to which we can all relate.

Who among us has not had a time when so many of our own "demons," (*and you are free to define your demons however you like, but we all have them*) how many of us have not had those demons pulling us every which way, in all directions…confusing us to the point that we don't even know our own name, tormenting us until we forget who we are…or worse…we fear that others have forgotten us, that we are no longer known. We have been robbed of our identity by our own personal legion of "demons."

I think this is where *we* can most relate to that man who fell at the feet of Jesus, no longer knowing who he was.

And again, we heard what happened next in the reading. The man's demons ask to be sent into the swine, Jesus does so and the man is free and in his right mind again and the swine jump the cliff into the sea.

We could spend some time talking about the usual. Why do the demons want to be sent to the swine? Why did Jesus do what the demons asked of him? Why did they jump to their death right after? Much is written about these questions if you are curious.

But I want us again to be intentional again about staying with the story path we have been following so far today.

The man.

The man is clothed.

He is in his right mind again. The man is inspired by what has been done for him so much so that he wants to go wherever Jesus is going.

But Jesus tells him to return to his home. Jesus also instructs him to tell everyone about the good thing that God has done for him. And in my mind, he is greeted by name in his community when he returns, and he proudly gives his name when asked. He is known once again!

The healing that Jesus has provided, the miracle that has been performed is the reclaiming of the man's identity as a child of God.

This is not simply a personal healing story about an outcast who is exorcized of that which is tormenting him and forcing him to be isolated.

This is a story about a restoration to community.

A story about the reclaiming of one's identity in Christ.

A story about the transformation that is possible when we are known and loved!!

I must confess that despite my requests for intentionality and staying on a certain path where this story is concerned, I have to admit that my mind wanders somewhere else when I read this story from Luke. My mind wanders to a friend of mine.

His name is David.

David was an outcast.

He left home for good reasons at 13 years old, with a less than desirable outcome. He was homeless for more than 40 years. He traveled about, following the Grateful Dead and sleeping under bridges. He would find a place to stay put every now and then…a friend's carport...a burned-out abandoned house...but he was always on the move. He wasn't welcome anywhere, and he came to expect the stares, rude comments, and rejection he received from others because of the way he looked.

He stayed away from mainstream community for the most part because he just didn't fit their idea of "normal" David would tell you that he did every drug under the sun and drank more than he cared to talk about sometimes. David had a temper and was he very, very stubborn.

David had demons, just like the man in Gerasenes.

David knew what it was to be nameless, to be judged and identified as *"less than"* because of his demons, just like the man in Gerasenes.

David knew what it was like to be an outcast shunned by his community, just like the man in Gerasenes.

But just like the man in Gerasenes, David knew Jesus, and Jesus helped David to be reminded time and again of his true identity as a child of God. David was known and loved by Jesus. It's true that David had to be reminded at times, just like we all do, but David *knew his name*. I met David last year right after he experienced a bit of good luck, met the right people, and was placed in an apartment at just about the same time he found out he was dying from stomach cancer. That little one-bedroom apartment he lived in was his castle, and David reigned over that place until he died on May 19th of this year.

His name is David.

My name is Lisa Kay Cook. I get more wrong than I get right most days. I desire to show love always, but I fail often.

I am a child of God, and I am known and loved by Jesus Christ.

What is your name...?

Closing Prayer:

God, you know us. You know our names and you delight in us. If we are honest Lord, it is the deepest longing of every one of us to be known and to be loved. You stand ready always to satisfy that longing. So thank you God, we are so blessed to be called yours. Amen.

Un llamado a Romper Paradigmas
A Call to Break Paradigms

Maria del Socorro Delgado

OBJETIVO: Que podamos ser libres de paradigmas y esquemas que obstaculizan nuestro llamado y vocación para realizar un gran ministerio en la obra de Dios.

INTRODUCCIÓN:

Pensando en personas que se atrevieron a romper esquemas quiero resaltar la participación de dos mujeres de Arabia Saudí (Wodian Ali Seraj Abdulrahim y Sarah Altar) quienes fueron las primeras deportistas femeninas de su país en competir en las olimpiadas de Londres 2012. Esta participación se constituyó en todo un éxito en la lucha por la igualdad de género, a riesgo de ser tildadas "prostitutas" como algunos de su país las llamaron según un titular que encontré en internet.

El titular decía:

Arabia Saudita: llaman prostitutas a las primeras deportistas olímpicas del Reino.

El condicionamiento social nos ha guiado por estereotipos que han encasillado tanto a hombres como a mujeres con capacidades intelectuales físicas y espirituales.
Me enfocaré en la mujer debido a que ha sufrido el rigor del rechazo y menosprecio. La biblia nos muestra lo difícil que ha sido para la mujer tener el reconocimiento de su valor y sus derechos como ser humano con relación al varón. Observemos tres casos de mujeres que se atrevieron a romper paradigmas que hasta ese momento se tenían, y cómo Dios da aprobación a los mismos.

1. CINCO MUJERES QUE DESAFIARON LAS LEYES DE SU CULTURA
    (Números 27:1-11)
    Maala, Noa, Hogla, Milca y Tirsa.

a.   Un momento crucial

Su padre, Zelofehad, de la familia de Manasés, había muerto en el desierto, sus hijos tenían derecho a su herencia por no haber participado en la rebelión de Coré contra Moisés, el problema es que este hombre no tenía hijos varones, solo tenía cinco hijas y estas no podían reclamar la herencia, ya que las mujeres no tenían ningún derecho de propiedad bajo las costumbres existentes de la época. A estas jóvenes les pareció injusto, y se determinaron con valentía a reclamar el derecho a la herencia que su padre había dejado.

El momento era crucial, ¡era ahora o nunca! El pueblo se preparaba para entrar a la tierra prometida, la tierra sería distribuida no podían dejar pasar la oportunidad. Si callaban arriesgaban a quedarse sin la herencia de su padre.

b.   Un caso nunca antes visto (Números 27:4)

Fueron directamente a Moisés, al sacerdote Eleazar y a toda la congregación para presentar su caso públicamente: "¿Por qué será quitado el nombre de nuestro padre de entre su familia, por no haber tenido hijo? Danos heredad entre los hermanos de nuestro padre"

Estas jóvenes se exponían al rechazo y quizá a una disciplina severa por cuestionar las leyes que Dios había dado al pueblo de Israel.

c.   Dios juzga el caso y da su veredicto a favor de las mujeres (Números 27:7)

"Bien dicen las hijas de Zelofehad; les darás la posesión de una heredad entre los hermanos de su padre, y traspasarás la heredad de su padre a ellas". La resolución de Dios fue en favor de las hermanas. Estas jóvenes tuvieron derechos legales de propiedad por primera vez al igual que los hombres, el nombre de su familia no quedaría en el anonimato gracias al valor de estas cinco mujeres.

d.   La ley es modificada (Números 27:8-11)

El decreto se aplicó a las doce tribus, el caso fue ampliado para incluir otras instancias. Este caso sentó un precedente para las generaciones futuras.

2. LA MUJER CANANEA, rompe con los esquemas religiosos y sociales de su tiempo: Mateo 15:21-28

"Partiendo de allí, Jesús se retiró a las región de Tiro y Sidón. Una mujer cananea de las inmediaciones salió a su encentro, gritando: Vers. 21 y22

    a.   Esta mujer hace un llamado angustioso al que todo lo puede "¡Señor, Hijo de David, ten compasión de mí!"

    b.   Expone su necesidad : "Mi hija sufre terriblemente por estar endemoniada"

    c.   Al parecer su presencia no es grata: "Jesús no le respondió palabra. Así que sus discípulos se acercaron a él y le rogaron:

    Despídela, porque viene detrás de nosotros gritando.

    No fui enviado sino a las ovejas pérdidas del pueblo de Israel. Contestó Jesús. Vers. 23 y 24

    d.   Ella sabe bien que no es digna, no pertenece al pueblo escogido, es una forastera pero a pesar del rechazo y de las barreras que se estaban levantando en ese momento no desfallece, insiste en actitud de humillación y súplica. "La mujer se acercó y, arrodillándose delante de él, le suplicó: ¡Señor, Ayúdame! Vers. 25

    e.   Los argumentos de Jesús son más contundentes: "No está bien quitarles el pan a los hijos y echárselos a los perros" Vers. 26

    f.   La respuesta de ella quita todo argumento, barrera, obstáculo y abre la puerta para ser aceptada, escuchada y elogiada por Jesús mismo. "Si, Señor pero hasta los perros comen de las migajas que caen de la mesa de sus amos. ¡Mujer, que grande es tu fe! Contestó Jesús. Que se cumpla lo que quieres.

    Esta mujer, al igual que las cinco hijas de Zelofehad recibió respuesta a su solicitud.

3. LA MUJER SAMARITANA (Juan 4:1-42): Otro caso de alguien que venció barreras sociales es el de la mujer Samaritana. Después de su encuentro con Jesús y quedar al descubierto todo su pecado por el cual era rechazada socialmente, al ser perdonada y restaurada no hubo barreras para que ella quedara libre y saliera corriendo para contarle a los hombres de su pueblo que había visto al Mesías. Así se constituyó en la primera mujer en predicar el evangelio de Jesús.

CONCLUSIÓN:

Que gozo hacer memoria de aquellas personas que fueron valientes para aceptar el llamado de Dios y decidir a riesgo propio servir para el Reino de los cielos, cruzando barreras culturales, prejuicios sociales, y que rompiendo esquemas y paradigmas abrieron el camino e impactaron la sociedad y fueron instrumentos útiles para la gloria de Dios. Mujeres como Louisa Woosly primera mujer ordenada de la iglesia Presbiteriana, que ha sido inspiración para quienes habiendo recibido el llamado se han aventurado a servir con los dones que el Espíritu Santo les ha dado para que el cuerpo de Cristo sea edificado.

APLICACIÓN:

La historia se escribe todos los días, Dios nos ha dado libertad, construyamos la historia. La mujer está llamada a conquistar; de hecho ha conquistado muchos espacios hasta hoy. Esta es una conquista de actitud y de pensamiento. Esta conquista eleva nuestro status como ser racional, emocional y por supuesto espiritual.

ORACIÓN:

Gracias Dios por el respaldo a nuestras antecesoras, y por todo lo que se ha logrado hasta hoy, pero todavía tenemos que continuar aceptando desafíos, ayúdanos a ser perseverantes, a no abandonar la lucha aunque los obstáculos estén delante de nosotras.

El Amor Que Transforma Vidas
The Transforming Love

Esperanza Díaz

(1 Juan 3:1-9; 2 CRON. 34:1-8, 26-33)

TEMA: EL AMOR TRANSFORMADOR DE DIOS

PROPÒSITO: Reconocer el amor transformador de Dios y aceptarlo en mi vida.

TESIS: Todas las obras de Dios han sido realizadas por amor. Un amor sin igual, un amor incluyente pero a la vez excluyente. Un amor que se abre para que todos puedan recibirlo, pero un amor que al llegar a El todo lo que le es incompatible tiene que salir…

INTRODUCCIÓN:

Cuando le hablan de amor ¿EN QUÉ PIENSA? ¿Corazones? ¿Flores? ¿Promesas? ¿Invitaciones?... o tal vez decepciones? soledad?, desengaños y traición?... confusión y temor?

El Señor tiene un mensaje de amor realmente profundo y transformador… UN AMOR QUE ROMPE BARRERAS Y QUE DERRIBA MUROS, UN AMOR QUE LIBERA Y QUE RENUEVA… ESTE AMOR TRANSFORMADOR QUIERE HOY EL SEÑOR OFRECERLE

La historia de Dios con el hombre es una historia de amor:

Cuando Dios creó al mundo lo hizo por amor

Cuando Dios creó al hombre y a la mujer como ayuda idónea lo hizo por amor

Cuando Dios creó a la familia lo hizo por amor

Cuando Dios escogió un pueblo lo hizo por amor

Cuando Dios hizo pacto con este pueblo lo hizo por amor

Cuando Dios castiga a su pueblo lo hizo por amor

Cuando Dios exige santidad lo hace por amor

Cuando Dios Envió a su hijo para tomar nuestro lugar en la cruz lo hizo puramente por amor

Cuando Dios creó una iglesia lo hizo por amor

Cuando Dios nos dejó su palabra y leyes lo hizo por amor

Cuando Dios nos ofrece libertad de la esclavitud del pecado... lo hace por amor

Cuando Dios nos hace sus hijos y nos lleva a ser parte de su familia... lo hizo por amor.

Dios es amor... ¿Cree que hay suficientes muestras de este amor?

CONTEXTUALIZACIÓN:

1 Juan es una carta escrita en un contexto bien especial y parecido a nuestra época. En un contexto de acomodamiento del cristianismo a tradiciones y costumbres en ocasiones huecas (palabras acomodadas, estilos cristianos sin ningún significado en la vida diaria...) SI DECIMOS QUE... ENTONCES DEBEMOS... y con un peligro muy grande por la aparición de la doctrina de los gnósticos que declaraban la maldad de la materia y que por lo tanto Cristo no había estado realmente encarnado, no podía un Dios bueno estar envuelto en una materia mala. Esto también llevó a la teoría de que para acercarnos a Dios era necesario solamente el conocimiento y nada tenía que ver la conducta... al fin y al cabo la materia es mala, "Dios no atiende a lo que se haga con el cuerpo". Esta doctrina llevó a una confusión entre los creyentes de la época, pues llegaron a dudar de la encarnación de Cristo y a descuidar el nivel de compromiso y vida llegando a dejar que el pecado se hiciera parte de su vida diaria.

Los cristianos se estaban dejando contaminar como lo hicieron los israelitas en la época de los grandes padres del pueblo.

Juan llega a atacar esta doctrina y las consecuencias que estaba teniendo en la vida de la iglesia y del cristiano en particular.

Juan era viejo, quizás el último de los apóstoles que quedaba vivo, duró casi hasta el fin del primer siglo... pero a pesar de su edad luchó vigorosamente contra cualquier cosa que pudiera corromper la fe que le había inspirado durante tantos años.

Entonces: Esta es una carta para personas que han creído y seguido al Señor, para quienes de una u otra manera se llaman cristianos y aún para quienes tienen algunas prácticas que les puede distinguir como cristianos... por ejemplo venir a la iglesia, compartir con otros cristianos, cantar coros... sin embargo si usted es nuevo, si viene por primera vez, también las enseñanzas de esta carta serán muy apropiadas pues en últimas el anhelo del escritor era *explicar cómo la fe en Cristo debe afectar la vida personal de una manera radical*

LA VIDA QUE VIVE EL HOMBRE REVELA LA FUENTE DE LA CUAL NUTRE SU VIDA.

Pero, entonces debemos preguntarnos:

¿Cómo nos puede transformar el amor de Dios?:

1.   **Nos hace sus hijos**:

Para que esto fuera posible fue necesario:

1.1   **Un sacrificio**: entregó a su hijo, a su único hijo para darnos salvación. Juan 3:16

EL SEÑOR Jesús entregó su vida en rescate por muchos: mateo 20:28

1.2   **Un acto de fe y entrega**: a los que le recibieron y creen en su nombre Juan 1:12

Dios no solo nos llama sus hijos… El nos hace sus hijos

2.   **Nos transforma a su imagen**:

2.1   **Nos hace incompatibles con el mal** Vrs.3:1

Concepto de incompatibilidad:

Incapacidad para unirse o para existir conjuntamente. Es sinónimo de rechazo-repugnancia.

2.2   **Nos exige pureza y santidad** Vrs.3

Nos llama a cumplir la ley y a dejar el pecado Vrs.4

Esta demanda no es nueva:

Desde el mismo momento que Dios decidió crear un pueblo para sí, puso normas específicas, ninguno que fuera parte de su pueblo podría incumplirlas y vivir fuera de ellas… no era lógico que un pueblo de un Dios santo conviviera con el pecado.

El pueblo luchó pero no pudo, su contaminación fue clara. Sin embargo hubo reyes que "hicieron lo bueno ante los ojos de Jehová" Ejemplos claros como: El Reinado de Josías: el rey que detuvo el deslizamiento acelerado en que iba el pueblo hacia la perdición, la corrupción… la destrucción total.

Su historia nos ilustra claramente lo que necesitamos hacer para purificarnos del mal:

*Tomar decisiones claras: aunque era hijo y nieto de dos reyes que hicieron lo malo ante los ojos de Jehová, él decidió agradar a Dios. Andar en los caminos de Dios y seguir los buenos ejemplos que encontró en su historia. Ninguna historia de pecado y desamor en su vida y en la de su familia debe impedirle buscar un cambio radical y una solución profunda y total.

*Buscar al Señor: De corazón y con convicción Josías aun siendo un muchacho dedicó tiempo a conocer más de Dios y acercarse de corazón a su Dios. Pero no se quedó allí. El Señor nos invita a buscarlo en tanto que está cercano... que si llamamos él nos escuchará, él dice que se deja conocer de quienes con corazón sincero le buscan.

*Arrojar el pecado de su vida: En todo lo que tenía que ver con su reino, derribó los ídolos, los altares dedicados a la idolatría y de raíz sacó la infidelidad y la corrupción espiritual de su vida. ¿En qué manera hoy el Señor le está pidiendo que haga esto en su vida? Rom. 12:1 dice: Así que, hermanos, os ruego por las misericordias de Dios, que presentéis vuestros cuerpos en sacrificio vivo, santo, agradable a Dios que es vuestro culto racional. Nuestro cuerpo debe ser para el Señor un altar, un altar de entrega total, sin reservas.

1 CORINTIOS 6: 20 Porque han sido comprados por precio, glorificad, pues, a Dios en vuestro cuerpo y en vuestro espíritu, los cuales son de Dios.

¿Puede usted seguir el ejemplo de Josías?

En una época en que nos están enseñando que nosotros somos los dueños del cuerpo y hacemos con él lo que queramos, pecamos en fornicación, adulterio, pornografía, homosexualismo... y decimos: Eso está bien, con tal de que no le haga mal a nadie...con tal de que haga buenas obras y con esto tape el pecado. El Señor nos llama a entregar todas estas cosas y destruirlas así como hizo Josías...a purificar nuestra vida, a no dejar que estos ídolos hagan más parte de nuestra vida... El Señor nos dice: hoy es día de entrega total.

Como Josías, debemos tomar decisiones radicales... aun cuando creamos que nos van a criticar, que vamos a encontrar rechazo... JOSÍAS ESTABA MÁS INTERESADO EN AGRADAR A DIOS QUE AGRADAR A QUIENES LE RODEABAN... al fin y al cabo el amor que ofrece Dios es eterno, profundo. Fiel y sanador... ¿ENCONTRARÁS EL MISMO AMOR Y ACEPTACIÓN EN EL MUNDO?

Recordemos lo que Juan dice: "todo aquel que peca no ha visto a Dios ni le ha conocido"

2.3 Implica renuncia y entrega:

2 Corintios 10:4,5: *Porque las armas de nuestra milicia no son carnales, sino poderosas en Dios para la destrucción de fortalezas, derribando argumentos y toda altivez que se levanta contra el conocimiento de Dios, y llevando cautivo todo pensamiento a la*

obediencia a Cristo.

La batalla es continua, estando en el mundo, en el momento en que estamos… las luchas se hacen muy fuertes. Por más que intentemos con nuestras propias fuerzas no podremos vencer las tentaciones, los malos hábitos, aún los malos pensamientos, solo las armas de Dios pueden hacerlo… Generalmente estos versículos son usados para guerra espiritual, sobre todo para pelear contra espíritus y no es del todo equivocado, pero tristemente no atendemos casi a lo que sigue diciendo el versículo: DERRIBANDO ARGUMENTOS Y TODA ALTIVEZ QUE SE LEVANTA CONTRA EL CONOCIMIENTO DE DIOS: la mente llega a ser nuestra mayor enemiga cuando queremos dejar nuestra vida en actitud de entrega, humildad y sacrificio total ante Dios… ¿no siente en su mente un rechazo cuando se le habla de sometimiento, entrega, obediencia, sacrificio?

¿Qué cosas ha rechazado su mente que le impide llegar al conocimiento real de Dios?

Recordemos que Juan escribió esta carta para atacar el concepto de que solo el intelecto me lleva a Dios, Juan nos motiva a dejar que EL SEA EL REY DE NUESTRAS VIDAS… QUE NUESTRO PENSAMIENTO SEA SOMETIDO EN EL ALTAR COMO UN SACRIFICIO DE ENTREGA Y FE.

¿Cuáles son los argumentos que se levantan contra el conocimiento de Dios? Muchos han luchado diciendo que la mayoría tiene la razón… ¿si muchos lo hacen yo por qué no? La historia ha probado una y otra vez que la mayoría no siempre tiene razón. Cristóbal Colón probó que la mayoría estaba equivocado en creer que la tierra era plana. Nicolás Copérnico probó que la mayoría estuvo equivocado en creer que el sol giraba alrededor de la tierra. Luis Pasteur probó que la mayoría estuvo equivocado en creer que los gérmenes tienen un principio espontáneo.

Pensamientos que justifican el pecado, nos alivian la conciencia PERO NOS ALEJAN DE DIOS.

¿Qué argumentos debe hoy usted entregar?, ¿Qué fortalezas debe derribar en el nombre de Jesús?... estas fortalezas se oponen a Dios y le llevarán a la perdición total… ES TIEMPO DE DERRIBARLAS

3. **Al amor de Dios nos da vida y razón de vivir:**
3.1 **Nos hace instrumentos de adoración a su nombre:**
    HEB. 13:15, 16: "Así que ofrezcamos siempre a Dios, por medio de él, sacrificio de alabanza, es decir, fruto de labios que confiesan su nombre"
    1 Ped. 2:5: Vosotros también como piedras vivas, sed edificados como casa

espiritual y sacerdocio santo, para ofrecer sacrificios espirituales aceptables a Dios por medio de Jesucristo.

3.2 **Nos da Su Palabra para guiarnos**: LUEGO de TERMINAR LA OBRA DE PURIFICACIÓN, JOSÍAS **Volvió a la Palabra de Dios: Redescubrió la Ley que estaba perdida, SE HUMILLÓ y actuó y llevó al pueblo a actuar con base en lo que allí estaba escrito.**

Su fervor y entrega hicieron eco en las lejanas y acabadas regiones de Israel…

3.3 **Nos da vida en lugar de muerte**:

EL QUE CREE EN EL HIJO TIENE VIDA ETERNA; PERO EL QUE REHUSA CREER EN EL HIJO NO VERÁ LA VIDA, SINO QUE LA IRA DE DIOS ESTÁ SOBRE ÉL. Jn. 3:36

"Pero Dios, que es rico en misericordia, por su gran amor con que nos amó, aún estando nosotros muertos en pecados, nos dio vida juntamente con Cristo (Por gracia sois salvos)…" Efesios 2:4,5

CONCLUSIÓN:

● **LA CRUZ lugar de rescate, de intercambio**… entrego mis pecados, mis temores, mis dudas y recibo salvación, restauración, el rescate: la liberación del dominio de Satanás para recibir la liberación y la inclusión en la familia del amor. En los brazos del salvador.

● **Los brazos del Salvador estuvieron abiertos en la cruz** y continúan abiertos aún más después de la resurrección para recibir a todo el que viene a él para brindarle su amor. Pero queda claro que quien se acerca a El para recibir su amor… no podrá salir de allí igual. El llamado a restauración y regeneración es para todos. La decisión es personal. Sería ilógico y hasta irreverente decir que el amor del Señor me ha dejado igual y que aún a pesar de tenerlo en mí mi vida no ha cambiado… ES TIEMPO DE VENIR A SUS PIES Y RECIBIR SU AMOR LIBERADOR El no te rechaza si vienes a El en humildad… pero si le rechazas hoy… tu recibirás las consecuencias.

● **LLAMADO:**

● **¿CONSIDERA USTED QUE ES CAPAZ DE SANAR Y LIBRAR SU ALMA?** ¿Se considera capaz de vencer las obras del diablo? Una respuesta sincera deberá ser: No… y esto nos da descanso pues la biblia nos deja claro que no somos nosotros, nuestra condición nos lleva a reconocer que somos débiles y que aún cuando queremos hacer el bien, el pecado quiere siempre apoderarse de mí, pero esta no debe convertirse en una excusa para pecar, sino en una oportunidad para acercarnos más AL TODO PODEROSO: Es JESUCRISTO EL ÚNICO QUE PUDO HACERLO

- "1 Juan 3:5,8 "Y sabéis que EL apareció para quitar nuestros pecado y no hay pecado en Él...el que practica el pecado es del diablo; porque el diablo peca desde el principio. *PARA ESTO APARECIÓ EL HIJO DE DIOS, PARA DESHACER LAS OBRAS DEL DIABLO.*

ES TIEMPO DE VENIR A LA CRUZ, ABANDONARSE EN LOS BRAZOS AMOROSOS DE Jesús, LOS ÚNICOS BRAZOS QUE DAN UN AMOR QUE TRANSFORMA, SANA Y SALVA. Un amor que da vida en lugar de muerte, un amor que vence el mal y las obras del mal en mi vida, un amor que me hace un adorador y fiel hijo de Dios.

VEN A SUS BRAZOS DE AMOR HOY.

Misses to be Avoided

Gloria Villa Diaz

We are familiar with tests. Students take tests periodically to prove they have assimilated knowledge in their classes. Doctors ask for lab tests to make sure our bodies are working perfectly. Skills are tested before a candidate gets the job he/she applied for. The Gospel for today helps us to examine our individual and communal approach to Jesus Christ.

We as Christian Cumberland Presbyterian Church believe that Jesus Christ sustains the creation, (Colossians). Jesus Christ is the closest image of God we have. Therefore He is the only who can show us the divine and eternal Creator and owner of the universe, (John 15). Jesus Christ is the one who erased any wall or curtain that could separate us, human creation, from the almighty God. In his crucifixion Jesus washed away every poor decision we took against ourselves. Also Jesus took away every wrong action we did against our loved ones and neighbor. Jesus cleansed every bad thought we had against God. With his resurrection Jesus Christ freed his creation to be back in relationship with the eternal Father. As a result Jesus Christ remains central for us Christians as Jesus is the foundation of God's covenant with the people. In the same way Jesus is the foundation of our relationship with God.

Mark 6:14-29 tells the sad story of an infamous man named Herod Antipas, the king of Galilee, and his relationship with John the Baptizer. As John was the messenger sent before Jesus, Herod's response to John would determine his future connection with Jesus. In Herod's time Jesus was known as a popular prophet and a potential political leader. At the same time Jesus, the one we receive as son of God, was famous for doing massive public campaigns that included healings and food festivals. Therefore in Herod's mind there would be two options, either to join Jesus as political strategist, or destroy Jesus' political dreams. Herod didn't want a political opponent in his territory.

Herod gathered information about Jesus from many sources. Herod's supporters, the Galilee Chronicles, and of course the vocal messengers who would amplify or distort what they saw and heard. Herod was informed that Jesus made once a humongous public campaign that ended in a food festival for 5000 attendees. Herod knew that people claimed Jesus to be a healer of the blind, a healer of the deaf, and a friend of the poor, the aliens, and the sick. That news must puzzle Herod's heart because the new leader in town would jeopardize Herod's political power and his relationship with his boss, the roman emperor. In other words, Herod defined Jesus as other political adversary, not a prophet, nor spiritual leader, no maybe the Son of God.

Herod's story apparently does nothing to do with us today as we claim neither to be politicians nor see Jesus as a political leader reigning against our nation. In fact, we today pretend to have no problems with any political leader. We would have problems to follow the law, and law has to do with politics, but we claim to have no difficulties with a political figure in particular. Also we recognize that our leadership over some people is done with good intentions. But we have problems when we feel that Jesus wants to have the control of ourselves.

Jesus was a political intruder for Herod; while Jesus is an intruder into what we love the most, our private lives. It is what we are taught through personal testimonies, through the Bible, through the church and through the Holy Spirit. The first thing we know about Jesus is that He becomes an intruder in the places where we, controllers of our lives, don't let others to come.

Besides, Mark 6:14-29 refers to how a chain of very poor personal decisions made Herod to change his perception of Jesus from a political enemy to a Zombie. Instead of seeing a leader, Herod saw a monster he was scared to dead of confronting personally. What did Herod lead to make those poor decisions and then be afraid of Jesus?

Let's say now that there are "misses" which are not good to hang on with. When we think of "misses", it comes to mind: the multimillionaire Donald Trump and his Miss USA and Miss Universe pageant. Those misses are beautiful women with physical, intellectual and spiritual attributes. However, the gospel on Mark is not referring to that kind of beautiful ladies.

The Gospel of Mark refers to some very dangerous behaviors that would be inserted in the life of any person, even church people. If reinforced, those behaviors will lead individuals and/or groups to a fatal relationship with others and of course with God.

These "misses" were present in the life of Herod and they, the "misses" that are strange behaviors led him to have family problems, then to imprison an innocent, next to kill John the Baptizer, and finally to see in Jesus a monster instead of a savior and friend.

We cannot assume that Herod had to react in self-defense against any enemy. Herod was not protecting his government or his kingship. That would be a valid excuse for what he did. However Herod the king of Galilee became famous to Christianity, not because he achieved several political goals as he did, but because he acted as a vulgar killer and then, out of his mind, Herod was petrified because He saw in Jesus a super powerful specter that must be destroyed along with his followers.

What are those behaviors that have form of misses but are not ladies?

The first miss that misleads the relationship with Jesus Christ and with any other person is:

1. Misconception concerning who Jesus Christ is and what Jesus Christ does. It occurs when the information about who Jesus is not confirmed by different sources, but is rooted on lose comments.

Herod heard about Jesus by John's sermons many times. What did Herod heard? John the Baptizer begged his audience to await *"the Lamb of God who takes away the sin of the world"*. John made sure everybody knew Jesus was the expected Lamb. Jesus will take human sins away! John proclaimed his personal experience when He baptized Jesus on the Jordan River. John told everybody that the heaven was torn open and the Spirit descended on Jesus like a dove. And a voice came from heaven saying of Jesus: *"You are my Son, whom I love; with you I am well pleased."* (Mark 1:11). John proclaimed openly: *"Jesus is the powerful one who will baptize everybody with the Holy Spirit."* John preached that "Jesus was before the humanity with God as Jesus was God. Through Jesus, the world receives grace and truth." (John 1:1-18). John preached publicly and privately. He made sure Israelites, including his governors, would be open minded to welcome Jesus as the hope to the entire nation.

Herod had the opportunity to question personally Jesus as he did to John the Baptizer. Jesus was walking through Galilee cities, villages, and towns. Jesus drove in on roads Herod controlled. But, unfortunately, Herod lost the opportunity to hear Jesus' voice, to see Jesus' face, to stare at Jesus' gestures. Herod didn't know who Jesus was from Jesus' own lips. He limited himself to some references brought by third parties. The other day Beto, one loved pastor as called to help Jim and Richard in their ministerial conflict. Beto listened to Jim friends' version of the problem but forgot to listen to Richard's version of the conflict. As consequence, instead of helping two dear brothers in Christ, Beto intervention made Jim and Richard to end far from each other.

We are to be careful with the information we have regarding to Jesus because that information should lead us to meet Jesus as the son of God. What it's expected is that we dedicate our lives to meet God's presence through Jesus, to explore Jesus Christ's divinity. We serve Jesus Christ according to the eternal love of God and the gifts we have. We join others to hear God's actions as the body of Christ. We gather to enjoy God's deeds among us. Through the Bible we refresh our relationship with Jesus Christ. During our daily routines, we hear, see, smell, and taste many powerful acts of Jesus in heaven and on Earth. We adore Jesus because without Jesus our lives have no meaning. On the light of these events we make sense of our lives and our personal and collective experiences. Then, we are encouraged to embrace those who can't believe or are lost. Our NDIC ministry is supported by our belief that there is enough space for every person in God's kingdom. The prisoners, the ex-offenders, the homeless, their relatives and the day-laborers are included in Jesus' salvific plan.

However, the truth is that we are tempted to reduce our faith to a bunch of moral codes Time to time. Or in the other hand, we tend to play to be our own god. As consequence, Jesus is erased from our ethics and our god is anything but the clown of our misery, a ghost that becomes our worst nightmare, as happened to Herod.

If the misconception about Jesus Christ persists, it leads to:

2.   Misbelieve concerning the intentions of Jesus Christ: Misbelieve or disbelief occurs when there is a lack of trust in Jesus. This lack of reliance makes people do not experience salvation, freedom, joy and peace from Heaven.

In Mark 6, we read Herod got a false believe about Jesus because he missed the most of John's sermons. Herod got puzzled every time John spoke but Herod reduced all John's sermons to a personal attack he couldn't overcome. Time later, Herod became guilty of killing John the Baptizer without a legal, fair trial, or political reason. Herod felt bad because in his heart grew a mountain of guilt. When Jesus became known in Galilee, Herod concluded that John resurrected. The problem was not the resurrection. Herod was afraid that Jesus would hurt him, kill him, or destroy him in revenge for John the baptizer. This misbelieve made Herod a very scared man who saw in Jesus a powerful enemy that came from the other world.

A guilt loaded person like Herod bears a painful feeling of self-reproach. He/she perceives others as judges that are condemning him/her all the time. This condition becomes a barrier to enjoy open and safe relationships with others. When ex-offenders who come for first time, they say "I didn't do what I was accused of." But at the same time are angry, accusing clerks, bosses, workmates of being idiots, stupid, and other pejorative qualifications. The way to be free of the misery of a guilty conscience is meeting Jesus Christ because Jesus is the only one who takes away all sins of misbelieving and guiltiness. Then the heart and mind of whoever believes in Jesus is free to be in relationship with God and others.

Nevertheless, if not overcome, misconception and misbelieve, will gladly invite one more miss:

3.   Misunderstanding concerning the relationship with Jesus. If the shame continues, it appears a strong disagreement within oneself and the world surrounded.

Herod couldn't get along with John. Even though Herod called John a righteous and holy man, Herod couldn't overcome John's sermons on his marriage with his brother's wife. But worse than an illegal marriage, Herod forgot that it was said that Jesus, the popular prophet, was the Lamb of God who could take away his past.

The inconsistency in Herod is not found in a dogma or instruction. The contradiction was not with the sermons and pastoral counseling. The conflict stated because due to misconception and misbelieve Herod couldn't get along with himself and with others like Jesus. It was very sad for me to hear one of the members of the church to say: "Jesus makes miracles in my life everyday" but at the same time was complaining of others members of the church because "they are not as generous and loving people [like me]." She moved to a different congregation, I hope so.

We tend to think that attendees leave the church for problems with liturgy or theological perspectives. But the reality is that it is impossible to live oneself in accordance with a conscience that censure and blame regret 24 hours at day, seven days at week and the 12 months of the year. The only self-defense is the same read in Genesis 3. After Adam and Eve realized their wrong actions, Adam blamed Eve and Eve blamed the serpent. A person with a heavy load of guilt learns to blame the world, to live in denial, and to hide her/his own misery. The natural step down in this road is written in Genesis 4:8. Cain killed his brother Abel. Centuries later, Herod killed John the Baptizer, and most likely wanted to kill Jesus as well.

Of course, Herod didn't plan to kill a good man during his birthday party. But a good intention of a birthday party turned to be a nightmare. Three siblings agreed to celebrate mothers' day with a big party at mom's house. They bought a beautiful dress for mom; daughter took their mom to the hair stylist. Mom looked like the queen of the house. During the celebration the two brothers started discussing about the next family celebration. They were a little drunk. The argument escalated to the point that they felt mutually offended. One shot the other and mother's day ended in funeral with other son in jail.

Herod Antipas was not a cruel person. History doesn't say Herod Jr. was a killer or a king who agree with massacres. Herod was not as his father Herod the Great who killed toddlers and babies in Bethlehem 30 years before. Herod Jr was a person trying to fulfill his personal, family and public responsibilities. But the truth is that his hands were bloody stained and his soul was tortured by the shadow of his memories with John. Jesus' fame reinforced Herod's miserable condition.

Reflection:
>
> We are called today by Mark 6 to examine ourselves. Do we live with any Miss mentioned above?
>
> Misconceptions about Jesus Christ move us away from his forgiveness.
>
> Misbelieving about Jesus Christ moves us away from faith in him.
>
> Misunderstanding about Jesus Christ moves us away from relationship with others.

In consequence:
>
> It is arrogance to trust in own-good intentions.
>
> It is dangerous to trust in own wisdom.
>
> It is very risky to live a self-centered life.
>
> It is not sufficient to hear about God's word.
>
> It is no enough to be puzzled by God's word.
>
> It is necessary to listen to, to question, and to pray the word of God. Then, it is good to sit next to Jesus Christ to enjoy his relationship, his salvation and his presence, sometimes alone, sometimes with the saints at church.

If any "miss-behavior" is discovered within us, we are on time to cast out what the Holy Spirit guides us to throw away. If we are not sure on what we believe about Jesus Christ, we should organize, synthesize and summarize our faith. Then, we can compare our faith with our creeds because they are examples of a way to sum up the Christian faith. They, the creeds give us a safe environment to grow up in relationship with Jesus Christ.

Upon the creeds, we can look for people of faith and how they commit themselves to God. One example I find of relationship is given by responsible parents, including moms, dads, grandmas, and foster parents. They take time to meet personally their children and children's friends. Those parents have a tendency to ask their children about their friends saying something like, Julius, How did you meet your friend Grace? Where does she live? Does she have siblings? Who picks her up at school?

All these questions are not intended to put others aside, but to guide the children to faithful, healthy, and solid relationships while they are growing.

In the same way, let's not only look like Christians but act as Christians. Let us question our knowledge and relationship with Jesus. Let us inquire on our assumptions about what we think as religious people or what we think is the truth about Jesus. As the Holy Spirit brings us close to Jesus, books, the Bible, our Bible studies along with our service to others are good companions to grow faithfully in relationship with Jesus. Our attitude to worship God and our joy to meet others will grade our level of relationship with Jesus. At the same time let Jesus to imprint himself in our life. Let me share one story:

After 6 years of marriage my husband and I discover that we had problems with fertility. We were ready to invest much of our time, efforts and money looking to have a baby while we attended the seminary. Lab tests were the beginning of the diagnostic: our obstetrician affirmed that even we had a primary infertility it would be easy for us to have a baby. My husband and I followed all his instructions to get pregnant. Then we prayed to God dedicating the baby to Jesus without understanding what we were doing, but it sounded spiritual. We were excited, happy, and triumphant.

However weeks later we received the sad news that the baby was dead. The doctor just advised us to wait several months before trying again to get pregnant. I was frustrated and very disappointed. As student I was able to attend classes on theology, read about it and discuss diverse perspectives of church, religion, and faith. But when classes were over and so my homework, I felt empty and worthless. One day while walking inside the mall I saw a maternity clothe store. A deep angriness against God blossomed from a hidden part of me. I got scared of myself because it was new for me that I had that kind of sentiment inside me. This event happened several times and it was triggered always for those maternity clothe stores. I shared my experience with others but no one said anything; I prayed but anything happened.

Months later while I was walking through a very crowded street I felt the warm presence of Jesus next to me. I was glad to feel God in the midst of many people. Then, Jesus said to me with a very soft voice: "Gloria, you are mourning for a person you will never know. However I mourn everyday for all these people you see because I know them inside out but they reject me." Next, without words, Jesus took my pain out of my heart and let me live without that suffering. Jesus has been with me as my confident friend and restorer of my life.

Prayer:

"Search me, O God, and know my heart; test me and know my anxious thoughts. See if
there is any offensive way in me, and lead me in the way everlasting."
In your mercy forgive what we have been and done without you,
help us to overcome what we are in the midst of our mis-relationship with Jesus,
and direct what we shall be,
so that we may delight in your will and walk in your ways, as your loved ones.
Let us show up your everlasting love in the world to the glory of your holy name. In
Jesus Christ we pray, Amen.

The Hem of Jesus' Robe

Virginia Espinoza

(Mark 5: 25-34)

The world is a cynical world. People in general don't believe in everyday miracles. Case and point, let us look at Thomas as he is told by fellow disciples that they have seen Jesus, listen to what Thomas says to the disciples, ".... Unless I see the nail marks in his hand and put my finger where the nails were, and put my hands into his side, I will not believe it." (John 20: 25). So, just as one of Jesus' own disciple did not believe in the wondrous miracle that took place, we too, have our doubts and in so doing we lose sight of all the miracles that happen all around us. In this world of "show me and I will believe" the story from Mark calls upon us to look at this story through the eyes of faith. This is about witnessing to believers as well as to unbelievers.

Now let us look at this woman who believed that just touching the hem of Jesus' robe would heal her, it showed a great deal of faith, but, the story is not about the garment healing as much as it shows us that Jesus is the healer. Jesus and not the garment is the healer and not just our physical body but also our spiritual body. To be completely well is to be healed body and soul. The woman's faith led her to Jesus, led her to reach out to the last person who she believed could help her. All of her physical resources were gone, the physicians had done what they could for her and yet she was not healed. Jesus was her last resort.

In verses 27, 28 Scripture says, "When she heard about Jesus, she came up behind him in the crowd and touched his cloak, because she thought, "If I just touch his clothes, I will be healed". So, as we look at this passage let us look at this story as if this woman represents the Church. If look at it this way it means that the church is slowly bleeding to death and the only hope we the church have is to touch Jesus again. There are people today and in communities throughout the country that are bleeding to death. The only hope and answer is to touch Jesus again. By reaching out to touch the hem of Jesus we can began the restoration and healing of the Church. The world needs to touch Jesus and touch others with the healing power of Jesus Christ.

Let us look and think about this passage as if this woman, not only had an issue of blood, but, were there other issues in her life? We can place ourselves alongside this woman because her issues may very well be ours also. Let us look at some issues that apply to us today. Then let us ask ourselves, "What are the issues in our lives that need healing?"

1.   **A physical issue:** The issue of blood was a physical issue. This woman suffered for twelve years. Every day, every hour, every second, she was aware of her physical condition. As women we can relate to this illness and we know the length she would have gone to ease the suffering. Maybe, there is someone sitting next to you who knows how this woman felt, maybe, there is illness in our family that has drained and exhausted us. The hopelessness and despair can be very overwhelming and when all hope is gone and we have nowhere else to go reach out and touch Jesus. The story of Mark tells us that we should reach out to Jesus first. Touching Jesus is all that matters, for Jesus is the healer of all our illnesses. We must understand something very important here. God is never late. God does not work on our time-line. Living in this world we live under natural laws and natural laws are controlled by time. In 2 Peter 3: 8, he writes, "....With the Lord a day is like a thousand years and a thousand years are like a day." God has a perfect time and the impossible becomes possible when God's perfect time meets our natural time.

2.   **A financial Issue:** The second issue the woman had was a financial issue. If we have ever had an extended illness we know what that can do to our financial status. The medical treatment was very crude for a woman with a female hemorrhage as this illustration gives an excerpt from a rabbinical book quoted by Lightfoot: "Let them dig seven ditches, in which let them burn some cuttings of vines under four years old. Let her take in her hand a cup of wine; let them lead her away from this ditch and make her sit over that. Let them remove her form that and sit her over another. At each removal you must say to her, 'Arise from thy flux'." This is an illustration of what this woman suffered. The tragedy was, she did not get better but rather her condition worsened. She was also broke.

Today we could say she sold her house, car, TV, furniture, jewelry, everything she owned. She had no more resources, no CD's, no savings, NOTHING, NOTHING WAS LEFT. We can all relate to that and we can feel the despair.

This is where grace and mercy came to her through a man called Jesus, her only hope. In 2 Corinthians 8: 9, Paul writes, "For ye know the grace of our Lord Jesus Christ, that, though he was rich, yet for our sakes he became poor, that ye through his poverty might be rich." Jesus came so that we might have life and have life abundantly. We must understand the verse above is not only for our spiritual existence but for every area of our lives. Whether it is our spiritual, physical, or material existence, God wants to treat us better than we deserve.

3.   **A family and friends issue:** In Leviticus a woman with an issue of blood was regarded as unclean and anything she touched was unclean (Leviticus 15: 19-27). For twelve years she was an outcast. She knew how it felt to be cast out of the community. She knew the loneliness of being ignored and shunned by people, even, the women who had once been her friends. She knew loneliness especially if she were married. For twelve years she was not allowed to touch her husband or her children, if she had children. She was not allowed to walk in the streets where there were people. She was not allowed to sit on anything in public places. No one dared to come and visit. She was all alone in the world. In fact the law decreed that if she was caught in public, they had a right to kill her.

In her approach to Jesus she took an overwhelming risk. She dared to come to him in the midst of the crowd and then she dared to touch a man, even if it was just the hem of his garment. Her act was punishable by law, yet, for her, a death sentence had been passed on her for twelve years and she had nothing to lose and everything to gain.

4.   **A faith issue:** The last issue had to do with faith. How many of us can relate to this? How many of us today realize that after twelve years of loneliness and being shunned by her community that she would have a faith problem? With each passing year, day, month, hour and moment her level of faith grew smaller.

Maybe, you also, have a faith issue. Maybe, you also feel it's not worth the trouble to believe anymore. Maybe, you are just going through the motion each day, and each Sunday, you sit quietly in your pew and wonder what you are doing here? Then, listen, reach out and touch the hem of Jesus' garment and renew your commitment to him. Life will never be the same for you again.

I thank God that God is only looking for faith as big, or rather as small as a mustard seed. With faith the size of a mustard seed your life will take on new meaning and vitality. One of my favorite scriptures is from Hebrews 11: 1, "Now faith is being sure of what we hope for and certain of what we do not see." God calls on us to just believe. Believe in the Word that became flesh and dwelt among us.

When we look at this story by Mark, there are two things that stand out to me.
1) Desperation; the woman had nothing to lose. She had already lost everything. Her pride, self-esteem, and self-worth were gone. She had no dignity left so she got down on hands and knees and crawled her way through the crowd, this she did to touch his garment. Her only thought was, "…If I but touch his garment I will be healed." Her faith gave her the determination to reach out to him.

2) She DARED to touch to Him; she had to touch him. As we read her story we must understand that to touch anything around her became unclean. Her uncleanness would make Him unclean. Yet, she knew that all her hope was to get to Jesus, the One person who could bring her healing and wholeness. His cleanness would make her clean, his purity would make her pure.

How desperate are you? Would you risk your very life to reach out to Jesus?
So many of us just sit in our pews and do nothing. We think, there is nothing I can do, but, we are only defeating the powers that we have. Jesus gave us the power to help others in their trials. To give hope, to those dying in despair. A kind word doesn't cost us anything, a smile may give someone hope to continue to live.

Today, it doesn't matter how your life looks. It doesn't matter what issues you have. It is impossible for us to change Jesus by touching Him. You see, the change takes place in us when Jesus touches us.

Healing is a powerful manifestation of God's Kingdom here on earth but it comes with the insistence that we respond by our faith. When we look at our situations, sometime, I think we forget how powerful the God we worship is, God's power is made available at the point where human possibilities are exhausted. When we have nowhere else to turn, God is patiently waiting for us. Miracles are not merely self-evident, objective events in the world, but require the response of faith, just like the woman in Mark's story, her miracle began in desperation and ended in indescribable JOY!

God's mercy is shown not simply to the well-to-do and deserving, but especially to those who are down and out without hope in the world. God's power cannot be deterred even by the power of death; hope is a possibility even in the face of apparent hopelessness.

Today, dare to touch Jesus. Everything was done for us on Calvary. No amount of money or programs or whatever we can give can repay Him. What Jesus did he did out of love and then gave it freely to us. In Isaiah 53: 5, the writer says, "But he was pierced for our transgressions, he was crushed for our iniquities; the punishment that brought us peace was upon him, and by his wounds we are healed." Many things could be said but I believe this tells us that by His blood we are healed and made whole. It is ours for the asking.

Be bold like the woman in Mark's story, touch Jesus and be made whole, then in turn pass it on to someone in desperate need of Jesus' touch and healing.

If Walls Could Talk

Nancy J. Fuqua

(Daniel 5:1-6)

Good Morning and to God be the Glory

Let us pray….. Amen

Just the other day, I heard the song writer say "Early this morning when I arose I didn't have no doubts, because I knew the Lord would take care of me". Can I get a witness here today? Do you know that the Lord will take care of you In the word of God Jesus said if you don't cry out the rocks will and I don't want know rocks crying out for me. In every opportunity I get I will let the world know that I am a sanctified witness for the Lord.

Let me tell you this and I will get on with the message for today.
You know there is another song that comes to mind when the song writer said "I went over to my window, while looking through the shade, just a few feet away in a tree I saw robin and he was singing a song. I don't know what he was saying, but I believe he was saying thank you Lord for another day. Now if a robin can say thank you Lord, we can do it to". Now Let's give God a hand clap of praise Amen, Amen!!, Amen!!!

I invite your ears and heart to this passage of scripture

Daniel 5:1-6 (New Revised Standard Version) which reads as follows

¹ Belshazzar the king held a great feast for a thousand of his nobles, and he was drinking wine in the presence of the thousand.

² When Belshazzar tasted the wine, he gave orders to bring the gold and silver vessels which Nebuchadnezzar his father had taken out of the temple which was in Jerusalem, so that the king and his nobles, his wives and his concubines might drink from them.

3 Then they brought the gold vessels that had been taken out of the temple, the house of God which was in Jerusalem; and the king and his nobles, his wives and his concubines drank from them.

4 They drank the wine and praised the gods of gold and silver, of bronze, iron, wood and stone.

5 Suddenly the fingers of a man's hand emerged and began writing opposite the lampstand on the plaster of the wall of the king's palace, and the king saw the back of the hand that did the writing.

6 Then the king's face grew pale and his thoughts alarmed him, and his hip joints went slack and his knees began knocking together....

From this scripture I bring this thought: "**If walls could talk**" - what would they tell on you?

Looking at the scripture that was read in your hearing we find that "King Belshazzar held a great feast for his one thousand nobles. The wine flowed freely. Belshazzar, heady with the wine, ordered that the gold and silver chalices his father Nebuchadnezzar had stolen from God's Temple of Jerusalem be brought in so that he and his nobles, his wives and concubines, could drink from them. When the gold and silver chalices were brought in, the king and his nobles, his wives and his concubines, drank wine from them. They drank the wine and drunkenly praised their gods made of gold and silver, bronze and iron, wood and stone," (The Message)

A national festival is not in itself sinful; nor was it the eating and drinking in moderation, but the excess, and the spirit in which it was done, that made King Belshazzar's feast not agreeable with God.

All that he did at this party gave God heartburn that was out of this world. Their overdoing was a great sin, but their defiance of God and the mockery in using the sacred vessels brought from Jerusalem was a far greater sin.

If those walls could have talked wonder what they would have been saying about old King Belshazzar. You see the king and his lords, by using the holy vessels of the temple for their idolatrous festival, hurled defiance at God, and showed their contempt for His power over them. They forgot that God was the Almighty King who did according to His will in the armies of Heaven.

You know when liquor or shall I say self rising punch start talking a person can get courage they never had before and will do and say anything that come to mind. **My, my, my If Walls Could Talk**

Well pastor I don't know why you are preaching this to us. We don't do anything like that. But I am here to remind you that when Holy Communion is taken without faith to discern the Lord's body; In whatever way religion is dragged from its lofty and holy sphere, and made to be treated like a party with the party goer having no respect for the Lord's Supper, then and there we have a repetition of Belshazzar's sinful acts against God. When the Sabbath is made a day of pleasure, of visiting, feasting, and writing letters — and not a day of Worship and Praise of God; When the house of God is used for anything but the purposes of religious worship — then we have treaded upon that unholy ground as seen at Belshazzar's feast.

But let us leave this concern about the desecration of holy things and observe the party feast for a moment. It was one of great splendor. All you could eat, all you could drink, they were partying hardy. But the party got stopped. Daniel 5:5 says "Suddenly the fingers of a man's hand emerged and began writing opposite the lamp stand on the plaster of the wall of the king's palace, and the king saw the back of the hand that did the writing. **If wall's could talk what would they have said about this party. Well in a way these walls were talking when the handwriting appeared on the wall out of know where. They spoke so loud and clear that Daniel 5:6 says the old** king's face grew pale and his thoughts alarmed him, and his hip joints went slack and his knees began knocking together....

Now look at the scene. What is this a picture of? Can you express the whole of that revel or shall I say that wild party in one word? I think I can, and this is the word — godlessness.

If Walls could talk) This poor, luxurious, profane king, who comes up, drinks, trembles for an hour before us in the blaze of splendor, and then passes away swiftly into chaos and old night — this old king would never have been heard of, but for "the fingers of a man's hand that wrote ever against the candlestick upon the plaster of the wall of his palace." What message he has brought to us. **If Walls Could Talk.** There is nothing interesting in this man. He does nothing, says nothing, is nothing but made famous by his reaction to the hand writing on the wall. If men/women will not take the trouble to read the warnings of yesterday, tomorrow's fingers will write a word on their walls which will scare their eyeballs, and make their knees shake! We all ought to take kindly to the warnings of all history, **(If Walls could Talk)**

Let me come home for a minute. Are we partying like the old king and not paying attention to God's word. Does He need to do the handwriting on the wall for us today? We ought to be real and pass for what we are; and be what we pass for; If we pass for a Christian, we ought to use the passwords of the Christian religion; We ought to take heed to the warning in the words Mene, Mene, Tekel Peres that were written on the wall. If we don't we will be found out. But stop! before we blame King Belshazzar and other light kings, let us ask a question — Are we doing what we profess to do? Are we living the holy life that God has called us to? Are we ruling our households in the fear of God? **(If walls could talk)** Is there spiritual equality, love, purity, the law of truth, swaying the family? Is there a kingdom of God there? **(If walls could talk)** Ask yourself this question if you profess to have a conscience, a presiding God on your side. Are you taking it easy, and making light of your responsibilities, of the charge which God has laid upon you, and thinking that God don't see? **(If Walls could talk)** **The word of God says** "Let integrity and uprightness preserve us, O God of our salvation."

Wait a minute, wait a minute, I wish my walls could talk, I know they would not say Mene, Mene, Tekel Peres. I do know they would tell you how much I love the Lord, because he heard my cry and pitted my every groan. **If walls could talk** they would tell you how I praise Him with a tongue that never get tired!!!. They would tell you how I read his word and "Lean not to my own understanding"!!!! How I lift my hands in holy praise to God everyday of my life!!!! **if walls could talk** they would tell you about my praise and worship of God. They would tell you "I praise God everyday! With knees bent and body bowed when I pray in the walls of my home; **If walls could talk** my walls would tell you how I call on the name of Jesus in the midnight hour; saying here I am Lord leaning and depending on you. They would tell you I call him my all and all hear me right now; they would tell you I call him my wheel in the middle of a wheel. **If walls could talk;** they

83

would say I call him my battle ax in the time of war. They would say I call him my Lawyer in a courtroom and surly they would tell you I call him Dr. Jesus my doctor in a sick room,

Finally if my walls could talk they would tell you, I shout hallelujah when I just can't hold my peace. **If walls could talk what would they tell about you and your praise unto our Lord God almighty.**

I close with this thought from Daniel 5:24 "Therefore he sent the hand that wrote the inscription", Meaning God did. What would the wall tell on you if God sent the hand to write on your wall? To write on the wall of your heart.

Amen
Amen
Amen

Nueva Vida En Cristo
New Life in Christ

Michele Gentry

(Salmo 103:1-5, 20-22)
(1 Juan 3:1-2)

somos hijos adoptivos de Dios—1 Juan 3:1-2

¡Fíjense qué gran amor nos ha dado el Padre, que se nos llame hijos de Dios! ¡Y lo somos! El mundo no nos conoce, precisamente porque no lo conoció a él. Queridos hermanos, ahora somos hijos de Dios, pero todavía no se ha manifestado lo que habremos de ser. Sabemos, sin embargo, que cuando Cristo venga seremos semejantes a él, porque lo veremos tal como él es.

Hace años colaboraba con entidades oficiales en Colombia para prohijar la adopción de niños y niñas Colombianitos por familias europeas. Niños en la mayor parte abandonados, algunos entregados por una mamá que no los podía criar, que los amaba tanto que prefería entregarlos antes de ponerlos a sufrir. Y algunos que fueron retirados de situaciones de abuso.

Niños y niñas, a veces bebés, más frecuentemente de 3 a 5 años, y ocasionalmente de más edad.

Al final de los trámites cada uno ya era "criatura nueva".

- registro civil nuevo—y el viejo sellado;
- cambio a veces de nombre—aunque los nuevos papás se eforzaban por mantener
- el nombre al cual estaba acostumbrado el niño o la niña, tampoco iba a dejarlos con nombres que eran incomprensibles, o ridículos, o denigrantes en su nuevo país;
- ciertamente cambio de apellido;
- cambio de nacionalidad—con pasaporte nuevo;

85

- hasta aquí todo más bien fácil, pero luego llega el cambio a otro país,otro idioma, otra casa, otras comidas, otro clima, otras costumbres, otra familia—abuelos, tíos, primos y a veces hasta hermanos.

Este último paso es siempre el más difícil.

HISTORIA DE UNA NIÑA ADOPTADA

- Hubo una niña de 6 años que necesitaba una familia. Y una familia que deseaba tener una hija. La solución: adopción.
- Primero llegó el libro de vida nueva que enviaron los padres nuevos con muchas fotos para que la niña empezara a familiarizarse con su entorno futuro.
- Luego llegaron los padres adoptivos y con la niña se fueron a vivir a una hotel a conocerse.
- La vida en los primeros días fue de resistencia absoluta por parte de la niña; no quería saber nada de nada, especialmente del idioma raro que hablaba esas personas.
- Pero llegó el día en que todos asistían a una fiesta en mi casa para celebrar el cumpleaños de uno de mis hijos. Hubo torta de chocolate. La mamá ofrece un pedazo a la niña diciendo (en noruego)—*KAKE* -. La niña rehusa la palabra y la torta. Después de tres intentos la mamá se da por vencida. Sintiendo la tristeza de la niña la invito con señas a la cocina y le sirvo su torta. Regresó a la sala con plato en mano y en toda el pasillo la escucho decir en voz muy baja: kake, kake, kake ... ¡Por fin se derrumbó el muro de resistencia y la familia se integró!
- 10 años después la mamá y la niña regresan a Colombia a visitar los sitios de la infancia. Luego de caminar y observar durante tres días le preguntamos a la niña qué pensaba. Su declaración me impactó: esta gente parece a mí por fuera pero por dentro es muy diferente. Es decir, ya era persona nueva, completamente integrada a su familia y vida nuevas.

Esa niña no escogió su familia, pero personas muy sabias la seleccionaron de varias que buscaban hijita.

Imagínate que empiezas tu vida de nuevo y te llevan al inmenso almacén de papás donde puedes pedir un papá a la medida, ¿que clase de papá escogerías? Pues la mayoría escogería
- uno con brazos fuertes y manos cariñosas, dispuesto a brindar cuidados,
- un hombre trabajador pero al mismo tiempo dispuesto a escuchar todo lo que

quisiéramos contar,

- un varón sabio para ayudarnos a diferenciar entre lo bueno y lo malo, para ayudarnos a escoger bien, a caminar correctamente,
- pero dispuesto a perdonar cuando nos equivocamos, a educar, a guiar.

Así, lleno de tantas cualidades pediríamos un papá.

Creo que muy pocos de nosotros nos fijaríamos en su estatura, su belleza física, o la cantidad de dinero que tuviera en el banco. Sólo que sea un buen, muy buen, papá.

La buena noticia es que hay un papá así y que nosotros podemos escogerlo. Aunque no pudimos escoger el padre terrenal, sí podemos escoger el mejor padre de todos—el Padre Celestial y si se lo pedimos, Él nos adopta.

La niña de mi historia no tuvo que "ganar" el privilegio de pertenecer a la nueva familia. La aceptaron tal como era, sin imponer condiciones.

Igual nuestro Padre Celestial. Sólo pide que expresemos nuestro deseo de formar parte de Su familia—recibiendo a Cristo Jesús—para hacer efectivo de una la adopción.

A cuantos lo recibieron, a los que creemos en su nombre, les dio el derecho de ser hios de Dios. Estos no nacen de la sangre, ni por deseos naturales, ni por voluntad humana, sino que nacen de Dios. (Juan 1:12-13)

HIJOS ADOPTADOS
Cuando llegamos a Cristo, el Padre Celestial nos adopta

- nos da un nuevo registro civil—registrado en el Libro de Vida del cielo y en la iglesia en las Actas de Bautismo o de reafirmación de fe—con el viejo registo civil
- sellado.
- un nuevo nombre—que sólo conoce nuestro Padre Celestial y que supuestamente nos lo revelará cuando lleguemos a Su presencia
- ciertamente un nuevo apellido—aunque el mundo todavía nos reconoce por el apellido "civil" que tenemos, todos ya somos "de Cristo". Ya no somos Ricardo o María, Johan o Michele sino Ricardo de Cristo, María de Cristo, Johan de Cristo, y Michele de Cristo.
- además, somos ya ciudadanos de un país nuevo—el cielo, con pasaporte—de manera

que cuando lleguemos a la frontera, se nos franqueará la puerta—¡de una!

• pero—siempre hay un pero—todo esto implica integrarnos a una vida nueva, con nuevas costumbres, nuevo idioma, y nuevos hermanos y hermanas.

¿Y QUÉ ANHELA DIOS DE SUS HIJOS E HIJAS ADOPTIVAS?
Lo que quiere cualquier padre, cualquier madre.

Dios desea tener una verdadera relación con nosotros.
- en Colombia hay un número significativo de hijos de padres secuestrados, hijos que fueron bebés cuando el papá fue secuestrado o que nacieron después del secuestro;
- esos muchachos se han criado viendo fotos de su papá, escuchando historias de ese papá, pero no hay verdadera relación;
- cuando en fin llega el papá a la casa—si tiene suerte y sobrevive—el papá y el hijo tienen que tomar un tiempo para conocerse, para formar una relación

Así para que la niñita de mi historia se integrara en la familia fue necesario tener el **deseo**, y abrir vías de **comunicación**.

Así como la familia adoptante deseaba formar una verdadera relación con su nueva hijita, Dios desea que crezcamos y maduramos en nuestra relación con Él. Es decir,
- que estrechemos nuestra nueva relación con Él,
- que le conozcamos como es Él,
- que mostremos ganas y gozo de ser Sus hijos,
- que hablemos con Él con frecuencia
- que nos integremos con nuestros hermanos y hermanos en la fe.

ABRIR ESPACIO PARA DIOS
- para relacionarnos con Dios tenemos que aprender sobre Él y aprender de Él. El Domingo por la mañana no es suficiente! Si el Domingo no es suficiente, entonces? **dedicar parte de cada día a edificar la relación**

Como Padre, Dios también desea que nos parezcamos a Él
Entre mis hijos hay uno que ciertamente a primera vista no se parece a su papá—es mucho más alto y mucho más rubio. Pero en su manera de hablar y caminar, es igualito a su papá.

Y es médico como el papá. Los tres trabajamos en la misma institución y a veces causa risa cuando los veo a los dos alejarse por un pasillo de la clínica—el alto y el bajo, el gringo y el latino—los dos con sus batas blancas, los dos con el mismo paso lento, ambos con la misma postura.

Pero, si Dios es espíritu, ¿cómo parecerse a Él en el campo físico?
Tener un ejemplo es mucho mejor que tener un descripción. El refrán chino dice que "una imagen vale más que mil palabras"—nuestro "imagen", nuestro ejemplo es Jesucristo.

Les he puesto el ejemplo, para que hagan lo mismo que yo he hecho con ustedes. (Juan 13:15)

PARECERNOS A CRISTO
saber más de Dios y de Cristo a trevés de un tiempo diario para lectura bíblica y **meditación** (que lleva a la aplicación práctica), el estudio bíblico de la iglesia y/o participación en un grupo pequeño de estudio y oración, y usar lo aprendido para imitar a Cristo -

Seguir el ejemplo del amor de Cristo
porque Cristo es la expresión del amor de Dios para nosotros—un amor puro y sin intereses personales; un amor que está siempre renovado y renovándose; un amor que se brinda sin condiciones ni ataduras.

Seguir el ejemplo de la vida con propósito de Cristo
Jesús declara su propósito en Lucas 19:10 *Porque el Hijo del hombre vino a buscar y a salvar lo que había perdido.* En nuestra vida como comunidad de fe hacemos muchas cosas: adoramos, proclamamos la Palabra, gozamos de confraternidad (la compañía unos de otros), estudiamos, y buscamos extender el Reino de Dios por mediode ayudar otros en la acción social, y compartir de Cristo testificando de Él. Todas estas cosas haremos también en el cielo menos trabajar para extender el Reino de Dios—eso es nuestra tarea aquí en la tierra.

Seguir su ejemplo en la oración.
La comunicación es la mejor manera de forjar una relación. Jesús habló mucho con su Padre.
• Oró en adoración, contemplando las verdades y características de Dios. Nosotros también hemos de orar así.

- Cristo oró por las necesidades de otros, y nosotros hemos de elevar oración de súplica otras personas, especialmente por los que aún no conocen a Cristo.
- y también hemos de pedir por necesidades personales.
- La única forma de oración que no hizo Cristo fue la confesión—porque nunca pecó. Pero nosotros debemos presentarnos ante Dios conscientes de nuestras fallas para pedirle perdón, y aceptar ese perdón.

CREAR UN AMBIENTE PROPICIO

Hay que administrar bien nuestra vida nueva—nuestra vida espiritual cuidando nuestro entorno

- al comprar tenis nuevos, finos y por lo fino, caros—¿el primer fin de semana los usa para jugar fútbol en un campo mojado y enlodado?
- al comprar una camisa fina, azul oscuro- al lavarse ¿se extiende al sol?

Entonces,
- ¿vamos a inundar nuestro espíritu constantemente con imágenes de violencia?
- ¿llenar los oídos todo el día con música que no aporta nada edificante? ¿Con palabras que no son propiamente lenguaje del cielo?
- ¿saturar la cabeza sólo de ideas huecas y situaciones artificiales sacadas de "telebobelas"?

No digo que no hay espacios para cine sano, para música, para mirar televisión. Pero sí, debemos seleccionar lo que vemos, leemos y escuchamos para evitar ambientes que pueden dañar nuestra nueva vida espiritual, utilizando los conocimientos aprendidos de nuestro Padre Celestial y el ejemplo de Jesucristo para empezar a discernir—evaluar a la luz de los valores del Reino de Dios—las acciones y actitudes que ocurren en el mundo alrededor.

En todo esto Dios nos ayuda permanentemente.

Es más, Dios no espera que lleguemos al cielo para integrarnos completamente en Su familia. Nos coloca en una parte de la familia aquí para que tengamos quien comparta nuestras alegrías y nuestras tristezes, quien nos ayude y nos apoye—nuestra Familia en Dios aquí en la iglesia local.

Mire bien a tu derecha, a tu izquierda,

Estas son las personas que Dios ha escogido para acompañarte en tu camino al cielo.

A estas son las personas hay que amarlas.
Al amar en la tierra sabremos cómo amar en el cielo.
Al amar a los de nuestra familia en Dios, nos preparamos para seguir amándolos en la eternidad.

Nunca olvidamos de nuestra vida "vieja"—sus costumbres, sus palabras, sus gustos. Volver atrás de atractivo porque implica reasumir lo conocido, lo cómodo, en vez de enfrentar lo nuevo. Ciertamente creo que los niños salieron de Colombia para Noruega, Holanda, Francia, o Canadá en algunos momentos anhelaron volver a hablar en español y comer fríjoles con arroz en vez de harenques con papas. Pero su mayor bien estaba en aprender a vivir una vida nueva.

Así también nosotros. Y ocurrirá que—como la niña que volvió a visitar a Colombia 10 años después—llegará un tiempo en que encontramos con la realidad que somos "extranjeros" y "peregrinos" aquí, que nuestra ciudadanía verdadera sí es del cielo donde nuestro Padre adoptivo, el Padre Celestial nos espera en la puerta acompañado por nuestro hermano mayor, Cristo Jesus.

Por ahora, mire a las personas en su alrededor ...
Extienda su mano a alguien en su familia en Dios.
Diga, ¡que bueno compartir esta familia contigo!
Alaba, alma mía, al Señor
alabe todo mi ser su santo nombre.
Alaba, alma mía, al Señor,
y no olvides ninguno de sus beneficions.
Él perdona todos tus pecados
y sana todos tus dolencias;
Él rescata tu vida del sepulcro
y te cubre de amor y compasión;
Él colma de bienes tu vida
y te rejuvenece como a las águilas.
Alaben al Señor, ustedes sus ángeles,
paladines que ejecutan su palabra y obedecen su mandato.

Alaben al Señor, todos su ejércitos,
siervos suyos que cumplen su voluntad.
Alaben al Señor todas sus obras
en todos los ámbitos de su dominio.
¡Alaba, alma mía, al Señor!
Salmo 103:1-5, 20-22

Putting our Baskets in the Water

Linda Glenn

(Exodus 2:1-10)

I'm a mother with two daughters, and I've had some grave concerns for my 2nd daughter. Our first-born daughter—Heather—has always seemed to know where she is going and what she is doing. The second-born—Amber—not so much. Amber sometimes can be easily influenced by those around her. Again, both daughters are lovely, but a friend of mine explained their difference like this: "Heather is like this mother-earth goddess with this strong, quiet beauty that draws people in. But Amber oozes sensuality and sexuality—even though she doesn't recognize it."

My friend is right. The mother in me worries about the predators who prey on such young women as Amber...

Interestingly, our scripture text names no character in our story except Moses. Yes, Moses' father (Amram), mother (Jochebed), and sister (Miriam) as well as Pharaoh's daughter (Bitya) have names elsewhere in the Bible, but here in the text they are unnamed. The focus is clearly on Moses' beginnings-Moses, who becomes the deliverer of God's people.

Just prior to our day's text, we discover that the Egyptians are afraid of the Israelites because they outnumber them and *are stronger than they are*. So they enslave the Israelites and force them into hard manual labor to build Egyptian cities, hoping to wear them down. When that doesn't work, the Egyptian Pharaoh orders the Hebrew midwives to kill the Israelite boys when they are born. When *that* doesn't reduce the population, Pharaoh decrees that all Israelite baby boys are to be thrown into the Nile River.

Thus, into this setting is born a baby boy to a man and woman from the Levite tribe. As with *all* mothers and their children, this mother "saw that he was a special baby" so she hides him. But that doesn't work for long. So she waterproofs a basket with tar and pitch, puts the baby in the basket, and lays it *strategically* among the reeds along the bank of the very same river the Egyptians have been told to drown the Israelite baby boys. She is working toward life for the baby in that river instead of death. She instructs the baby's sister to keep watch.

I say she placed the basket strategically because who should "happen" to come—as likely was their custom—down to bathe in the Nile at that particular place not long after the baby has been put in the water?? Pharaoh's daughter and her attendants. And naturally, the baby is crying by that time, so Pharaoh's daughter's heart melts when she opens the basket bobbing there in the reeds. As one would expect, she recognizes an effort to save a Hebrew baby.

And who should "happen" to appear at the princess' side who "happens" to know a Hebrew woman who could nurse the baby? (As if Pharaoh's daughter doesn't know this woman is the baby's mother—plausible deniability though!)

You see? Strategic. Moses' mother loves her baby and wants to give him the best shot at survival in these dangerous times. She doesn't know that *he will one day be their people's deliverer*; she only knows she wants him to live. And she does what she can to make that happen, trusting the outcome to God—and the soft heart of a woman who hears a crying baby.

So I'm a mother who has concerns for her daughter. I realized as I was praying the scripture that I was in a similar place as Moses' mother in that Amber with her easy empathy for others and striking looks may end up in a position she never intended, far away from the faith she has practiced all her life. Like Moses' parents, we kept Amber safe as long as we could. But the time came when we could no longer do that. We had to place her in the waterproofed basket of college and put her in the water of uncertainty so she could continue to grow into the young woman God created her to be.

But also like Moses' mother, I made some strategic moves in "waterproofing" her basket and maneuvering the external circumstances. Senior year, Amber began talking about which college she would attend. After we clarified that she could go to any college that the Tennessee Hope Scholarship of $4,000 would take her, she narrowed her choices to UT-Chattanooga (4-5 hours away), UT-Martin (less than an hour away), and Austin Peay State University (around 2 ¼ hours from home). Austin Peay also "happens" to be the college her older sister was already attending.

We faithfully toured each campus. Her father and I cheered her on when we returned to each campus for her French horn auditions. All three schools offered scholarships; Austin Peay offered the most—perhaps in part because her sister had made sure that key professors knew just how beautifully her little sister played.

It just so "happened" that-as I already knew-the Martin music department was spread all over kingdom-come, meeting in buildings literally all over the city, while they were building a new music building-a building they stopped construction on for several years. Although her father and I had known all this, we let Amber discover the inconvenience for herself. So Martin was out.

So, she said, UT-Chatt is where she wanted to go. "Okay," I responded, "but the deadline to respond to their offer is coming soon, and you'll need to get your paperwork in." Could I have been more helpful in getting the paperwork together? Maybe. So it "happened" she missed her deadline.

Now you know why Amber is completing her third year at Austin Peay. This is actually the first year her sister has not been there watching out for her. Now, like Moses with Pharaoh's daughter, Amber is living in the Egyptian palace of college away from our strategies and influence and I have to trust that God is still at work in her life.

Like Moses' mother, I love my child and want to give her the best shot at survival in these dangerous times of growing into adulthood. Like Moses' mother, I don't know what Amber will become; I only know I want her to live and become the young woman God created her to be. And I have done what I can to make that happen, *trusting the outcome to God*—with a little help from her older sister!

If you are a parent, putting your precious child in the waters of uncertainty that can mean death or life-even with a waterproofed basket and watchful sibling-is an act of faith. You do what you can and trust God to be at work in the process.

Some of you are not parents yet. Still, we *all* have loved ones and situations we are inclined to worry over, be concerned about. It might be a health issue or the future. Maybe

financial safety or— well, you know what you work not to worry about.
Whatever or whoever that is, we carefully place them in our waterproofed baskets and strategically put them in the water.

There are no promises. We don't know the outcome. We can't control the outcome. We watch, standing ready to help in any way we can.

Then they're off to the Egyptian palace away from us and our loving influence. We entrust them to God who does have a vision of the desired outcome which is far greater than our limited vision of simple safety.

My friends, I invite us and challenge us all to place our child, our loved one, our situation into our water-proofed baskets of faith and put our baskets in the water!

God is in Control: Easter Sunday

Melissa R. Goodloe

Santa Claus, Tooth fairy, The Easter Bunny, a pot of gold at the end of the rainbow
Some things we believe in change with age!

Vitamins, fountain of youth, diet pills, anti-aging creams
Some things give us false hope!

Farmer's almanac, Ford or Chevy, Democrat or Republican, Jesus Christ
Some things we put all our belief in and would never waiver!

Earthquakes, Tsunamis, Tornados, Wild fires
Some things are beyond our understanding and control!

Economy, abortion, homosexuality, abuse
Some things come with stronger opinions than others!

Virgin birth, marginalized, crucifixion, resurrection
Some things we focus on occasionally!

Faith, Hope, Peace, Love, forgiveness
Some things we have not found!

Mercy, Grace, eternal life
Some things we cannot earn!

God does not control some things—God controls all things!

The Centurion soldier went to work that morning like he always did! Maybe he took the same route to work he always took, maybe his wife made the lunch she always made, maybe he thought it would just be the same old same old at the site of the crucifixion. However as the day went on and the noon hour was met with darkness that lasted until three

I am sure he was beginning to think this is not an ordinary day! As Jesus cries out "My God, My God why have you forsaken me" (which scholars believe Jesus was praying aloud scripture found in Psalm 22) he was giving us a message.

Jesus was giving us a message of HOPE. Even though believers in God may feel abandoned when they suffer, in reality God the Father is closer than ever. What earthly father would not desire to be near his son when he is suffering? Certainly an earthly father is not more loving than God the Father.

As Jesus breathes his last breath the centurion is most likely thinking, the way we all do at the end of a work day,--that this will soon be over and I can go home.

Yet scripture tells us that the temple curtain was torn in two from top to bottom. Now this curtain was not some little curtain it was what separated the people from the holy of holies. The holy of holies was so sacred that only the priest could enter in and they tied a rope with bells around their waist or ankle so that if God struck them dead for some reason they could be pulled from the holy area of the temple. This curtain was thick and wide enough to cover the entrance from top to bottom. Symbolically it is what separated the people from God. As this curtain rips imagine there is nothing standing in the way between you and God. Jesus took the sin so the path is clear.

Not only did this take place but the earth shook and the rocks split and the tombs of the saints were opened.

I don't know about you but I have been through a tiny earthquake and it was enough that I never want to go through another one… especially not one that has rocks splitting and tombs opening. The centurion saw all this and was terrified and said "Truly this is the son of God!"

It took Jesus death on the cross, unnatural events, and natural disasters to get this proclamation! Yet his belief in Christ guarantees his new life in heaven.

We have the rest of the story…Scripture tells us that Jesus resurrection took place 3 days later—just as he said.

We know that it is recorded that people saw the dead saints appear in the city after the resurrection.

We know that he appeared to the disciples after the resurrection.

Many of us try to control our own lives, our situations, the ups and downs, but we are no more in control of our own lives than the Centurion was that day. We can control some things but God controls all things.

Of all the things I mentioned in the beginning of the message the only ones that matter are the ones many of us have not found…These are the things that Jesus died upon a cross to convey to us…

FAITH:

"Now faith is the substance of things hoped for, the evidence of things not seen"(Heb.11:1).

HOPE:
"I saw the Lord always before me. Because he is at my right hand, I will not be shaken. Therefore my heart is glad and my tongue rejoices; my body also will live in hope" (Acts 2:25-26)

PEACE:

"And the peace of God, which surpasses all understanding, will guard your hearts and your minds in Christ Jesus" (Phil. 4:7).

LOVE:

"To love him(Jesus) with all your heart, with all your understanding and with all your strength, and to love your neighbor as yourself is more important than all burnt offerings and sacrifices." (Mark 12:33)

FORGIVENESS:

"Therefore, my brothers, I want you to know that through Jesus the forgiveness of sins is proclaimed to you" (Acts 13:38).

What will it take for you to believe?…an earthquake, the dead walking, an innocent man dying on a cross…it has already happened…**BELIEVE!**

God does not control some things…God controls all things.

"Jesus looked at them and said, "With man this is impossible, but not with God; all things are possible with God." (Mark 10:27).

Witness

Susan Carole Guin Groce

(Luke 24:36-48)

This passage in Luke takes place immediately following the Road to Emmaus encounter, where two travelers, unknown to them, are greeted by Jesus. They don't recognize him until the have stopped for a meal and he breaks bread with them. Then he disappears.

Then Jesus suddenly appears to the disciples.

He bids them peace and to stay calm, because they were terrified. Can you even imagine how frightened they were?

Jesus assures them he was not a ghost, but a physical resurrected reality! Jesus was before them wholly and hungry.

Let's ponder that for a moment.

Where do we see Christ and we stand in disbelief instead of awe?

Do we see it in children, but we are in disbelief because they are "too young?"

Do we see it in the homeless, but ignore it because of their situation? Do we encounter Christ in unbelievers, but discount it because they haven't made a profession of faith?

ABC has a segment in the show 20/20. Some of you may be familiar with it. It's called "What would you do?" On the show, they stage situations where people are in need and wait and see what your average person will do. In one episode, a lady, actor, was faced with a very large prescription bill at the pharmacy. She was on medicare and a fixed income. Remember this is a staged event. As she is pleading with the pharmacist to cut her a deal, the pharmacist, an actor, too, is not budging. They stage this scenario several times over the course of a few hours. What they find is complete strangers come to this woman's aid and offer to pay either a portion or all of her prescription bill.

The host interrupts as they are in the midst of paying and asks them, "Why are you doing this?" One woman's response, "because that's what we're supposed to do—take care of one another." The host was in disbelief, as were the actors, that someone would do such a thing. They were in disbelief instead of awe.

Jesus in his conversation with the disciples is addressing the confusion surrounding his death. Luke is straight forward in telling us that Jesus is present in his real, physical being. After his meal of boiled fish, Jesus draws their attention to the scriptures—what he had taught them before his death and what he was to fulfill. Luke discussed the Messiah's suffering, resurrection and preaching of repentance and forgiveness in Jesus' name. Only now are the disciples able to understand, only now are they capable of comprehending. Jesus doesn't point out which specific scriptures are fulfilled, but that all scripture finds its ultimate fulfillment in Jesus.

His resurrection appearance to the disciples is the beginning of a transition from Jesus' ministry to the ministry of the church.

Jesus tells them about their mission as witness and testifiers. The story, the one story of God's faithfulness and justice and mercy, is now entrusted to the disciples to proclaim to the world.

Jesus calls the disciples to go forth and proclaim repentance and forgiveness of sins in his name. The message is very clear, they are to share the good news of God's mercy.

Even though Jesus will be leaving them very soon, Luke assures Jesus' followers that they and we are not left to our own devices in the work of being a witness. The Spirit will come at Pentecost and will give us the power we need to be effective witnesses.

So what does it mean to be a witness? We assume we know. . .right?

1.	One who sees an event.
2.	Gives factual, credible info about something happening.
3.	Testify as to what has taken place.

The disciples were witnesses.

As a people of faith, we consider ourselves to be witnesses as well. But we have a problem. How is it that we can be witnesses of or for or to something that we've never seen for ourselves? We weren't there. We weren't there. And if being there like the disciples is the only criteria, we've obviously missed the boat by about 20 centuries and we might as well just go home.

In the gospel sense of being a witness, though, we believe that the "there" continues to be present to us, among us and with us "here." The risen Christ meets us and stands among us here today—in the midst of all our doubts, confusions and hesitations, in all our successes, triumphs and rejoicings, and in all our powerlessness and weakness. The risen Lord stands among us, offers a word of peace and says, "Why are you frightened, and why do you have doubts? Look at my hands and my feet; see that it is I."

We are witnesses of these things.

There's a song that some of you may have sung as a child at a summer camp or Vacation Bible school called "Jesus My Lord." The verses went through a litany of ways in which we could or might see and know Jesus for ourselves. But the song, the chorus ended like this:

Have you ever stood at the table,
with the Lord there in your midst?
Seen the face of Christ on each other?
Then I say ... you've seen Jesus my Lord.

Have you seen Jesus my Lord?
He's here in plain view.
Take a look, open your eyes.
He'll show it to you.
We are witnesses of these things.

Fredreick Buechner, in his book Listening to Your Life says, "Just as Jesus appeared at his birth as a helpless child that the world was free to care for or destroy, so now he appears in his resurrection as the pauper, the prisoner, the stranger, the one who on his hands and feet still bears the marks of finitude and human suffering. He appears in every form of human need that the world is free to serve or to ignore. The risen Christ is Christ risen in his glory and enthroned in all this glorious canvas, stained glass and architecture as Redeemer and Judge. But he is also Christ risen in the shabby hearts of those who, although they have never touched the mark of the nails, have been themselves so touched by him that they believe anyway. However faded and threadbare, what they have seen of him is at least enough to get their bearings by." (Buechner, Frederick, Listening to Your Life (San Francisco: HarperCollins Publishers, 1992), p. 100.)

We are witnesses of this risen Lord. We have beheld his hands and his feet, his presence with us.

But part of being a witness of the risen Christ also involves bearing witness to his life, death and resurrection.

We so much want people to know, don't we? We want people to know, we want to bear witness to the grace and presence of the Christ that has met us.

But, soon as someone starts talking about "bearing witness to Jesus Christ," our skin crawls or we break out in a sweat, or the hair on the backs of our necks might be apt to stand up, for we've all have those experiences or encounters with people who cram Jesus down our throats whether we want or are ready to hear about what they have to say. "Bearing witness" conjures up visions of crazy people with bullhorns or the guy with the crazy rainbow wig at the football game that holds up a big sign that reads John 3:16. Or TV evangelists that rants and rave on almost every network on Sunday mornings—bearing witness by scaring people. Or people who beat us over the head with the Bible in the name of Jesus Christ.

We so want people to know, so we rush head-long into the world to shout the good news from the mountaintops and to whoever will listen. Oftentimes, though, we move too quickly from being a witness of the risen Lord to bearing witness to Jesus Christ. Or we, as preachers, give people a kick in the pants and say something to the effect of: "So you've seen and met Jesus? Great. Now get out there and tell everyone you meet about what it is you know, about what it all means. Bear witness to your faith." But so often we end up—as the church, as individuals—giving answers to questions that people are not asking.

So listen again to the Jesus in Luke: "These are the words that I spoke to you while I was still with you—that everything in the law of Moses, the prophets and the psalms must be fulfilled. Thus it is written, that the Messiah is to suffer and to rise from the dead on the third day, and that repentance and forgiveness of sins is to be proclaimed in his name to all nations, beginning from Jerusalem. You are witnesses of these things. And see, I am sending upon you what my Father promised; so stay here in the city until you have been clothed with power from on high."

We are not called simply to exist. We are not called just to survive. We are not even called to be successful. We are called, as churches, as believers, to be faithful to Jesus Christ and to serve the world as he served it, to love the world as he loved it, to give our lives away to the world as he gave his life away.

As we live and move in the tension between being witnesses and bearing witness, between the already of Easter and the not yet of Pentecost, we know, experience and believe that in every age there rises again the need to tell the story of our life—what has happened to us in our community, how we came to believe, how we reason about things and what we see from our point of view. To bear witness to the risen Christ who meets us again and again, showing us his hands and his feet, and who speaks to us and to the world a word of resurrection hope.

We tell our children this truth, this presence we know, and want to know and are still learning—when they ask where God is or why we love them.

We tell the story to ourselves when once again we have let another down, done the thing that is hard to forgive or broken the promises and trust of another—the story which bears witness and calls us to repentance and reminds us of God's love and grace.

You share it with a friend who is in a dark place, who finds herself crushed by the weight of the world, unable to see any light on the road that lies ahead.

You share it with someone you visit in the hospital as you and they watch their life slip away, as you pray together and wait.

We bear witness to this risen Christ even as we stand at the foot of an open grave, mud on our shoes and tears on our faces, when all we're able to do or say save a shred of faith and hope we have left is to point to the one who defeated death, who rose from the tomb to meet us.

As ones who have seen and heard, as ones who live in the glorious tension between being witnesses and bearing witness, we tell, share and live our faith.

We are witnesses of these things.

Now, we must follow Jesus' words and proclaim it.

La Adoración o Servicio del Creyente, Ha de Ser en Obediencia Respetuosa, Pues Dios es Soberano Señor

The Responsibility of the Believer is to Be Respectfully Obedient to God, Our Soverign Lord

Luz Dary Guerrero

Introducción:

El propósito del pueblo de Dios o creyentes en Jesucristo como Salvador del hombre pecador es: adorar a su Señor y Dios. Entendiéndose al <u>Señor</u> como: propietario, dueño y amo de la vida del creyente, y <u>Dios</u> como: la persona o ser objeto de devoción y fervoroso culto, es decir, a quien venera este pueblo. Entonces la adoración o culto en amor del creyente es todo su ser integral. La biblia señala en muchos lugares la alabanza y adoración de los creyentes, el Salmo 145: 10-13 es uno de ellos:

"Señor, Tus obras todas Te darán gracias, Y Tus santos Te bendecirán.
La gloria de Tu reino dirán, Y hablarán de Tu poder,
Para dar a conocer a los hijos de los hombres Tus hechos poderosos Y la gloria de la majestad de Tu reino." [+]
También Isaías 43:7, 21, nos dice: "A todo el que es llamado por Mi nombre Y a quien he creado para Mi gloria, A quien he formado y a quien he hecho....El pueblo que Yo he formado para Mí ,Proclamará Mi alabanza". [+]

Igualmente Dios exige no tener ni adorar otros dioses porque El, es Dios celoso que castiga tal acción. Éxodo 20: 3-5, Isaías 45:18.

El Salmo 96, es una exhortación al pueblo que El Señor ha formado, a la adoración que implica respeto es decir, acatar Su palabra en humilde obediencia y sumisión. (ampliar un poco lo que involucra estas acciones en la vida del creyente).

1. El mundo y todos los que en el hay, deben adoración al creador, El es El Señor, esto es lo justo.

Detengámonos en los versículos 1 al 6 y detallemos:

1-Canten al Señor un cántico nuevo; Canten al Señor, toda la tierra.
2-Canten al Señor, bendigan Su nombre; Proclamen de día en día las buenas nuevas de Su salvación.
3-Cuenten Su gloria entre las naciones, Sus maravillas entre todos los pueblos.
4-Porque grande es el Señor, y muy digno de ser alabado; Temible es El sobre todos los dioses.
5-Porque todos los dioses de los pueblos son ídolos, Pero el Señor hizo los cielos.
6-Gloria y majestad están delante de El; Poder y hermosura en Su santuario.[4]

El escritor bíblico comienza con acciones que el pueblo de Dios debe realizar: canten, bendigan, proclamen y cuenten, todos estos verbos están en imperativo es decir que es una exigencia inexcusable en la vida diaria del creyente; en la relación con El Señor, es nuestro compromiso realizarlas, Su amor en nuestras vidas nos mueve a ejecutar Su voluntad pues lo amamos, debe entonces salir de nuestros labios sonidos melodiosos que hablen de las obras maravillosas del Señor acontecidas en el pasado, presente y futuro, como dice un famoso cantante cristiano "Jesucristo es el motivo de mi canción, otra canción no tengo que cantar...", y no solo nosotros, toda la naturaleza también hace lo propio a su creador, hasta los árboles del campo cantan; la alabanza en el reino de Dios abarca totalmente todo lo creado. Debemos exaltar, enaltecer Su nombre decir, quien es El con todos sus atributos, como hemos visto Su gran poder en muchas formas y ocasiones, debemos pregonar todos los días, día tras día, sin falta, contar a las personas con quienes nos relacionamos las buenas noticias del plan que Dios diseño desde el principio de todo, para salvar a la raza humana, (que esta muerta en sus delitos y pecados) la buena noticia, que es posible tener vida nueva y eterna, y esta declaración no es solo para los que están cerca nuestro, sino para todos los pueblos y naciones para todos los conjuntos de personas que tienen diferentes idiomas y tradiciones, es deber del creyente apoyar a otros, que pueden ir a lugares apartados a repetir esta noticia de salvación y las asombrosas obras que ha realizado y realiza nuestro buen Dios y Señor. Proclamar que el reino del Señor se ha acercado.

---

[4]La Biblia de las Américas.

Y cual es la razón por la cual es nuestra necesidad u obligación, hacer todas estas cosas, pues porque EL ES, es grandioso, admirable, eterno, soberano Señor, este es el principio de nuestra adoración, nuestro Dios es aterrador, El domina sobre todos los dioses que el ser humano se ha inventado: dinero, belleza, poder, conocimiento, posesiones, afectos y mil cosas mas que consideramos mas importantes, todo esto son solo, amuletos o fetiches inventados por el hombre pero, EL ES, es El Señor creador de los cielos y la tierra y todo lo que en ella hay, El es todopoderoso y nada o nadie se compara al eterno soberano Señor en cuya presencia como rey permanecen personificadas como su corte, la perfección y magnificencia; el dominio y preciosidad divina están presentes en Su tabernáculo.

2. Todos los pueblos le dan gloria, porque El Señor reina y juzgará con justicia.
Versículos 7-10, miremos:

"Den al Señor, oh familias de los pueblos, den al Señor gloria y poder.
Den al Señor la gloria debida a Su nombre; traigan ofrenda y entren en Sus atrios.
Adoren al Señor en vestiduras santas; tiemblen ante Su presencia, toda la tierra.
Digan entre las naciones: "El Señor reina; ciertamente el mundo está bien afirmado, será inconmovible; El juzgará a los pueblos con equidad."

No solo debemos publicar en alta voz para que sea notorio el reinado del Señor en esta tierra y que las voces de Su pueblo sean en honor al salvador, declarando solemnemente que el reinado del Señor ha comenzado desde hace mucho tiempo, debemos también entregar voluntariamente las vidas que El nos ha concedido, en sometimiento voluntario a Su dirección y autoridad y no solo las nuestras sino la de nuestras familias, de allí la gran responsabilidad, de ser ejemplos y testimonios vivos para que nuestros familiares sean testigos del poder del Señor al transformar la vida de Su pueblo y recibir la alabanza por tal hecho, El merece la gloria por las obras que el creyente realiza cuando es transformado en una nueva creatura, debemos ofrecer nuestra obediencia afectuosa permanentemente, pues estamos delante de Su presencia, nuestra adoración debe ser honesta, verdadera, sincera, recordando siempre que hemos sido separados del resto de los hombres para reflejar, el poder de Dios que opera el la vida de los nuevos integrantes de este reino, en el cual se nos ha apartado para ser sal y luz, al resto de los mortales, es así como debemos presentarnos delante de El, en santidad, no olvide mi hermano que nuestro Dios es temible y aterrador, de tal forma que ante Su presencia tiembla toda la tierra, convirtiéndose esta en otra razón, por la cual debemos decir a todo el mundo, que es Dios Rey, es soberano, aunque todos los seres humanos no lo reconozcan, la tierra fue creada por Su palabra, es por ella que existe y se sostiene; incluso en el futuro, cuando regrese por segunda vez, lo hará como juez justo y juzgará a toda la raza humana con su habitual dignidad y rectitud, que no nos quepa la menor duda, todos absolutamente todos tendremos una sentencia, seremos hallados: culpables o inocentes.

3. **Gozo y alabanza de toda la creación, a causa de Su juicio fiel a la tierra y a todos los pueblos.**

Versículos 11-13

"Alégrense los cielos y regocíjese la tierra; Ruja el mar y cuanto contiene;
Gócese el campo y todo lo que en él hay. Entonces todos los árboles del bosque cantarán con gozo Delante del Señor, porque El viene; Porque El viene a juzgar la tierra: Juzgará al mundo con justicia Y a los pueblos con Su fidelidad. "*

Finalmente, el salmista motiva, anima, a todos los seres creados por El Señor, a que se regocijen y proclamen con júbilo de forma espectacular y escandalosa como el rugido del mar (ante el cual el ser humano solo puede estar quieto y escuchar), que el regreso de su creador es como juez fiel, con un juicio exacto y puntualmente cabal para todos las personas de todas las regiones de todas las lenguas y todas las culturas, de TODO cuanto existe, este mis hermanos en nuestro Dios, El Señor, quien tiene todo el poder, honor, gloria y majestad, no hay nadie como El, ¡ que maravilla ! ¡ como no asombrarnos y admirarnos en El ! ¡Aleluya!.

El es nuestro Señor nuestro Dios, al cual adoramos y servimos en obediencia, Su poder y soberanía son motivo suficiente para no cesar de hablar de El a todas las personas con quien nos relacionamos, contarles la transformación que ha causado en nuestras vidas y familias, proclamar sin vergüenza que el Dios que revelan las escrituras, la santa Palabra de Dios, es El único Dios verdadero, real y veraz en Su proceder.

Aplicación:

Amados hermanos en la fe de nuestro Señor Jesucristo, es mi deseo que cada uno de ustedes pueda entender, conscientemente las Escrituras, para profesar esta verdad, que nos confronta y obliga a proclamarla y además a reflexionar seriamente sobre nuestros hechos, es nuestra responsabilidad el no estar obedeciendo la Palabra de Dios en la vida diaria, debemos entonces preocuparnos por nuestras propias actitudes y ojala sea este el tiempo de tomar decisiones con madurez y compromiso sincero, el que se demanda de alguien que pertenece al pueblo del Señor, dejemos la inactividad la pereza de actuar de cada día y vivamos, actuemos como El Señor demanda del creyente.

Le animo entonces mi hermano a encarnar la Palabra de Dios en su vida para que tenga testimonios que contar a otros, para que pueda ver la transformación milagrosa que El Señor puede obrar en su vida, entonces no podrá callar las maravillas que usted mismo haya experimentado, logrando así impactar a las personas que la rodean, familiares, conocidos y por que no, hasta desconocidos, tengan de que hablar y reconocer el poder transformador de nuestro Todopoderoso Señor y Dios. Sea un verdadero, adorador y siervo fiel al soberano Señor.

The Call

Donna Stockberger Heflin

(John 1:29-31; 35-42
1 Corinthians 1:4-9)

January 20, 2008

Some of us remember those childhood days of playing outside with a sense of joy, excitement, freedom and adventure. And then it happened. The door would open and we would hear "the call."

We may appear no different but we are because we have heard "the call." The way it happens at our house is this... In the waning daylight the call into the yard can be heard for our eight year old daughter. "Leanah its time to come in." No response. Leanah goes on playing hide-and-seek with her neighborhood friends. To any one passing by Leanah looks no different from all the other children caught up in the excitement and frenzy of the game. But, she is different. She has been "called in." Everything has changed.

In the same way we Christians experience a similar thing. We may appear no different from those around us caught up in the frenzy of life. But, we have a ringing in our ears, God's summons to believe and obey. We hear the distant but clear calling, "Come, follow me." It sounds over the cry of the baby, the urgent ring of the cell phone, the whisper of success... Over it all can be heard the sometimes soft but urgent calling of God.

Now this thing of being called is tricky and important. It is easy to get confused. Especially the way we use it these days. We think of being called to something specific and major. We talk about being called to the ordained ministry. Or being called to a special, usually, full time service. This weekend we recall with respect and appreciation the ministry of one of the visible ministries of our time; that of Martin Luther King, Jr. And that's where some of us leave this thing of being called. We leave it to the professionals. We leave it with those called to big and visible ministries.

On one hand we listen to the call of the disciples and it's neatly separate from what's going on with us. After all they were called and we're just ordinary people. So we're safe.

Jesus said to a couple of ordinary guys, "Come and see." They were exactly like us. They were called to be disciples. No matter what our life situation is when we are called by God, as we each are called in our Baptism, we are, like those first two, called to be disciples.

From the very beginning, God called not individuals, but a community. From the vantage point of communities outside the Christian faith the idea of "call" makes no sense.

Then there's this other sticking point. God does not call us to a job or to fulfill a particular role. God's first call to us is not to work but rather to "abide". Our call is to a relationship. Jesus says "come and see." Or "follow me." To respond to such a call to relationship is different than responding to a call to a particular job. We often think of call in terms of being productive. After all, that's what society tells us. "Let's see the product!" To be called into relationship to be called "to follow" that is to enter into a mystery, to enter into the holy....That means moving out into uncharted territory. Jesus simply says "follow me." He calls us first to himself-to a personal intimacy and shared life. That is what matters and has to be central.

If we look at Jesus call from the perspective of what is left behind, it is a call to repent. If we see it from the perspective of what comes next, it is a call to seek him first, to know him, and to make that relationship the central focus of our lives. Early in my ministry I was all about the product of ministry. What could I do that showed concrete results? You know me I'm one of those "task" oriented, list making people. In those early years I was frustrated. I learned it wasn't all about the product. It has more to do with the people. Ministry has more to do with relationships. It is about relationships with God and each other.

I needed to slow down to listen and wait. I was racing to get to a destination when in reality it is more about the journey and the relationship.

When we are called it is primarily to be held for awhile and not to go anywhere. By and by it will lead us somewhere. But we won't know where for a while. Maybe for a long while. The call to the disciples to walk away from everything is disturbing. This makes the call frightening and frustrating. We might know something very powerful is going on, something that has to do with all our life and much more. Then, because we live in a society that insists that for something to be valuable, it has to produce, we start looking for what we are called to "do." We need time to "be". Time to "be" with God. We need time to listen and wait.

So it was with the disciples they stayed close to Jesus for a while. They learned and came to know him. Then, long before they thought they were ready, Jesus gave them ministry to do. For some these ministries were dramatic, for others they were quiet and invisible.

The call, will always in some form or other find expression in ministry. There can be no real, abiding, and sustaining ministry without relationship with Christ, without obedience to him as he calls us to himself.

We are called to be disciples. That call came with our baptism. And that call to relationship and ministry will haunt us, and track us down; it will trouble our sleep and whisper in our ears at the worst possible times. It will grow stronger and weaker and stronger again. It may seem to go away. But it always comes back. For, finally, it is a call to life, to joy, and to true peace.

Aspects of our call may shift and change. After all real life brings shifts or transitions and new learnings that are both the expected and unexpected. Again we are called to abide for a time, to listen and wait, to soak up the holy and discern God's call for us in this particular place and time. That not only happens to us as individuals but also to congregations, presbyteries and denominations.

One of Carrie Newcomer's songs has sort of become my mantra. Hear the words of a couple of stanza's...

"Holy is the dish and drain The soap and sink, and the cup and plate And the warm wool socks, and the cold white tile Showerheads and good dry towels And frying eggs sound like psalms With a bit of salt measured in my palm It's all part of a sacrament As holy as the day is spent.

Holy is the place I stand To give whatever small good I can And the empty page, and the open book Redemption everywhere I look Unknowingly we slow our pace In the shade of unexpected grace And with grateful smiles and sad lament As

114

holy as the day is spent And morning light sings "Providence" As holy as a day is spent."

I continue to be a list making, task oriented person. Early one morning this week I had the words of this song in my head as I was taking sheets off a bed. The dishwasher was empty. Breakfast was over. The girls were getting dressed for school and I was trying to get just two more things done before car pool time. You know the moment...just let me get this done without interruption. And then it happened a cell phone was thrust into my face by thirteen year old daughter Laura. She needed my husband Robert and me to make a decision before school. Right behind Laura was Leanah hairbrush in hand for my help with her waist long hair. My family will tell you that I'm not all graceful in the face of interruptions. And there I stood with a cell phone and dirty sheets thinking to myself... "Now God please remind me just what is so holy about this moment?"

As I was brushing Leanah's hair it hit me. This is what is holy. This moment. This is part of my calling right now in this place and time. And all too soon that calling with be transitioned into that of an empty nest mom. This relationship is what is holy.

And so my prayer of repentance begins. "Lord please forgive me for my impatience when my lists are interrupted. "For Holy is the place I stand To give whatever small good I can. And morning light sings "Providence" As holy as a day is spent." Amen.

¿Por Qué Nosotros No Podemos Dejar De Decir Lo Que Hemos Visto Y Oído?

For We Cannot But Speak The Things Which We Have Seen And Heard

Luz María Heilbron

(Lucas 5: 27 - 32)

Idea Central:

Jesús rompe con los esquemas religiosos de los fariseos, y demuestra su simpatía y aceptación para con los pecadores, declarando el sentido de su misión.

Propósito:

Demostrar el valor de una persona en el Reino, y motivar una respuesta de acción en la tarea de ser testigos y evangelistas en el Reino.

Introducción:

He pedido a estos hermanos que nos compartan como y cuando fue que ellas recibieron la invitación de asistir a la iglesia, porque me pareció muy importante resaltar con testigos, el hecho de que si da resultado invitar a familiares y cercanos a la iglesia, que vale la pena intentarlo y persistir, porque Dios obra aunque a veces parezca que no hay buena respuesta a la invitación.

Tal vez algunos de ustedes están aquí después de que alguien tuvo la paciencia de insistir y más aún alguien oró mucho tiempo por su conversión.

Como ustedes saben el lema de trabajo para el 2.012., apunta hacia la responsabilidad que tenemos de ser testigos y anunciar el mensaje del evangelio de Cristo.

Podemos repetir juntos el lema:

"porque nosotros no podemos dejar de decir lo que hemos visto y oído" Hechos 4:20

Les invito a leer Lucas 5: 27 - 32

La propuesta para esta reflexión es la siguiente:

AFORISMO:

Cuando una persona verdaderamente experimenta el perdón y la Gracia de Cristo, se convierte en testigo ferviente y hace participes a otros de la salvación y la Gracia recibidos, compartiendo con entusiasmo las buenas nuevas de salvación.

El llamamiento y posterior invitación que Jesús le hizo a Leví me sirve de base para desarrollar el tema e invitación que quiero exponer en esta mañana para ustedes. Usaré el lema a modo de pregunta como tema del sermón:

Así que el tema y título de este sermón es: *¿Por qué nosotros no podemos dejar de decir lo que hemos visto y oído?*

No podemos dejar de decir lo que hemos visto y oído porque:

1. Porque nuestras vidas han sido transformadas por el perdón y la Gracia de Cristo. Vers. 27 - 28

El relato va precedido de la sanidad del paralítico y la declaración que Jesús hace sobre la potestad que El tiene para perdonar pecados.

El evangelio de Marcos nos da una descripción más amplia de la escena…
Dice Marcos que después del encuentro con el paralítico, Jesús volvió a la orilla del mar y toda la gente venía a Él y les enseñaba y mientras eso sucede dice el relato que él vio a un publicano sentado en el banco de los impuestos llamado Leví *y le dice sígueme.*

¿Qué conocimiento tiene Jesús de Leví?   ¿Qué ve Jesús en Leví aparte de su pecado?
Era un recaudador de impuestos, llamado publicano en la escritura, son presentados en los evangelios como una clase típica de individuos moralmente reprobados, y eran especialmente despreciados porque trabajaban en beneficio de Roma y porque explotaban y oprimían a los contribuyentes hasta el límite. Eran considerados traidores y contados como pecadores tanto en su vida personal como en su profesión...

Aparte de saber quién es Leví Jesús ve más allá de la apariencia externa de este hombre, sabe que es un hombre con muchas riquezas pero con un enorme vacío y pesadumbre en su corazón, un hombre insatisfecho cuestionándose su manera de vivir pero sin encontrar la alternativa que le ayude a mejorar su condición de vida.
Jesús sabe exactamente cual es la condición moral del hombre que tiene en frente, y este encuentro no es producto de la casualidad, es el encuentro y la invitación de uno que hace

tiempo lo tiene en su mira, de uno que sabe cuanto dolor y necesidad de aceptación y perdón se esconden en esa vida aparentemente feliz.

¿Qué sabe Leví de Jesús?

Seguramente ha escuchado sus enseñanzas, habrá oído decir que hace milagros y que se muestra especialmente compasivo con los desvalidos y rechazados por los líderes religiosos. Pero en este día, Leví no ha tenido que esperar a que alguien le cuente algo de Jesús, en este día el posiblemente ha sido testigo de la sanidad del paralítico y tal vez quedó sensiblemente impresionado al oír decir a Jesús "tus pecados te son perdonados" y es que en el fondo de su corazón Leví hubiera querido que esas palabras fueran dirigidas a él, el necesitaba el perdón y aceptación de Dios, pero ante las autoridades religiosas el es un individuo moralmente reprobado no merecedor de pertenecer al pueblo de Dios.

¿Qué sentimientos se despertaron en el pensamiento e interioridad de Leví, Cuando vio que Jesús se acercó y cuando lo escuchó decirle <SIGUEME>?

Me he hecho esta pregunta: ¿acudió el llanto a sus ojos? Supo entender que Jesús sabía todo de Él y sin embargo le brinda aceptación incondicional, y qué de su profesión, puede un individuo con la clase de vida y la fama de ladrón que tengo, ser un ¿qué...? ¿Discípulo tuyo?, pero frente a todos sus pesares, El se encuentra con la mirada compasiva y la mano extendida de Jesús, por eso es entendible la prontitud de la respuesta a la invitación de Jesús, no necesitó más explicación, sintió que a partir de ese momento su vida su pecado era perdonado y su vida tomaría otro rumbo. *Lo dejó todo, por un amor así vale la pena dejarlo todo.*

En segundo lugar: no podemos dejar de decir lo que hemos visto y oído...

2. Porque hay gente que también necesita recibir la Gracia y el perdón que nosotros hemos recibido. Vers. 29 -30.

Hermanos...cuando alguien ha sido rescatado de una vida de dolor y miseria, cuando ha pasado de muerte a vida, lo que desea es dar a conocer y ayudar a otros a encontrarse con la fuente que le trajo esperanza y significación a su vida.

Eso fue lo que hizo Leví.

Leví hizo una gran fiesta no solo para celebrar su nuevo estado de vida sino para abrir las puertas de la oportunidad para que sus amigos conocieran y escucharan a Jesús.

Es una fiesta diferente a las que ha hecho antes, en esta ocasión su invitación es sincera, los amigos lo perciben, algo ha pasado con Leví, entenderán la razón del cambio cuando tengan la oportunidad de ver y oír a Jesús, Leví tiene la esperanza de que sus amigos encontrarán en Jesús la Gracia y el perdón que el encontró. La admisión de Leví al grupo de los discípulos llevó a otros miembros de esta despreciada clase a que siguieran a Jesús.

Jesús entró en compañerismo inclusive al compañerismo de la comida con aquellos que eran los más despreciados por la religión judía de su día.

El hecho de Jesús aceptar comer con los pecadores constituía un gesto de amistad y aceptación.

En tercer lugar: no podemos dejar de decir lo que hemos visto y oído, porque...

3. Porque el concepto sobre la forma de obtener la salvación debe ser explicado y corregido Vers. 31 - 32.

La pregunta hecha a los discípulos, provoca la intervención y la aclaración de Jesús.

Su deber estaba con los necesitados a quienes invitaba al arrepentimiento, aquellos que se consideraban justos no eran de su principal interés.

Su ministerio era para los pecadores como el del médico para los enfermos. Jesús buscó a los pecadores.

La respuesta expresa la compasión de Jesús hacia los pecadores, a los que va dirigida su misión, pero al mismo tiempo constituye un ataque a la justicia autosuficiente de los fariseos.

Jesús corrige el concepto de la salvación por obras, no son los actos de piedad lo que conducen a la salvación, lo que recibe la aprobación de Dios es la búsqueda de un corazón que declara su necesidad y se arrepiente.

Los que no se reconocen enfermos, no llaman al médico ni lo reciben, no tienen curación posible, Nadie puede acercarse a Jesús, a menos que se confiese pecador. La colocación de este relato a continuación del de la curación del paralítico resulta muy adecuada en los evangelios. La fe que obtiene la curación exige arrepentimiento.

Concluyendo entonces esta meditación, ¿por qué no podemos dejar de decir lo que hemos visto y oído?

1.   Porque alrededor nuestro hay personas como Leví que necesitan saber que Dios los perdona y quiere transformar sus vidas.

2.   Porque tal vez sin saberlo nosotros, esa persona llegará ser un instrumento de servicio en la obra del Señor. ¿Saben quién es Leví? El autor del evangelio de Mateo, Leví

y Mateo son la misma persona, y a..¿cuántas personas habrán encontrado y conocido a Jesús en la lectura del evangelio según San Mateo?

3.   Porque muchos pecadores pasarán a la eternidad, sin saber que la oportunidad de la salvación era una oferta precisamente para ellos, pero nunca lo supieron, porque alguien Que creyéndose bueno tuvo la osadía de declararlos condenados porque no eran santos y nunca llegaron a saber que el perdón se recibe cuando se admite que se es pecador y admitiendo que se es pecador se recibe la Gracia y recibiendo la Gracia es como se llega a ser santo.

Bien hermanos, como dice el refrán:

"A buen entendedor pocas palabras bastan".

Oración:….

Nothing is Trivial to God

Donna Lee Hollingshed

(Matthew 25:31-46)

Does anyone else besides Glen and me watch "Jeopardy?" We watch it every night; it's our tradition, right after supper, to watch it and compete with the contestants, and each other, every night at 7:30. Before we met-actually decades before we met-we both were watching "Jeopardy," and many times, both of us would have won big it, and have gotten all that fame and acclaim, and money, that goes along with winning a game based on the knowledge of trivia.

Trivia-you have heard of it, I'm sure. It is usually called "useless knowledge," and is considered things which are unimportant. I never thought it was useless. By reading World Book Encyclopedia cover-to-cover, and I filled my head with enough trivia to win a place on the Rockmart High Academic Bowl team, and then receive a scholarship to Berry College. My head full of useless information made the difference between lots of college loans, and only a small college loan. It looks like trivia was definitely not useless to me.

But at times, the world sees things that are important to us as useless, and even sees some people as unimportant. The world sees people who are homeless, people who are old, who have gotten sick, and who have to have help to get around, can be seen as useless. People who don't look like the world's idea of beautiful, who are from the wrong side of the tracks or side of the world, who have to live in homeless shelters or even on the street, who don't dress as well, or don't talk like the news anchors on TV, or don't have a job, can be seen as unimportant, and their wants and needs can be seen as "trivial." The world sees them as trivial people who have trivial needs; and having those needs met could be the difference between life and death.

Please open your Bible to Matthew 25:31-46. Let us pray.

Let's just see who is important and who is not, according to Jesus Himself.

[31] *"When the Son of Man comes in his glory, and all the angels with him, he will sit on his glorious throne.* [32] *All the nations will be gathered before him, and he will separate the*

people one from another as a shepherd separates the sheep from the goats. [33] He will put the sheep on his right and the goats on his left.

[34] "Then the King will say to those on his right, 'Come, you who are blessed by my Father; take your inheritance, the kingdom prepared for you since the creation of the world. [35] For I was hungry and you gave me something to eat, I was thirsty and you gave me something to drink, I was a stranger and you invited me in, [36] I needed clothes and you clothed me, I was sick and you looked after me, I was in prison and you came to visit me.'

[37] "Then the righteous will answer him, 'Lord, when did we see you hungry and feed you, or thirsty and give you something to drink? [38] When did we see you a stranger and invite you in, or needing clothes and clothe you? [39] When did we see you sick or in prison and go to visit you?'

[40] "The King will reply, 'Truly I tell you, whatever you did for one of the least of these brothers and sisters of mine, you did for me.'

[41] "Then he will say to those on his left, 'Depart from me, you who are cursed, into the eternal fire prepared for the devil and his angels. [42] For I was hungry and you gave me nothing to eat, I was thirsty and you gave me nothing to drink, [43] I was a stranger and you did not invite me in, I needed clothes and you did not clothe me, I was sick and in prison and you did not look after me.'

[44] "They also will answer, 'Lord, when did we see you hungry or thirsty or a stranger or needing clothes or sick or in prison, and did not help you?'

[45] "He will reply, 'Truly I tell you, whatever you did not do for one of the least of these, you did not do for me.'

[46] "Then they will go away to eternal punishment, but the righteous to eternal life.

Here, Jesus does not mince words; He says what the world was thinking-that if they did not see Him personally, in the flesh, in a needful state, that He was not there, and so, they should not be held responsible. First, He was talking to the "sheep," about people who needed things that they could not get on their own, and people who had to have them to stay alive:

- people who were hungry and thirsty, and who had to have food and water to stay alive;
- people who were new to the place, who maybe didn't know how to speak Aramaic, and needed help in getting around;
- people whose clothing was so raggedy and worn out, who had to have something warm to wear;
- people who were sick, with all kinds of diseases, and who were avoided by their family and friends, who couldn't take care of themselves anymore; and
- people who were in prison, who were shunned and forgotten by friends and family-Trivial People. The LEAST of these! The Sheep didn't notice they were the LEAST of these, but the Goats did.

Now, a little bit of word study from good old Strong's Exhaustive Concordance will help us understand just why the King in the parable was so angry with the Goats. The King used the words, "the least of these" two times: once to the Sheep and once to the Goats. The Hebrew word that Jesus used for our word "least," means unimportant. It means, the people who were not important to anyone-the outcasts, the people who had been driven out from somewhere, probably driven out from their homes, who had been forced out-by whom? Who made "the least" of Jesus' brothers and sisters outcasts? Could it be some of the same people who were criticizing Jesus for hanging around with "sinners," with outcasts who were sick, unacceptable, immoral people? Could it be the Goats? Who were they driving out, shunning, avoiding? The least of these. The trivial people who had trivial needs.

Do you remember the woman in Mark 5, who had had a bleeding sickness for twelve years? And no doctors could help her? Society thought she was unimportant-in fact they thought she was unclean, and if you touched her, you'd be unclean, too. She was may have been an outcast, driven out of her community. Probably people thought she, or even her parents, had committed some really bad sin to make her as sick as this. So, she bravely went up to Jesus and just reached out and touched His robe-just touched it, with her finger-and as soon as she did, she was immediately healed. Power went out of him and into her, and she was well again. In fact, Mark says that she felt in her body that she was free of her suffering. She was one of the least of these, but Jesus had seen her faith as important enough for her to be healed. The Goats would now have to take her back into her community again.

Getting back to the King, He speaks to the. The Goats started to make excuses-why, when did we see You, Lord? We saw those vagrants, those panhandlers with their dirty kids, but we didn't see You, Lord. We heard those people babbling, standing there in dirty old clothes, coughing up a storm, but You weren't there. We didn't hear about You going to prison, either, since of course, we never have been in there ourselves, no, we were following the Law and being good people-no, we would see You in a place like that? No, that is for the least important people, and we wouldn't be there. So the King sent the Goats off to everlasting punishment-but He sent to Sheep off to everlasting life.

The Sheep got it-anytime we take care of people who need help, who are seen by the world as trivial, the least important people to be bothered with, it is like we are taking care of Jesus, Himself. What did He call those trivial people? "My brothers and sisters." He looks beyond our faults and sees our needs, and we need to be just like Jesus, and do that also. The world sees their needs as trivial; but their needs, and our needs, are not trivial to him. Our sicknesses, both physical and spiritual, are able to be healed by Him, if we just reach out and touch him, If we can have the faith of the outcasts, the unclean, the unimportant people. IF we can see Jesus-because He will be right there in the middle. And if we do get into the group of trivial people and help them, and take Summer Lunches, and work with Backpack Buddies, and take care of them when they are sick, give them clothing when theirs is worn out, and go visit them when they are in jail, we will be doing it to Jesus. Just as much as we help the least person with the most trivial needs, we will be doing it to Him. If we want to be important, according to Jesus, we must become the servant of all. "For," He said, "It is the one who is the least among you all who is the greatest."

"Least?" There's that word again. Trivial? Not in Jesus' book.

The Present of Christ's Presence in the Present

Linda Smith Howell

(John 20:31)

This third Sunday of Eastertide the lectionary calls us to stretch beyond what is physically seen, or touched or heard. We are called to what faith is all about, what Christ calls us to be so that he can guide us to become a people of faith. Notice I said "to be" not "to do". This congregation is filled with people of great willingness to do. Each of you offers your talents and skills to the work of the church beyond all expectations. You take that old hymn, "We'll Work 'till Jesus Comes," as your anthem until you are almost worked to death. In truth, I worry that we are so busy doing for Christ, that we lose the spiritual blessing of being with Christ as he desires us to be. Today's scriptures call us to be and to receive Christ's presence in ways we perhaps overlook, or fail to practice.

John 20 tells us about the resurrection and appearances of Christ to his followers. It begins with Mary Magdalene at the empty tomb, and ends with "But these are written that you may believe that Jesus is the Messiah, the Son of God, and that by believing you may have life in his name. (John 20:31 NIV)" It is in the in-between of these two stories we find our teaching for today.

In Verses 19-28 we encounter the disciples hunkered down behind locked doors for fear of the Jews. We can imagine the anxiety and hopelessness of their plight as they wonder when the locked door will be forced open and they will be arrested. Their strength is failing and their hope weak as they wait and try to support one another.

Suddenly, without prelude, Jesus comes and greets them with the *peace of God.* After Jesus speaks he shows the disciples his hands and side so that they will know it is he who has appeared. As the disciples attempt to recover from the shock of his presence with them, Jesus speaks again. But when he speaks the word of peace this time, the peace he offers is from the *Lamb that was slain,* entwined with the very breath of God. A breath peace from God swirls around and through them, filling their spirits with peace, joy, hope and comfort as only the *Holy Spirit* can fill them.

Eight days later they are again together in the locked room, waiting, hoping for a word, a message from Christ. Thomas, who had not been with them when Jesus first appeared, is waiting with them this day. Again, with no preamble, Jesus greets the disciples with the gift of peace. Jesus turns to Thomas and tells him to touch his hands and side so that he will stop doubting and believe. Doubting Thomas does not need to touch or feel. He immediately believes and acknowledges Jesus as *My Lord and my God.*

The disciples received the perfect "present," yes, the perfect gift from their Master. They received the gift of his "presence" with them in the moment in the locked room. In a blink of an eye Jesus had turned their "present" existence from devastation into peace, joy, hope and comfort. The experience of Christ with them in his resurrected body carried them through the challenges they met as they lived their lives as the ones sent by Christ to spread the good news that God had given the world: news of salvation and the promise of new life in Christ. They are promised the presence of Christ's peace, hope, joy and comfort in that moment and all the other moments of their lives, if they but live in that hope of resurrection and life eternal in the presence of God.

Today we are not only the children of Jesus's twelve disciples, but are also the inheritors of the faith of all believers throughout almost two millennia. We are the ones throughout the age who have not seen the risen Lord, yet believe in our hearts God raised him from the dead. Yet we rarely receive the gift (present) of the presence of Christ in our daily lives. We go about doing the necessary labors of life: work, family time, chores, church services, church evangelism, caring for the church property, paying bills and keeping account of our finances and on and on. We are doing all the time. Even our quiet time reading scripture becomes a strictly study time, rather than a time to encounter and be in the presence of God in Christ. Our world appears to be becoming more and more task oriented, while what we truly need is to exist in a present moment in the presence of God.

So, the question bears asking, how do we prepare ourselves to encounter Christ spiritually within the confines of our busy lives. While The Spirit can and does teach us within the business of our active lives, finding time exclusively for God is helpful. Think about the position the disciples were in as they hid behind locked doors. Their circumstances dictated they live within the present. Their fears, anxieties and questions caused them all to wait and listen for help from God. They had their special hiding place where Christ chose to reveal himself as Lord and God. So, how do we prepare ourselves to encounter the living Christ? Here are a few thoughts I have had.

First, we are required to step away from doing. Finding a hiding place within our sphere of experience is enough. We are to be, to just exist in our special place. In our home in West Texas, my hiding place is on the upstairs balcony with a connecting door to a bedroom. There I spend time sitting in a comfortable chair by a small bistro table where a hot cup of Starbuck's coffee and my open Bible rest. Your hiding place could be the woods at the back of your house, your barn or shed, your spare bedroom, or any place you can imagine transforming into your special hiding place.

Second, we are asked to be in the present. To rest in being who we are in relationship to God. Our minds cannot be on the problems from yesterday or the challenges of tomorrow. I believe retiring to the present place can help us encounter Christ and be spiritually in his presence.

Third, I believe we cannot possibly write the script of how and when we will encounter Christ. Though God hears our prayers, the Spirit of God is not controlled by our thoughts, prayers, or demands. I know control is sometimes an issue for all of us. But our reality is control of any kind is an illusion. We can do nothing without God, because our very breath comes from God. We cannot come to God with clinched fists demanding God give us what we want. We can only come to God with open hands, hands that are able to welcome the presence of Christ.

Fourth, when we feel his presence, we receive an amazing blessing in our spirit. Our spirit is, in those moments, in tune with the spirit of God. It is Christ with us, offering us peace from the very breath of God. We experience the same peace, joy, hope and comfort the disciples received in the locked room.

Fifth, We are open in this moment to the teachings of Christ. Just as Christ had a word of instruction for the disciples, so he will instruct us. Then we can return again to our work with a new word from God to offer to the World.

This morning are you seeking a closer walk with Christ? Do you crave the peace, joy, hope and comfort Christ offers, but cannot find in your daily life? Then be still, be in the present with open hands and hearts, willing to welcome Christ's presence in your heart. Be the child of God you are, no pretense, no secrets. Wait for The Lord, for he is good, the giver of good and precious presents. He will revive your soul so that you can walk in his ways with confidence.

Yes, we too can receive the present of Christ's presence in the present. And with this gift, we breathe in peace, joy, hope and comfort from the breath of God. Amen!

Ms Helen's Funeral Service

Cardelia Howell-Diamond

(Isaiah 25:1-9)

You may be wondering why I would pick a passage from Isaiah for a funeral message. Too often when we think about the prophets we think of doom and gloom. We think of judgment, punishment, and fear. But when we think that way we do the prophets, and God a great disservice. We miss the point! Often we take the words and thoughts of these men and women and turn them into things they are not. We think of them as fortune tellers or future predictors. We treat Ezekiel, Daniel, and Isaiah as if they were only reading the palm of God. As if they were looking at his life and love lines giving their best guess as to his future actions. That my friends is more than a disservice, its just down right WRONG.

The prophets spoke the word of God to the people. They were the voices God used on earth to share God's work in the world. They were the messengers of not only God's displeasure, but also his joy. They were conduits of grace! (repeat!)

And today, as we grieve the passing of Ms. Helen, we all could use a little grace. The words of Isaiah this morning are words full of grace for the Hebrew people, God's children, and for us! Isaiah was writing to a people who had been in captivity. They had lost the land that God had promised to them. They had lost their place and standing in the world. They, who had dared to call themselves "chosen", were now outcasts. They were without hope.

When we find ourselves orphaned, no matter our age or status, we can feel lost, without an anchor in this world. It can be easy for us to pull away from one another, to let things divide us from our potential support systems because we feel so isolated already. We can find it hard to lean on family, friends, the church, or even God.

And in these times the words of Isaiah call us back. The voice of Isaiah calls us back to a relationship with God. It reminds us of who God is and what God is doing. Helen knew a relationship with God was important, even in the midst of suffering. She loved to hear the good old songs of God, loved hearing what was going on in her church family, and she prayed constantly for everyone she could. She held a deep love for her God.

129

The prophets, especially Isaiah, remind us that the living breathing God is not satisfied with a part of us, he wants all of us, all of our lives. Just as he wanted the whole being and heart of the Hebrew people.

And in this scripture Isaiah tells us of God's promise to enter into our lives and change them when we let go of our reigns and give back the control to the creator.
The text praises God, celebrates God, as active and real. It talks of a God who has worked miracles, rescued people, and has removed the strong city, the oppressors from their position. Isaiah shows a list of attributes for God that as his followers we should strive for, not to lift ourselves up, but to point others toward God. He speaks of caring for the poor, sheltering them from heat and bad weather. He speaks of sheltering the poor from those who would seek to abuse them, shutting their mouths so that they cannot devour the weak and needy.

And then Isaiah talks about the promised grace of God. He speaks of the heavenly banquet table where God will through a feast for all persons all nations who he calls his people. It will be lavish with wines and decadent foods, a far cry from what the Hebrew people have as exiled persons. It sounds like a party I want to be at! It sounds like a party Ms. Helen would enjoy.

But even more than the festivities a great thing is happening. God is removing the pall of death from his people. He is banishing death forever! The tears of his people will be wiped away by his gracious hand and all disgraces will be removed.

What an amazing picture! What a great thing to look forward to. I'm sure that many Hebrews took these words to heart. That they rejoiced in their souls over this picture of their promised future in God. Yes, what a comfort it must have been.

But guess what? It's not a pie in the sky by and by text we read this morning. No, my friends hear the good news! In Jesus Christ this has come to pass. The pall of death has been removed; our sins have been washed away! The feast sits before us for all who are willing to partake! Let us rejoice and be glad in the Lord, let us celebrate the very goodness of God. For you see we are the ones who get to proclaim the words at the end of this text. Also at this time people will say "Look at what has happened! This is our God! We waited for him and he showed up and saved us! This God, Jesus Christ, is the one we waited for! Let us celebrate, sing the joys of his salvation. Truly God's hand is upon us and this mountain!"

That is the good news! And it is the good news that we are called to share! We are to shout it from the rooftops, to proclaim it to all nations and all persons. It's good news that we remember here even as we gather to mourn the loss of Helen. Death is finished and new life has been given through the death and resurrection of our Lord. The banquets table is open for all who wish to come in and join the feast.

Have you accepted the invitation? Have you invited another to join you? Let me tell you friends the invitation is for all, and God is waiting on us to say yes to him!

But it is more than just saying yes to God. What the prophet Isaiah and the other great prophets were trying to teach the Hebrews is still what we need to learn today. We must respond to God by giving our all. It's not enough to want to be at the banquet table. It's not enough to make plans to go there, we have to get ready, get dressed, and actually show up! The prophets told us that it was not enough to pay lip service to God. We must clothe ourselves in the garments of Christ, we must be changed from head to toe! Sure, all of us here have responded to the extent that we've shown up, we're here today, we're sitting in the seats. But have we fully responded to God? Have we allowed ourselves to be changed to the way that God expects us to be?

When it comes to what we do with our lives, when it comes to what we do with our time, are we responding to God in such a way so that instead of focusing merely on what we expect out of life, we're focusing on what God expects out of us in life?

Are we responding to God, by making the effort to develop a relationship with God? God has removed death from the world and God is inviting us to the banquet to celebrate, inviting us to be God's people. And so God expects us to come and get to know God.

Ms. Helen responded. She lived out her days with a firm faith. It's shown by the love she has for her family, in the love she has for her church. And while Ms. Helen was not perfect, none of us is, she had accepted the invitation to come and see that the Lord is good.

You're invited. We're all invited. We're all invited to come and be God's people. That's the message that God has for us. The question is: do we accept that invitation? Because if we do, we need to respond to that invitation not just with our words, but we need to respond to that invitation with our whole selves with all that we are and with all that we have. After all, that's the kind of response God has expected throughout the ages. That's the kind of response God expects from us today.

Let us be those people spoken about in our text. Let us respond with all that we are so that the words of the prophet spill out of our mouths! "Look at what has happened! This is our God! We waited for him and he showed up and saved us!" The power of death has been taken away! Let us rejoice in knowing that Helen now lives with the Savior, seated at the banquet with Christ. Thanks be to God! Amen.

日期： 2014 年 2 月 9 日
講題： 時代英雄
經文： 士師記三章 7-11 節

Hero of the Era

Ella Hung

引言：

　　曾看過一個故事。17 世紀時，意大利有位物理及天文學家名叫伽利略，因為聲稱太陽在宇宙的中心，地球不是中心而且在運動著，而被異端裁判所審判，當他出來時，他的學生衝過來說：「老師，你頂住了？」伽利略回應說：「不，我招了。」學生震驚：「為甚麼？」伽利略：「因為我怕挨揍。」學生憤怒的說：「沒有英雄的國家真不幸！」伽利略搖頭：「不，需要英雄的國家才不幸。」

　　細想這句說話，實不無道理。中國人有句話說：「亂世出英雄。」若不是國教風雲，便不會讓一群中學生冒出頭；若不是電視發牌事件，相信沒有人會認識一位名叫伍佩瑩的顧問公司總監；我們更不願看到愈來愈多的劉曉波、趙連海、李旺陽被壓迫而揚名在外。唯有愈混亂不堪的處境，我們更盼望有些有能力的時代英雄可以幫助我們渡過難關。今天，我們在經濟政治困難中，期望有一位有能有德的領導者；在工作場境中，我們期望有良心的老闆；在家庭關係張力中，我們又會期望有人可以指點出路；甚至建立教會，我們期望教會領袖既可對內牧養關顧，又能外展佈道，幫助信徒紮根，並能關心社會，處處照顧到不同弟兄姊妹的需要，這樣的領袖當然了不起。恰恰像士師記所描述的情形，以色列民在困苦中，便自然的呼求拯救。上帝揀選和興起的拯救者有何條件呢？

　　上次講過士師記的序言，今早繼續士師記系列的第二講。從序言一章至三章 6 節中，我們得知在士師時代，以色列人其實陷入了一個循環中：離棄上帝、受壓迫、呼求、神拯救、國中太平。接著到了全

書的第二部份，三章 7 節至十六章，作者便以這個循環，或長或短的從南到北，記載十二位士師的事蹟。今天，我們所唸到的經文，首先出場的便是士師俄陀聶。短短五節經文，便交代了這個士師循環：

v7　　　離棄上帝
v8　　　受壓迫
v9　　　呼求
v10　　神拯救
v11　　國中太平

按照經文的記載，我們得知俄陀聶出場之時，「以色列人行耶和華眼中看為惡的事」，而這一個短句乃是本書主體中每一個士師出現前的開場白，也是俄陀聶作為一位領袖的挑戰。當時的處境是：

- 約書亞已經死了。（一 1，二 8）
- 那些看過耶和華為以色列行大事的長老已不在了。（二 7，10）

經文以兩個動詞來說明當時以色列人如何行惡：
1 / 忘記
這不是一時疏忽、忘掉，其實反映以色列民更深層的問題，在申命記中，神多次提醒以色列民，當他們不謹慎保守自己的心，輕忽與神所立的約，他們就會心高氣傲，忘記那位將他們從埃及地，為奴之家領出來的耶和華，背約和離棄上帝

2 / 事奉，亦即敬拜
當這些以色列民背約、離棄上帝，就自然的敬拜別神，經文中指當時的以色列人選擇了事奉諸巴力及亞舍拉，諸巴力與亞舍拉兩字均是複數，泛指以色列人所接觸並敬拜迦南人所拜的男神與女神。

這樣的結果是惹怒上帝，於是神將以色列人交到敵人的手中統治八年。這敵人是米所波大米王古珊 •利薩田。米所波大米是指巴勒斯坦以北，幼發拉底河與哈柏河之間，亞蘭人統治的區域。古珊 •利薩田似乎不是真的是某位古代君王的名字，反似是以色列人所給予的綽號，因為這名字的意思是「雙倍邪惡的古珊」，有誰會為自己改一個這樣的名字呢？就像我們會稱希特拉為希魔，而 689 或吳得掂，都不會這樣稱呼自己一樣。

總的來說，俄陀聶所面對的處境正是外憂內患，對外要面對雙倍

邪惡的敵人，對內的以色列民又不生性，甚至以色列人在苦難中向神呼喊，是否代表他們真心悔改呢？若是，他們應徹底離棄過去的惡行，何以當士師一死，他們又故態復萌，又去行耶和華眼中看為惡的事呢？

英雄不易為，風光的背後總有許多挑戰。但上帝所興起的時代英雄，首要條件是有上帝的靈在他身上。

主點一： 時代英雄 -有上帝的靈在他身上（v9-10）

v9　　以色列人呼求耶和華的時候，耶和華就為他們興起一位拯救者救他們，就是迦勒兄弟基納斯的兒子俄陀聶。

v10　　耶和華的靈降在他身上，他就作了以色列的士師，出去爭戰。

俄陀聶是迦勒的姪兒，換言之，他與迦勒一樣，都是歸化猶大支派的外族人。從約書亞記十五章以及士師記第一章，我們也知道他奪取了基列西弗而娶了押撒成了迦勒的女婿。或許我們也可以稱他為士師中的樣板人物，為以後出場的士師定下基調。而俄陀聶與押撒的婚姻，歸化的外邦男子與以色列女子聯婚，更與士師當代的其他以色列人與迦南人結合成了一強烈對比。可是除此之外，聖經對俄陀聶便沒有很多的描述，甚至他奪取基列西弗也只是一句簡單的帶過去，他是否有驚世之才？用了甚麼軍事策略？我們一無所知。

論背景，俄陀聶只是歸化的外族人，論才幹，亦沒有多著墨。只肯定「耶和華的靈降在他身上，他就作了士師，出去爭戰。」

應用：

弟兄姊妹，上帝所要使用的人，從來都不論背景和才幹，後來的幾位士師，他們更不是品格特別高尚的人，但他們也會被揀選，為神爭戰。今天，我們都是上帝的戰士，在這個歪曲的世代，神也會藉著祂的靈來更新我們，並賜我們恩賜和能力，去完成神所托付的使命。或許有時我們都會內外受敵，工作家庭的張力，個人的軟弱，影響我們與神的關係，不要說要事奉，就在生活上都難以作好信徒的見證，總覺得那是屬靈偉人才能做到的事，自己心裡願意，肉體卻軟弱了。

例子：

感謝主！我們身邊總有許多見證人在激勵著我們。我認識不少弟兄姊妹在學校或職場建立查經小組或團契，招聚基督徒同事彼此守望和成長。有些弟兄姊妹幼嬰剛滿月便回團契事奉，甚至孩子未滿一歲，夫婦雙雙委身啟發十多個星期擔任組長。從前在耀道堂有些初中生，大膽的在學校建立團契，自己領詩講信息，我問他們如何預備信息，他們說將在教會聚會中所聽到的，回校分享就是了。在我們教會，也有大學生，同樣的去學帶查經，然後回大學團契作帶領的工作。弟兄姊妹，他們都不像是顯眼的人，可能你根本沒有發現他們，可是在職場上、在學校中，他們正是為上帝爭戰的勇士，你與我都可以是。

上帝的靈除了賦予我們能力，也是一種急迫、不能抗拒的力量。而人所要做的便是順服上帝的主權完成使命。

主點二：　時代英雄 - 順服上帝的主權

上帝的拯救者，使命是將以色列人從敵人手中救拔出來。但從經文我們可以肯定，由始至終，唯有耶和華是那位拯救者。

v8　　耶和華的怒氣向以色列人發作，就把他們交在米所波大米王古珊·利薩田的手中。以色列人服事古珊·利薩田八年。

v9　　　以色列人呼求耶和華的時候，耶和華就為他們興起一位拯救者救他們，就是迦勒兄弟基納斯的兒子俄陀聶。

v10　　耶和華的靈降在他身上，他就作了以色列的士師，出去爭戰。耶和華將米所波大米王古珊·利薩田交在他手中，他便勝了古珊·利薩田。

　　三節經文的主動權都在上帝。是上帝把以色列民交在米所波大米王手中；是上帝興起拯救者；是上帝降祂的靈在拯救者身上；也是神自己將米所波大米王交在俄陀聶手中，便打了勝仗。當我們一口氣唸這幾節經文，是上帝以行動去拯救一群行了「惡」的百姓，俄陀聶只是當靈降在他身上，便作了士師，出去爭戰。聖靈固然賦予人爭戰的能力，在塑造領袖上，扮演一個重要的角色，但更重要的是只有耶和華是真正的王，所有領導者都先要服從這位真正的王，他們才能長久和成功地帶領百姓。這是全本舊約所表達的一貫思想，就是將來以色列地上的王，都只是耶和華的地上代表，無論有多少領袖，但真正的王，是耶和華自己。

　　就是在士師記中，除了俄陀聶，耶弗他也是有「耶和華的靈降在他身上」，基甸則是「穿在身上」，而參孫是耶和華的靈大大感動，可是並不代表這些士師毫無缺欠，反倒一蟹不如一蟹。上帝的靈降在拯救者身上，目的不是要彰顯神的能力這麼簡單，而是這些能力是否推進上帝的救贖計劃。

應用：
　　今天，神同在的應許，讓人得著恩賜和能力，我們所以問的是，這些恩賜怎樣回應這個時代的需要？於建立人的生命有何益處？

例子：

　　早前，台灣有一位女牧師，聲稱自己過去十幾年，不住的檢鑽石，甚至於帶領禱告時有鑽石從天掉下來，於是網絡瘋傳這段「信耶穌得鑽石」的影片。及後又有另一女子記曾經於禱告後發現自己手上有閃閃金粉的超自然現象。姑勿論這些所謂神蹟是否真有其事，即便有，事實上我自己也試過敬拜禱告後面上出現金粉，我自己並不知道，還是有人發現的，然而那又如何？問題是上帝的靈降在人身上是為了甚麼？不是為了我們有超自然的屬靈經歷，而是為了拯救在困苦中的人。所以我們所追求的不是超自然的能力，而是有能力去建立人的生命，將人帶到上帝面前，一切拯救只有從上帝而來。我們可以誇的是甚麼呢？唯有基督而已。

　　因此時代英雄，有上帝的靈在他身上，會得順服神的主權，更會回應時代的需要。

主點三：　時代英雄 - 會得回應時代的需要（v11）
v11　　　於是國中太平四十年。基納斯的兒子俄陀聶死了。

　　剛才已說過，士師記的作者並沒有記載俄陀聶有任何策略、特殊的誓言或是別人從旁協助而能獲勝，反之，即使國中太平四十年，他還是會死的。無論多顯赫的英雄，都有人最大的限制，就是都會死。聖經裡提及四十年，多指一代。「太平」，從約書亞記、士師記及歷代志，都是指戰亂結束後，社會歸於平靜，人得到安息的意思。作為最正面的士師，俄陀聶所能服事也只是一代。按聖經記載，他死後，以色列人又行耶和華眼中看為惡的事」，於是又陷入士師循環中。

應用：

　　弟兄姊妹，在預備這篇信息之時，這節經文一直縈繞在我心中。

「國中太平四十年。基納斯的兒子俄陀聶死了。」我不住的默想，上帝給我兩個提醒：

1 / 人人必有一死，屬靈偉人也不例外，當然不是他們一死，便完全沒有了影響力。就好像剛返天家的滕近輝牧師，他對華人教會的影響是毋庸置疑的。然而，我們所仰慕的不是這個人，而是這位牧者敬虔的態度，否則就像以色列人般，當士師死去又追隨別神。

例子：

在滕近輝牧師的追思會中，滕師母分享滕牧師是一位真誠宣講神話語、熱愛讀經事奉、生活簡樸的人。他看得最多的書，就是聖經，看得很有趣味，雖然他也看很多其他的書，「但都是因為別人邀請他為新書寫序，所以看了很多書！」她說無論有沒有人邀請他講道，他都經常看聖經，在家中寫作準備，因此他的聖經「看爛一本又一本……而生日願望就總是希望能『講道到一百歲！』」滕牧師對講道是十分渴望的，甚至有時自言自語，不來是一個人也在講道，實在是很愛上帝的話語。」詩篇第一篇中說：「惟喜愛耶和華的律法，晝夜思想，這人便為有福！」

每一個時代都有不同屬靈前輩值得我們去學習，過去有楊牧谷牧師、鮑會園牧師、滕近輝牧師；今天有鮑維均牧師、孫寶玲牧師、李思敬博士。可是上帝提醒我說不要把他們成了上帝，也不要以為上了他們的課堂或是聽了幾張碟便代替研讀上帝的話語，他們也只是人，是每一個世代上帝所揀選所使用的人。

2 / 第11節給我的第二個提醒是我們都是這時代的英雄，要回應這個時代的需要。我們生於這個時代，這是地方，必有神的心意。我們回應的就只是此時此刻，目前的這個身份，盡力的被主使用。在家中，我們是父母兒女；在學校，我們是學生；在職場，我們有不同的位置。該被提升時，我們不要卻步推讓，謙說自己不及前人的經驗；該退下來時，又當悄然讓賢。要知道，神揀選，並不論背景地位，而是願意順服主的人。

例子：

最近聽到一個見證。一對新人在婚宴上答謝父母，其中新郎特別感激媽媽在他反叛的時候不離不棄，直到如今。他稱媽媽為

soulmate，靈友，對母親來說是何等尊榮。這位母親就是英雄，拯救了兒子的一生，不是因為她有多能幹，而是她有多倚靠神，在她的位分中盡了本份。

結語：

　　2006年，著名的《時代》周刊選的風雲人物是「你you」，即是我們中每一個的普通人，不是大人物，不是別人，是你和我。這是因為我們把向來由少數人控制的傳媒主導權奪過來。今天，在上帝的國度裡，無論我們是甚麼背景，有甚麼才能，有多大限制，只要相何上帝的揀選，願意順服上帝的主權，回應需要，便是時代英雄。

讓我們一同禱告。

Women are Always Starting "Stuff"

Versey Jones

(John 4:25-29)

Introduction: To the women of the church, visiting women and women everywhere, we salute you for your united and untiring efforts, your patience, and your contributions to the Church, society and the world. We salute you for your motherly attitudes, your beauty, your brains and all the contributions you have made to mankind and the world.

If we were to paraphrase Proverbs 31 we could say that in many things women excel, if we were to sum up the book of Proverbs we could do so by saying it is a book that teaches moral and ethical principles. When we read Proverbs we find words like wisdom, instruction, understanding, justice, judgement, knowledge and learning, but the word wisdom is especially noted, and it is interesting to note that the book speaks of wisdom as she, and I think that as women we do have wisdom, maybe not the kind of wisdom that the world defines, but the kind that allows us to have "common Sense", the kind that allows us to run a household, soothe crying babies, smooth over rough places, and make things run smoother, and we don't do too bad on the professional level either, only a few weeks ago astronaut Mae Jemison was in our city to participate in a ribbon cutting ceremony held in honor of a new high school being named for her.

As women we have historically been known for starting stuff, and we must admit that some of the things we start are not always seen in a positive light, we sometimes gossip, we can sometimes be bossy, sometimes we get in the way, but we usually mean well.

But in the overall scheme of things we have to admit that the world is a better place because of women.

If we look around in our schools, government installations, businesses and other institutions we can see that women are visible in all these areas and the churches are no exception, God has work for women in the church too.

Because God has work for women to do; there are things that we need in order to continue our journey.

We must learn to sit at Jesus' feet and listen, if we don't listen we will not grow, if we don't listen we will be overcome with temptation and worldly things, if we don't listen we will become carnal minded.

If we become too busy we will forget that worship is more important than work, we will forget that many times we need to listen rather than speak.

If we are not in a Christian frame of mind we can become critical of others, causing them to become discouraged.

Our labor and works must be balanced by listening to Jesus. The Christian life for all of us, not just women, ought to set an example, an example of a Christian learning, an example of a Christian worshiping and an example of a Christian having times of prayer and devotion.

As women we cannot properly start things without the proper tools, without proper preparation, we have to be disciplined, we need the roadmap of Jesus and we must take advantage of every opportunity to serve Him, we must welcome those things that challenge our spirit and we do have challenges, but we must remember that we are all different, we have different personalities, and different temperaments, but God has put us among each other as believers, He has given us something in common, we are all baptized by one Spirit, we are baptized into one body and we are made to drink of one Spirit, in other words, the things that we have in common are the most important and if we do what we are supposed to do we compliment reach other.

It's like shopping for the perfect outfit, you want the perfect shoes, accessories and hat because these things pull everything together. Another very important thing to remember is that all work done in the church should glorify God, not us. Colossians 3:23 explains this very well: "And whatsoever ye do, do it heartily as to the Lord and not unto men..."

I feel the need to mention our subject and text, we have already said women are always starting "stuff", we confess that we are guilty as charged, that has been the case since the beginning, when Eve started a family with Adam, not on her own, but through the power of God.

As the world started to grow and multiply so did sin, strife and suffering, but we should not let this bother us because the best is yet to come, we suffer because the adversary attacks, but in the suffering God is preparing us for glory. How does He prepare us?

He does it by perfecting us, maturing us, he does it by establishing us, building our faith, by strengthening us, by placing us on a firm foundation; and because we are partakers of Jesus' suffering, we are also going to share in His glory, suffering is to make us like Jesus. Things of the earth are fleeting, temporary, but Jesus' glory is eternal.

We have said that women are always "staring stuff" some of those things don't put us in a positive light, things like petty attitudes, feeling shunned because someone failed to notice us and even small gossip, as I said; sometimes we are guilty but for the most part the Christian woman is about the Lord's business, most of the time she is that woman that Proverbs 31 describes.

We are known for things that we start, Job's wife started him talking when she suggested he "curse God and die", what she said may sound bad from our point of view but what Job said to her will forever be remembered: "Shall we receive good at the hand of God, and shall we not receive Evil?"

Potiphar's wife started something with Joseph, it started off wrong but God made it right, Joseph was accused unjustly and put in prison but God was with him even then, Joseph used this time to minister to his inmates, upon his release Joseph was placed in charge of the king's estate, second only to the king himself.

The woman with the issue of blood started something, all she wanted was to be healed, she had no idea that hundreds of years later we would still continue to teach the way to healing is to "touch the hem of His garment.", she started something.

When the king of Persia sent out the decree calling for the extermination of the Jews, Queen Esther intervened on behalf of her people, she started something by saying "If I perish, I perish"

In the book of Luke, we find a poor widow starting something by casting all she had into the treasury, her two mites started the phrase we call the "widows mite" She taught us the principle of giving our all to the Lord.

Martha started something when she said to Jesus "Lord if you had been here our brother had not died.", but she didn't stop there she went on to say "But I know that even now, whatsoever thou wilt ask of God he will give it thee" she started Jesus' reply: "Thy brother shall rise again, I am the resurrection and the life, he that believeth in me though he were dead yet shall he live."

Yes, it's true, women are always starting ("stuff") things.

What can you start?

The Difference a Dollar Can Make

Abby Cole Keller

(Luke 18:9-14)

When I was asked to preach this week on stewardship, I nearly ran for the hills. I took a few deep breaths and thought to myself, "I can do this! I will just focus on time and talents. That will be easy enough." However, after I agreed to preach, I was given further direction that focus had to be on financial stewardship specifically and not just time and talents. At this point I had some major second thoughts. Jamie was just lucky that I had already agreed and could not bolt for the door at that point.

Financial stewardship is a hard topic to talk about for anyone especially from the pulpit, and even hard for an Associate Pastor. I spent the end of last week struggling with where to even begin. What should I saw to a congregation that has always been so generous? How do I approach financial stewardship with people that have always proven to be so gracious with giving; gracious with their giving of time, of talent and of financial gifts as well?

I could stand before you today and preach on all the reasons that we are called to give to the church. I could list Scripture after Scripture that calls us as Christians to tithe. Give you Scripture that speaks to the evil of the love of money and the joy of a faithful giver. I could argue from the pulpit whether we should tithe based on gross or net income. I could get into deep theological debate over how we give not out of legalistic motives but out of thankfulness for all that we have been given. Where to begin? Where to begin?
I sat there listening to the service last Sunday and soaked in Jamie's excellent sermon on stewardship of time and talents; I did note his focus on time and talent and not financial giving; Don't think for a moment that did not go unnoticed by me, as I heard Jeorald Miller speak for the stewardship moment, I remembered that one year we called the stewardship moment "What My Church Means To Me". It occurred to me during that time that perhaps today I should take a similar approach. I could argue about the scripture and the theology behind good stewardship. I could beg you to give of your time and talents and tithing. I

could use good ol' Christian guilt in an attempt to get you to give. But we have all heard that before. We all know the reasons.

So today I think there is a better way. Today I want to share with you what your giving in the past has done for me. Hopefully that will give you a glimpse into the difference that your giving can make for one individual. I think the best reason to give is because you believe in the cause, because you can see that your giving can make a difference in the world, even if in a small way, even if only for one individual. My hope is that in my story you can see what a difference your support makes. Maybe the hope of that difference can move us all to be cheerful givers. So here it goes, and apologies to those doing the stewardship moment a little later on.

Here is what my Church means to me.

For as long as I can remember I have come to this church. This church has given me my roots in Christian Faith, and those roots run deep in the Cumberland Presbyterian church. This church and its people have given me the strength to grow into Christ's light and room to spread my branches in ministry and in life. You all have provided me with roots strong enough to support the person I have become and that will allow me to spread my branches even further in the future.

As I said earlier, for as long as I know, my family has come to this church. I can tell you exactly where we sat in worship as I was growing up. We sat on the pulpit side of the sanctuary, half way back, first full seat after the second radiator, right behind Mrs. Margerate Gaut and in front of the Allen and Sandy Jones and their girls Kendra and Andrea who were the same age as my sister and me. I remember a lot of wiggling in the pews, crawling under the pews and cuddling in parents arms during worship. Many of you may remember a lot of noise, great commotion, and live entertainment from that section.

I can still remember the old fellowship hall and Wednesday night suppers. I remember the clown ministry preforming after a few of the meals with Shelia Ricker, and Jonathon Freeman and a few others, although those details are a little fuzzy because I would have just been knee high to a gross hopper back then. I can still remember the old nursery and the really cool wooden boat that rocked or could be flipped over to be a bridge with

149

steps in Mrs. Andi's room. I remember going to Cherub Choir practice with Mrs. Dinah Rhea and Mrs. Dottie Flieshman. I remember singing songs and playing games all while learning about God and church. I remember Sunday School class with Mrs. Jean Jenkins who ended up becoming my grandmother in law, and Senior High Sunday School Class with Compton's, who always brought fresh doughnuts.

I remember going through confirmation class with Dr. Dan Freeman. I remember the weeks of class we underwent. I remember stressing about memorizing the Apostle's Creed and the Lord's prayer. I remember standing in the front of this very sanctuary by Jason Austin and Matt Buckles and several others getting baptized and joining the church. I remember the cool water rolling on my forehead and Dr. Freeman's large, warm hand placing it there.

I remember youth group activities. I remember lock in's and youth choir when there were only three of us. Sam McCamey and Andrea Jones were good sports to be dragged along. I remember Sally Anderson and all the love and support that she gave me throughout all of high school. She showed me the love and compassion of Christ and how to live that out in faithful ministry.

I remember the beginnings of the harvest auction, which we are about to celebrate later in November. I vividly remember how Sally used to pair a youth with an adult congregation member as a prayer partner. The prayer partner was to pray for us throughout the year and send us notes of encouragement. The prayer partner remained anonymous until the night of the Harvest Auction and then it would be revealed. I remember the year that my prayer partner must have done one heck of a job praying because I felt their support and love all throughout the year and all the years since. I remember the connection that was made and I am thankful that it stuck. That relationship has held true even into adulthood. It probably did not hurt that she sent me many treats that were delicious throughout the year either. That one prayer partner, so many years ago, has taught me what true Christian faith means and continues to show me how to be faithful even in the face of great adversity. She is one of the great Saints I have known in my life.

I remember trips to Resurrection in Gatlinburg. Two trips to Triennium at Purdue University. I also remember standing once again in the front of the sanctuary in my cap and gown with my graduating class. I think there were nine of us that year. I remember a lovely service and a great luncheon. I remember this church sending us out into the world with its love and support.

I remember feeling heard and loved, supported and encouraged by this church, by individuals and by the institution as a whole through my childhood and youth. There are countless others of you who supported me, loved me and prayed for me through my journey. My parents would tell you that you all must be one praying church because there is no other explanation for how I ended up here on this side of the pulpit.

Even when I left for college and seminary your love a support remained. I remember cards from circles sent faithfully to let me know that they were praying for me, and notes from individuals when I was away in school. I received scholarships that helped support both my college education and my seminary education, helping on only emotionally but physically.

Throughout my bout with cancer this church supported not only me but my parents. From visits, and cards, to food and offers of transportation in the snow, you all stood by us as a family. From pastoral visits to communion brought when I could not attend worship, you saw us through. This church has been where my life has been lived. This church is where I got rooted in my faith.

In seminary, they tell you not to go back to your home church ever to work. Never, Ever!! You can be a guest speaker or fill in the pulpit once or twice, but never go back to work at your home church for your ministry. They warn you that you will never be able to do real ministry there. They tell you that you will never be seen as a true pastor because to your home church you will always be that rowdy child in the pews. There is even scripture to support that! When Jesus went back to his home town the people would not listen to him. They could not get past the boy he was.

Despite the many, many warnings my home church was where I was called to after Seminary. I believe that God led me back here. While there are always challenges, while there will always be those people who still see me as a little girl, knee high to a gross hopper, wiggling in the pews and struggle to get over that hump to see me as their pastor, for the most part, my husband, children and I have truly been blessed by this church both in life and in my ministry. My kids feel the love and support of the body of this church. They have been blessed by so many extra grandparents and loving hands that there is no other place we would want to raise them in the Christian faith.

This is not only the place where I was baptized it is all so the place where I stood up front and brought both my girls to baptized. It is not only the church that strengthen me to face the world, it held me up as I sat in the front row at my daddy's funeral, provided meals, and food and cookies for visitation, which helped to make a difficult time less hard because we were support by a faith community.

This church is truly our home. It has held so many of the pivotal points of my life. This is where I was given the roots of my faith, the strength to grow tall and room to extend my branches. It is here that I have had the opportunity to live into God's calling for me. Throughout my time in ministry here I have also been blessed to see some wonderful works of the Spirit alive here as the church has spread her branches to cover this community with compassion and care, to show Christ's love in our world. I have seen empty halls during the week become jam-packed with groups coming in and out. I have seen the congregation become more connected, more prayerful, more mission minded. We have developed a warmth and a caring that truly speaks to the spirit of Christ and the body of the church, not only within these walls but reaching out into the world around us.

So when you prepare to give this year, take your stewardship packet home, pray over what God is calling you to do and to give. Remember this is why you are giving. Give not out of guilt, give not out fear or for legalist reasons, like the Pharisee in this morning scripture but give as you are able. You, like the tax collector, are but a sinner who desires a better world. Give because you believe in this church, because you believe in its mission and its work in this world. Give because you believe in what this church is doing and what it can and will do in the future. Give because you are part of something bigger than yourself. Something that is helping to bring the word of God to the community around us, and without your support that cannot happen.

Know that when you give, you are not just helping pay the light bill or repainting the windows, you are not just giving to support the staff salary or fix the leaking roof. When you give, you are giving to make a difference in the lives of people, of individuals. You are helping provide community and support, love and compassion. You are giving to maintain a church home, full of love and grace. You are providing a warm sanctuary for people are who worn and battered, who are seeking peace. You are providing hope for children who hear the word of God no where else but inside these walls. You are providing comfort and companionship to older adults who can no longer get out into the world.

I Am Calling You

Mary Kathryn Kirkpatrick

(Jeremiah 1:4-10)

Jeremiah 1:4-10

⁴ Now the word of the Lord came to me saying, ⁵ 'Before I formed you in the womb I knew you, and before you were born I consecrated you; I appointed you a prophet to the nations.' ⁶Then I said, 'Ah, Lord God! Truly I do not know how to speak, for I am only a boy.' ⁷But the Lord said to me, 'Do not say, "I am only a boy"; for you shall go to all to whom I send you, and you shall speak whatever I command you. ⁸ Do not be afraid of them, for I am with you to deliver you, says the Lord.' ⁹Then the Lord put out his hand and touched my mouth; and the Lord said to me, 'Now I have put my words in your mouth. ¹⁰ See, today I appoint you over nations and over kingdoms, to pluck up and to pull down, to destroy and to overthrow, to build and to plant.'

Jobs

When we look for a job, we hunt. There is an art to job-hunting. We prepare resumes and find appropriate interviewing clothes. We go to school for years in order to prepare for a job that we don't yet have. We have been trained to pursue our jobs.

Jeremiah had a job tossed into his lap. He was not looking for this job. God simply came up to him and appointed his job to him.

When we interview, many of us stretch the truth just a little bit to help our cause. Jeremiah stretched the truth to turn down a job. He was probably about 18 years old, yet he tried to make himself look worse by claiming to be only a boy. Jeremiah did not want the job that God was offering him.

What would you do if God offered you a job? Would you turn it down?

Danger!

We all know certain jobs that are overflowing with danger. Loggers, pilots, roofers, steel workers, truck drivers, and miners come to mind.

Jeremiah probably considered the job of a prophet to be overflowing with danger. Why? Prophets speak for God. They are often sent to proclaim unpopular news to the people. God sends prophets to foretell events -- usually horrible ones. For example, "If you don't stop your wicked ways, you are all going to die!"

Prophets were people in the Bible such as Isaiah, Nathan, Elijah, Elisha, Jonah, Micah, Daniel, Ezekiel, Balaam, Samuel, Miriam, Deborah, Noah, Moses, ...oh, there are more! At least some of those names probably conjured up memories of difficult jobs given by God. Who wants to be called to be a prophet?

A prophet's job is full of danger. You have to go and tell people something that they don't want to hear and that you don't want to say. People make fun of you. They talk about you. They run from you. They try to kill you.

Jeremiah's Call

Jeremiah's call from God follows a pattern. First there is the call. Then an excuse. Then reassurance. Then a promise.

He clearly hear's God's call appointing him to be a prophet to the nations.

His excuse? "Ah, Lord God! Truly I do not know how to speak, for I am only a boy."

The reassurance? "You will go. You will speak. And do not be afraid because I will rescue you."

The promise? A consecration. A blessing. God reached down and touched Jeremiah's mouth, symbolically giving him the words that he would need. God said, 'Now I have put my words in your mouth."

God Calls Us All

God calls us. God initiates the call. God takes divine initiative. The first hymn that we sang today was, "We Are Called to Be God's People." Do you believe that? We are called to be God's people, God's servants, God's prophets. That's what the hymn says. God calls us. God initiates the call.

We are all called to do something. The call can be as simple as to write a letter of encouragement to somebody. And the call can be as difficult as to create a new, forgiving relationship with someone who has wronged us.

You might be called to break through your hesitation to visit a sick friend. Or to make peace with a son or daughter.

You might be called to work at the Food Pantry or to join the Prayer Group on Wednesday nights.

You might be called to serve as a Sunday School teacher, an elder, a deacon, a committee chair.

You might be called to be a minister.

You might be called to join this church.

We All Make Excuses

Just as God calls us all, we all make excuses! Every call has a conflict. Every call meets resistance.

When God called Moses, he really protested. He had a litany of fears. At various times in Moses' story, we heard him say, "Who am I? They'll never believe me. I have limited skill. I am insecure about my personal identity. I am afraid of being rejected." Moses. We know his story. God provided for him in every single protest, with every single excuse.

The prophet Isaiah had a profound sense of personal sin. "Woe to me! For I am a man of unclean lips!" (Isaiah 6)

My own favorite prophet story is the story of Jonah. When God told him to go give the wicked people of Nineveh a message, Jonah got on a ship that was sailing in the opposite direction!

We laugh at Jonah, but we all make excuses of some kind! While some of us might physically run from God's call, I can think of several other excuses. See if any of these fit you.

> I am only a woman.
> I am too old.
> I do not hear very well.
> I don't have time for this.
> I don't know how.
> I have never done that before.
> I am not very persuasive.
> If I were really supposed to, God would make it a whole lot easier.
> Excuses. We all make them.

Our Call Stories

One of my seminary professors had each of us describe our call story to the class. While all of the stories were extremely interesting, they were all so different. At the same time, they all had common themes. We heard God call us. We made an excuse. We were reassured, usually by the person we would have thought least likely to reassure us! And we were equipped. I wish that you could have heard these call stories. They reminded me of how creative God can be...how God can get our attention...how many ways that God can speak to us!

Teaching Disciple Bible Study

About 15 years ago, when I was in another church, and in my pre-pastor life, I committed myself to study a 39-week Bible class. Most people only want to take a 4- to 6-week class. But this was a commitment. I did not really think that I had the time in my very busy schedule to take the class. It required daily and weekly reading and thinking. For 39 weeks. It required me to attend a 2 1/2-hour class each Thursday evening. For 39 weeks.

After the study ended, our class leader called me and suggested that I might be the right person to lead the next study. My excuses were multiple. What? I just took the time out of my very busy schedule. Now you want me to spend more time being trained? And then I need to commit to 39 more weeks? I don't think so! I have never taught a Bible class! I don't have time!

In sharing my disbelief with a friend, she said, "Get thee behind me, Satan!" She was telling me that Satan was making these excuses for me. Let me tell you -- that got my attention!

My whole mind jerked around. What if I really should lead this class? What if God can really use me? What if God can really help me? What if God can use me to help others?

I led the next class. It was difficult, but it was a blessing. Nothing in my life was harmed by the blessing. I struggled, I worked, I thought, I learned, I thrived. And so did others in the class. God helped me. God used me.

And if I had missed that opportunity, just think of the blessings I would have also missed.

Missed Opportunities

Think of some of the missed opportunities in the Bible.

In the story of the Good Samaritan (Luke 10:25-37), the priest and the Levite both miss an opportunity to help the man from Jerusalem who had been stripped, beaten, and left for dead beside the road. The priest and the Levite see him and avoid him. A missed opportunity to help another human being.

In the story of the Rich Young Ruler (Luke 18:18-23), a wealthy man asks Jesus what he must do to inherit eternal life. He already follows the Commandments and follows the Law. When Jesus responds, "One thing you still lack. Sell all that you have and distribute to the poor, and you will have treasure in heaven; and come, follow me," the Rich Young Ruler becomes very sad. For he knows that he cannot give up his earthly riches. A missed opportunity to follow Jesus and receive treasure in heaven.

Caught Opportunities

Hearing those missed opportunities might help us recall other stories of people who DID respond to a call. People who CAUGHT an opportunity!

The Samaritan helped the man who was dying alongside the road. He showed compassion for a foe and, according to Jesus, he earned the chance to receive eternal life.

The disciples who Jesus called to follow him were an interesting lot! They were 12 men, full of faults and shortcomings. Not a single one of them was a scholar or a rabbi. They had no extraordinary skills. They were not refined, not particularly religious. They were ordinary people, just like you and me.

But God chose them for a purpose-to fan the flames of the gospel that would spread across the face of the earth and continue to burn down through the centuries. He selected and used each of these regular guys to carry out his exceptional plan.

What if they had not caught the opportunity? They might not have understood what they were doing when Jesus was alive, but they became the pioneering leaders to the New Testament church because they answered a call from God.

A Challenge to Us All

The word of God challenges us. Jeremiah's call is serious. It is challenging. It's probably inconvenient. Our call, no matter what is might be, is serious, challenging, and probably inconvenient.

The precious gift that God gives us, though, is this. Even when we recognize that we are not up to the task, God says, "Do not be afraid of them, for I am with you to deliver you." God assures us. When God calls us, God enables the disabled.

I Am Calling You

(My cell phone rings. I answer.)
Hello?
It's God!
Yes, I thought it might be you. (pause)
Oh, yes, I'll be sure to tell them that. (hang up)

God says all of us should be on the alert for a call from God at any time. God loves you and is going to be in touch. And when God calls, be sure to listen and respond!

Baptism of Christ

Sherry Whitaker Ladd

(Matthew 3:13-17)

One thing that we recall in Jesus' baptism each year at this time is our own baptisms. John Calvin wrote that Jesus "undertook baptism with us that the faithful might be more surely persuaded that they are engrafted into his body, buried with him in baptism, that they might rise again to newness of life."

The second sign, "the Spirit of God descending like a dove," was probably visible to all the people, for Luke recounts that "the Holy Spirit descended upon him in bodily form like a dove" (Luke 3:22 NRSV). The descent of the Spirit, and the form of the dove itself, represented to Israel God's mighty workings in the world. At creation, "the Spirit of God was hovering over the waters" (Gen 1:2 NIV). After the great Flood, the dove carried the news to Noah of the receding waters (Gen 8:8-12). The descending of the Spirit signified God's workings in the world; therefore the arrival of the Messiah would have been marked by the descending of the Spirit, in this case, in the form of a dove.

Later, Jesus would read from the prophet Isaiah (Isa 61:1-2), "'The Spirit of the Lord is on me, because he has anointed me to preach good news to the poor. He has sent me to proclaim freedom for the prisoners and recovery of sight for the blind, to release the oppressed, to proclaim the year of the Lord's favor'" (Luke 4:18-19 NIV).

The church uses the dove as a symbol for the Holy Spirit; however, the bird itself was not important. The descent of the Spirit "like" (or "in the form of") a dove emphasized the way the Holy Spirit related to Jesus. The descending Spirit portrayed a gentle, peaceful, but active presence coming to anoint Jesus. It was not that Jesus needed to be filled with the Spirit (as if there was any lack in him) because he was "from the Holy Spirit" (1:20) since his conception. Rather, this was his royal anointing (see Isa 11:2; 42:1).

John the Baptist, and we who study this important event, can learn not only who the Messiah was, but also what kind of Messiah he would be (how his power would be demonstrated and used). His nature was revealed not by a thunderclap or lightning bolt, nor by an eagle or a hawk, but with a gentle dove. Jesus the Messiah would have a different way and a different message than even John expected.

The word baptize in the Greek had many meanings. There are two words used in the New Testament from Greek. The words are *bapto* and *baptizo*. There are three distinct usages, a mechanical one, a ceremonial one, and a metaphorical one.

The mechanical usage can be illustrated by the action of the smith dipping the hot iron in water, tempering it, or the dyer dipping the cloth in the dye for the purpose of dying it. These instances of the use of our Greek word, give us the following definition of the word in its mechanical usage. The word refers to the introduction or placing of a person or thing into a new environment or into union with something else so as to alter its condition or its relationship to its previous environment or condition. This was the main usage of the word in Greek.

Observe how perfectly this meaning is in accord with the usage of the word in Romans 6:3-4, where the believing sinner is baptized into vital union with Jesus Christ. The believing sinner is introduced or placed in Christ, thus coming into union with Him. By that action he is taken out of his old environment and condition in which he or she had lived,

Baptizo in the ministry of our Lord and John was, like the theocratic washings and purifications, a symbol whose design was to point to the purging away of sin on whom the rite was performed (Matt 3:6; John 3:22-25). John's baptism was in response to the repentance of the individual (Matt 3:11). It was connected with his message of an atonement for sin that was to be offered in the future, and the necessity of faith in that atonement (Acts 19:4).

John's baptism had looked ahead to a coming Saviour. Paul's baptism, or Christian baptism now looks back to a Saviour who has died and who has arisen again (Acts 19:5). That the rite of water baptism is the outward testimony of the inward fact of a person's salvation, and that it follows his act of receiving Christ as Saviour and is not a prerequisite to his receiving salvation, is seen in the use of the preposition *eis* in Matt 3:11 where the translation should read, "I indeed baptize you with water because of repentance." While the act of Christian baptism is a testimony of the person that his sins have been washed away, it also pictures and symbolizes the fact of the believing sinner's identification with Christ in His death, burial, and resurrection (Rom 6:),

The Greek Orthodox Church views the baptism of Christ in this way: When Jesus was baptized, He was in no need of cleansing because He was without sin. However, by Jesus' divine nature He purified the waters of the Jordan and through them the whole creation.

The metaphorical use of *baptizo* we find in Matt 20:22, 23; Mark 10:38, 39; Luke 12:50. A metaphor is the use of a word or phrase literally denoting one kind of object or idea in place of another by way of suggesting a likeness or analogy between them, for example, "the ship plows the sea." In the above passages, our Lord is speaking of His sufferings in connection with the Cross. He speaks of them as a baptism

The words were uttered while He was on His way to Jerusalem to be crucified. John the Baptist had announced His coming and had baptized the multitudes. Our Lord's disciples had been baptizing during the three years of His ministry. The words *baptizo* and *baptisma* which are used by Matthew, Mark, and Luke had by that time become the technical and common Greek words used to describe the rite administered by John and our Lord's disciples. Our Lord used the rite of baptism as a metaphor to speak of His coming sufferings.

You may remember the episode of *The Andy Griffith Show* in which the Women's Historical Society had discovered that a living descendant of a Revolutionary War hero was living right there in Mayberry. The news generated excitement and curiosity throughout the town as people made plans for recognizing the hero's relative. Barney Fife, of course, twisted his own family tree to the point that he put himself in line for the honor. The rest of the townspeople felt special just because someone among them was related to the hero.

Everyone was shocked when the news came. A careful analysis of the genealogical records determined that the hero's descendant was Otis Campbell, the town drunk. Despite instructions to find a "substitute Otis" for the presentation, the real Otis showed up for the ceremony. When the ladies gave him the plaque which they had engraved especially for him, Otis gave the plaque to the town. He said, "Just because you're the descendant of a hero doesn't make you one. So I would like to present this plaque to the town of Mayberry, to which I am just proud to belong."

Well, aren't we all? Aren't we all just happy to belong, to be included! We can refer to this part of our baptism as incorporation. We are included, incorporated into the body of Jesus Christ. This incorporation came about as a result of a love that was determined to draw us in. And long after the act of baptism, that love holds us together without ranking us as more or less important, allows us to disagree with each other without deserting one another, and leads us to use our different gifts without any need to compare them with somebody else's gifts.

God's Refination

Jenny Lam

地點：金巴崙長老會 道顯堂主日崇拜
講題：上帝也煉金
經文：雅各書 1 章 1-12 節
主題：上帝藉試煉，使人磨練出堅毅忍耐的意志，人若能憑信心，並依靠上主的來經歷
　　　試煉，最終能得到生命的冠冕。
目的：當遇到困難險阻時，只要憑著對上主的信心及堅毅忍耐的意志，最終能夠渡過難
　　　關。

大綱：　一、引論：
　　　　二、本論：煉金四部曲
　　　　　　1.　Rejoice 喜樂
　　　　　　　　「我的弟兄們，你們落在百般試煉中，都要以為大喜樂。」（雅1:2）
　　　　　　2.　Rely 信靠
　　　　　　　　「但忍耐也當成功，使你們成全、完備，毫無缺欠。」（雅1:4）
　　　　　　3.　Request 祈求
　　　　　　　　「你們中間若有缺少智慧的，應當求那厚賜與眾人、也不斥責人的上帝，
　　　　　　　　主就必賜給他。只要憑著信心求，一點不疑惑。」（雅1:5-6 下）
　　　　　　4.　Reflect 反省
　　　　　　　　「上帝啊，祢曾試驗我們，熬煉我們，如熬煉銀子一樣。祢使我們進入網
　　　　　　　　羅，把重擔放在我們的身上。祢使人坐車軋我們的頭：我們經過水火，祢
　　　　　　　　卻使我們到豐富之地。」（詩 66:10-12）

　　　　　　三、結論：
　　　　　　　　1.　憑信心依靠上主來經歷試煉，最終能得到生命的冠冕。
　　　　　　　　　　「忍受試探的人是有福的，因為他經過試驗以後，必得生命的冠冕，這是
　　　　　　　　　　主應許給那些愛他之人的。」（雅 1:12）
　　　　　　　　2.　我的回應

願我口中言語，各弟兄姊妹的心懷意念都蒙上帝悅納：

人生試煉又是甚麼呢？作學生的面對考試升學；作老師的面對三三四學制的改變與適應；作兒女的面對如何與父母的溝通；作父母的面對兒女的教育，生活和經濟的壓力；作夫妻情侶的面對感情的煩惱；作朋友的面對互相之間相處的問題；作僱員的面對工作的擔子和挑選；作上司的面對公司業績和管理，甚至每個人也會經歷生老病死等，這一切都是每個人都會經歷的試煉，又可稱為考驗。

我們會否覺查覺到的上帝是藉著人生中很多的試煉來訓練我們，祂把我們人生中混入了不同的元素令我們成長，如像煉金術的目的是通過一些化學方法，再加或減一些元素將一些鐵、鉛、銅、銀等賤價金屬轉變為黃金這貴價金屬。而我們應該用怎樣的態度面對這些試煉時，從而自我成長呢？原來「上帝也煉金」。

本論：煉金四部曲

《雅各書》是一本《基督徒成長手冊》，短短 5 章經文就涵蓋了早期的基督徒在面對人生的試煉時的應有態度，並如何以實際行動活出信仰，本書的對象，按當時而論是寫給"散在十二個支派之人（雅 1：1）；換句話說，即是給分散在羅馬版圖的猶太籍基督徒。"十二支派" 這詞是對猶太人的一種通稱，表明他們是上帝立約的子民（太 19：28，徒 26：7），也表示對象也我們地上各世代的所有信徒，跨越時空到今日的世代，《雅各書》仍是一本幫忙我們基督徒成長的指引。本書寫於大約主後四十五年左右，相當於使徒行傳第八章十二或十五之前，即耶路撒冷會議之前的時間，因此是新約書信中最早的一卷。當時耶路撒冷教會正在大受逼迫之後，從本書起首從雅 1：2-3 安慰信徒忍受試煉的話，即看出此書作者很關切是信徒遭遇試煉時的境況來作出安慰的，是次証道集中雅 1：2-12 也可稱「為上頭來外面的試煉」，我概括了為「上帝也煉金」下有四個 R 的情況會產生，它就是「煉金四部曲」。

1. Rejoice 喜樂

雅 1:2 我的弟兄們，你們落在百般試煉中，都要以為大喜樂。

「試煉」一詞的意思，希臘文用的是 peirasmos' 可譯作試煉、考驗或測驗。當小麻雀學飛時，牠要試煉雙翼，經試煉後，則能如意地滑翔於空中。又如煉金，當金經過火煉後，一切雜質被火熔化，煉成更純更美的金。所以，試煉不是破壞和拆毀，乃是造就和鍛煉。人經試煉後，更趨成長。「落」字在原文上為不預備之試煉，不是預備的，乃出人意外的試煉。

喜樂是絕對不可能強迫出來的，每個人經歷考驗，遇到因境時都會有情緒，經文提醒我們落在百般試煉中仍要喜樂，而且要喜樂在試煉當中，因為面對的困難情況可能未必可以即時改變，但我們應該用另一個角度去面對困境，可能有新的體會，最緊要是仍有樂觀的態度來度過這個困境，否則可能只會憂愁的停在困苦當中走不出來，困苦時間揮之不去。

我認識一個朋友，她有先天性的罕見眼疾及弱視，當年是全港首個病例，只有左眼只有常人一成視力，右眼又有青光眼，她沒有瞳孔，多年來她看東西一向有重影和眩光，有時候會朦朧一片，慢慢更會失明，她讀書也比其他人吃力，後來她認識了耶穌，才發現她很幸福，在僅餘的視力也能學習和生活，還學人上山下海，於是認識她的人也發現她常常哈哈笑而不發覺她是視障，感謝上帝賜給她一對特別的眼睛，令她更珍惜用眼睛看世界的時候，她慢慢長大而眼睛也接近失明了， 2009 年一些基督徒醫生被感動了，為她作了未有人做過的眼睛重建手術，令她重見光明，經歷過 30 多年灰暗的日子，這種

考驗卻讓她學懂以耳和心來聆聽別人的需要，珍惜每天打開眼的時候，仍感恩和喜樂，那個人就是我了…其實我們在試煉當中要常存喜樂，因為我們的正向思維能夠反轉我們對不利的環境看法，使我們能容易度過難關。

2. Rely(reliable) 信靠
*雅 1:4 但忍耐也當成功，使你們**成全完備，毫無缺欠**。*

我們常常只是靠著自己的能力來面對很多事情和困難，以為自己可以勝過一切，我們常常以為自己能夠堅持的時候，亦是令自己更走不出困境，就好像我們閉上眼睛來單腳企起來，大家便只能單靠自己的能力來堅持，你們會發現自己較難站立得住，最終甚至跌倒，因我們閉上眼便失去焦點 Focus，我們失去了眼球作依靠，協助耳髓去保持平衡。相反開眼企，我們就有眼睛作依靠，當收集到既影像後轉為電波，再加耳髓發出既資料傳送到大腦，經大腦分析後再傳送到身體各部份的筋肉去調節平衡。約翰一書 1:5 說：「上帝就是光。」約翰福音 8:12 說：「耶穌對眾人說，我是世界的光，跟從我的，就不在黑暗裡走，必要得著生命的光」。上帝的指引就好比眼睛，幫助我們在試煉中站立得住，甚至可以堅持耐久一些。當我們面對試煉時，我們有沒有承認自己有軟弱的地方和錯失呢？其實只要憑信心相信主耶穌基督，依靠我們的上帝，我們就能經歷考驗，我們會在試煉中訓練出堅毅和耐力，並能驗出我們人生有甚麼破口，就好像檢查車輪有否漏氣，要先打氣進去，讓它有壓力，用力量去擠壓，然後再放進水裡，就可看出有否漏氣了。試煉一定會有壓力，正如經文所說，我們要有忍耐的意志，然後環境才讓自己軟弱的地方慢慢顯露出來，再去修補，我們才會成長和完全。「成全完備」在英文 NIV 譯本翻譯成 mature and complete，意義亦是我們自身會更成熟和完美，也指我們對人、事和信仰等態度 mature and complete。「**成全完備，毫無缺欠**」也是**雅各書的核心**，希望所有信徒也能達至。

3. Request 祈求
雅 1:5-6 下 你們中間若有缺少智慧的，應當求那厚賜與眾人、也不斥責人的上帝，主就必賜給他。只要憑著信心求，一點不疑惑。

正如經文所說，縱然問對困難，只要憑著信心求，一點不疑惑，真是知易行難，因為我們始終會信心不足。

2008 年 11 月世界各國正經歷金融海嘯，溫家寶總理曾說過：「目前情況下，信心是比金子還貴重的東西。」我們不要心懷二意，只要憑著信心祈求上帝的幫助，一點也不疑惑，這樣就會得著智慧，因為智慧能轉變對我們不利的環境，更加成為我們的祝福，一切的事情始終都會過去，所以不要因為現在的得失、升高或降卑而傷心難過，反而要樂觀面對，這就是智慧。

聖經中約伯從腳掌到頭頂長滿了毒瘡，這種皮膚病很可怕，初時隆腫，後會潰爛，使人身上佈滿蟲子，口腔發出惡臭，全身皮膚脫落，四肢如火燒般疼痛那麼痛苦，換了是平常人已經忍耐不到了，更何況是要一點不疑惑，只要憑著信心祈求上帝的幫助。約伯正面對著人世間最深的痛苦，但他仍能說：「難道我們從上帝手裡得福，不也受禍嗎？」憑信心領受上帝所給予人超乎常人的耐力，去抵受一切身體和心靈的痛苦，這份智慧能讓人接受一切困境遭遇。

4. Reflect 反省
詩篇 66 篇就是以色列人被仇敵壓迫，蒙上帝的拯救，滿心讚美上帝的詩歌。*詩 66:10-12 上帝啊，祢曾試驗我們，熬煉我們，如熬煉銀子一樣。祢使我們進入網羅，把重擔放在我們的身上。祢使人坐車軋我們的頭：我們經過水火，祢卻使我們到豐富之地。他們面*

對試煉時，反思自己為何會有困境，明白上帝是藉熬煉銀子來鍛鍊他們，上帝並沒有離棄他們，相反是帶領他們離開困境，帶他們到豐富之地，所以就歌頌讚美上帝。

美國總統華盛頓在 1789 年 4 月 20 日就任美國首任總統時，他把手放在聖經上宣誓，並在講辭中說：「上帝的神聖賜福，顯明在我們的前途，祂及時的指導，智慧的判斷，是這個政府成功的倚靠。」並即時宣告第一個全國的感恩節。華盛頓反省到自己能從紛亂困難的北美洲中建立聯邦國家就任總統，不是單靠自己個人的功勞，而是要承認這一切都是上帝的賜福和保守，他只順從上帝的旨意行前面的路，所以要感謝上帝，並謙卑祈求祂的保護和恩寵。

當我們面對試煉時，我們嘗試反思上帝要我們學習甚麼的功課。

結論：

當我們憑信心依靠上主來經歷試煉，最終能得到生命的冠冕。

雅各書 1:12 是對前 11 節的總結，*雅 1:12 忍受試探的人是有福的，因為他經過試驗以後，必得生命的冠冕，這是主應許給那些愛他之人的。*這裡的試探與之前所說的試煉是同義詞，我們在試煉中的常存喜樂，以及這些試煉本身都能夠建立我們的品格，並使我們達至完美成熟。

杏林子《凱歌集》有一首詩《你知道嗎？》：

你知道嗎？

你知道蠟燭要經過燃燒才會發光嗎？
你知道橄欖要經過壓榨才會出油嗎？
你知道美酒要經過醞釀才會芬芳嗎？
你知道柿子要經過風霜才會香甜嗎？

你知道嗎？

金子要經過提煉才見精純。
鑽石要經過琢磨才見光華。
寶刀要經過鍛鍊才見鋒利。
麥子要經過死亡才見重生。

你知道嗎？

天空若沒有風雨的肆虐，就顯不出彩虹的美麗。
溪流若沒有礁石的阻擋，就激不起浪花的飛舞。
小徑若不是曲折穩密，就顯不出它的幽靜。
梅花若不經一番寒風徹骨，何處聞得芳香撲鼻？

你知道嗎？

沒有經過流淚的雙目，永遠看不到人間的疾苦。
沒有經過流汗的耕作，永遠不懂收獲的歡樂。
沒有夏日炎陽的烤灼，永遠不知樹蔭的清涼。
沒有漫漫長夜的等待，永遠看不到曙光的重現。

你知道嗎？

你知道受苦越深，離神也越近嗎？
你知道環境越刻苦，也越能造就人的信心嗎？
你知道打擊越重，也越能造就人的信心嗎？

你知道世途越坎坷，人生的閱歷也越豐富嗎？

你知道嗎？
  失敗教我們吸取經驗。
  錯誤教我們學習謙遜。
  挫折教我們培養勇氣。
  損傷教我們懂得珍惜。

你知道嗎？
  沒有試煉，你永遠不知生命的潛力有多深？
  沒有重擔，你永遠不知生命的耐力有多大？
  沒有痛苦，你永遠不知生命的韌力有多強？
  沒有缺陷，你永遠不知生命的內涵有多美？

你知道嗎？
  「萬事都互相效力，叫愛神的人得益處。」

就讓杏林子所寫的詩句，作為彼此的鼓勵，上帝是藉試煉令我們知道人生是何等佳美。這個生命的冠冕是榮耀的、寶貴的、是別人都能看到的，那就是由試煉而生的堅忍毅力、成熟、完備和智慧。當上帝把這個冠冕交給我們時，別人就會從我們的身上看到我們那平靜安穩、生命經過煉淨的冠冕，但願大家的經過人生的試煉以後，人人頭上都有這樣一個美麗的冠冕。

2.回應—祈禱

慈愛的父上帝，*我們當稱頌祢，使人得聽讚美祢的聲音。祢使我們的性命存活，也不叫我們的腳搖動。父上帝啊，祢曾試驗我們，熬煉我們，如熬煉銀子一樣。祢使我們進入網羅，把重擔放在我們的身上。祢使人坐車軋我們的頭；我們經過水火，祢卻使我們到豐富之地。*我們從心裡承認我們是軟弱的人，當我們面對生命中的困境時，真是會灰心氣餒，人生缺乏方向，有時候真是想逃避，不願意面對那些困難，但我們明白原來父上帝是想藉人生中不同的經歷來試煉我們，讓我們從中得以成長，並結出更多聖靈的果子，我們真是要多謝祢。願主耶穌基督進入我們的心，成為我們生命中的救主，讓我們人生有了依靠，有了方向，有了指引，並賜我們能力和信心，從而走出一個又一個人生的困境，使我們得以完備，最終得著父上帝賜給我們生命的冠冕。祈禱奉主耶穌基督的聖名，阿們！

Step out and Follow the Leader[5]

Paula Shepard Louder

(Mark 6: 6b-13)

This Summer Extension School marks the beginning of what my husband and I both hope to be my last three blocks of studies with the Program of Alternate Studies. During the past 2 ½ years, we have been comparing my husband's seminary education with that of my PAS experience. Our conclusion, both are good, one not noticeably better than the other based on the needs and goals of the individual student. Both have good content and training, but in both instances there is only so much classroom learning because at some point, the candidates are going to move out into the real world. Teachers leave college and apply their trade with children. Mechanics learn in a classroom, but eventually must work on cars. Medical professionals must take their medical knowledge and apply it to real people. The best education available is not complete until we get out there and apply what we have learned!

So it is with Christianity as well. We see this in our text today of Mark 6. Jesus is teaching his disciples how to do the work of ministry and now, he is taking them to the next level. Jesus seems to be saying, "All right, you have heard me preach, you have seen me heal the sick, raise the dead, calm the storm and even drive out demons, and you have seen me love people who have never been loved before. You have witnessed what a servant of God must normally do, and now it is your time to do it. I did not choose you to sit around, to be spectators. It is your time to step out, go tell and do." I'm sure that you are aware that "step out, go tell" is the slogan of the 10 year evangelism program that is being implemented by the Cumberland Presbyterian Denomination. In fact, we are now in its second year. But I'm here today to say, that 2000 years ago, long before the CP church was organized that Jesus instigated his own Step out: Called to go, sent to share campaign and

---

[5]Presented at the Program of Alternate Studies Summer Extension School at Bethel University, McKenzie, Tennessee, 2012.

the guidelines for that evangelistic ministry can be seen in the passage that we have read today.

The first thing that we see is a model. Verse 6 says that Jesus went around teaching from village to village. The wonderful part about that is that *Jesus leads by example*; he was out there doing ministry first. Jesus wasn't teaching behind a large mahogany desk in heaven and pointing his finger; he was there demonstrating how they could and we can be dynamic servants. Notice that Jesus doesn't wait for people to show up. He left Nazareth and went to them. The theme for CPWM this coming year (which was presented at General Assembly) is *meeting people where they are*. We all realize that hanging CHURCH above our door will bring in very few people. We might think, well, people know what church is and what we do, but not until they actually experience the church in action, not until they share in our Christian fellowship, not until they are shown the love of Christ will church have meaning in their lives. In many of our Christian circles we talk about getting people to come to church, but we don't talk enough about motivating witnesses to go out, minister to people and invite them. This is what Jesus is talking about.

Sure we need to pray for people, but likewise we need to go where they are. Based on Jesus's example; most of the ministry of the church should be outside the walls of the building with the people in our community. It is teaching our children right from wrong, it is talking about the Bible in our conversations, and it is reaching out to our neighbors and those that God has placed in our lives. It is accepting our calling to bring the message of a loving Christ who can change lives, families and communities. Meeting people where they are.

In verse 7 we are told that ***Jesus sent his disciples out two by two***. In the Jewish tradition and during Jesus's time on earth it was customary for there to be a witness, thus the need for two. Another advantage in going out by twos was and is that each could strengthen and encourage the other, especially when faced with rejection. Our strength most assuredly comes from God, but He meets many of our needs through our teamwork with others. As we serve Christ, we should not try and go it alone. I think this is difficult for many of us as ministers. We feel that we are the leaders, we are the ones to do it all alone, for after all we are "super preacher." But even one of the greatest preachers of all time, the Apostle Paul, did not go it alone. On his first mission trip, Barnabas, the son of encouragement, was his companion. We all need "sons of encouragement" in our lives; we need people who will love us, people who will build us up when life gets us down. Ecclesiastes 4:9 says *two are better than one, because they have a better return for their work. If one falls down, his friend can help him up. Pity the person who falls and has no one to help him up.* Pity the person who thinks they can do God's work all by themselves. Let's pray that God will send us a Barnabas and let us also pray that we might be a son of encouragement to another.

The second part of verse 7 says that *he gave them authority over evil spirits.* Just as Jesus equipped his disciples, he equips us as well. Jesus isn't asking us to minister under our own power. He is not asking us to face the world empty handed, He is giving us HIS power. The Bible gives us example after example of ordinary men and women who were able to accomplish extraordinary feats because God gave them authority over kings, over diseases, corrupt religious leaders, over evil - whatever was needed the power was bestowed. If we were in this ministry thing by ourselves, we would all be looking to quit. But we are not alone, and we need to remember Philippians 4:13 that reminds us *that we can do all things through Christ who gives us strength.*

Jesus wanted his disciples to know (and that includes us today) that God's call will never lack God's supply. Jesus provides us with the necessities for ministry as demonstrated in verse 8 where the disciples are instructed to take nothing but a staff, no food, no bag, no money. He further instructs them to take only the clothes on their backs and a pair of sandals. These instructions were given so that they would depend entirely on God to take care of them. This was a short mission trip - perhaps a training mission - in order for the disciples to gain an understanding of what ministry was going to be like. In Luke's account, Jesus asked his disciples to look back on their experience and what they had lacked. The answer was, of course, nothing. In other words, there was never a time when what was needed wasn't there. God always took care of them. This story teaches us that when we step out in faith to serve Him, we will receive whatever we need.

Another reason to totally rely on God is to be totally committed to the mission instead of being preoccupied with material things. In our time, there are so many things that claim our time, things not of a spiritual nature, we live such comfortable lives that it is easy to forget that we are on a mission. That mission is to win people for Christ and to be ministers to people who have needs in their lives. It really makes no sense to spend all out time gathering "stuff," none of which we are going to take with us to the next life.

We all know people whom we desire to come to see and love Christ, but sometimes, for whatever reason, they are not open to spiritual things; we continue to pray for them, we know God isn't finished with them yet, so we place them in God's care and remain open for God's leading. ***We aren't always going to be able to reach people, we are not always going to have the desired result, but we must always remain faithful.*** In verse 11 in the "shaking of dust from the feet", Jesus made it clear that the listeners were responsible for what they did with the gospel. The disciples were not to blame if the message was rejected, as long as they had faithfully and carefully presented it. We are not responsible when others reject Christ's message of salvation, but we do have the responsibility to share that gospel clearly and faithfully. God did not call us to be successful - he called us to be faithful. (Dr. Virgil Todd)

Perhaps one reason that we are sometimes reluctant to **step out and tell**, is because (like the disciples) we are instructed to "preach" a gospel of repentance (verse 12). People need to have a change of mind and a change of heart - people need to change their minds toward their feeling toward sin, and they need to change their lives as they set their priorities and turn to live their lives in accordance with the teachings of Jesus. It is not too difficult to see where this might become a problem. Most of us do not like our flaws pointed out to us, nor do we really enjoy taking advice on how we must change our lives. Sin is not a popular topic. Today people tend to gloss over sin saying times have changed; we need to adapt. Sin is sin. If it was wrong in Jesus's day, it is still wrong today, and we are called to proclaim that message. But the message of repentance is only part of the example we are given in verses 12 and 13. Yes, the disciples went out and preached that people should repent. They met a spiritual need, one that would have a bearing on their souls, on eternity. But they also dealt with immediate needs. "They drove out many demons and anointed many sick people with oil and healed them." God's servants are to demonstrate the love of God and minister to the whole person. To come full circle, we are to **meet people where they are**.

Just as God called and Jesus trained and sent the disciples to help the hurting people of Galilee, He is sending us to the hurting people of our local congregations, our communities, and beyond. We do our ministry, and others are encouraged as we do and they in turn become participants in ministry and not merely spectators. One of the greatest joys is to see people catch the vision of serving God in their lives. Being a faithful servant of Jesus means we will see changed lives - selfish lives become selfless, bitter lives become filled with forgiveness and then in turn extend forgiveness to others, and greedy people become generous with time and talents.

Again, some will gladly receive the message of Jesus Christ and some will not; Jesus did not say that all would. Some will reject the message but that does not give us reason to stop. We are to continue to share with others, using all our God given gifts, the life that is available in Christ.

God sees us in our faithfulness as we serve in our community, He sees as we take each step toward greater commitment to Him. We matter enough, everyone here, and all people for God to send His only son to die for each of us so that we might have eternal life, and in response, we are now sent as His servants to **step out** and **to tell** that message to others whoever and where ever they are.

Let us pray: Our most gracious heavenly Father, we are so thankful that you loved us enough to send your Son to die for our sins. We are also thankful for the example that He has set before us for ministry. Empower us as your servants and may we in turn be examples to a hurting world in need of a Savior and may all the praise and glory be yours. AMEN.

Wake Up!

Tiffany Hall McClung

(Mark 4:35-41)

I have a confession to make. I sometimes get very angry with God. Maybe I'm all alone in this with a group like this. Maybe not. Where I know that I have some company is in the disciples, those twelve we hear so much about. Don't you just love those wacky guys? I mean, come on, sometimes I'll be reading scripture and I find myself wanting to scream, "How stupid can you be? It's all right there in black and white. Can't you understand who this is? It is Jesus! Don't you get it?" I find myself wanting to scream at those twelve and then I hear that still small voice or sometimes what feels like a Zen stick.

Do you know about this? Persons on Zen retreats sometimes ask to receive the Zen stick. What the Zen stick is is a big stick that the monk in charge carries around with him as people pray and meditate in the room. By the way, this kind of prayer can often be sitting perfectly still on a tiny cushion while staring at a white wall for up to 45 minutes at a time. And, you think that sitting through long "preacher prayers" is difficult! Anyway, if you are sitting there meditating and you have asked to receive the Zen stick, the monk will watch you and if you begin to dose off or fidget, he will come up behind you and when you least expect it, WHACK! He hits you on the shoulder. The Zen stick. It brings you back to focus. It helps you remember why you came there. So, that inner voice, that voice of God which does still speak to us if we will only listen. It is kind of like my Zen stick.

And, I get angry with those stupid disciples. Why would you question Jesus? Why couldn't you just have faith and trust? And then, and then, WHACK! My zen stick. "Tiffany, why would you question me? Why don't you have faith and trust?"

I have another confession to make. I wanted to stand up here today and be eloquent. I wanted to speak to your needs, to talk about struggles you may be going through. I wanted to stand up and say, "Yes, I'm mad that Jesus sleeps through the storm." I wanted to tell you it is okay to be mad too. And, while I still believe that all this is true. WHACK! Zen stick during my sermon preparation. WHACK! And it hit me. I'm supposed to have Jesus in my heart, right? RIGHT?

You have probably heard it all your life. "Mommy, where does Jesus live?" "Well, sweety, Jesus lives in your heart." Right? Ring a bell? Well, I'm not one to be that literal and frankly if I were a child and I heard that, it would probably scare me out of my mind, but as a Christian, I do know where this saying comes from. Because as a Christian, I do know that Christ is both outside of me and within me all at the same time. Hear this from the word of God. This is Jesus actually praying for you, for me, and for all people. John 17:20-23. [Read scripture.]

Yes, I am a seminary trained ordained minister, but I will not stand up here and pretend that I understand how all this works, but guess what. The disciples didn't understand either. And, what is really wonderful is that we don't have to understand. It just is. Christ lives within me. Christ lives within you.

So, I wanted to stand here and sound eloquent as I accused the Christ outside of me of not caring if we perish in the boat. I wanted to shake Jesus awake and remind him that there is a storm. I wanted to point my finger at God and say, "Why is there so much pain in this world? WAKE UP!" I wanted to raise my fists to the sky and shout, "Don't you care that people are still judged and mistreated because of the color of their skin? WAKE UP!" I wanted to confront the sleeping Christ and beg, "Please stop the wars in our world, bring peace to Iraq, to Darfur, to the streets of US cities. WAKE UP!" I wanted to look everywhere outside of myself and cry to the Jesus sleeping there on that cushion, WAKE UP!

WHACK! Christ is within me. When do I allow that part of Christ to sleep? When do I pass by someone in anguish and never think of her again? When do I allow Jesus within me to sleep through storms in my marriage? Storms with my family? Storms with my friends? When do I let Jesus be comfy on that cushion while I am comfortable with spending an hour a week with God? When do I respond to hatred with hatred? When do I use violence to confront violence? When do I use rules, regulations, and yes, even Holy Scripture to hurt other people? When do I abuse myself? When do I abuse others? Sleeping Christ within me, wake up, wake up, wake up!

Maybe you are ready to wake that Jesus inside your heart, but I've got to warn you, when you wake up Jesus, something's gonna happen.

And, that brings us back to those 12 again. There they are, scared out of their minds. Feeling that they are looking death in the face and they are mad. They are mad that Jesus can catch some winks in the middle of their storm. And, so here they go once again, they are stepping into places that they may not be ready for. When you wake up Jesus, something's gonna happen. And they do, and it does. Something amazing happens. That storm that was raging in that sea, it ceased its raging.

None of us can know how they really felt or what they really thought, but I bet they were glad that they went stepping into places that they may have not been ready for. When those waters became peaceful again, when that boat stopped rocking, when the lightning died out, I bet they were happy they had made their way to that comfy cushion where Jesus rested his head. At least I bet they were mostly happy.

When you wake up Jesus, something's gonna happen. And it did. And their lives were saved, but do you remember what they did next? They became even more afraid and asked, "Who is this that he can calm even the sea?"

What did they expect? Why did they wake him in the first place if not because they believed he would calm the storm? But, apparently they didn't because they were shocked and terrified when he did. They couldn't believe their eyes, "My goodness, this guy just did something and the storm just stopped." When you wake up Jesus something's gonna happen.

What did they expect? Did they just want their buddy next to them when they died? Was he that good at praying that they woke him to send up some prayers in the midst of perishing? Or did they just need the cushion he was sleeping on for a life preserver? What were they thinking? Apparently they were expecting anything except what happened because it frightened them and led them to question who Jesus really is.

When you wake up Jesus, something's gonna happen.

So, be careful. Think before you go there. Or maybe don't. Like the disciples, see the sleeping Christ within you and know that it is time to say, "Wake up!" Without even thinking it through, see the storm and know it is time to say, "Wake up!" When that happens, you may be shocked by what you find, but won't it be worth it? Won't the storm come to an end? And, yes, it may even lead you to ask some questions about who Jesus really is, who God really is, and even who you really are, but isn't that why we are here? Isn't that how we grow in our relationship with God? And being in a true relationship with our creator, isn't that what being the child of God is about? Learning more and more about how to be better and better and seeing more and more of how God can never fit into any box that we create?

I've got to warn you, if you are ready for this, it could take you on a wild ride. You may end up involved in things you never planned. You may be at church a lot more. You may be forgiving that one person you thought you never could. You may change your opinions. You may put self last and the community of faith first. It may take you on a wild ride indeed. But if you keep that Jesus within awake and you listen for that still small voice or if you will just keep asking for that Zen stick, then I promise you, Whack! God will bring you back to focus, God will help you remember why you are here, God will help you be kind to those who are difficult to live with, God will help you seek justice in our world, God will help you deal with tragedy, God will help you, God will help you, God will help you. Whack! Don't forget. Wake up! Wake up that Jesus in your heart. Wake up! Wake up your compassion. Wake up! Wake up that love of neighbor and of enemy. Wake up! Wake up your sensitivity. Wake up! Wake up and listen for the Holy Spirit in your life. Wake up! Wake up Jesus and get ready, now, get ready, I'm warning you, get ready. Because when you wake up Jesus, something's gonna happen.

The Price

Rhonda McGowen

(John 19)

As I read the scriptures I want you to think about something that is your salvation was free? all you had to do was ask, believe and confess BUT it was not free it was paid for by our Lord and Savior Jesus Christ. So the next time you commit a sin or invite someone to salvation remember the scriptures and what the PRICE of SALVATION cost. Let's begin we will be reading from John 19 from the ESV Bible.

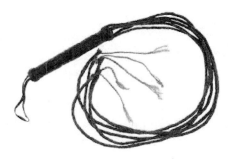

Verse 1: Then Pilate took Jesus and flogged him. Flogged some translations say scourged Jesus. Flogging or Scourging was a long process of whipping. His hands were tied above His head. Then, He was brutally whipped with a "flagellum," or a "cattail," which was a short whip of several heavy tentacles, the ends tied with small balls of lead, rocks, or bone fragments. Kinda of like this one here. It produced deep, large, painful bruises and intense pain. Cutting deep into the subcutaneous tissues, it literally tore the flesh off His back, exposing the muscles. The flesh from the back would have hung from His body and would have been open and bleeding the purpose? Was to weaken a person. According to Jewish law a person was allowed only thirty-nine lashes or forty minus one because it was believed that forty lashes would kill. However, Romans allowed it to continue till the soldiers were too tired to continue or they were told to stop (Luke 23:16; 1 Peter 2:24).

Verse 2: *And the soldiers twisted together a crown of thorns and put it on his head and arrayed him in a purple robe. They mashed a crown of sharp thorns into His scalp.* These thorns were large and ugly and not like the little thorns on rose bushes we have today. The beating would have caused the large ugly sharp

thorns to dig into His scalp, causing a lot of bleeding. The soldiers continued to attack our Lord and hit Him across His face. By this time, Jesus would have been unrecognizable. The purple robe represented royalty and statue. It was worn by those in power because the dye used to make it was very expensive and hard to come by.

Verses 3-6 *They came up to him, saying, "Hail, King of the Jews!" and struck him with their hands. Pilate went out again and said to them, "See, I am bringing him out to you that you may know that I find no guilt in him." So Jesus came out, wearing the crown of thorns and the purple robe. Pilate said to them, "Behold the man!" When the chief priests and the officers saw him, they cried out, "Crucify him, crucify him!" Pilate said to them, "Take him yourselves and crucify him, for I find no guilt in him." they continued to make fun of him and strike them with their hands this* after being beaten and having a crown of thorns placed on His head. They were trying to humiliate Him By putting on Him a purple / scarlet robe. Purple during this time was a very expensive dye. The color purple was found for example in the materials used for the Tabernacle and Temple. The color purple is associated with royalty.

Verse 7 *The Jews answered him, "We have a law, and according to that law he ought to die because He has made himself the Son of God."* Their original charges having come to nothing, they give up on this angle, and as Pilate was throwing the whole responsibility upon them, they retreat into their own Jewish law, saying that His claiming equality with God He ought to die; and telling Pilate that it was his job, to protect their law.

Verses 10-11 *So Pilate said to him, "You will not speak to me? Do you not know that I have authority to release you and authority to crucify you?" Jesus answered him,"You would have no authority over me at all unless it had been given you from above. Therefore he who delivered me over to you has the greater sin."* Pilot was upset that Jesus refused to answer him because he believed he deserved to be respected and answered. Then Pilot says Do you not know that I have authority to release you and authority to crucify you?" and Jesus tells him just how little power he has by telling him, "You would have no authority over me at all unless it had been given you from above. Therefore he who delivered me over to you has the greater sin." Jesus answered Pilot affirming that He was just who He claimed to be and that Pilate had no power over Him, and the power he did have was from heaven. He then told Pilate that the greater sin was not his for throwing up his hands and letting them do what they wanted, but was of the Jews who were forcing him to do. So Jesus statement also shows that it was God's plan that Jesus be betrayed and crucified the only way for the sin debt of the world to be paid in full. It was God and God alone that allowed Pilate to even have the opportunity to give the order and Jesus was willing to follow through all the pain of His flesh being torn from being beaten, the poking, cutting and stabbing agony of the thorns on His head, the humiliation of the Jews, and the rejection from you and me. Oh did you hear what I just said, the rejection of you and me yes we were guilty to. But Jesus was looking down through history at us when He was dying for us.

Verses 12-16 *From then on Pilate sought to release him, but the Jews cried out, "If you release this man, you are not Caesar's friend. Everyone who makes himself a king opposes Caesar." So when Pilate heard these words, he brought Jesus out and sat down on the judgment seat at a place called The Stone Pavement, and in Aramaic* **Gabbatha***. Now it was the day of Preparation of the Passover. It was about the sixth hour. He said to the Jews, "Behold your King!" They cried out, Away with him, away with him, crucify him!" Pilate said to them, "Shall I crucify your King?" The chief priests answered, "We have no king but Caesar." So he delivered him over to them to be crucified.* Pilot had the authority and could have freed Jesus but was very afraid of the people because he did not want to stand up for Jesus so he gave into what the people wanted. Not much difference in us today is there well think about it if you are around a group of people who want to do something are you willing to stand up for what is right or do as Pilot did and try to wash your hands of it. Hmm Prayer in schools come to mind if all the Christians had stood up one woman could not have had prayer taken it out, just saying. So Pilot turned Jesus over to be crucified.

Jesus shows that He was/is completely one hundred percent obedient servant when He suffered for you and me along with each and every person that has ever or will ever walk on the face of this earth. When the leaders demanded Jesus to be crucified Pilot turned Jesus over to the people.

Verses 17 *and he went out; bearing his own cross, to the place called The Place of a Skull, which in Aramaic is called Golgotha.* Jesus carried His own cross. This was a sign of guilt. We see here, Jesus someone who did not deserve to be punished being punished and He carries the cross and bears our guilt, our sin and covers us with HIS blood. He fell to His knees under the weight of the cross, the Roman soldiers force Simon of Cyrene's help; now, Jesus carries all of our burdens! Even in a state of severe trauma, He did not allow His power to override His physical pain.

Verse 18-27 *So they took Jesus, and he went out, bearing his own cross, to the place called The Place of a Skull, which in Aramaic is called Golgotha. There they crucified him, and with him two others, one on either side, and Jesus between them. Pilate also wrote an inscription and put it on the cross. It read, "Jesus of Nazareth, the King of the Jews." Many of the Jews read this inscription, for the place where Jesus was crucified was near the city, and it was written in Aramaic, in Latin, and in Greek. So the*  *chief priests of the Jews said to Pilate, "Do not write, 'The King of the Jews,' but rather, 'This man said, I am King of the Jews.'" Pilate answered, "What I have written I have written." 23 When the soldiers had crucified Jesus, they took his garments and divided them into four parts, one part for each soldier; also his tunic. But the tunic was seamless, woven in one piece from top to bottom, so they said to one another, "Let us not tear it, but cast lots for it to see whose it shall be." This was to fulfill the Scripture which says, "They divided my garments among them, and for my clothing they cast lots." So the soldiers did these things, but standing by the cross of Jesus were his mother and his mother's sister, Mary the wife of Clopas, and Mary magdalene. When Jesus saw his mother and the disciple whom he loved standing nearby, he said to his mother, woman, behold, your son!" Then he said to the disciple, "Behold, your mother!" And from that hour the disciple took her to his own home.*

Jesus was nailed onto the crossbeam, through His wrists (not hands because the person would easily slipped off the cross), with large, heavy, nails approximately the size of railroad spikes. These spikes were driven through the body and deep into the wood of the cross. Several soldiers would have been responsible for the process of placing Jesus on the Cross. The feelings, pressure and pain of these spikes being driven through would have been extremely painful. Being a massage therapist I know that the medial and ulnar nerve run in the wrist and hand and a spike/nail into this area would hit the medial nerve. This would cause extreme pain and agony as the muscles would begin to cramp and jerk. The soldiers would have been careful not to pull the arms tightly, but allow them some movement. The top board would be pulled up into placed , and tied most likely. Then His left foot was pressed backward against a block a small board this was used to prolong the crucifixion. Then, with knees extended, feet on top of each another, toes facing down, one spike was used to nail through the arches of His feet into the bottom block. The knees would have some movement. During this agony, the pain would be overwhelming. In crucifixion, dehydration is a major factor. The lungs struggle relentlessly to pull in as much oxygen as possible but it is in vain, when this happens carbon dioxide levels in the blood way up. If you have ever seen someone who is going through low oxygen and high carbon it is not pleasant. I have with my granny they placed her on a bypap and it helped and she did get to come home. Something Jesus did not get. This makes the person struggle harder to breathe more and the heart begins to beat as fast as possible to oxygenate the blood.. When the heart beats faster it will become tired and the person will die the blood pressure becomes so high that blood leaks. The only relief is if the person can drink water. So the Lord says, "I thirst." Hoping to lengthen His life and suffering, they soak a sponge with wine, and put it onto a hyssop branch.

Verses 28-30 After this, Jesus, knowing that all was now finished, said (to fulfill the Scripture), "I thirst." 29 A jar full of sour wine stood there, so they put a sponge full of the sour wine on a hyssop branch and held it to his mouth. 30 When Jesus had received the sour wine, he said, it is finished," and he bowed his head and gave up his spirit. We see that this final statement of Jesus was a loud cry. The last words of Our Lord and Savior Jesus Christ was "It is finished Jesus is letting everyone know that He paid for your sins in full on the cross each and every one of them.

Verses 31-37 *since it was the day of Preparation, and so that the bodies would not remain on the cross on the Sabbath (for that Sabbath was a high day), the Jews asked Pilate that their legs might be broken and that they might be taken away. So the soldiers came and broke the legs of the first, and of the other who had been crucified with him. But when they came to Jesus and saw that he was already dead, they did not break his legs. But one of the soldiers pierced his side with a spear, and at once there came out blood and water. He who saw it has borne witness His testimony is true, and he knows that he is telling the truth—that you also may believe. for these things took place that the Scripture might be fulfilled: "Not one of his bones will be broken." And again another Scripture says, they will look on him whom they have pierced."*

The Jews want Pilate to allow them to break the legs of those on the cross since the Sabbath is coming he agrees so they go and break the legs of the first but when they come to Jesus He is already dead. However one of the soldiers take his spear and stabs Jesus when he does this blood and water flows. The soldier most likely hit the heart because we see blood and water this come flowing out from the stab of the sword , this could have come from the pericardium which is the sac that surrounds our hearts. When this takes place the one who saw it becomes a witness and he states that His testimony is true. This took place so that scripture could be fulfilled. None of Jesus bones were broken and scripture states that they will look upon Him who they have pierced.

Verses 38-42 *after these things Joseph of Arimathea, who was a disciple of Jesus, but secretly for fear of the Jews, asked Pilate that he might take away the body of Jesus, and Pilate gave him permission. So he came and took away his body. Nicodemus also, who earlier had come to Jesus by night, came bringing a mixture of myrrh and aloes, about seventy-five pounds in weight. So they took the body of Jesus and bound it in linen cloths with the spices, as is the burial custom of the Jews. Now in the place where he was crucified there was a garden, and in the garden a new tomb bin which no one had yet been laid. So because of the Jewish day of Preparation, since the tomb was close at hand, they laid Jesus there.*

Jesus was buried in a borrowed tomb by Joseph of Arimathea. Jesus was willing to sacrifice Himself for you and me? He took each step of His life just for us. He was born, lived, witnessed and died for us.   Each one of Jesus last agonizing steps would have been filled with pain and agony and yet He never stopped he took step after step, insult after insult, slap after slap, whip after whip, nail after nail, breath after breath, thorn after thorn just for you. Now if Jesus can do that for you can you tell His story to others so that they can know who He is and what He did for them. After all that is our job as brothers and sisters in Christ. Do it today and when you feel scared, shy or fill in the blank remember what He did for you, the steps He took for you. And remember He died for everyone the neighbor who drives you crazy, the drunk, alcoholic, murderer, draw a line and fill in the blank He died for each and every one of us. So tell someone today about Jesus.[6]

[6]The English Standard Version Bible translation was used for all scripture quoted. The King James Bible was used for reference and research as were *Matthew Henry's Commentary on the Whole Bible* and *William Barclay's Bible Commentaries*. The websites Bible Gateway (biblegateway.com) and Bible Study Tools (biblestudytools.com) were also used.

Sheep or Goat? Trouble Everywhere!

Judy Madden

(Matthew 25:31-46)

My husband David and I have two daughters; they are 20 and 23 years old. When our girls were younger we used to hunt together for this crazy character in the "Where's Waldo?" books. We would all pour over each page filled with small vignettes of activity in a larger scene, looking for Waldo who was always wearing the red and white-stripped hat. Sometimes we would search for hours, just trying to find this one silly man.

Our scripture for today is the parable of the Sheep and the Goats. In this passage each group was told that Jesus was with them, one feeds Jesus and the other does not. But both groups ask Jesus the question, "When were you with us? "

Jesus is everywhere and with all of us! What allows us to see Jesus and what blinds us to Jesus is the question. In "Where's Waldo" what allowed us to find Waldo is intensely studying the picture before us… To find Jesus we need to be watchful, to search, to be looking for Jesus.

Let's stop and look at the people around us…. Jesus is among us right now.

All of us have a bit of Jesus in us.   You see it is that God's light, the light of Jesus that lives within us and shines through us everyday! Sometimes I think we may have a little bit of temporary dementia, and we forget that important fact.

So Let's dig into the scripture for today…..Matthew Chapter 25:31-46.

The Sheep and the Goats

"When the Son of Man comes in his glory, and all the angels with him, he will sit on his glorious throne. All the nations will be gathered before him, and he will separate the people

one from another as a shepherd separates the sheep from the goats. He will put the sheep on his right and the goats on his left. "Then the King will say to those on his right, 'Come, you who are blessed by my Father; take your inheritance, the kingdom prepared for you since the creation of the world. For I was hungry and you gave me something to eat, I was thirsty and you gave me something to drink, I was a stranger and you invited me in, I needed clothes and you clothed me, I was sick and you looked after me, I was in prison and you came to visit me.' "Then the righteous will answer him, 'Lord, when did we see you hungry and feed you, or thirsty and give you something to drink? When did we see you a stranger and invite you in, or needing clothes and clothe you? When did we see you sick or in prison and go to visit you?' "The King will reply, 'Truly I tell you, whatever you did for one of the least of these brothers and sisters of mine, you did for me.'

"Then he will say to those on his left, 'Depart from me, you who are cursed, into the eternal fire prepared for the devil and his angels. For I was hungry and you gave me nothing to eat, I was thirsty and you gave me nothing to drink, I was a stranger and you did not invite me in, I needed clothes and you did not clothe me, I was sick and in prison and you did not look after me.'" They also will answer, 'Lord, when did we see you hungry or thirsty or a stranger or needing clothes or sick or in prison, and did not help you?' "He will reply, 'Truly I tell you, whatever you did not do for one of the least of these, you did not do for me.'" Then they will go away to eternal punishment, but the righteous to eternal life."

This has always been a difficult passage for me. I have stayed away from it like it was the plague! Seriously, what does this mean? I thought Jesus died for all and yet here he is separating nations, people, sheep from goats? What happened to forgiveness? What happened to grace? Where's God? The God I know and love through Jesus the Christ! Where's God in all this? I feel like I am hunting Waldo all over again…. This sounds like the God before the New Testament, before the cross, before Jesus! But wait, this is Jesus telling this parable!

As I began to search for the answers to my questions I discovered Matthew 25:31-46 is the final parable of Judgment. There are three parables of judgment in Matthew 25. Here is Jesus, trying to explain one more time what is important. I imagine that Jesus may be at this point getting concerned that his message must sink into the minds of his disciples the ones who will be carrying on Good News in his absence.

This is the final parable that Jesus will tell, the final planned lesson to his disciples before his is tried and crucified. These are Jesus' final words of instruction to us! And this story, this instruction is about judgment. We have heard that we should not judge and yet in just a couple of days following the telling of this story Jesus will be tried, judged, sentenced, and crucified by many who just days before celebrated him! The disciples will be crushed when Jesus dies, but here Jesus is telling them, hold tight to my promises. Here Jesus is telling his disciples, that he will be the judge; judge over *all the flock*, the sheep and the goats! There are no two ways about it; we will be accountable for our actions, or lack of actions here on earth.

Judgment originates from the Greek word *krisis*, to sift, to separate, to decide or judge. This is the same origin for our word 'crisis' which means a dangerous or worrying time, a critical moment. And for us when we are at the point where we are in the midst of being divided into sheep and goats this will be a dangerous time for us if we are not prepared!! I like the German word for crisis; it is *Torshlusspanik* which means 'shut—door-panic', a fear of being on the wrong side of a closing gate! I would say in this scripture, this is a good description of the judgment that was taking place from the people's point of view.

The story of the sheep and the goats appears to be in a similar pattern as the other judgment parables in Matthew 25. A common thread throughout is the inclusion of everyone at the beginning of all three parables. These Judgment parables all begin with inclusion and move to exclusion throughout the story. At the beginning of Matthew 25 we find the parable of the ten maidens; five were prepared and five were not, and the door to the party was literally shut on the five who were unprepared. *The Ten maidens were all invited to the party.*

At verse 14 we enter into the parable of talents. This time three servants are given talents to take care of and return to the master upon his return. The two servants who wisely invested the talents were commended and the one who hid his talent away was scolded for his misuse of the talent. *The servants were all given talents.* Now comes the final parable… the judgment of the sheep and the goats. *Sheep and goats were all part of the herd.*

At first glance this story of the sheep and the goats appears to be focused on doing good deeds. But our works do not get us into heaven... so why the separation??? It says here if you treat people well, you will be rewarded, if you don't you will find yourself headed to eternal punishment.

But let's look again at this story, a little more closely, and in connection with the other parables. The main character of the 10 maidens, the bridegroom, is missing, at the beginning of the story. He finally shows up late at midnight. The next parable, the parable of the talents, the master hands out talents for his servants and then takes a trip and is absent while these servants try to figure out what to do with the responsibilities they have been given. These two stories include warnings about living prepared for the return of Jesus.

In this third parable of the sheep and goats, Jesus has returned! Jesus is not only present; he is everywhere! Those known as the sheep and the goats just thought he was gone. Growth often occurs in the actions of the individuals while in the absence of the master.

All three judgment parables are tied to the origin of the word; Crisis. It is a crisis here! Not knowing if we are going to be a part of the sheep or the goats! Because we think we are part of the sheep but are we really? It appears that this symbolism of these animals may be used because of their behaviors within community or the herd. Sheep have a tendency to travel and stay clustered together, easy to lead; while goats on the other hand often stray away from the herd and are more independent and aggressive, hard to lead, and will wander off on their own with no regard for the rest of the herd. The sheep also know the voice of their shepherd and the shepherd knows his sheep. Many pictures of shepherds depict the shepherd actually carrying their sheep on their shoulders. There is a relationship between the shepherd and the sheep.

John 10:27 reads, "My sheep listen to my voice; I know them, and they follow me." We, by the death of Jesus on the cross, have been invited to be a part of the Kingdom of God! Jesus included us all! But how many of us will hear our shepherds voice? Jesus says in John 10:14 "I am the good shepherd; I know my sheep and my sheep know me, just as the Father knows me and I know the Father and I lay down my life for the sheep."

So what separates them? What makes some of them fall on the side of the good and blessed and some on the side of the evil and cursed? It wasn't so much what they did, but what they did not do that caused the separation. The maidens who were not prepared, found the door closed after they returned, the servant who did nothing to strengthen the talent, was the one whose talent was taken away, and here it is the goats who did nothing when they saw need, or maybe they did not even see the need…. maybe they were just to busy. They were the ones separated from the flock. The Sheep and the Shepherd are relational and other minded while the goats are non-relational and me oriented.

This passage is the final lesson. One, in which Jesus wanted to make an impact on his disciples. He wanted to make sure that they understood the message! You see it wasn't that the goats could not be a part of the herd. They already were in the care of the Good Shepherd's love. They knew Jesus was the Shepherd….. But Jesus is asking…. Do you know me? Do you know me in such a way that you will respond to others for me? Do you know me in such a way that you can see me on the side of the road? Do you know me in such a way that you realize it is me who is in need of water? We can all fill up every minute of every day doing good deeds, we can work hard for the church putting in multiple hours every week doing great things for the kingdom of God, but do we know Jesus? Good deeds done *in response to God's love*, indicate we have a relationship with Jesus.

This is a very personal discussion for me, someone who has spent at least 40 hours a week at church for the last 15-20 years. I have recently been struggling with the question: Am I more committed to the church or to Jesus? You see there is a difference there. I know that I have a relationship with Jesus but could I be more committed to the church, doing great things that point toward Jesus and yet not be spending enough time with Jesus myself? So even though I thought I was doing all the right things, the right deeds, am I really building a relationship with Jesus? Do I truly know Jesus? This can be a very troubling discussion and yet we see here in the Bible time and time again trouble and reassurance are found side by side.

"In this world you will have trouble. But take heart! I have overcome the world." John
16:33

We are told in this story that the sheep will be given their inheritance and the goats will receive punishment.   We think we are with the sheep, but how do we know for sure? Trouble and reassurance together remind us we cannot be *complacent*.

It is by our own doings, by our own choice, ….. that we may find ourselves on the side of the goats. This second part of this parable where Jesus is talking about the goats… I don't believe he was saying this with a heavy hand, I believe he was saying it with a heavy heart… Saddened that any of his children would have to be put on the side of the goats. The goats, they were complacent, happy with life as it was, feeling they were blessed.

To me, the most intriguing part of this new world that Jesus tells us of in the New Testament is that as soon as we think we know something specific, there is a catch, a change, a new way of thinking about it. We cannot be complacent, thinking there will be tomorrow, or next week, or next month, or next year to make things right with Jesus, to stop the busyness and spend time listening for God and reading God's word. This parable should be moving us to realize that we need to act now! Find time for God in our lives everyday. God wants to be involved in all we do! Opening up our schedules to make time may be difficult, but margins in our lives enable us to be aware of Jesus' presence in our lives.

I love to preach, and more importantly I love to prepare to preach! It is in the preparation that I find quality time of relation building with Jesus. My eyes and ears are more aware of what is happening around me. I am consciously and unconsciously looking for God in everyone and everything around me.   As I was working on this message I was wondering what illustration I could use that I had experienced to bring this message to life for you.

So on Monday afternoon I was returning from the library, driving down Berry Street I saw a man on the corner ahead with a bucket asking for donations. The man visually was having a difficult time with life. This is it, I thought, I usually pass these folks by thinking that they are working the streets, but in lieu of what I had been studying maybe I should give him something. I really need to start carrying McDonald bucks in my car, that would be a better thing to give than money, I thought to myself. The man was working his way down the lane and then all of the sudden he went to the next lane over! The light turned green and I missed him. That's odd, I thought to myself…. Was that a chance to help Jesus and I missed it?

As I drove into my hometown, up four-lane street, a woman in a pink workout suit caught my eye. She was probably in her 70's, well dressed, standing next to a mailbox on the sidewalk. That's a nice color on that woman I thought. It was 5:15pm. I went home to touch base with David and then I was going to go to my office at the church to finish this message. 5:45pm. I leave my home and head toward the church, in the distance, I saw what appeared to be a person walking in the street. Probably crossing the road to go into the neighborhood I thought. As I got closer I noticed it was the same lady in pink. Now she was in the middle of the street. "God protect her going across the street I prayed." I slowed down watching in the rear view mirror, she wasn't crossing the street. She was now walking on the other side of the street into oncoming traffic. Cars were passing her, and the car in front of me was making a u-turn. "They are probably turning around to check on her"… "How nice", I thought. *__Turn and check!__* my gut told me. I turned; the car in front of me did not stop. There was a man on the sidewalk… he kept on walking, She was on the other side of the street; a median strip separated us… I drove quickly back to my house, parked in my driveway and walked toward the street. The lady in pink was out of my view. Two girls were jogging on the sidewalk, another man walked by on the opposite side of the street. "Surely one of them got her to the sidewalk", I thought. I turned the corner and there about two houses away I saw her in the turn lane. I walked out onto the median strip and called out to her, "hello, how are you today?" The woman started walking toward me, she had stepped onto the median strip. Cars were passing us left and right; the woman said 'hello'. She was hot, tired. Trying to access the situation I said, "nice day for a walk." She replied 'it's getting hot." "Where are you walking to", I asked? "I am trying to get home", she replied. "Where is that?" "Everman" (a town approximately 10 miles away). That answer affirmed my concern. "My name is Judy", I told her. "My name is Grace", she replied. "Grace, nice to meet you Grace. That's a lovely name; do you have a last name? " She remembered her last name and her phone number. "My house is right there I said, would you like to sit with me in my yard and I will try to call your house?" She did, and fortunately the phone number was the number of her son.

Fifteen minutes later a police car pulled around the corner, followed by her family in another car. I waved them to the side patio where we were sitting in the shade drinking

192

a glass of cold water. A very relieved gentleman came through the gate, shook my hand and said "Momma what are you doing here?" We spoke for a few minutes more and it was time for her to leave. "Goodbye Grace, thank you for the visit"...... she stretched out her arms and gave me a hug and a kiss. "Thank you", she said. I called the number she gave me again that night. I spoke to her daughter in law who told me Grace was doing well and would be moving from the facility she was in to an Alzheimer's home on Wednesday.

But what if I wasn't paying attention? What if I wasn't thinking about the scripture on my way home when I was driving? What if I had been thinking why is the car in front of me driving so slowly, I have a sermon deadline! I might not have seen Grace. *And then, What if I didn't turn around? Would I have been separated with the goats?* We could drive ourselves crazy wondering if we were doing enough, judging our own actions. Jesus tells us that he is the judge; we need not worry about that.

Jesus died for all! He is the good shepherd of both the sheep and the goats! He is telling us that everyone is invited to the party, to sit at the right hand of Jesus. All of us, no matter what we have done in the past are worthy of a relationship with God! Not by our doings, but by the sacrifice of God through Jesus. Jesus does not exclude anyone! Thanks be to God!

Jesus is not saying in this parable... these sheep they have racked up an excellent record of good deeds. But Jesus is saying these, the sheep, have a relationship with me, because of their relationship with me , because of their trust in me, because even when they didn't think I was present they poured out my love to others, their faith, their faith in our relationship.... That is the deciding factor.

Jesus recognizes us, knows our names, our innermost thoughts, and has seen how we built a relationship with him through helping 'even the least of these', even and most especially when it made us uncomfortable to do so. To find Jesus we need to be faithful. That way we will know Jesus when we see him. Jesus is cheering us on to be in the side with the sheep that's why he told this parable last... this isn't a parable of doom it is a parable of love, that Jesus the King of Kings, the Lord of Salvation has saved even the silly sheep who didn't even recognize him so that we would understand, Jesus is all about Love.

Grace, the lady in pink, had walked over a mile to get to my house from the nursing home. During our conversation I said," you've walked a long way"…. Grace replied, "I had to, or I would not have seen you."

Jesus continues everyday to invite all of us to be sheep in this life!   Amen.

Earthly Treasures

Melissa Malinoski

(Luke 12:13-21)

As Americans we are taught, really we are told, that we should succeed in life. And part of success is how much wealth, how much money we have. We should have enough money to have nice cars, a nice home, good clothes, and the newest gadgets and phones. That is what we hear from television.

Everyone wants to be a millionaire and wants to make money any way they can get it. There are those who want to win it on television through game shows. There are those who have some talent like singing, baking, or who knows what else that try and win it by their ability. There are those who try and make money just by letting someone follow them and film them.

Have you seen the show Honey Boo Boo? I must admit that I watched a few shows because of all the hype about this Southern Georgia family who are about as redneck as you can get. They are making a great deal of money letting people film them and all their antics. I heard a television commentator last week say, "Do you think this show is perpetuating the stereotype that all southerners are dumb red necks"? The other person said, "I think they know what they are doing and making a lot of money letting people laugh with them not just at them".

There are those who are millionaires by the time they are in their twenties with internet start ups. Like Mark Zucherberg who started Facebook who was a billionaire by the time he was 23. I have even heard about a couple who are millionaires selling golf clubs on the internet out of their garage. Those people have an idea and capitalize on it.

There are those with the talent to act, sing, or play ball that make unreasonable amounts of money. Why because we the consumers are willing to pay to be entertained.

It is fun to go to a game, watch a movie, or attend a concert. It gives us an escape from our reality and some people make a great deal of money to entertain us.

It seems we all want to succeed anyway we can. There are lots of us regular people who play the lottery or gamble and try to make our dreams of wealth come true. I am not against having a little fun and buying a lottery ticket. One of my son's friends grandmothers bought a ticket every week for years and even won small amounts several times and even thousands of dollars once. I do find it a bit heartbreaking though when people in line at the gas station seem to use their last dollar to buy a ticket. They are filled with hope that the ticket will change their lives for the better and most of the time their hopes are dashed and they lose.

There are those who work hard for what they have in life. They have gone to school or worked in a profession and succeeded. America is filled with the entrepreneurial spirit, for generations we have been taught that with hard work and a little know how we can succeed. Just the other day at work a co-workers 12 year old daughter brought around a flyer she had made to sell her homemade cookies. She has been creating her own businesses since she was 6. She is determined to succeed and who knows in a few years she may.

That entrepreneurial spirit is nothing new in America. It has been alive and well since our country was founded. There was the most interesting show on History channel about the men who made America. It told the story of men like Carnage, Rockefeller, and Vanderbilt. I have visited Biltmore in North Carolina Vanderbilt's southern home and it is massive. To image that beginning in 1889 Vanderbilt built the largest home in the United States. It has so many rooms including an indoor pool, bowling alley, and an elevator all built in the 1800s. The show also featured Henry Ford. The man who made the assembly line part of car manufacturing which led to the sell of many cars.

Henry Ford once asked an associate about his life goals. The man replied that his goal was to make a million dollars. A few days later Ford gave the man a pair of glasses made out of two silver dollars. He told the man to put them on and asked what he could see. "Nothing," the man said. "The dollars are in the way." Ford told him that he wanted to teach him a lesson: If his only goal was dollars, he would miss a host of greater opportunities. The man should invest himself in serving others, not simply in making money.

Wise truth filled words from a man who had great wealth, but seemed to understand that life is more than money and possessions. The old saying that money is the root of all evil seems true many days. It is not a new phenomenon or only an American issue. Greed and lust for money and the power that money brings have been around for a long time and it doesn't seem to be going away anytime soon.

Greed, lust for money, status, power, and lust for things were an issue during Bible times. The story of Jacob and Esau in the Old Testament where the younger brother tricked the older out of his birthright and tricked his father to receive his blessing shows that greed is nothing new to the human family. So when a man in the crowd appeals to Jesus to tell his brother to share his inheritance Jesus could not have been surprised.

In ancient Israel the practice of primogeniture was persistent. That means that the first born male had special rights to the inheritance and to status. The firstborn male was the principal heir and successor to be the head of the family. Obviously this caused problems in many households. I know families who fuss and fight today over furniture or china at the death of a family member. Feelings are hurt when someone believes they should get granny's quilt. Imagine if there were multiple brothers and sisters and only one received everything. I am sure Jesus knew many who received little to no inheritance.

Jesus responded to the man with a wise story filled with truth. He told the story of a rich farmer who had produced so much that he had nowhere to store his crops. So the man decided to build new barns. Not only did he build new barns he tore the old ones down and replaced them. So the man said to himself I have so much now I can retire. I can do what I want, have a little fun, eat, drink, and party. And then what happens? The man dies. Jesus said, "So it is with those who store up treasures for themselves but are not rich toward God."

Wise, truth filled words from a man who lived what he preached. A man who owned nothing and had no place to lay his head. Words from God.

We can hear these words from God that we should not store up earthly treasures, but heavenly treasures and know they are truth because that is how Jesus lived. Yet, it is hard to hear those words from people who are only trying to get us to give money to their church or mission and they are living the high life. They are driving fancy cars, wearing designer clothes, and are covered in jewelry. And if we do know people who choose to give all they have away, owning no property or clothes we often don't listen to them because by societies standards they seem crazy.

But these words from Matthew's gospel, "Do not store up for yourselves treasures on earth, where moths and vermin destroy, and where thieves break in and steal. But store up for yourselves treasures in heaven, where moths and vermin do not destroy, and where thieves do not break in and steal. For where your treasure is, there your heart will be also". Were spoken by Jesus who lived what he preached and calls us to follow him.

But how? We are taught that it is foolish not to save for a rainy day. We are told to have enough savings to live for months. We are told to save for our children and grandchildren so that they can go to college. We are told we need to save a great deal of money for retirement so that we can live well. The show Honey Boo Boo really is silly and foolish. However, Honey Boo Boo's mother, Momma June, said that she took all the money that they made the first season and put it in savings accounts for her daughters and grandchild. That seems so wise compared to the foolishness that happens on the show. It seems wise compared to so many movie stars who blow all their money on stuff and wind up losing all they have. So what are we to do? We can't take it with us when we go.

Leo Tolstoy once wrote a story called "How much land does a man need?" about a successful peasant farmer who was not satisfied with his lot. He wanted more of everything. Here is how Tolstoy tells the story: One day a farmer received a novel offer. For 1000 rubles, he could buy all the land he could walk around in a day. The only catch in the deal was that he had to be back at his starting point by sundown. Early the next morning he started out walking at a fast pace. By midday he was very tired, but he kept going, covering more and more ground. Well into the afternoon he realized that his greed had taken him far from the starting point. He quickened his pace and as the sun began to sink low in the sky, he began to run, knowing that if he did not make it back by sundown the opportunity to become an even bigger landholder would be lost. As the sun began to sink below the horizon he came within sight of the finish line. Gasping for breath, his heart pounding, he called upon every bit of strength left in his body and staggered across the line just before the sun disappeared. He immediately collapsed, blood streaming from his mouth. In a few minutes he was dead. Afterwards, his servants dug a grave. It was not much over six feet long and three feet wide.

I am not so sure that Jesus is saying that we can not have any earthly wealth, but that we can not let the money blind us to what is right and good. If we seek wealth at any cost it will cause us to do things that we shouldn't and to not do things that we should. If we think that are responsibilities in life are done when we accumulate a certain degree of wealth or secure our future than we are merely viewing life as means of collecting possessions.

Luke's gospel clearly tells us that our relationship, our attitude toward earthly material possessions has a direct impact on our relationship with God. It is not that God does not love us if we have earthly wealth it is that the wealth becomes an obstacle. We are blinded by the dollars in front of our eyes and wealth often takes priority over everything even God.

The man who asked Jesus to tell his brother to divide the inheritance knew that Jesus was powerful. If Jesus told his brother to divide the inheritance than it should be so, but he was trying to use Jesus so that he would get wealth. He was placing wealth above all else.

What can we do to heed Christ's call to store up riches in heaven and not on earth? We can keep our priorities straight keeping God first in our lives. We can strive to not let money or all that goes along with money come between us and Christ. We can also not let money come between us and doing good works. Following Christ isn't easy, but it is our calling.

Let us go out and live a Christian life striving to follow in Christ's way. Amen.

What Happens When Jesus Comes to Town?[7]

Theresa Martin

Matthew 21: 1-11

I remember when I was a little girl and would visit my relatives in Cookeville, Tennessee, what a special event it was to go to town. This was way back when Cookeville was a small town with almost all the stores located on Main Street, including the one movie theater, the Princess. My relatives lived on farms in the country and the only day they had time to shop was on Saturday. Monday through Friday, you went to school or to work and on Saturday, they took time to go to town to buy whatever they had to have and to dress up and see friends and neighbors. Every Saturday—at least when I was visiting—felt like a special occasion. Time to go to town. It was a big deal to me.

We remember this day on the Christian calendar as Palm Sunday. What happened on Palm Sunday? Crowds were gathered in the big holy city of Jerusalem. I can only imagine what Festival time must have felt like for Jews close to Jerusalem. Every Jewish man who lived within 15 miles of Jerusalem was required to go to the Temple to observe Passover and the feast of unleavened bread. There would have been thousands and thousands crowded around the city ready to celebrate.

Some scholars say that as Jesus was riding into Jerusalem that first Palm Sunday during that Passover celebration that there were two processions entering the City, each representing a kingdom. From the West was the power of Rome and Pilate leading military troops. From the East came the one called Jesus. He was riding on a donkey, like the beloved king David. He was greeted with shouts of Hosanna and Son of David, King of Kings, Lord of Lords, Mighty God of Mighty Gods and Prince of Peace. He came in the name of, and represented, the Kingdom of God.

---

[7]Preached on Palm Sunday at Prospect United Cumberland Presbyterian Church, Cleveland, Tennessee.

Two kingdoms, entering the Holy City of Jerusalem from opposite directions during the Passover week in which the people were celebrating liberation from slavery. Can you imagine the sounds? From one side the sound of marching feet, military cadence, symbolizing that kind of power and control. From the other side came sounds of God's people shouting Scripture—quotes from the passage we know as Psalm 118. These groups were headed toward a mighty collision. When Jesus comes to town, powers collide and forces clash. There will be battles for power and control!

The people around the gate called Beautiful were overjoyed to see Jesus coming on a colt / fulfilling Zechariah 9:9. Many spread their cloaks on the road. Others spread branches they had cut. Those who went ahead and those who followed shouted: "Hosanna! [a Hebrew expression literally meaning Save us! Which had become an exclamation of praise!—**Praise you for coming to save us! Please Lord, please save us**.] Blessed is He who comes in the name of the Lord! [Psalm 118:25-29] Hosanna in the highest! They were quoting what we know as Psalm 118. "O Lord, save us; O Lord, grant us success. *Blessed is he who comes in the name of the Lord*. From the house of the Lord we bless you. The Lord is God, and He has made His light shine upon us. With boughs in hand, join in the festal procession up to the horns of the altar. You are my God, and I will give you thanks; you are my God, and I will exalt you. Give thanks to the Lord, for He is good; His love endures forever." Blessed is he who comes in the name of the Lord was the regular greeting with which pilgrims were addressed when they reached the Temple on the occasion of the great feasts. This was a conqueror's hello or greeting, a psalm, a song of praise to God. A song of hope and assurance that the Jews used to remember God's deliverance of them and look toward the future. When they said Hosanna, they meant not to praise Jesus but to plead with God to **break in and save** His people. *Hosanna means Lord, save us now!*

The people wanted help and protection NOW. They were looking for a Savior!

Jesus was riding into Jerusalem knowing his days were numbered and that he needed to do what had to be done. The city was very crowded with Jews celebrating the Passover and two days later, the Feast of Unleavened Bread. The 'common people' around Him adored Him. Many of the religious leaders, people in positions of power were jealous of Jesus. He was surrounded with tension / facing adoration on one side and suspicion on another with tremendous tension pulsing from both sides

Application: What happens when Jesus appears? What would we do—really?

What would happen if Jesus came to town today? Would we line the roads and spread our coats for him to go across? Would we grab flowering branches from the trees to wave in praise? Would we wait for Him to enter a stadium to preach? Would we stay in our living rooms and wait for Him to appear on the news? What would we do? Would we clap our hands—use our palms to sound our excitement? Would we form a group to sing and shout praises? Would we take our joy to the streets—become a flash mob and go viral on you tube? ***Would we take time*** / make time / to celebrate Jesus' saving power?

When we lived in Memphis and I worked at Memphis Theological Seminary, there was a huge funeral procession down Union Avenue, the street in front of the seminary. . It's one of the busiest intersections in Memphis, TN where Union crosses Central Avenue. Firefighters had been killed while fighting a fire and one of the funeral processions went through town as it went from Christ United Methodist Church (one of the biggest churches in a town of BIG churches) to the cemetery. The road was blocked for hours. All day traffic was shut down in mid-town Memphis on busy, busy streets. At intervals they brought in fire trucks. They fully extended the ladders of the trucks so that they met in the center of the street. and hung huge American flags down from the ladders. People lined the streets for hours to stand in respectful silence as the hearse and the procession went. People wanted to show they cared / that they grieved with the family who had lost a loved one while trying to put out a fire. What was I doing? The procession went by about 100 feet from me. I could see some of it from my office window. But I was too busy putting together presentation packets for an afternoon meeting to go outside and make a picture of the people and the flags and the loving care being shown by the citizens of Memphis I didn't take time / make time to get involved that day.

I wonder, if Jesus rode by and I was busy working, would I have time to stop and say, "Hosanna!" Or would I feel like I needed to say, "I'll catch you later, Jesus. Don't move too fast. I want to be with you but I'm busy right now." I hope I wouldn't do that. But I am an American. I do have a "to-do" list. Every day I have a "to-do" list. Things to do. People to see. Places to go. The people in Jerusalem stopped what they were doing to take care of urgent happenings. Jesus was in the city! What would we have done? Would we have been skeptical like the leaders of the Jews? Would we have lined the roads to watch?

Would we have been one of those waving branches and yelling: "Blessed is He who comes in the name of the Lord! Save us, Lord Jesus! Praise you for coming to save us!" Where do we stand in the story? Where do we want to stand? What does God want us to do?

If Christ came to America today, what would happen? Do you think he would ride in a parade? Do you think they'd have a ticker-tape parade in his honor? Would we gather around big screens to watch? Look for it on You tube? Sit back or stand up and shout?

In the church today:

Many churches try to re-enact the parade that we recall on Palm Sunday. We wave branches or palms and sing hymns. Often children bring in the palm branches and it can be a great memory—but God calls us to remember and **get excited / stay excited** about Jesus our Savior.. But if Jesus really came to town today, what would we want to do? Would we want to check it out? Would we want to applaud? Would we want to run beside the procession singing and shouting, rejoicing and shouting, Lord Jesus, save us!?

Truthfully, would we be

    1. excited or 2. scared or 3. too busy to participate?
        Where would we be?
        Where do we want to be?
        Where should we be?

As this week continues and we move toward Easter Sunday, as we celebrate what some call Holy Week, we will remember Jesus as He prayed in Gethsemane, as He went on trial, as He celebrated the Last Supper in the Upper Room, as He was nailed to the cross, and we get more and more excited as we Look Forward to Resurrection Sunday—Easter is coming!

Closing prayer:

All powerful God, we thank you for the saving power of Jesus Christ. Help us to BELIEVE in You. Help us live as people who are really excited about what Jesus did when He went to the cross and came out of the tomb resurrected! Help us to live for You—keep us so excited that we can't contain ourselves and we have to say what we believe to others and act it out in ways that surprise and amaze the world around us. In Jesus' name we pray, Amen.

Bridges

Brittany Meeks

Luke 7:1-10

I was told by a mentor recently that, "Seminary is the vessel upon which you have to sail through your entire ministerial career; don't go through it so fast that you build a shoddy ship." It was good advice, and I took it. A poorly built ship is dangerous not only to the captain but to all of those who are upon it. The same can be said of bridges. A poorly constructed bridge is at constant risk of crumbling away. Not only would this cause disrepute for the architect, but it puts those who are meant to journey across it in grave danger as well.

We have all heard that you shouldn't "burn your bridges" but, rarely do we talk about the importance of constructing those bridges well in the first place. I am not really sure why, fire, after all, is not the only thing that can destroy a bridge. If a bridge is shoddily built, fire may never even have a chance to destroy it because it will likely fall to pieces before adversity even has the chance to strike.

As a Church, and as leaders in the Church, one our most important calls is to build bridges, and it is unacceptable to build shoddy ones. When we do so we put the ministry to which God has called us at risk as well as all of those who trustingly journey along with us.

The author of Luke teaches us a bit about bridge building in the text we just read. One thing we are taught is that there is one bridge which God has already built. To understand what this bridge is, we need to clarify what the real miracle in this text is. The miracle isn't that Jesus healed the sick servant but that a gentile man who had never seen Jesus in person, who didn't even experience Jesus in person when he was pleading for a favor, had faith. A faith that Jesus, that God, acknowledged as more than sufficient.

What good news for us, we who have also never seen Jesus face to face, who did not witness his miracles or hear his lessons first hand—we, who have never washed Jesus' feet or followed him through Galilee and Capernaum—we are not at a disadvantage. We, like this gentile man, can have a faith that is more than sufficient in the sight of God.

But the miracle doesn't stop there, its even bigger than just that, he said if you, Jesus, speak the word it will be so. He displayed his great and miraculous faith by believing that Jesus didn't have to be physically present with his servant in order for his servant to be healed. Jesus does not have to be physically present for his word to be effective. That is the miracle then and the miracle for us today.

So then, if that is the miracle—what is the bridge? The bridge is between God and us, of course—it is a bridge that cannot be broken by time. A bridge that assures us that though Jesus may not be physically among us—his words are still affective and so our faith is not in vain.

That is the bridge that God has built. And thank goodness it isn't shoddy. If it were we would find our only comfort in a Book of memories of what Jesus once said and what Jesus once did for those people back then. If this bridge between then and now were shoddy, the word of Christ would not be effective or relevant for all times and places and there would be little to sustain the church or her people. The church could not survive if she had a past but no present. We would be in a very dire state because any faith we managed to have—as miraculous as it may be—would be in vain.

It would have been absolutely devastating if God had built a shoddy bridge. But God did not. God did not construct a questionable bridge, but an eternal one. God didn't create some chintzy, second-rate bridge prone to collapse and decay and neither should we. So what is it that this text teaches us about the bridges we are to build? First of all we see that in this story there is a relational bridge between the leaders of the synagogue and those who are considered the others, the outsiders. The local Jewish leaders, clearly had a great respect for this gentile man. If they had not, they would not have pleaded to Jesus on his behalf, nor would they have spoken of him as "deserving" something from Jesus. It is important that we too build bridges between ourselves and the other, the outsider. And it is unacceptable for those bridges to be shoddy. We are most at risk of building shoddy bridges with the other when succumb to the attitude that we have everything to teach and nothing learn. We must always remember that we serve a living and vibrant God who continues to reveal more to us daily. Therefore, we must learn from those we minister to, even, and perhaps especially from those with whom we are most uncomfortable. When we fail to learn from them we fail to see that the Spirit of God is at work in all kinds of people and we cease to be a dynamic Church who is able to reach out to all humankind.

There is a family in my church who has an Atheist son. He was raised in church but something that was said to him while he was in one made him never want to walk through a set of church doors again. Whatever was said killed his hope that there was a God. The day any church family believes that they have all the answers for him if only he would listen—and become unaware of what they can learn from him and his experiences—they will have built a shoddy bridge, indeed.

The day when our churches believe that God is a conservative or a liberal, we will have built a shoddy bridge because we will have failed to consider what we have to learn from people who are different than us.

We must never forget that we have as much to learn from those who we view as different, as outsiders, and as in need of ministry as they have to learn from us. The Jewish elders, the religious leaders—like us, who pleaded to Jesus on behalf of the Centurion would have missed out on many great lessons if they had excluded this man simply because he was a gentile, an outsider.

From this outsider they learned the value of truly caring about slaves—those who were the least, from this outsider—who gave them significant funds to build their synagogue—they learned what it meant to be truly generous, what it was to be humble and recognize their own lowliness, what it was to respect Jesus not merely as a healer but as one with authority from God, from this outsider they learned how to have authority and yet not demand of others what you think you deserve, and from him, from this gentile-outsider, they learned what true faith looked like. They would have missed out on a lot if they had built a shoddy bridge between themselves and this outsider. God did not build a shoddy build bridge when ministering to us, the outsiders, in the person of Jesus so neither should we build shoddy bridges when we minister to others.

This text also teaches about the importance of building good bridges between ourselves and those with whom we minister. The Jewish elders in this text seemed to view Jesus as one who could help them in their ministry. They did not hesitate to ask for his help nor did they treat him as a heretic like some other leaders had done. No, they saw value in his ministry and so they built a bridge between their ministry and his. It is important for us to do the same. To build positive bridges between ourselves and others with whom we minister.

If we as a Church will ordain women, then we should be willing to call them to our pulpits. In her book, Shall Woman Preach, Louisa Woosley compares the ministry of women to the building of the city wall in the book of Nehemiah. She points out that it was not only men building the wall, and if it had been, many breaches would have remained after its completion. Likewise, women are a vital part of ministry in this Church and when we ordain equally and yet fail to educate our congregations and fail to call them equally we begin to build shoddy bridges bound for decay.

Also, if we are serious about our desire to merge our Church with the CPCA from "the grass-roots"—then we need be serious about actually taking the "grass-root" measures of which we speak.

It is not enough to talk about getting our churches together for fellowship. It is not enough to hear about our desire to do it in Presbytery and General Assembly meetings. We as the leaders of the CP Church have a responsibility to go back to our congregations after we leave meetings such as this and to tell them about what is going on. We have an obligation to share with them about what steps are suggested, and most importantly it is our duty to propel our congregations towards actually doing these things.

If we don't then we are at risk of building a shoddy bridge because in reality when we merge will have still merged from the top down and not from the "grass-roots." If we fail to be active we will build a bridge between the CPC and the CPCA that will falter due to its poor construction before it has ever had a chance to face the fire of adversity. We cannot risk building shoddy bridges between ourselves and those to whom we minister or between ourselves and those with whom we minister because when they crumble—and if we build them poorly they will—there is no guarantee that those who we've left on the other side will continue to journey with us, even if we attempt to rebuild them.

Now hear me correctly

In speaking of calling women, the CPCA, and those who are different from us, I am not suggesting that our Church is already guilty of having built shoddy bridges. This Church has built a bridge between women and ministry that has been invaluable to me and all of the other women sitting in this room. All I am suggesting is that we keep that bridge in good repair so that it will remain in tact and so that the wonderful women leaders we have stay.

In regards to the CPCA, we are in the process—the process of building what could be a monumental and healthy bridge between our Churches. All I am suggesting is that we help what could—to be—by spending adequate time preparing the cables which will support it along the way.

And in encouraging us to learn from others, from outsiders, I am not suggesting that we bend with every wind and whim, but that we humbly remember that we do not know it all, and that we do have room to grow—so that as we build our bridges, others will actually be willing to join us in journeying across them.

We as a church have so many wonderful opportunities to be involved in something great on behalf of God. So Let us come together in courage and be the leaders we are called to be by building the bridges God has called us to build and by doing so well. And let us do it out of gratitude to God—who saw it worthwhile to build an everlasting bridge between us and God through the person of Jesus Christ. Amen.

Una Madre Sobreprotectora
An Overprotective Mother

Luciria Aguirre Naranjo

(Génesis 27:1-17)

Texto bíblico: Génesis 27:1-17

Propósito: Tomar el ejemplo de Rebeca para no cometer esos errores que dividieron su familia. Decidir depender de Dios y no de nuestros sentimientos y emociones.

Introducción

La celebración de la fiesta de la madre tiene defensores y detractores. En nombre de la mamá se mueve el comercio, hay ofertas, viajes, rifas, créditos y se utiliza el sentimiento para crear la necesidad de darle regalos como muestra de amor. Como cristianos, sabemos que la labor de una madre es trascendental en la vida de sus hijos y su familia, que no se puede celebrar un solo día del año y que la Palabra de Dios nos enseña que como hijos debemos honrar a nuestros padres todos los días de nuestra vida.

Aprovechando esta celebración vamos a ver la influencia de una mamá en una familia, en su esposo y en sus hijos, para que este modelo abra nuestro entendimiento, nuestro espíritu y no caigamos en los errores que ella cometió. Este es un mensaje de reflexión para advertirnos sobre las consecuencias de nuestras decisiones.

1. Solicitud de Isaac a su hijo mayor Esaú. V. 1-4
2. Rebeca escucha y prepara un plan V.5-10
3. Temor de Jacob de ser descubierto V.11-12
4. Premeditación de Rebeca V. 13-17

¿Cuáles fueron los errores de Rebeca?

1. Escuchó la conversación entre Isaac y Esaú

Cuántas mamás hacen lo mismo? Espían a su esposo e hijos para saber qué hablan o para conocer sus secretos. Si tú quieres saber algo debes preguntarlo y no espiar ni escuchar tras la puerta. Las mamás debemos enseñarles a los hijos lo que es correcto e incorrecto y en la medida que van creciendo debemos confiar en ellos y darles su espacio y su privacidad. Las madres debemos pedir sabiduría de lo alto para guardar el equilibrio entre ser flexibles y tener autoridad. Los extremos no son buenos y esto trae muchas dificultades, dicen que nosotros pasamos de ser la generación que le tenía miedo a los padres para tenerle miedo a los hijos. Las generaciones han tenido un cambio devastador porque antes había mucho autoritarismo de parte de los padres y ahora hay autoritarismo de parte de los hijos. Como madres debemos enseñarle a nuestros hijos las bendiciones de la obediencia y que cada decisión tiene unas consecuencias, que todos somos responsables de lo que hacemos o no hacemos y de lo que decimos o no decimos; que los errores se pagan caro. Si enseñamos a nuestros hijos desde que nacen y los vamos corrigiendo y acompañando en sus distintas etapas del desarrollo, podemos confiar en ellos y hablar abiertamente para que no haya necesidad de escuchar a escondidas como lo hizo Rebeca.

2. Solicitó la obediencia de Jacob su hijo menor, para engañar a su padre Isaac

Qué error tan fatal! Qué poca fe! Qué poca dependencia de Dios! Qué autosuficiencia!

Las madres debemos ser muy cuidadosas porque a veces manipulamos y coaccionamos para que nuestros hijos hagan lo que nosotras queremos. Rebeca quería algo bueno para su hijo pero se equivocó. Hay madres que engañan al papá y que hacen cosas al escondido. Hay madres que protegen a sus hijos del papá y esto no es bueno, ni saludable, ni honesto. Lo mejor que podía haber hecho Rebeca era orar y depender de Dios pero dependió de sí misma, de sus sentimientos y esto fue muy grave para toda la familia.

3. Pidió la maldición para ella y de nuevo solicitó obediencia para el engaño

Rebeca fue muy obstinada y no le importó pedir que Dios la maldijera con tal de seguir adelante con su plan.

Su intención era buena pero no tuvo en cuenta que al proteger a Jacob estaba haciendo algo en contra de su hijo mayor Esaú, que estaba enseñándole a su hijo a mentir, engañar y suplantar, que no estaba dejándolo madurar y ser responsable por sí mismo. Cuántas mamás se equivocan al sacrificarse por sus hijos sin enseñarles que todo en la vida tiene un costo, que todo se gana con esfuerzo, con estudio, con trabajo y con un comportamiento adecuado hacia los padres, hermanos y familia en general.

Una madre no puede pedir maldición para su vida porque esto trae maldición a su familia. Por el contrario, las madres debemos orar para recibir bendiciones y ser de bendición al esposo, los hijos, nietos, nueras, yernos y a todas las personas que nos rodean.

Rebeca no se equivocó una sola vez, su acción incorrecta se repitió y en ese momento ella no pensó en las consecuencias de lo que estaba haciendo. Esas consecuencias iban a ser de maldición y de división en su familia.

4. Preparó la cena, tomó los vestidos de Esaú – los más preciosos que tenía en casa- y vistió a Jacob. Hubo suplantación, engaño, mentira.

Las mujeres y sobre todo las madres son muy habilidosas en conseguir lo que quieren! Esta madre era buena cocinera y preparó la cena que le gustaba a su esposo, pensó en todos los detalles, buscó la ropa especial de Esaú para esa ocasión tan importante, vistió a su hijo Jacob y lo envió a recibir la bendición.

Qué bueno ser habilidosas pero siempre para bendecir, para unir, para ayudar, para perdonar, para dar un testimonio adecuado de que dependemos de Dios! Cuántas suegras han hecho planes perfectos para separar a su hijo o hija de la persona amada. Cuántas han hablado un poquitico de más para quedar bien y hacer quedar mal a otra persona. Cuántas han llorado y hecho un show para llamar la atención o conseguir lo que desean. Cuidado madres, nosotras estamos para bendecir, para ayudar, para unir a la familia, somos ejemplo y debemos enseñarle a nuestros hijos y familia en general, que ante toda situación primero vamos a la presencia de Dios, oramos y pedimos sabiduría antes de tomar decisiones. Que tenemos una fe real en el Señor Jesucristo y le pedimos su ayuda; solicitamos la guía del Espíritu Santo, para saber qué es lo correcto a los ojos de Dios, no dependemos de nuestras emociones y sentimientos porque estos son variables y poco confiables.

5. Cubrió con piel de cabrito a Jacob para que la suplantación fuera perfecta, premeditó bien su plan.

Qué madre tan detallista! Ella utilizó los recursos existentes para que su plan fuera un éxito. Premeditó muy bien el engaño de modo que le saliera perfecto. Cubrir a su hijo con la piel de los cabritos fue una gran idea!

Lo que esa mamá ignoraba era que estaba siendo enredada por el pecado. Cuando decimos una mentira necesitamos de otra para cubrir la primera y de otras para seguir manteniendo como verdad lo que sabemos que no es cierto. No podemos jugar con el pecado, jugar con el pecado es como jugar con fuego, algunos salen bien librados aparentemente, pero otros se queman, hay quemaduras leves pero otras profundas que dejan dolor y cicatrices. Mamitas nosotras somos las primeras maestras de nuestros hijos, las que les enseñamos lo bueno, lo malo, lo correcto e incorrecto. Si nosotras mentimos o engañamos luego qué podemos pedirle a nuestros hijos cuando hagan lo mismo? Las mentiras se descubren, salen a flote, aún más, a veces quien dice la mentira es quien la descubre. La Palabra de Dios enseña que no hay nada oculto que no haya de ser manifestado.

6. Envió a Jacob a engañar a su padre para obtener su bendición

El propósito era bueno, obtener la bendición, pero la intención y el procedimiento fueron un desastre! Es horrible pensar que una madre envía a su hijo a mentir y engañar a su padre. Esta mujer fue necia, fue muy irresponsable, utilizó su astucia y sabiduría de forma negativa. Esa mamá ni siquiera pensó en el dolor que iba a causar a su esposo e hijos, ella solo actuó por impulso, por un sentimiento de favoritismo y preferencia por su hijo menor. El nombre Jacob significa engañador suplantó 2 veces a su hermano para quedarse con su primogenitura y luego con la bendición de su padre.

Consecuencias

1. Odio entre los hermanos V. 41 aborreció Esaú a Jacob por la bendición. División familiar, venganza, resentimiento.

2. Rebeca le pide a Jacob que huya, su hijo se alejó y ella se quedó sin el hijo que más amaba v. 43

3. Por qué seré privada de vosotros dos en un solo día? Se le acabó la paz v. 45

4. Fastidio tengo de mi vida, para qué quiero la vida? V. 46 perdió el propósito, el norte de su vida. Desintegró su familia.

Conclusión - Aplicación

Proverbios 14: 1, 12 y 26

El ejemplo de Rebeca es una advertencia para nosotras. No cometamos esos errores que dividieron la familia.

v.1 La mujer sabia edifica su casa, la necia con sus manos la derriba.

Nuestra labor es de construcción no de destrucción.

v.12 Hay camino que al hombre le parece derecho, pero es camino que lleva a la muerte.

Nuestros caminos son humanos, limitados y nos equivocamos como lo hizo Rebeca. Aunque a nosotras nos parezca que el camino es derecho para evitar dolores y llanto consultemos con Dios, oremos y pidamos sabiduría para ser madres que bendigan a sus hijos, que les enseñen el amor a Dios, a sí mismos y al prójimo.

No forcemos a nuestros hijos a que hagan nuestra voluntad, oremos por ellos y con ellos para que busquen la voluntad de Dios en todas sus decisiones, leamos con ellos la Palabra y practiquemos los principios que Dios nos da en ella.

v.26 En el temor de Jehová está la firme confianza, la esperanza para sus hijos.

Si nosotras amamos a Dios, lo respetamos, lo obedecemos y lo reverenciamos, ese es un regalo eterno para nuestros hijos, si confiamos en Dios y en sus promesas nuestros hijos tendrán nuestro ejemplo y pondrán su esperanza en el Señor!

Mamitas no dependamos de nosotras mismas, de nuestros sentimientos o emociones porque nos podemos equivocar y hacer cosas que luego nos van a doler, a lastimar o a dañar la paz y la armonía familiar.

Oremos por nuestros hijos, busquemos primero que todo agradar a Dios y hacer su voluntad, si educamos y formamos a nuestros hijos en el amor y la obediencia a Dios, podemos confiar en que ellos tomarán decisiones acertadas y se dejaran guiar por el Señor. No forcemos las cosas, no los obliguemos a obedecer si es algo contrario a la Palabra de Dios. Cuando los hijos van creciendo los padres vamos envejeciendo. Ellos van siendo autónomos, responsables de su vida y nosotros estaremos allí para acompañarles, apoyarles, animarles, darles la mano cuando caen y presentándolos cada día y cada noche en la presencia de Dios para que él los guarde, los guíe y los bendiga.

Nuestros hijos no son nuestros, son un préstamo temporal de Dios! Son de Dios y debemos educarlos y formarlos en el amor hacia él.

Oración.

With God on the Mountain

Jennifer Newell

(Mark 9:2-10)

Mark 9:2-9: TRANSFIGURATION

2 Six days later, Jesus took with him Peter and James and John, and led them up a high mountain apart, by themselves. And he was transfigured before them, 3 and his clothes became dazzling white, such as no one on earth could bleach them. 4 And there appeared to them Elijah with Moses, who were talking with Jesus. 5 Then Peter said to Jesus, "Rabbi, it is good for us to be here; let us make three dwellings, one for you, one for Moses, and one for Elijah." 6 He did not know what to say, for they were terrified. 7 Then a cloud overshadowed them, and from the cloud there came a voice, "This is my Son, the Beloved; listen to him!" 8 Suddenly when they looked around, they saw no one with them anymore, but only Jesus.

The Coming of Elijah

9 As they were coming down the mountain, he ordered them to tell no one about what they had seen, until after the Son of Man had risen from the dead. 10 So they kept the matter to themselves, questioning what this rising from the dead could mean.

Before we climb the mountain, we need to put this scene in context, because that is the only way I seem to be able to make sense of it.

Only a few verses before this mountaintop experience, Peter shows signs that he finally gets it-that he finally knows who this guy is. This miracle-working guy who walks on water and forgives sins, who heals the sick and raises the dead, who feeds crowds with a handful of food and who teaches with authority: this guy is none other than the MESSIAH, the son of the Living God.

Well, it is good to have THAT finally resolved. Surely Jesus sighed with relief that SOMEBODY had connected the dots.

So Jesus takes advantage of this teachable moment and tells the disciples what being the MESSIAH really means: it means suffering and death on a cross at the hands of powerful people. It also means coming back from that defeat by rising from the dead.

But Peter can't seem to get past the suffering and death part: "No! You're a HERO, not a criminal. You're God's triumphant Savior, riding in on your white horse to right what is wrong, to restore what is broken. You are here to pull God's people up out of the humiliating circumstances of their lives, to kick those Romans out of town once and for all, to clean up the Temple and bring peace and dignity to us." No more talk about crucifixion: that's not for you.

And then, I am sure, Jesus sighed a very different sort of sigh. One minute, Peter gets it; the next, he's missing the point altogether.

So Jesus tries again. If you want to follow me, Jesus says, you get to take up a cross, too. This life I'm offering you is not one where you ride my coattails to fame and fortune. It's one where you will have to set aside your own ambitions, sacrifice your own comfort, let go of your life and your plans and take a stand for me AGAINST the powers of greed and selfishness, against oppression and hate.

Are you ready to do that?

Good grief. Is any of us ready for that life?

It's a bitter pill to swallow-a hard truth to wrap our heads around. Maybe that's why Jesus offers them a preview of the bigger picture, a glimpse of where all this heartache and suffering will eventually lead. These men need a good, healthy dose of glory to get them through the darkness that is headed their way.

Peter, James, John, and Jesus: high up on a mountaintop-far from the crowds pawing at the hem of Jesus' clothes, far from the scribes and Pharisees with all their trick questions, far from the realm where demons know Jesus on sight.

Cool crisp air…and a view like no other.

What they see is incredible: Moses and Elijah walking with Jesus in a dazzling array of glory and majesty.

Whites so white the OXICLEAN people are quaking in their boots; light bursting forth from every pore, shining through every seam.

This is the Shekinah glory of God...the glory that shone in that pillar of fire in the wilderness, in the Temple sanctuary, in the visions of the prophets. The glory that made Moses' own face glow when he came down off the mountain.

Moses and Elijah have been on the mountaintop before.

- Moses: the great liberator, law giver, and leader climbed a mountain and received the Law. He encountered God's glory on that mountaintop, and brought it back with him when he came down.
- The prophet Elijah climbed a mountain, too, and heard God's still, small voice...and when Elijah's time on earth was over, he rode a chariot of fire straight up to heaven.
- In that group of three, we see the Cross...the Law...the Prophets: all standing together, all pointing to the same God, all promising triumph, all reminding us of the truth of this broken world:
- a world that needs Law to help us sort out good from bad;
- a world that needs Prophets to speak truth to power;
- a world that needs a Cross, to reveal the ugliness of evil and the transforming power of love.

This is two semesters of theology right here in one mountaintop experience. But what they are experiencing is way more than just a powerful object lesson or a lifetime's supply of theology. What they get here is a life-changing, transforming experience of God's true self.

It's called a theophany: an experience of God that grabs hold of our hearts and minds and won't let go. Hard to wrap ourselves around it...hard to explain it, hard to help others understand it.

If you've ever had that sort of mountaintop experience, it might be hard to explain. I've had a few-a few experiences of God's presence that defy words or understanding. One was during a retreat, out in the woods, where you would expect this sort of thing. Another was as I was driving down Lee Highway, right in front of the Krystal restaurant: the last place you'd expect Jesus to reach out and grab hold of you.

And there was comfort and conviction in those moments, and both of those moments changed the direction my life was headed. And as hard as I try, I can't figure out how to share them with you in a way that does them justice.

It was overwhelming, to say the least…and all these years later, it still is.
These closest friends of Jesus are overwhelmed, too…and more than that, they are afraid. Not just in awe…they are face-down on the ground shaking-in-their-boots terrified.
This coming face-to-face with the mystery of the Divine, this up-close-and-personal glimpse of God's glory, is scary stuff. There is no logic to it-God is what God is, God does what God does, and even a taste of that overwhelms us.

- The disciples saw it when Jesus walked on water and again when he calmed the storm, and it scared them near to death.
- They'll hear it when he talks about resurrection later in this same chapter, and the text says they don't understand…and are afraid to even ask.
- In a week two, they will see it one more time in that empty tomb, and they will run like scared rabbits.

So it is no real surprise that they don't know what to do with THIS mountaintop experience.

Peter says, "let's build something: three houses, three shrines. And let's just stay here forever and ever." It's like when you take your kids to Disney World, and someone inevitably says, "I wish we could just live here."

I love Peter. Right after this supernatural subdivision plan of his, the text says, "he did not know what to say, for they were terrified." But that doesn't stop him. He still wants to chime in and saying SOMETHING. He doesn't know what to do, but he is going to bumble and stumble through this anyway.

Three houses: as if the three glorified men in front of him are equals. That's a huge compliment, you know, to be viewed as an equal to the likes of Moses and Elijah.

But of course, Peter misses the point again. Jesus is NOT their equal: he is not even in the same LEAGUE as those guys. Moses and Elijah were two special men, used by God in extraordinary ways. Jesus IS God.

And besides: this is not a time for talking or building. It is a time for listening and looking, for soaking it all in. A cloud overshadows them, and from the cloud comes a voice: "This is my Son, the Beloved; listen to Him!"

Just like at Jesus' baptism, God bridges the gap between heaven and earth, lays bare what has been hidden from view, but was there all along.
And this time, the message is directed not to JESUS but to his followers:

- Jesus IS the Messiah, and when he talks about suffering and death, you should listen to him.
- Jesus IS the Messiah, and when he says he will rise again, you better believe it.
- Jesus IS the Messiah, and when he tells you that you that the road ahead of you is not comfortable or easy or simple, you ignore that at your own peril.
- Jesus IS the Messiah, and when the days get dark and scary, and when the nighttime seems too long to endure, never lose sight of that fact.

And then it is all over. Elijah and Moses are gone, and Jesus says something Jesus says a lot in Mark: "ssshhh. Let's not talk about this. Until I am resurrected, just keep this to yourself."

Let's put ourselves in Peter and James and John's sandals for just a minute.

Imagine seeing what they saw and hearing what they heard and facing what they are about to face…and being told to keep it to themselves.

Maybe that's for the best, because what on earth could they say that would make any sense?

On that mountaintop, Jesus' divine nature is revealed in God's own way and on God's own timing. With 2000 years of hindsight and tradition, we often assume that Jesus' real nature, his real identity, is obvious. But take Mark's word for it: there was nothing obvious about it. These men had spent 3 years face to face with Jesus the Christ, and they struggled to get it.

Jesus' mission was not to make a big deal of himself. And sorry, guys, it was not to make a big deal out of his followers, either. He wasn't in it for the power, the prestige, or any of the worldly rewards of success. Jesus didn't work to impress Rome, or the Temple Priests, or even his own family.

Jesus did what he did and said what he said in order to point beyond himself…to God, whose kingdom was crashing the party even then, whose will continues to be worked out in a broken and blind world.

This Jesus: he is a paradox.

- He is God almighty, and yet he suffers.
- His name is glorified above all others, and yet he is so often misunderstood.
- He is majestic, and he is also a servant.
- He is headed toward ultimate glory and victory as king of kings and lord of lords, but the way to victory leads first to humiliation and pain and death.

This is the God we serve…the leader we follow…the truth we bear witness to with our words and our actions, in our relationships with others and in our worship of the Divine. Where does that leave us?

What's true in physics class and on the baseball field is true here, too: what comes up must come down.

God does not give us mountaintop experiences so that we can stay in that rarefied air forever. God does not show us glimpses of his nature so that we can turn a blind eye to the rest of the world.

God, in God's grace, offers us a taste of the BIG TRUTH of life, then God sends us back out into the world: refueled and refreshed and maybe a little bit mystified.

When the darkness comes, we can hold onto the LIGHT we've seen.

When the valleys are deep, we can remember the truth of the MOUNTAINTOP.

When life is messy, we recall that we serve a God who is in the business of cleaning up, like no laundry on earth can do.[8]

---

[8]First Cumberland Presbyterian Church, Cleveland, Tennessee, July 24, 2013.

Waiting on God

Sharon M. Notley

(Acts 16:16-34)

Have you noticed that it seems that all of life entails waiting? We wait at a stop light, *waiting* for the red light to change. When we are in a hurry, the wait seems to last forever. We wait for a person to cross the street and they seem to dawdle. We wait—sometimes hours—in the doctor's office for a fifteen minute consultation that costs us over a hundred dollars. Long lines at the checkout counter don't bring out the best in us either. How we handle the wait oftentimes determines our mood and perhaps the outcome of our wait.

A study was conducted with a group of children involving waiting. Several children were seated at a table. Each child had a piece of candy placed before him. The children were instructed that they could eat it. But, if they waited, they would be rewarded with another piece when the teacher returned--*if* they did not eat the first. Some gobbled it down as soon as the teacher left the room. Others sat on their hands, turned their back on the candy and sang songs to distract themselves from the temptation. Those who denied themselves received the reward. Sociologists and psychologists followed this group of children through life—those who waited, excelled in school, went on to college and generally became successful. Those children, who quickly gobbled up the candy, generally did poorly in school and also later in life.

Those children who waited, received the prize of a second piece of candy. How you and I handle our God-given waiting affects us, our family, our community, and ultimately our world.

In our Scripture today, Paul and Silas waited on God and received a reward that answered the desires of their heart.

Our Scripture reading in Acts finds Paul and Silas in the city of Philippi in Macedonia. They are on the way to the river which was a usual place of prayer for the

223

Jewish community. As they walk along, they are continuously oppressed by a slave girl with a spirit of divination. She made her owners rich by predicting the future. As they walked along, she kept saying, "These are servants of the Most High God, who are telling you the way to be saved." Notice, she was telling the truth, yet her manner was irritating Paul and Silas.

Ever notice that there is a way to say things. The same sentence or word has completely different meanings depending on how we say it.

The slave girl of our story was telling the truth, but shouting and mocking God and His disciples. She had to be silenced. She was interfering with the work of the Lord with her wicked torrent. However, Paul and Silas waited. They were waiting on God for the right moment. The slave girl kept up her harassment for several days, till finally, Paul was released by the Spirit of the Living Lord to rebuke the evil spirit within her. It left her at his word. Paul waited for just the right moment, when the Spirit of God, would join forces with his emotions, in order to effect a change.

WHEN HUMAN WILL AND THE SPIRIT OF GOD JOIN FORCES, CHANGE HAPPENS.

Now, that is empowerment!
When we pray and our prayers are half-hearted, we will not see effective change. But when we pray with fervency, our prayers are effective. Oftentimes when I pray, I ask the Lord to place His fervency in my prayers—and He does. The prayers of a righteous person are effectual.

Notice that Paul waited till God was with him and that it was God's will, before acting and rebuking the spirit. Anger alone would not have been effective. Only after days of prayer, did he feel the power of God come upon him. He was then able to cast out the spirit without harming the girl.

Once the evil spirit was out of her, she was useless to her owners. I find myself wondering: *what happened to the girl? Did she become a believer? Did she seek out Christians to hear the word of God that would explain what just happened to her? Or, did she not do anything at all?*

You see, AN EMPTY SOUL MUST BE FILLED.

God has given man a hunger for Him. We can place worldly pursuits in our soul, but the things of the world do not satisfy. Only God, His word, and the delights of God truly satisfy the hungering soul. It is only when we seek God and His will in the earth and in our own lives, that we find satisfaction. Worldly pursuits do not fill an empty soul—only God can fill us and satisfy us. Worldly pursuits and vain satisfactions leave us empty, craving something, and open us up to demonic oppression. We cannot throw out the bad without replacing it with something. If we choose the wrong thing, we will be in worse condition at the end of our lives than at the beginning.

Once the evil spirit was out of the girl, *how did the believers of Philippi respond?*

THIS EVENT DID NOT HAPPEN IN A VACUUM. *NONE* OF *GOD'S* WORKS ARE *EVER* DONE IN A VACUUM. THERE ARE *ALWAYS* WITNESSES.

The believers had a choice: *Would they take compassion on this girl and witness to her; would they choose to take her under their wing and disciple her?* True, she had issues that would have to be dealt with. Demonic activity in a human being has a source. Rape, abuse, being sold into slavery and being mistreated—perhaps she was sold into slavery by her *parents*, the very people she should have been able to trust. Perhaps they had abandoned and rejected her (this is purely conjecture on my part and may have not been the situation in her life at all)—yet she may have *felt* abandoned and rejected. Any of these issues mentioned are ripe playgrounds for the devil to enter in and wreck his havoc. Only the healing love of Jesus Christ administered to her through the Holy Spirit and Christ's disciples—ordinary people just like you and I—only the love and unconditional acceptance of the girl, combined with the word of God and the Spirit of God would bring about the healing she so deeply needed. She needed the love and compassion of Jesus Christ to fill her so that she could be made whole.

But the community of God was not the only one making the choice to help her--she had to make the choice as well. I wonder. Did she make it? Perhaps we shall meet her in heaven—perhaps not. We each have choices to make. The choices we make could have eternal consequences.

The slave girl's owners made their own choices as well. They reacted against Paul and Silas, and in their greed, incited the mob bringing civil charges against Christ's disciples.

Notice: The spirit if Anti-Christ is in the world. This spirit manifests itself by greed, idolatry, spreading falsehoods, deception, violence, perversion, and all manner of corruption in high and low places. The spirit of Anti-Christ wars with the Holy Spirit and with those who follow God. Suffering ensues. But, God has a plan! The world and the natural man—those who do not have the Spirit of God in them—have different eyes, different values than that of God. Natural man's eyes are veiled to the true work of God. God is surrounded by clouds and thick darkness (Ps. 97:2). It takes spiritual eyes to perceive God's activities in the world. We must put on the eye-glasses of the Spirit—Jesus Christ and His Holy Spirit—is He Who reveals the word of God to us. We must communicate with God listening and heeding His advice, to perceive those things that are of God. Therefore, whenever trouble comes, we should look beyond the natural to the Spiritual. God has made provision for us. Jesus prayed for us in the Garden on the night He was arrested. We are secure in Him—even when the devil is doing his worst!

Crowds are easily stirred, especially when the provocation is rendered as negative. Criticism, often motivated by thoughtless emotion, always comes before considered thought. Once the masses have been stirred up, they are hard to stop. Vigilantes and mob lynching are examples. The devil stirs emotions, but prayer cools us down to hear clearly from God. Once we are certain, then we should proceed. Assurance from God gives strength for our battle with Satan that always lies ahead. Every action of God encounters a reaction from the devil. If God said it, we can be certain that the devil will work hard to destroy it. The devil wants to wipe out from the earth anything that even faintly resembles God. If it is of God, the devil opposes it—and he won't be nice about it either.

The **good news** is that the shields of the earth belong to God. What that means, is that God *can* save us and *will* save us, but our salvation is costly. No Christian is immune to suffering. We live in a world that is controlled by the devil, and he wants to destroy us. The devil makes all manner of plans for our destruction. But thanks be to God, He edits those troubles and allows *only* those troubles that will edify and prosper us *in* God's kingdom, and that will bring glory to us both. After God edits and limits what He will allow the devil to do, God then walks with us in the midst of that suffering, no matter how grave. That's a promise.

Precious in the sight of God is the blood of His saints. Jesus paid the price—so should we.

Paul and Silas paid the price for their obedience. They did not *choose* to be severely flogged, or jailed in the deepest and darkest place in the dungeon, but they were. However, they knew the liabilities of their walk with Christ. As Christ was condemned by the world, they knew that they too, would face the same condemnation by evil people.

God knew what He was doing! He had a plan. He would carry it out despite the devil's opposition. Paul and Silas had to wait, **in faith**, for God's plan to be revealed.

WAITING *IN FAITH* IS DIFFERENT FROM JUST WAITING.

At the stoplight, drumming our fingers on the steering wheel is not waiting in faith. Cursing a slow-moving pedestrian is not waiting in faith. Silently fuming is not waiting in faith. Waiting in faith is expecting God's intervention and looking for it no matter what the devil throws in our path—or how long it takes.

WAITING IN FAITH IS PRAISING GOD FOR WHO HE IS. JUST REJOICING IN HIM AND KEEPING OUR EYES OPEN FOR HIS ANSWER IS WAITING IN FAITH.

The devil chose intimidation, and then used force in an effort to prevent the word of God from being spread abroad by Christ's ministers. Paul and Silas were falsely accused, flogged till the blood ran, and then thrown deep into the prison with their feet fastened in stocks—a prison reserved for only the vilest of prisoners. They were not going anywhere; they had no hope, seemingly. But *what did they do?* They praised God and sang songs and prayed.

A good lesson for us to remember is that when all seems lost and darkness in all its oppressive hopelessness looms overhead and threatens to envelop us, God notices our plight.

GOD HAS A PLAN.

God guards the lives of His faithful ones and delivers them from the hand of the wicked (Ps. 97:10).

God had a plan for Paul and Silas that affected more lives than their own.

GOD *NEVER* DOES HIS MIGHTY ACTS IN SECRET; HE ALWAYS HAS WITNESSES WHO CAN TESTIFY TO HIS WORKS.

The other prisoners were witnesses. They were hearing the word.

Corrie Ten Boom's sister told Corrie that even in the darkest pit, Jesus is there. In every hopeless situation—seemingly to us, but not to God—God is there ready to work His miracle-working power for those who believe in Him and actively place their trust in Him. Paul and Silas were actively trusting God by their prayers and songs of praise.
When do the birds sing, after the sun rises—or before? Before! God sits enthroned among the praises of His people. When He is seated on His throne, He enacts His judgments. The eyes of the Lord, search to and fro in the earth, seeking those whose hearts are steadfast towards Him.

He sees, He hears, He acts in favor of His people, and for His purposes. You are not here by mistake. God knows you and will come to your aid.

How do you respond in your times of darkness, when you have to wait on God? Do you sit hopelessly in self-pity, or anger, or frustration—to the devil's delight? Or, do you lift holy hands and praise God for all His goodness to you? God reacts to our praises and enacts His decrees in our favor when we praise him. He already had Paul and Silas' salvation planned **before** they were thrown into prison. God responded to their praises as a testimony to His power. God had a plan and He was working it out so that people could be saved.

God responded to their praise and trust in Him. He responded in a *most* unusual way. He caused a violent earthquake to shake the prison so that the doors were opened. Now, doors *can open* during an earthquake in the natural; *but,* God went one step beyond and struck off the chains that bound *everyone*. Now, *that's* supernatural! He left no doubt in the minds of His witnesses—the prisoners who were listening to Paul and Silas—that the Lord God Almighty was at work in that prison.

Notice: the chains were not struck on *only* the ministers Paul and Silas, but on *all* the prisoners.

God had a plan for Silas and Paul that was different from their own—different from what they had previously envisioned for themselves. Their plan was to make converts at the river, God preempted those plans with plans of His own. God's plans included suffering *and* glory!

DON'T BE AFRAID. GOD *CAN* AND *DOES* CHANGE *OUR* PLANS TO SUIT *HIS* PURPOSE.

Previously, Paul and Silas had been going to the place of prayer, congregating with those of like-mindedness, preaching along the way, inviting those they encountered to join them. But Scripture doesn't record any converts. It was only when God moved them to a place that they would rather *not* be, that they began to see what God had in store for them.

God sometimes has to force us to leave our comfort zone in order to produce fruitfulness in our lives. Paul and Silas were not producing the kind of fruit God desired, so He pruned them and placed them in a Philippian jail. While they waited in prayer and praised God in song, God acted. He caused a mighty earthquake to hit the jail.

—This is just a thought, but it is worth our consideration, perhaps God had Paul and Silas wait before rebuking the evil spirit in the girl, because an earthquake was about to happen. He didn't want Paul rebuking the spirit till the time was right. *Then* He gave Paul release to rebuke the spirit—*just so that Paul and Silas would be thrown in jail **at just the right time!***—As a result of God's timing, and Paul and Silas' obedient response, the earthquake struck and **lives were saved!**

I think of Haiti and Chile, two countries that sustained great damage due to two ferocious earthquakes. We have had two more since, both 6+ on the Richter scale: Mexicali, Mexico in Baja California, and another in China. The media reports the great damage in Haiti and the lives that were lost, but it records very little of the humanitarian efforts that are now taking place. The media speaks nothing of the lives that have been changed for the better because of the quakes. The news media criticizes, but has no eye to see the souls that have been transformed and added to the kingdom of God because of the quakes. Only through eye-witness reports of Christians who have been transplanted by God from their zones of comfort to the hellish region of Haiti, do we get an understanding of the glorious hand of God at work in those regions of devastation.

Paul and Silas saw first-hand the purposes of God in their own suffering: They saw the Philippian jailer and his household receive salvation that night.

Many prisoners were there to eye-witness the earthquake and the response of God to prayer and praise. Shackles were let loose and the prisoners were set free. But only Scripture, the testimony of Paul and Silas, and that of the jailer and his household record the salvation experience of the Philippian jailor. The prisoners were witnesses to the effects of the earthquake, but were not privy to the jailer and his household as the events occurred. Only afterwards did they become aware by the transformed life the jailer evidenced. Perhaps he shared his testimony with them.

One might by conjecture assume that just as the jailer washed Paul and Silas' wounds and gave them something to eat, that perhaps thereafter, the prisoners were treated more humanely in that prison.

The jailer, not only was saved from suicide, but he was also--if we continue on with the chapter--saved from disgrace, *because*, the next morning the magistrates sent word to the jailer to release Paul and Silas. Fortunately for him, he had prisoners to release. The devil intended for the jailer to die in disgrace. God had other plans. Consider the change that was evidenced to the prisoners. They saw God at work in answer to prayer. They saw His mighty hand at work by striking their chains. The jailer was changed, which in all probability changed how they themselves were treated.

Our penal system is based on Christian precepts. Nowhere else in the world are prisoners treated as humanely.

Scripture does not record what happened to those prisoners. Perhaps some of them received Christ as well. You and I will never know from this side of heaven, what changes of heart happened in that Philippian jail. But I am certain, that when we get to heaven, we will meet some of those people and hear their own stories first-hand. What a delight awaits us! What a day of rejoicing that will be as they tell us the story of God's actions in their lives—the stories we all long to hear.

So the next time that we find ourselves waiting and tempted to wallow in self-pity, frustration and perhaps despair, remember Paul and Silas and the Philippian jailer. Remember that as we wait, God is at work. He is working in our best interests and in that of others. He is working for our deliverance, fruitfulness, and His own glory.

GOD WILL NEVER ASK US TO DO SOMETHING FOR HIM THAT COSTS US NOTHING.

He wants us to be a blessing to others. To be a blessing to another is to be a vessel of God that He uses to prevent misfortune in the lives of others. To be a blessing to another can prove to be costly.

But along with the cost, will also come the equipping. Paul and Silas paid the price. They were flogged severely and thrown into a vile prison. But, after they had paid the price, God delivered them. God does not ask us to do something and then leave us bereft. He *always* provides the ability to do. He then rewards us substantially for our efforts.

Paul and Silas were rewarded, not with gold or silver, but with a testimony to the goodness of God in their lives. They were filled with an inner satisfaction that they had pleased God. They were blessed with peace with God—and they had an experience with God that no one could take away. They had joined forces with God and had unity with God that could *never* be replaced.

God showed them His goodness and they were richer for it. So the next time waiting comes into your life, consider it *a God wait* and see what He has planned.   Amen.

Not What But Who

Lisa Oliver

(Matthew 4:12-23)

Prayer of Illumination

God of Light and Life,

We praise you for the Amazing Grace and Love that you shower on us! We praise you for the gifts of life and family and friendships. We praise you for the gift of this community of faith called Mt. Tabor and for its long standing witness and light in this community. We know that it is only by your grace that any of us are here, and we praise you for bringing us together again to worship you!! We come today having been through darkness of our own, some of our own making. In this time of worship we ask that you would fill us with your light just as you are the Giver of Life and the breath that we breathe. We ask that you shine the light of your love on us, today tomorrow and always. Shine Your Light on these Scriptures. May we hear the message you have for each one of us. Surprising as it may be, there may be different messages for each of us in this one collection of thoughts. Help us to be open to how you are moving in our lives and in this worship service. This we pray in Jesus' Precious and Holy Name! AMEN!

Matthew 4:12-23[9]

[12] Now when Jesus heard that John had been arrested, he withdrew to Galilee. [13] He left Nazareth and made his home in Capernaum by the sea, in the territory of Zebulun and Naphtali, [14] so that what had been spoken through the prophet Isaiah might be fulfilled: [15] "Land of Zebulun, land of Naphtali, on the road by the sea, across the Jordan, Galilee of the Gentiles— [16] the people who sat in darkness have seen a great light, and for those

---

[9]**New Revised Standard Version Bible**, (Division of Christian Education of the National Council of the Churches of Christ in the United States of America, 1989).

who sat in the region and shadow of death light has dawned." [17] From that time Jesus began to proclaim, "Repent, for the kingdom of heaven has come near." [18] As he walked by the Sea of Galilee, he saw two brothers, Simon, who is called Peter, and Andrew his brother, casting a net into the sea-for they were fishermen. [19] And he said to them, "Follow me, and I will make you fish for people." [20] Immediately they left their nets and followed him. [21] As he went from there, he saw two other brothers, James son of Zebedee and his brother John, in the boat with their father Zebedee, mending their nets, and he called them. [22] Immediately they left the boat and their father, and followed him. [23] Jesus went throughout Galilee, teaching in their synagogues and proclaiming the good news of the kingdom and curing every disease and every sickness among the people.

Not What But Who

You want me to do what? Seems like would have been the first question that crossed the minds of the disciples. These guys were on their boats and heard Jesus calling them to follow him, and so they did. And instead of fishing as they knew it, Jesus would make them fishers of people. We have no indication that this thought crossed Andrew, Peter, James or John's minds. It appears they stopped everything and without hesitation decided to follow wherever Jesus was going. Last week we talked about what questions and thoughts they might have had…. And Gospel of John tells the story a little differently about how the disciples were called. We can get bogged down in why there is a difference, or we can simply accept that different writers have a different purpose and likely had differing audiences in mind. Additionally, we can put these Gospel stories together and get more of the big picture.

We can get blown away by these mythical spiritual giants who can walk away at a moment's notice from everything and everyone they knew to follow Jesus. And maybe we have been there with this text, and just overlook it because there is no way we can even relate to this kind of faith, adventure or whatever you want to call it. It's not realistic for us to grasp. I submit to you today, that we may be overlooking the biggest and more important reality here.

The call to the disciples is
1)   An action: To follow Jesus

2)   A Promise: Jesus will do something

3)   For the Community: Is for People, not Fish

In order to answer the call, the disciples had to take action and follow Jesus. To follow Jesus as we know from reading Scripture and our own lives is not always easy. To follow Jesus is to be in close proximity and be open to go where he goes, and do what he does or asks us to do. To follow Jesus means we should find ourselves in opposition to the world more times than not. To follow Jesus is to know and understand what Jesus would do and why Jesus would do it. We may not always get it right, but we have to be ready to try and willing to go. To follow Jesus means we may have to go and minister to people who are not like us, who may not live in safe areas, who may need us to do something for them that we have never done before. Jesus went to those who needed him. He didn't live among the rich and famous and powerful. He was with the poor and the sick. To follow Jesus may make us uncomfortable. To follow Jesus we may see things we haven't seen before, the good the bad and the ugly. To follow Jesus, is an action!! Following Jesus requires that we get up and move and do!!!!

In the call to the disciples, Jesus makes a promise that He will do something. In this case he says He will make them Fishers of People. The promise includes teaching them by parables, by showing them how to relate to others and what they are capable of doing as he empowers them to do what he has called them to do. Did they know what it meant to be Fishers of People when they accepted the call? Probably not but we can guess that since Jesus said it they wanted to know more about it. Jesus is going to make us Fishers of people; He is not going to leave us high and dry. He will be with us to teach and guide us. Sometimes we will be taught through parables and preaching. Sometimes we will be taught through experiences and trying out what we have learned. Sometimes we will be taught through miracles that we either experience or witness. Jesus used all sorts of ways to teach and train the disciples. Rest assured these are all still available to us, and especially in Scripture where we can learn from what has been handed down to us.

All of these points are critical, but this one is the umbrella of the call, and that is: The call is for the Community! It is for people not fish! These are fishermen who had been on boats in the water, and the call is for disciples on dry land (since that is where we live so we can breathe!!). It is people who need Jesus and need to know about Jesus. These were skilled men with fish, who now had to make the transition from being on separate boats to coming aboard a metaphorical boat together and fish the same metaphorical sea on dry land. The Disciples had made their living pulling fish up out of the sea, but now Jesus has called them to pull people up out of the darkness into the light!

I am not sure we understand that we are called to be in relationship. There is the delicate balance between doing and being. Often times we get caught up in the doing, we forget to be. Even us well-meaning and hardworking folks who want to do whatever we can do to help others and make a difference in this world can be so overwhelmed by what has to be done, we find we open our mouths and our Marthas come out! Right, our Martha's come out and say, Lord can't you tell Mary she needs to come in here and help me? I am so overworked and I don't have enough time or the energy to do all that is required of me. And well, it's just not fair that I have to do all of this…. Mary needs to be helping me. And she is in there with you …. I would love to get to visit with you and spend time with you, but I have all this stuff to do and as soon as we get this done, I can be right in there with you… This is when we know we have become a human doing and not so much a human being. As you may recall, Jesus is not so much interested in the stuff that Martha felt had to be done, but said Mary has chosen what is right, and he did not send her in to help Martha.

The call is for building up of the Body of Christ. People are required for the Body of Christ to function. People are the ones who are given the gifts of the Spirit which are used to bring grace and blessings to others. When we are working within our Spiritual gifts, it doesn't feel like work. It comes natural and we have all the energy we need to do what God has gifted us to do. People are best caught and attracted to the Body of Christ through relationship. Often we think of evangelism as how we bring others into the community. And it is true, evangelism is how it is done. However, evangelism and evangelical may have somewhat negative connotations due to some perceptions about what it means to be evangelical and Christian. Some of us have experienced what was said to be evangelism, but amounted to having a piece of paper with the Gospel story on it shoved in our hands as if we were in desperate need of salvation, though this person had no knowledge of our spiritual journey or perhaps our salvation experience. Again, possibly well-meaning and hardworking folks trying to do what they feel God called them to do. While it did not work for me, as I was already saved, it is highly possible others came to know Christ through their efforts. So I cannot discount what they did, maybe I can ask that they consider an alternative, which would be to develop relationships that are strong and healthy and teach about the love of Jesus Christ, through their words and their actions.

Building up the Body of Christ calls on us to step into the world of those we love and love them, as well as into the rest of the world and love them! Jesus came into the world as God made manifest in human form. The Epiphany that we celebrate is the light of the World coming into our lives and offering a relationship that will transform us into who God intends for us to be. Jesus is all about relationships. And he goes to those who are willing to receive him. He doesn't force himself on anyone. He offers us choice and a better more abundant life in Him. Our relationships should have some reflection of Jesus in them. Not all of them will, and we will have to let some of them go. And we will have to shake the dust off our shoes and continue on our journey to wholeness and blessing in Jesus Christ.

The call the disciples had is the very same call we have. Come, follow me and I will make you fishers of people! Sometimes our vocation lines up with our call from God and we get to do what we are called to do for a living. Sometimes our call does not line up with our vocation, if that is the case, find a way to live out your call in the church or in the community. What is your call?? What is it that God is asking you to do?? If you feel like you don't have the resources or the opportunity to serve the community in some way, you can always pray. You may never know what impact your prayers have, but know that they are heard by God. If you think you have done your job, given all you could give in years past and time for others to work while you get some rest, think again! As long as you have breath, you can serve God. You can pray and take on particular prayer requests to be an advocate for and take to God, our Father, Creator of the Universe to ask for God to intervene! What more important role could you play in the life of another??

The challenge for this week is to think about your relationships. Consider one or two in particular that are challenging for whatever reason. Pick one of those (or both of those) and spend some time praying daily for that person and whatever causes the relationship to be challenging. Maybe it is a past hurt or a misunderstanding, or something quite a bit deeper than that. What if we all did that this week?? What if we started doing this every day ???? What could happen?? How might we change the world by praying for not only those we love but those who make it hard to love them?? Could we experience some of what the disciples did by dropping everything to follow Jesus, just by dropping everything and having this prayer time not only for our beloved but also for our not so beloved?? Could we be transformed by God through our prayer time? Absolutely! What if we are changed enough that the relationship doesn't seem so challenging? What an improvement in our world already. What if this started an avalanche of change in the world and we wouldn't have to worry about School and Mall Shootings anymore?? Maybe we could be the agents for ushering the Kingdom of God in a major way!!

And one final word, there is a church in the Shackle Island Community near Hendersonville called St. John's Missionary Baptist Church. A few years ago they placed a banner over the front door of the church that says, "Go Fish." The banner reminds us what our job is, to go fish! My niece, who notices everything, was asking me something about the church and when I asked her which church she was talking about she said, "You know, the Go Fish Church!" I knew exactly which one she was talking about. What if Mt. Tabor Church was known as the Go Fish Church? What if all Churches were known as the Go Fish Church? What if we were all about our jobs of fishing for people?? When we leave today, let's Go Fish! AMEN!

Doubt

Susan Parker

(Isaiah 12: 1-6)

Today for a few minutes, I would like for us to think about doubt. If you are like my church, you don't talk too much about doubt. In most churches, most of the time, we talk a lot about faith, but not so much about doubt.

You may be saying, why would she talk about doubt, in a church? We are here because we believe, because we have faith. Yes, we are, but if you are like me you have also had times of doubt. I would dare say, there are very few people who have not had some doubt regarding their faith.

Even people like Mother Teresa, who was one of the greatest servants of God we have known in our lifetime. Someone who spent her life in the poorest, neediest place on earth, Calcutta India. She ministered to those with leprosy, tuberculosis and aids. The untouchables they were called. But she touched them and she worked to establish 133 other such ministries around the world. Many people would say that no one in modern times has even come close to the work she did for God. But Mother Teresa suffered terribly in her life with doubt.

Mother Teresa wrote in her letters about years of feeling far away from God. She had doubts and felt distanced from God. She wrote, "Such deep longing for God and repulsed, empty, no faith, no love, no zeal." And, "I utter words of community prayers and try my utmost to get out of every word the sweetness, it has to give, but my prayer of union is not there for I no longer pray."

Best selling Christian author, Phillip Yancey said, "Doubt is something almost every person experiences at some point, yet something that the church does not always handle well. I am an advocate of doubt. I am also impressed with the evidences in the Bible of doubt." (End quote) Let's consider the story of Doubting Thomas we call him. When, even though he was walking on this earth with Jesus, he could not believe Jesus was really resurrected. He said, "Unless I see the mark of the nails in his hands, and put my finger in the mark of the nails and my hand in his side, I will not believe."

How did Jesus respond to such doubt? You would think he might be frustrated or angry with Thomas. But he simply said, "Put your finger here and see my hands. Reach out your hand and put it in my side. Do not doubt but believe." And we know what happened, the scripture reveals his believing again, when he said, My Lord and My God!" (John 20:26-28)

You might look at it this way. Thomas' doubt had a purpose, he wanted to know the truth. His doubt is evidence not of a lack of faith but of a desire to have faith. He was brave enough to be straight forward with Jesus and say, "Help me!" Jesus also cut us a little slack here didn't he? In the twenty-ninth verse, he told Thomas, "You struggle to believe and you have seen and touched my wounds. Blessed are those who have not seen and yet have come to believe." That's us! Jesus acknowledges it will not always be easy. That if Thomas had doubt, then surely we might!"

But what about when you doubt? What do we doubt? That God is God? That Jesus is Jesus? That we are saved? That we are a child of God? That we are doing the right things? That we are where God wants us to be in life? Maybe one or all of these things.

How does doubt feel? Let me use my sweet, wonderful husband of 33 years, as an example. I do not doubt that Paul loves me. I know with certainty that he is faithful and honest when he tells me he loves me more than anything on this earth. That I am his everything. All that mushy, love talk. I know that today-- this morning.
But last week, when we were out of sorts with one another and I thought he was short and snappy with me and he really just kind of ticked me off because he was being a knucklehead, I might not have been so sure about just how much he loved me. Well, if he really loved me why would he act like a knucklehead? Maybe for a few minutes, I doubted, if he really really loved me more than anything on earth. I thought for a short time, he loved himself more than me! Before I spoil our Sunday afternoon and rehash, our little grumbling time, we better move on.

Now what does this have to do with Jesus? Well, sometimes, we may be rocking along just fine and we are absolutely sure of Jesus' love for us and ours for him. We are counting on him daily and "walking and talking with him" just like the song says. Then, for some reason, we get out of sorts. We feel down a bit. Maybe discouraged. Maybe our spouse hurt our feelings. Maybe you are sick, in pain, hurting, struggling with loss, financial problems or depression.   At these times, we may start to question. Does God really love me? Does he even care? I think he's just forgotten me. I'm not sure he's really there?

Let me say, that sometimes, it is in our times of darkest despair we feel God closest to us. That's the beauty of his love, that when we are at our lowest, he is carrying us along. But sometimes, before we get to that point where our despair brings us close to his face; we doubt.

Have you ever cried out in despair? Have you ever doubted that Jesus was there for you? I have. I still do sometimes. I doubt myself. I doubt I am doing God's will. I doubt he really cares for me. I just sometimes struggle. It helps me to know others like Thomas, Mother Teresa and Phillip Yancey struggled too. But for just a minute let's look at what we can do when we struggle like this. How can we overcome our fear and doubt?
One Sunday when I was traveling to church thinking about just what I believed, my pastor, Pat Driskell, preached, "How do I know the things we believe about Jesus are true? What evidence do I have Jesus was any of what we believe? Can we prove it? Can we like Thomas, touch his wounds? No, we can't. But we make a choice. We make a conscious choice to say we believe. We believe in spite of what we cannot believe. We just decide, I will believe--even though I don't understand, I shall believe. That's what we call faith. It is a choice and we choose to say yes."

When we experienced salvation, we simply said, "I believe." We confessed, most of us in public, and accepted Jesus as our Savior. We state that we believe he died for our sins and was resurrected from the dead to reign as Lord. We choose to believe and accept this.

So one thing we can do to overcome doubt, is to reaffirm in our hearts our belief and even if in bad times, we may feel distant from this experience, we still claim Jesus as our

Savior and hold on to him. How can we do this? Stay in church, read our Bibles, talk about our doubt with someone whose faith you respect. And focus on your faith and the wonder of it, not the doubt.

Again, think about your relationship with a spouse, brother, sister or parent. What you think about them influences what you think about them. Get That? What you think about them influences what you think about them. For example, I can wake up every morning and look at that sweet man and I can say, "You know he really irritates me. He snores sometimes, he thinks about himself a lot, he looks pretty old, doesn't have any money to speak of, etc etc." OR I can wake up every day and think, "I am the luckiest woman in the world. Paul is so sweet, considerate, kind and full of love for me and everyone around him. Thank you God for such a blessing!"

What we think about Christ in our lives, will become what we think about Christ in our lives. We can influence whatever happens in our lives just by our attitude.

A second thing is to express our belief out loud. Just say it-in word and deed. Even if the world is falling down around us, we can just proclaim it. And proclaim it to others as well. Someone once said, we may not *know* we are Christian at all times, BUT we can *show* we are. What did Mother Teresa do during her despair? Did she stop her work? Did she say I can't help these people because I have doubt that God really loves me or knows me? NO, she kept saying it by her actions. She proclaimed it by her deeds.

As a matter of fact, one of the ways we see Jesus and know he is alive in this world is through what others show us. We cannot be Thomas and touch his side. But we can see his love at work. I see him all the time in my church. There are giants of the faith like Jane and Linda and many others. Even when I'm down, I can see by how they love that Jesus is alive and well.

During my struggles, I tried to practice these two things myself. Choose to believe and proclaim that belief to myself and others.

Then last week I was on my way to church thinking once again that surely if there was a God, the world could not be in the mess it is in. If people of faith were in this at all, there could not be millions of hungry children while many of us are overfed. There could not be places in the world where dysentery and malaria kill so many when they were so easy to eradicate. I hit the steering wheel and said, "How can all this religion stuff be real? *How can this be real and have so little result*."

Again, the pastor just that Sunday, preached about the parable of the man who invited guests to his home and they did not come. He did not give up, he invited some more. And when those were not enough, he sent folks back out to invite some more! He did not give up. Do not give up the pastor implored. Whatever you are facing, do not give up. Perhaps I shall not give up.

I shall choose to believe , I shall proclaim Christ over and over and I will not give up. Yes, sometimes when I am angry and hurt at my family, friends or even the church, I may doubt but I will still keep the love of Christ in my heart.

The scripture from Isaiah we read at the beginning of the message speaks to me about this. "Surely God is my salvation; I will trust, and will not be afraid, for the Lord God is my strength and my might; he has become my salvation." Surely God is my salvation.

I love music. One of the ways I sooth and quiet my troubled soul sometimes is with music. My favorite hymn is, "The Solid Rock." The words tell us what we need to know about overcoming doubt, "My hope is built on nothing less than Jesus blood and righteousness. I dare not trust the sweetest frame but wholly lean on Jesus name." My favorite verse-"When darkness veils his lovely face, I rest on his unchanging grace. In every high and stormy gale, my anchor holds within the veil." And the chorus-"On Christ the solid rock I stand, all other ground is sinking sand-all other ground is sinking sand."
I guess it comes back to another thing my pastor said one time. I asked him how to preach about things I didn't know about? He said, "Preach what you know." I know my hope is built on Jesus' name. No matter how weak and limp my faith, I choose to lean on Jesus and build my hope on him.

And my earnest prayer? When you have doubts, fears and uncertainties, may you make a choice to build your hope on Jesus.

Let us pray: Dear merciful, forgiving God, please forgive our unbelief. Please help us to have stronger faith. Help us to feel your presence in our hearts and show it to the world in our love. Amen.

Hunger Pangs[10]

Lisa Peterson

(Psalm 63: 1-5)

My friend, Ms. Nell, who is well into her 80s and has threatened to shoot me for telling it, has shared many stories of growing up as a Southern child of the Great Depression. As lean and drastic as those years were for most families, Ms. Nell's were made even harder by the death of her mother when Ms. Nell was only six or seven years old. Being the youngest, Ms. Nell's older brothers and sisters were already out of the house and starting families of their own by that time: which left Nell, her sister Sara, who was just a few years older than she was, and her father alone to grieve.

"But then daddy went plumb crazy with grief," says Ms. Nell. "And he just up and ran off."

Which left the care of Ms. Nell and Sara to their older siblings. But times were beyond tough. Their older sisters and brothers could barely feed themselves and their growing families. At first, they tried to shuffle the little sisters between their homes, but even on that temporary basis, none of them could manage the extra expense of two more mouths to feed. So finally, Nell's favorite brother found a little shack for the girls to live in:

"Lord, it was way out in the sticks," Ms. Nell always remembers. "I don't think nobody could have found us if they tried."

But it was still close enough to the town where her brother had found work, so that once a month when he got paid, he could buy the sisters a bag of groceries and go out to

---

[10]Sermon preached at the "Taste and See Women's Spirituality Conference" July 2010, Dyersburg, Tennessee.

check on them. For the rest of the time, those two little girls, now around eight and eleven years old, were left on their own. But, by the grace of God, they survived together.

Ms. Nell tells of how she and Sara chopped wood to stay warm. How they hauled water from over a mile away, and how scared she was when Sara made her go alone. How the girls rarely had a chance to go to school because the only school still open was too far to walk-even if they had had enough clothes to keep them warm during the bitter cold of winter. Still, they weren't ungrateful or even angry for what life did or didn't hand them. Not even for the snow that blew into the shack through the cracks in the walls.
Because as Ms. Nell remembers, one winter when the food ran out earlier than it was supposed to, she and Sara gathered it up, shaped it into balls, and sprinkled them with salt and pepper for their meals.

But salt and pepper snowballs can only carry an empty, aching belly so far. And after a few days, Ms. Nell was so hungry that all she could do was cry. She cried, and she cried, and she cried until finally, Sara promised that if Nell would just stop crying, even for a little while, somehow, someway, Sara would do her best to find them something to eat....And that promise worked (at least temporarily), because soon the tears had dried, and Sara and Nell were on their way out the door: faces washed, hair brushed, hearts set on finding a way to satisfy the gnawing, gut-wrenching, ever-increasing pangs of real, bodily hunger.

The girls walked for a long way that day before they saw any signs of life. Eventually though, they saw a wisp of smoke rising from a chimney and made their way to an old cabin:

"And then, Sara grabbed me by the hand, raised her head high like she was the Queen of England and marched us up on that porch," Ms. Nell always recalls with a laugh. "The next thing I knew, she was knocking hard on that door, and I was so scared, I jumped back behind her, hid my face in her skirt, and began crying all over again..."

But in the midst of her tears, first the wood door opened, and then the screen door, and those two little orphaned girls found themselves looking up into a kind, brown face.

"Can I help y'all?" the woman in the doorway asked softly.

And even though she was scared to death, Nell has always remembered her big sister's answer:

"Um, ma'am, yes ma'am. Um…I'm here cause of my little sister. She's awfully hungry ma'am. We haven't had anything to eat for days…but I'm not hungry ma'am. Not at all. But my little sister, she is. She's so hungry she won't stop crying and…"

And before she could finish, the kind-faced woman was inviting them into her home.

"Oh, no ma'am," said Sara. "We don't want to be a bother."

"Well then," said the woman. "Y'all just wait right here." And she closed the door.

But soon it was opening again, and the woman was handing those two starving girls a flour sack filled with home-made biscuits, smoked ham and bacon.

"I declare, I think it was the most food I had ever seen in my life," exclaims Ms. Nell, even after all these years. "And before we left, she made us promise that if we were ever hungry again, we would come right back, anytime…We never did. But believe you me, we could have…We sure could have….You know that night, we nearly made ourselves sick with all that food."…

"But oh Lisa," Ms. Nell said, throwing up her hands, "It is the worst thing in the world to be that hungry. I don't ever want to be that hungry again!"

I will praise you as long as I live, and in your name I will lift up my hands, declares the psalmist. My soul will be satisfied with the richest of foods; with singing lips, my mouth will praise you.

Whenever I read those words, I can't help but think of Ms. Nell and her savior, Sara. Seeing those now aging eyes light up like a little girl again as she anticipates that first taste of ham biscuit after so much hunger. Listening as she describes that day so long ago as one of the holiest in her life-the day she was given life and hope that life would go on. Feeling the joy that radiates from her as she describes what it was like when she realized that the aching emptiness inside her was about to be filled with the most precious of gifts.

"Oh Lisa, it's the worst thing in the world to be that hungry."

Ms. Nell never fails to remind me of that painful truth in many of the stories from her childhood. And I know that first and foremost, she's remembering the physical hunger she endured. But deeper even than the physical pain, I know Ms. Nell is also recalling the tremendous spiritual and emotional hunger that came from being a little girl lost, abandoned in an unfriendly world in which she was powerless.

I also know that I, who have two refrigerators in my house, a freezer in my garage, and a few pounds more on my person than I need, will probably never be able to say that I know what it's like in any way, shape or form to be physically hungry. Although I am also aware that some of you here in this sanctuary this morning can. But even if we've never had to go without food until our bellies ached, there's probably not anyone here that doesn't know what it feels like to be spiritually and emotionally hungry in this life:

To wake up, maybe even in the wee hours of the morning, with a gnawing deep within that not even the heartiest breakfast will satisfy.

To go through days and weeks, months, maybe even years, aching with an emptiness inside that cries out to be filled.

And to spend large amounts of time, perhaps even large amounts of money, grabbing at all sorts of things that the world says will most certainly fill us up. …

That's why I personally have struggled with weight gain all my life. Somewhere along the way, I let the world convince me that food, especially food made with lots of sugar and plenty of chocolate, could satisfy my hunger pangs. It's why others grab a VISA and go shopping, emptying out their bank accounts and filling up their houses with stuff. It's why other folks pick up a bottle and drink their way to bottom after bottom. And why still others volunteer, and volunteer, and volunteer until they're beyond exhausted, or jump from one romantic relationship to another, or one job to another, or are always looking for better and bigger houses, or cars, or vacations.

The truth is that deep down inside so many of us, there is this gnawing, gutwrenching emptiness, begging to be filled: And oh my friends, it is the worst thing in the world to be that kind of hungry The problem is, the world's solution is to keep piling our plates with food that isn't any more filling than Ms. Nell's salt and pepper snowballs.

But then, we're here this morning, at least in part, because we already know that. We've stepped away from our homes and our offices, our children, our churches, our crazy schedules, and our too long to-do lists, because we've already had more than a taste of the empty calories the world offers us, and we know we are not even close to being full. So we've washed our faces, brushed our hair, packed our suitcases, and made our way toward a place where we know we will find life and love and real nourishment that always satisfies.

Last night, we had a good-sized helping of the goodness of God. We truly beheld God's power and glory as we sang praises together. One or two of you were even lifting up your hands, while others were still standing quietly clinging to God's. It doesn't matter how we came. It just matters that we did. And today, we are being invited to taste and see even more of God's goodness and mercy and love.

So on God's behalf, I invite you to hold your heads up high; grab hold of a sister in the faith if you need to, and get moving. March right up on God's front porch today and knock on the door. There is no need to be afraid. Just tell God you're hungry. And then get ready for a feast…because there is no end to the delicacies She will surely put in your flour sack. Amen!

The Towel of Jesus[11]

Pam Phillips-Burk

(John 13:1-14, 34-35; 21:15-17)

It started out like a typical Passover - one like every other annual holy event. They weren't expecting anything unusual to happen. The elements were the same as always. The prayers - the same. The conversation, nothing out of the ordinary Passover conversation. Well - there was that parade coming into the city, which was a bit odd, but other than that nothing really usual or unexpected. That is until Jesus stood up from the Passover table, took off his outer garment and grabbed a towel. Now that was odd. He then took a bowl of water and knelt down and began to wash his disciples feet. THAT was certainly unusual. They had never experienced THAT element in the Passover liturgy. They were shocked; I imagine confused, or maybe curious as to what their teacher was up to. You see, in those days, the common footwear was sandals and the roads were dusty, so when a guest entered a home, the host would have his household slave wash his guests' feet. It was a lowly, menial task. So it was a shocking thing for Jesus to perform this task during the Passover meal.

Jesus went around the whole room where they were gathered, washing his disciples feet. When he came to Peter and knelt down, Peter protested. Surely, his Teacher would not wash his feet. But Jesus insisted on this act of servanthood. He insisted in order to model for them what it meant to be a leader. He was teaching by example that to be a follower of The Way - they would need to become a servant of all.

After he had finished this task of love he gave them a new commandment - "love one another." Jesus demonstrated that Love is an **ACTION** word. Love is more than an emotion or feeling. Love is action. And sometimes that action requires sacrifice. Humility. Patience. Hard work. Love one another, Jesus says.

---

[11]Presented on the occasion of the ordination of Rev. Nobuko Seki.

We know the rest of the story. Jesus was betrayed by one of his disciples. He was beaten and abused and put to death on a criminal's cross. He was buried in a cold tomb with the entrance sealed by a heavy stone rock. For everyone present that was the end. The Teacher and this new way of life were dead. But the good news is that God's story has no ending. On the third day, Jesus came back to life and the story continues.

In the 21st chapter of John's Gospel, we get a tiny glimpse of what Jesus did between his resurrection and his ascension. He was bumping into his followers all over the place. Popping into a crowded room, even though the door was bolted; meeting people on a road to Emmaus and having dinner with them. One of the very last things that he did was host an early morning breakfast on the beach for his disciples. Can't you just imagine that breakfast conversation with his friends gathered around the campfire? Whatever the topic, Jesus wanted to have a little chat with Peter; a conversation about what it meant to be a servant leader. "Do you love me Peter? Do you really love me?" Evidently Peter was dismayed with Jesus' persistent questioning about his commitment. "You know everything about me, Lord. You KNOW I love you. "Do you really love me, Peter? Then FEED my lambs. Peter, TEND my sheep. FEED my sheep, Peter. Remember what I did at the Passover? Remember, Peter? Put on my towel of servanthood and love those whom I place in your care. Remember Peter, that **Love** is an action word."

This whole model of servanthood was very important to Jesus and he wanted his disciples to follow the example. In Mark 10:45, he says as much - "For even the Son of Man did not come to be served but to serve, and to give his life a ransom for many." And later in the great hymn of the church found in Philippians 2:6-7: [Jesus] *who, though he was in the form of God, did not regard equality with God as something to be exploited, but emptied himself, taking on the form of a slave,"* a servant. This is the type of leadership that Jesus desires for his ministers to model - servant leadership; pastoral leaders that will wear the towel of Jesus with grace and humility. As ministers we do not exploit our position or our role. As ministers of Word and sacrament, we are called to stoop down and wash the feet of the lambs and the sheep that the Servant Leader places in our care.

The towel of Jesus - that is what we are here to celebrate today; the towel of servanthood. During this service of ordination for Nobuko Seki, Japan Presbytery will confirm God's call on her life to the Ministry of Word and Sacrament. It has been a long and difficult process to arrive at this place today for Nobuko and Presbytery. There have been many, many conversations and meetings of discernment and prayer; countless seminary classes; hundreds of papers and tests and books; more conversations; more discernment. There have been internships and assessments. There have been questions, maybe doubts, some fear perhaps. And now the journey continues with her ordination; with Nobuko wrapping the towel of Jesus around her neck in the form of a pastoral stole. That is what the stole represents - the towel of Jesus, the towel of servanthood.

I've seen evidence within Nobuko of a servant's heart. And you have as well. Many of you have been blessed and nurtured by her servant heart. She is a dedicated Christian, an extremely hard-worker. I have been amazed during these years of study and preparation at her focus and stamina. She has been able to gracefully juggle many, many responsibilities with grace and humor. Whenever she and I have talked these past few years about her studies and her work, it has always been positive and uplifting. She has never been satisfied with "just getting by." She has always completed her tasks with great care and detail, always going the "extra mile." Nobuko has embraced every opportunity given her to model a servant heart, a servant's lifestyle. Japan Presbytery has been, and will continue to be, blessed by her servanthood.

As a Cumberland Presbyterian Minister of Word and Sacrament, Nobuko will be called upon to TEND and FEED the people that God will place in her care. She will feed them God's Word as she preaches and teaches and counsels. She will invite them to the feast of Holy Communion, the meal in which she will break the bread of life and lift up the cup of salvation, and offer this feast to the lambs of God. She will put on the towel of Jesus as she helps to initiate new believers into the household of faith through Christian baptism. She will wrap the towel of Jesus around her neck every time that she counsels one who is struggling or hurting. She will put on the towel of Jesus whenever she walks into a hospital room or a nursing home. She will wear the towel of servanthood as she helps to lead folks into acts of love and compassion in a broken and hurting world. At first, that towel might feel a bit strange or uncomfortable. There is no other Cumberland Presbyterian clergy woman in Japan Presbytery for her to talk with or confide in. She is the first. Certainly she will have her sisters across the seas available through technology, but more importantly through prayers. Eventually, though, that towel around her neck will begin to feel familiar.

While she will always be "the First," she will also be known to you and to others, as Pastor Seki, Nobuko sensei.

I think it is providential that Nobuko is being ordained THIS year, this year when we are celebrating the 125th Ordination Anniversary of another "first" within the Cumberland Presbyterian Church. The Rev. Louisa Woosley was ordained as the first CP clergy woman in 1889. There were struggles, doubts, challenges, questions, and even major disagreements with the church regarding Louisa's call to put on the towel of Jesus. Why couldn't she just be a missionary - or an educator? Those were the roles that women were filling during those days. Why couldn't she just stay home and take care of her husband and children? Why? Because God's call in Louisa's life was so strong and clear she could do nothing else. So she persevered, as did Nolin Presbytery. And the kingdom of God has been richly blessed and enlarged by their determination and dedication. It has been noted that Louisa preached over 6,000 sermons, and that well over 7,000 people came to the saving knowledge of Jesus Christ. Rev. Woosley truly wore the towel of Jesus throughout her ministry. And I suspect that neither she nor Nolin Presbytery had any clue what God had in store for her and the Kingdom. And neither do you, Nobuko and Japan Presbytery. All you know is that you are remaining faithful to listening and discerning God's call. You've taken this first HUGE step in ordination - and now the real journey begins.

So, Nobuko- take the towel of Jesus and wrap it snugly around your neck as you go about doing the work that God is calling you to do. I look forward to seeing what God has in store you, for Japan Presbytery, and for the lambs and sheep that you will tend in the years to come. I look forward to the amazing things that will happen in the Kingdom of God because of you now wear the towel of Jesus. Amen.

NOTE: There is a theory that the pastoral stole originated from a type of liturgical napkin called the orarium. It is often linked to the napkin, or towel, used by Jesus in washing the feet of his disciples. Therefore, the pastoral stole can be viewed a the towel of Jesus, the towel of servanthood.

Gone Fishing[12]

Patricia J. Pickett

(John 21:1-14)

Evangelization?

The thought of this enormous challenge scared me to death. Driving home from Presbytery my head hurt. It was announced at Presbytery that every minister was to do his/her part. How could I be part of this huge movement within our denomination considering my ministry was to persons who are diagnosed with intellectual disabilities? What kind of report could I possibly give to Presbytery? As a chaplain at a state institution I was a different kind of pastor, yet, I was expected to be part of this evangelization effort. I wasn't even sure I could define evangelization.

As I drove the rolling hills of Highway 12, a family story popped into my head. My parents had invited another family for Sunday dinner. When the father of the other family was invited to say grace before meals, I looked up and when he was finished, I soundly embarrassed my parents by asking if they were Catholic. The mother of the other family said, "No, darling, we're Lutheran, why do you ask?" "You didn't say the right prayer," I said. The adults looked at one another and I continued, "If you want to go to heaven you have to be Catholic," I said matter of factly and went about eating my drumstick. Those were my first attempts at evangelism and I don't even remember the event.

It was many years later that I bumped up against the story we find after Easter in the Lectionary. It tells about the apostles fishing all night only to come up with empty nets. Jesus tells them to cast their nets to the opposite side. John does not record the conversation, but other gospel writers describe the back and forth between Jesus and the doubters. After all, when did they see Jesus fish? They were the fishers. They were the

---

[12]I preached this sermon at Presbytery. I also made clay fish pins that I gave to everyone.

ones who made their livelihood through understanding the sea. In the end, they gave in. What a surprise! The nets were full to breaking.

What is more striking to me than the large haul of fish is Jesus NEVER said to throw any fish back into the sea! I'd like to repeat that if for nothing more than just myself:

Jesus never said to throw any fish back.

Throwing out nets gets more diversity than a rod and reel. You get all kinds.

When Jesus fed thousands, what did Jesus say after all had eaten?

Gather up the leftovers!!!

It seems like Jesus is into conservation of the human kind for the fish and even the bread are often considered metaphors for human beings. The fish obviously become the object of our evangelization. The baskets of bread leftover from the sermon in the plain can refer to the marginalized that also need to be gathered up.

Think for a moment…do we have leftovers? What is a leftover? Why aren't our churches filled to the brim with a diverse catch? Why do we look out and see mostly over 50 year olds? If our hairdressers don't tell, we all know that gray and/or white is the real color of our hair. Now, let's take all of us over 50 and graying, or already white…shouldn't there be a lot of wisdom here? We're not just newly born. We've lived lives with all kinds of experiences. It shouldn't take a committee to solve this…we all should come to the table bursting with ideas…alive because we have experienced abundant life. Isn't that the way it should be? Or could be?

For starters, I'm going to tell you what I've been thinking. We throw out those nets and we become the fishers we were commanded to become. Jesus didn't tell us to throw any fish back into the sea. Jesus simply said, "GO FISH!" So, if we happen to get some fish in our nets that we've never seen before, what do we do?

We get to know them. Then we love them.

And you say, "But, what if we pull in an Arab, a homosexual, a mentally ill person, a mentally retarded person, a homeless person, a poor person, a person of color?

We tell the good news…and if it is THE GOOD NEWS…REALLY the GOOD news…the same Good news that Jesus came to tell, people will believe us. People will believe us when we feed the hungry, clothe the naked, visit the imprisoned,

What I've learned at CBDC is that preaching is through action. My people can't talk. My people can't read. My people don't give any money to build buildings. My people only understand actions. How do I love them? I love them by anticipating their needs. I love them by putting my arm around someone who let a tear slip out of her eye but can't tell anyone that her wheelchair is uncomfortable. I love them by spending extra time watching someone brush their teeth when I really want to go home. But that person just learned to brush his teeth that day. So, I stay. I love them by laughing with them and crying with them. Some of you may say, "Well, I don't even know any persons with disabilities like that. I respond, "It doesn't matter. We all are disabled in one way or other. We love people, plain and simple because that is what evangelism is really all about.

Did Jesus ask the gentile woman if she was a Jew before he healed her? Did Jesus ask the Centurion if he believed in Yahweh before he raised his son?

Our goal is to evangelize through love. Why? Because EVERY ONE… EVERY ONE was created in God's image. That means black and brown and yellow and red and white and all the different cultures that color all the world views. EVERY SINGLE ONE. Just being tolerant is not enough and sometimes tolerance comes across as arrogant. Falling in love is a God-thing. In order to PROCLAIM the Good news…not our good news, but the good news that Jesus proclaimed we MUST take tolerance to a new level. We don't throw any of the fish back. We take care of leftovers. We love all the "fish" into the Good News. Evangelism then, is nothing more than going fishing and our fishing license has no limit.

Padre Perdónalos
Father Forgive Them

Zenobia Rivera

(Lucas 23:34)

Ya que estamos en este lugar, vayamos al calvario para aprender como fuimos perdonados y por favor quedémonos allí para aprender como tenemos que perdonar.

Allí muy junto al calvario vemos en primer lugar lo que es el pecado, su crueldad, y alcance que incluye la intención de matar manifestado en el asesinato del Señor del amor.

Veamos algunas de las cosas que Jesús el Rey de reyes tuvo que soportar:

- El acto culminante de matar dentro de la malicia humana. Le vemos soportando la mayor vergüenza y pena de muerte de su tiempo histórico y sin embargo solo nos hace un llamado urgente a sentir lo mismo que él… una misericordia profunda por quien nos hace daño, no buscando nuestro propio provecho sino el de los demás y esto solo se logra manteniendo nuestra mirada fija en Jesucristo. filipenses 2:1-11 y hebreos 12:2.
- El extremo del sufrimiento personal. En medio del físico dolor de tortura y muerte, aún cuando había un grito de dolor real, también había un canto de alabanza por encontrarse haciendo la voluntad del Padre. salmo 22:1-18.

Allí junto al calvario estando en agonía de muerte, el amor trajo un encuentro entre el cielo y la tierra para todos aquellos a quienes ama. Vemos a Jesús orando e intercediendo por sus indignos asesinos en el acto mismo de su crimen. Pide perdón pleno e inmediato por ninguna otra razón más que por su ignorancia. Solo la gracia y el amor podían sugerir y aceptar la condición humana. La humanidad puede pecar tanto que muchas veces ni se percata de lo que hace por su propia ignorancia.

Jesús nos ensena desde la cruz:

- A perdonar las mayores injurias para que usted y yo no tengamos excusas, porque solo el perdón abre las puertas del cielo para toda bendición. Marcos 11:25.
- Nos enseña a orar por los demás aún los enemigos hasta el último aliento de nuestras vidas, con el mismo amor con el cual Jesús dijo padre perdónalos porque no saben lo hacen. Lucas 23:34 y hechos 7:59-60.

Había algo en este ruego que me confundía al principio y me hacía preguntar con reverencia ¿En qué sentido Cristo se refería a la ignorancia? Pues sin duda la ignorancia estaba manifestada en contra del clamor del evangelio de las buenas nuevas. La ignorancia en cuanto a la falta de conocimiento y en cuanto a la intencionalidad de no querer saber por miedo u otra razón no nos da ningún derecho a violentar y atacar lo que es desconocido y menos lo que venía de Dios que no era comprensible para muchos. En Colombia decimos "La ignorancia es atrevida" porque puede conducirnos a conclusiones equivocadas sobre Dios, el perdón, la salvación y el bienestar.

La ignorancia de los enemigos de Cristo y su intencionalidad en cuanto a rechazar el significado de la venida del Mesías no les quito el privilegio de que aun estando en rebeldía seguir podían si querían estar dentro del terreno de la misericordia donde el perdón era una posibilidad que la misma cruz estaba supliendo a través de la muerte de Cristo. Quizás es verdad que muchos seres humanos no saben lo que hacen cuando rechazan a Cristo; pero aún así Cristo les sigue amando y rogando por perdón en medio de su ignorancia.

Mientras haya vida siempre habrá para los pecadores de la raza humana un evangelio de perdón en las dos direcciones para con Dios y para con el prójimo.. No les parece algo sublime que aquellos que por ignorancia, terquedad o simplicidad persiguieron al maestro, en vez de recibir juicio, solo pudieron arrancar del corazón de Jesús un clamor de intercesión y perdón. Aún cuando los humanos no podemos saber plenamente todo y tenemos muchas veces una ignorancia injustificada, Dios nos sigue ofreciendo y permitiendo que podamos ser perdonados. Es por este clamor de "Padre perdónales porque no saben lo que hacen" que miles y millones de personas fueron y seguirán siendo transformadas por la muerte y resurrección de Cristo. Hoy tú puedes preguntar ¿Qué pecado hay en mí que mi Señor que tú no puedas perdonar? Y ¿Qué ha hecho mi hermano o mi prójimo contra mí que yo no pueda perdonar?

¿Hay en tu corazón heridas hoy? Déjalas junto al calvario. Te aseguro que hoy mismo Dios te hará entender sobre cómo funciona su justicia y tu herida será sanada. Ahora bien, si ere alguien que se ha sentido perdonad, sanado y amado, recuerda perdonar. Solo el perdón puede sanar el alma; pero si aun después de saber del mensaje de Jesús desde la cruz y no te puedes perdonar a ti mismo o no puedes perdonar el pasado de un ser querido, fija de nuevo tu mirada en Jesús en la cruz del calvario y si crees que tu sufrimiento es mayor reclámale; pero si ves que no es así, simplemente perdona de la misma manera que Jesús exclamo Padre perdónalos porque no saben lo que hacen. lucas 23:34.

Oremos hoy junto a la cruz del calvario. Por favor no carguemos más con esos pecados de resentimiento y amargura que lo único que pueden hacer es hacernos perder las bendiciones y hacer que nuestras oraciones no tengan respuesta. Mi deseo es que hoy sea un día especial para quedar en paz con Dios, con nosotros mismos y con nuestro prójimo a través del perdón.

Love—the Most Excellent Way

Linda Rodden

(1 Corinthians 13:1-13)

In the movie, "The Preacher's Wife," a pastor becomes overwhelmed with the demands of ministry, and enters into conflict with all those around him. In frustration, he prays, "Oh God, help me!" In response, God answers his prayer by sending an angel to help him sort out his priorities. You see, the pastor was so busy doing ministry that he lost his ability to love. He forgot how to love his wife, his son, the people of his church, and a troubled youth. In his busyness, he forgot the most important element of ministry—to love others; and as result, he lost the joy of ministry as well. We find Paul prior to today's text teaching the Corinthian Church about spiritual gifts. You see, Paul was responding to a conflict that had developed in the church. As Paul is teaching, he pauses in the middle of his lesson to speak about love, as well as reminding us of other fruits of the Spirit. Why, did Paul feel a need to do this? Well, what better time than a conflict to remind brothers and sisters in Christ about the love of God. What was the problem that the church was dealing with anyway? It seems that some in the church felt that their spiritual gifts were more important than others. Does this sound familiar? You see, pride can sometimes get the best of us! Paul responds to this challenge by stating in verse one, that you may speak like an angel; but without love as your motivator, you are a resounding gong, or a clanging symbol.

The pastor in the movie had lost his focus. Ministry became a burden for him, because he allowed the busyness of doing ministry to dominate his life. His pride of wanting things to be perfect caused him to lose touch with the very people that he was serving. Why, because he forgot the most excellent way. What motivates our ministry? Are we motivated by love or pride? Have you ever suffered with pride? No, I am sure none of you have. However, some ministers that I have been privileged to hear are very gifted speakers and deliver their message in a more eloquent way than I could ever hope to do. Some deliver messages that can be very inspiring and persuasive. Some are highly respected for their homiletic skills. As I watch them interact with their people, though, I think they could use some lessons about how to love people. The Apostle Paul says, if we have not the love of Christ in our hearts for our listeners, we are ineffective.

Paul goes on to tell us that others may have the gift of prophecy and can fathom all mysteries and all knowledge. Education is needed and helpful, but sometimes we Christians, whether ordained or lay ministers, can get so puffed up about our knowledge and accomplishments that we seem to ignore the truths of the Bible. Some tend to think that they are smarter than God. They seem to preach their gospel rather than the Gospel of Christ. Pride has a tendency to sometimes make us think we are God rather than a servant of God. I have had some Christian ministers tell me they do not believe that Jesus was born of a virgin, they try to explain away his miracles and even have gone as far as to say they do not believe Jesus was resurrected. Do we believe that the Bible is the inspired Word of God? Are we limiting God's power? In my Bible, it states that with God, all things are possible! Yes, I know men wrote the Bible and the Church placed it together, but do we not believe that God's hand was directing all those events? I do not understand how people can call themselves Christians, let alone a minister of Jesus Christ, and not believe in the resurrection! Is not the resurrection of Christ the hope that the Christian Faith is founded upon? Because of God's great love, He sent His Son into the world to be the sacrifice for our sins and to overcome death and the grave. The Gospel of John tells us, "Greater love has no one than this, that he lay down his life for his friends". But Jesus did not just lay down his life for his friends, but his enemies too. Yes, because Jesus loved his enemies, we too must love those who are unlovely and in doing so, teach them of the love of Christic. Sometimes, actions speak louder than words.

There is a story of a pastor who decided to use the drive-thru at the local fast-food restaurant. After ordering, and moving forward, the pastor began his wait for his food. After some time, he noticed that the car in front of him was not moving although he had already received his food. The pastor waited, but as more time passed by, he became more angry and more impatient because after all he was in hurry to get to a session meeting. Finally, the pastor could not take it any longer, sticking his head out the window he yelled at the driver angrily, "Hey pal, can't you get that heap to go?" When the man turned around, the pastor's face turned red when he realized that the driver was a member of his congregation!

If we lose our focus of the most excellent way, the church and our world suffers. Our focus needs to be doing what is best to share the good news of Jesus Christ. We must share the good news with our world, because Jesus did not stay in the grave. Because Christ was resurrected, those that confess their sin and place their faith in Him, can look forward to resurrection as well. How can we be effective witnesses of the love of Christ if we doubt the truths of His Word and do not demonstrate his love toward others? If we Christians do not believe and do not demonstrate the love of Christ with each other, how can we expect the world to believe what we preach? In John 13:35 we are told, "they will know we are his disciples by our love". We must see others through the loving eyes of Christ in order for anything eternal to be accomplished. Everything else is merely a resounding gong or a clanging cymbal.

But then Paul tells us in these same verses that we may have the faith to move mountains, we may give all our possessions to the poor and even surrender our bodies to the flames; but if we have not love, we gain nothing. In Hebrews 11 it tells us, "Without faith, it is impossible to please God". Paul emphasizes in this passage that we may be among the most faithful to God; but if we do not love others, God can not effectively use us to build up his kingdom. You know, I had an instructor in Clinic al Pastoral Education at St. John's by the name of Sister Carol Atchity. Her nickname was "Buzzsaw". I learned many lessons from Sr. Carol. Some of them were painful lessons. I think the most important lesson, however, was that when dealing with people we must be present and genuine with those whom we minister to. You see, people can read us like a book. We cannot pretend to love people. They know if we are being genuine or not. We can go through the motions of preaching, teaching, and encouraging. We can shake hands and smile, but if we are not genuine in our love for others, they will sense that. If they sense we do not love or care about them, we can forget about impacting their lives for Christ. We must genuinely love those we serve. If we do not love them, then we need to get down on our knees and ask God to show us how to love them.

Well, Paul decides in verse four to address the characteristics of love. Paul states, "love is patient, love is kind, love does not envy, or boast. Love is not proud, rude, or self-seeking. It is not easily angered, and it keeps no record of wrongs. Love does not delight in evil, but rejoices with the truth. Love always protects, always trusts, always hopes, and always perseveres." If these characteristics describe the love that we should display in our lives and in our churches, then why do we as Christians talk and gossip behind our brothers and sisters' backs? Why are we rude to one another and worse yet to unbelievers? Why are we angry with one another? Why do we keep a record of wrongs? Why do we seek our own way? Why? Could it be that we are not loving one another as Christ loves us? What are we telling the world by the way we treat each other? Does our lives reflect God's love? You know, people were drawn to the early church, because of the way they cared for one another. They shared everything. They shared their faith wherever opportunity afforded itself. They shared their possessions, so no one would be deprived. They ate together. Now that is one tradition that we seem to still do well today! We must learn to love and forgive as God has loved and forgiven us so many times. Do we love those in our church, in our Presbytery, in our Denomination?

The American Baptist, Harry Emerson Fosdick, shares this story of Abraham Lincoln. He shares that no one treated President Abraham Lincoln with more contempt than his Secretary for War, Edwin Stanton. He called the President, "a low cunning clown," and nicknamed him, "the original gorilla". When President Lincoln heard these words, he said nothing. In fact, he made Stanton his war minister, because he was the best man for the job and continued to treat him with every courtesy. The years wore on. The night came when the assassin's bullet murdered Lincoln in the theater. In the little room where Lincoln's body was taken-there stood Stanton looking down on President Lincoln's silent face. Those standing close by heard Stanton share these words, "There lies the greatest ruler of men the world has ever seen". You see, the patience of love had conquered Stanton's heart in the end!

Paul shares in verse three that, "Love never fails". Do we want a successful ministry? Then we must love the Lord our God with all our heart, our soul and our mind and love those he has entrusted into our care.

Paul's following thoughts remind us how temporary our lives and gifts are and how eternal love is. Paul continues by saying, "where there are prophecies, they will cease; where there are tongues, they will be stilled, where there is knowledge, it will pass away". Paul continues, "That now we only know in part and we can only prophecy in part." For the best is yet to come! Paul tells us that when perfection comes, meaning our Lord Jesus Christ, imperfection will disappear. Thank God! When Jesus comes again, we won't even

263

be using our gifts anymore. We are going to be caught up with Him and forever be with Him. Then and only then will we know Him fully! So, Paul stresses that we are not to be childish! We don't have much time! We do not need to be wasting precious time arguing over whose gift is more important, or what is the best music to use, what carpet works best, or this or that or something else in the church. Yes, gifts must be discovered if they are to be used in the Body of Christ for the church to function in the way it is intended to. Music and carpet decisions have to be made. However, we should not allow these things to divide and cause us to lose our focus. The church's first and foremost focus should be on our mission to make disciples and share the Gospel of Jesus Christ with those who do not know Him as Lord and Savior! We must all work together to the glory of God, not ourselves. We will not always agree, true; but, we do need to remember to love and respect each other in our disagreements. You say, but they hurt me! Yes, Christ did not say it would be easy. I am sure it was not easy for him to love those who spat on him, cursed him, beat him and crucified him. And yet, he prayed, "Father forgive them for they know not what they do." Are we loving and encouraging the Body of Christ to love God and each other? Leaders of the church are responsible to teach the love of Christ, not only in words but in actions as well. We are to encourage and equip others to serve and demonstrate the love of Christ in their lives for the purpose of building up the church. If we love those we serve, we will encourage them to grow in their faith and to love as Christ loves.

Paul summarizes by sharing that these three remain-Faith, Hope and Love. He ends with emphasizing, once again, the greatness of love. Only through faith in Jesus can we learn to love God with all our being and to love each other as God so loved us. So, I challenge you, my brothers and sisters in Christ, to go, serve and love others in Jesus' name. Amen

In the Garden

Missy Rose

(John 20:1-18)

Early on the first day of the week, while it was still dark, Mary Magdalene came to the tomb and saw that the stone had been removed from the tomb. So she ran and went to Simon Peter and the other disciple, the one whom Jesus loved, and said to them, "They have taken the Lord out of the tomb, and we do not know where they have laid him." Then Peter and the other disciple set out and went toward the tomb. The two were running together, but the other disciple outran Peter and reached the tomb first. He bent down to look in and saw the linen wrappings lying there, but he did not go in. Then Simon Peter came, following him, and went into the tomb. He saw the linen wrappings lying there, and the cloth that had been on Jesus' head, not lying with the linen wrappings but rolled up in a place by itself. Then the other disciple, who reached the tomb first, also went in, and he saw and believed; for as yet they did not understand the scripture, that he must rise from the dead. Then the disciples returned to their homes.

But Mary stood weeping outside the tomb. As she wept, she bent over to look into the tomb; and she saw two angels in white, sitting where the body of Jesus had been lying, one at the head and the other at the feet. They said to her, "Woman, why are you weeping?" She said to them, "They have taken away my Lord, and I do not know where they have laid him." When she had said this, she turned around and saw Jesus standing there, but she did not know that it was Jesus. Jesus said to her, "Woman, why are you weeping? Whom are you looking for?" Supposing him to be the gardener, she said to him, "Sir, if you have carried him away, tell me where you have laid him, and I will take him away." Jesus said to her, "Mary!" She turned and said to him in Hebrew, "Rabbouni!" (which means Teacher). Jesus said to her, "Do not hold on to me, because I have not yet ascended to the Father. But go to my brothers and say to them, 'I am ascending to my Father and your Father, to my God and your God.'" Mary Magdalene went and announced to the disciples, "I have seen the Lord"; and she told them that he had said these things to her. (John 20:1-18)

When I was a child, my family had a huge garden. It was ridiculously big. I mean, what family of four needs an entire acre to plant their garden? We had so much yellow crookneck squash that we were filling a wheelbarrow a day with the stuff. We froze it and put it up till our freezer couldn't take anymore. Then we fed it to the pigs till they wouldn't come to the fence anymore. Our neighbors began to avoid making eye contact lest they be forced to accept another bag of yellow crookneck squash. We had a problem with over-abundance. (And I won't even get into our cucumber problem).

Gardens are fascinating entities. When I began to consider today's scripture I was drawn to the fact that Mary had mistaken Jesus for the *gardener*. It's fascinating to me that the tomb from which Jesus was resurrected was in a garden. It reminds us of another garden in scripture.

And the Lord God planted a garden in Eden, in the east; and there he put the man whom he had formed. Out of the ground the Lord God made to grow every tree that is pleasant to the sight and good for food, the tree of life also in the midst of the garden, and the tree of the knowledge of good and evil. (Genesis 2:8-9)

In the creation account we learn that humanity was put into a garden full of all that was needed to sustain life. Creation was in perfect balance. The tree of life and tree of the knowledge of good and evil coexisted in God's good creation. All humanity had to do was choose wisely. Follow God's instruction concerning life and death and all would be well. We know how *that* turned out. Soon enough we are evicted from God's good and balanced creation into a broken and fallen one. And the resulting curses fall down like rain. By all rights, God should have been done with us. Left us to suffer the consequences of our actions. Our disobedience. Our desire to be gods ourselves. But God wasn't done with us yet.

Our Jewish brothers and sisters worship the LORD on Saturday. It is the seventh day. It is the day of completion and the day of rest. God commands this day of rest to reflect on who God is and who we are as God's people. We Christians have shifted this day to Sunday, the first day of the week. Why is that?

Early on the first day of the week, while it was still dark, Mary Magdalene came to the tomb and saw that the stone had been removed from the tomb. (John 20:1)

The Gospel of John speaks frequently in terms of darkness and light. Early on the first day of the week, creation was in darkness. We've seen this before. In Genesis, God speaks into the darkness and chaos and says, "Let there be Light!"

When it was time to plant our huge garden every spring, I was entrusted to plant a good portion of it. I was very proud of this opportunity. Now that I'm older I realize that anyone with an aging back and knees will almost always trust a young person willing to plant all day. Never the less, I was proud and protective of my work. I diligently chopped the weeds out of that garden. I lost the battle halfway through the field peas, but I did my best to chop out the nuisance threatening to choke out my seeds.

Like a garden, our souls are a mixture of seeds. More seeds are planted all the time.

Seeds of love and peace,
Seeds of humility and mercy.
But also,
Seeds of bitterness and bigotry,
Seeds of doubt and despair.
Seeds of fear and hate.

We are in desperate need of a Gardener to tend to the potential chaos of our souls. What seeds have been scattered in your garden? What is growing there? Which seeds are thriving in the garden of *your* soul? Which seeds are being choked out?

My background in the restaurant has given me a second language of sorts. Some refer to it as restaurant lingo. For example, to '86' a menu item is to make it temporarily unavailable. "86 salsa, we need to make more." Another term is "Being in the weeds." You are "in the weeds" if you've reached your limit and you are now behind. Being "Deep in the weeds" is to be hopelessly overwhelmed. People actually begin to shut down mentally at this point. The hopelessness of the situation makes them move and think slower. And often mistakes begin to pile up, one after another. The only way to recover is if someone steps in and helps. We can find ourselves "Deep in the weeds" in our lives as well.

Be comforted on this the first day of the week that the Gardener is there. God is able to step in and stop the chaos. Folks, creation is not yet finished! While Genesis says that God rested on the seventh day, we know that God is NOT resting in the midst of our suffering. On the first day of this new creation God speaks into the chaos, "Let there be LIGHT!"

The Gospel of John begins with an insight into God's redemptive work.
In the beginning was the Word, and the Word was with God, and the Word was God. He was in the beginning with God. All things came into being through him, and without him not one thing came into being. What has come into being in him was life, and the life was the light of all people. The light shines in the darkness, and the darkness did not overcome it. (John 1:1-5)

The Gardener in the Resurrection redeemed what was broken in the first garden. But there was a cost. There was suffering. We are given a glimpse of the suffering of God incarnate in yet another garden, the Garden of Gethsemane.
"Father, if you are willing, take this cup from me; yet not my will, but yours be done." (Luke 22:42)
The fully human side of our Lord and Savior knows our suffering all too well. The deadly choice of disobedience in the Garden of Eden was redeemed by Jesus' choice in Gethsemane In perfect obedience to Love, he chose to enter into the darkness.

And the darkness did not overcome it.

In Christ, God is at work in the garden of your soul. You are not meant to hopelessly suffer in chaos. You are meant to thrive and flourish! (More yellow crookneck squash than you can imagine kind of flourishing!)

This is the promise of resurrection! You are redeemed. What was corrupt and dead is no more. New life is at hand!

You Are A New Creation!

After resurrection, we cannot hold on to the chaotic life-choking weeds of our past. We are to look forward to a greater future that God has in store for us through the power of Christ's resurrection the sustaining power of God's Holy Spirit. Friends, by this power, *all* of creation is being made new! And that is Good News!

Amen.

Una Vida Que Da En El Blanco
A Life That Hits the Bullseye

Josefina Sánchez

(Efesios 2:1-10)

Introducción

El juego de tiro al blanco siempre me ha hecho pensar en la vida. La vida es como ese juego, tu la vives y el propósito es dar en el blanco! Vivimos en una sociedad que define el dar en el blanco en la vida de la siguiente manera: Dar en el blanco en la vida es tener la casa de los sueños, el cuerpo de la Barbie y el dinero del Kent, la mente Eistein, la habilidad deportiva de Michael Jordan, la salud de Dr. Chopra, la capacidad tecnológica de Bill Gates, los dotes artísticos de Botero, el espíritu investigativo de Patagayo quien descubrió la vacuna contra la malaria. Mencionando solo algunos de los iconos en nuestra sociedad que se presentan como ejemplos de dar en el blanco en la vida, desde la infancia se nos vende una idea de lo que es dar en el blanco. Esta idea nos ha puesto a correr una carrera in alcanzable, no importa cuánto nos esforcemos solo unos pocos darán en el blanco que ha definido nuestra sociedad. Si preguntáramos algunos de los de los personajes que hemos mencionados si piensan y sienten que han dado en el blanco tengo la leve sospecha de que la respuesta seria he logrado, he tenido éxito, he adquirido, soy famoso pero..... no se si he dado en el blanco. Dar en el blanco es algo que requiere tener claro el propósito de la vida, El propósito o la meta de la vida esta ligada inseparablemente al autor de la vida. El autor de la vida que para nosotros los cristianos, es el único, soberano, poderoso Dios a través de su hijo Jesucristo "nos dio vida", en palabras cortas dar en el blanco en la vida es tener vida, uno puede vivir y estar muerto. Tener vida es imposible a no ser por la intervención de Dios y por nuestro alineamiento su propósito.

El apóstol Pablo nos ilumina en como todos los seres humanos tenemos la tendencia a desviarnos, confundirnos, en nuestro esfuerzo por dar en el blanco. En primer lugar andamos muertos en nuestros delitos y pecados, caminamos siguiendo la corriente de este mundo, nos conformamos a los planteamientos del príncipe de la potestad del aire, vivimos en los deseos de nuestra carne, haciendo la voluntad de nuestra carne y de nuestros pensamientos y nuestro fin será la muerte. El blanco de de una vida vivida desde esta perspectiva bien parecida a la perspectiva de nuestra sociedad es la muerte.

Pero supuesto, el apóstol está hablando de una condición pasada que no atañe a nadie que es en la actualidad cristiano. Porque un cristiano sin lugar a duda tiene plena claridad de lo que es dar en el blanco en la vida, el cristiano sabe que dar en el blanco es vida, es experimentar vida aquí y después de la muerte. Algunos piensan que el cristiano realmente no necesita reenfocarse, o reorientarse pues el ya tiene la clave para dar en el blanco. Sin embargo esta carta es escrita para las iglesias en efesios, y el apóstol Pablo no tiene reserva en volver a recordarles que significa que Dios les ha dado vida en Jesús. Permítame ir con usted por lo menos por cuatro aspectos que a mi manera de ver caracterizan una vida que da en el blanco es decir que experimenta vida plena:

1. Una vida que apunta al blanco tiene una identidad basada en la obra de Jesús (Efe 1:3-14)

Es una vida que no tiene dudas de quien es, sabe que es un hijo o hija aceptado, amado, completo, que tiene toda bendición espiritual en Cristo. Es una vida que no solo sabe esto sino que ha decidido que su identidad no va a ser definida por lo que la sociedad dice sino por lo que Dios dice en su palabra acerca de usted.

Usted está aquí posiblemente porque es un cristiano, usted ha decidido ver en Jesús el hijo de Dios que es Amor y señor y que ha venido a redimirle del pecado a re direccionar su vida, a restaurar su vida, a darle una nueva identidad a hacer de usted esa nueva creatura que estaba desde la eternidad en la mente de Dios. Conoce usted que dice Dios de de usted? Ha escuchado usted esa dulce voz en su palabra? Ahora la siguiente pregunta no solo usted lo sabe pero los cree en la profundidad de su ser en ese lugar donde se agolpan los pensamientos y sentimientos que le empujan a optar por una identidad basada en el estatus económico, en su capacidad intelectual, física, en su éxito o su belleza? El cristiano sabe y cree que dice Dios de El y quien es en Cristo.

2. Una vida que da en el blanco entiende el lugar que tiene con Jesús (Ver 4-6)

El cristiano es plenamente consciente de que aunque ocupa un lugar espacial en esta tierra también de manera misteriosa está sentado en los lugares celestiales con Cristo. Es decir los cristianos somos bichos raros tenemos la posibilidad de percibir realidades espirituales. Nuestros sentidos físicos no están atrofiados en cuanto a la realidad espiritual y la interacción de esta con la realidad espacio temporal. Esta conciencia de su lugar les da una perspectiva de la vida diferente, el cristiano puede ver la vida en el cuadro grande, con esta perspectiva, la vida y el universo son sencillamente un punto en la inmensidad de Dios, es similar a la vista que tiene alguien que va en un avión, es una vista panorámica, del mundo su historia y la intervención divina en los dos. Por el contrario son aquellos que tienen extraviado el blanco su lugar se reduce al espacio físico material. Son como el niño piensa que el mundo es su ciudad. Por otro lado estar sentados en los lugares celestiales nos permite discernir el actuar de el príncipe de este mundo, este discernimiento nos permite ser mas efectivos en nuestro esfuerzo por ver la obra de Dios en nosotros y otros. Finalmente el estar en este lugar nos recuerda que nuestra vida biológica tiene un significado de propósito, mayordomía, servicio y eternidad. Nuestra vida biológica no es una maquina que anda por qué tiene que andar.

En palabras de C.S Lewis el cristiano es un anfibio que vive en dos mundos uno espiritual y otro físico material con un significado transcendente en estos dos mundos. Es decir, impacta de manera efectiva en los dos realidades. Vale la pena entonces preguntarnos somos realmente consientes de estas dos realidades en nuestra vida, es imposible dar en el blanco si no. Dialoga nuestra realidad física con la realidad espiritual? Vivimos una vida que ignora la realidad espiritual?

3. Una vida que da en el blanco tiene un status un poco diferente al status que promueve nuestra sociedad (ver. 8-9)

El estatus del cristiano está basado en la Gracia de Dios, sabe que es por pura gracia y no por sus meritos, capacidades, habilidades, belleza, logros o estatus que tiene todas las bendiciones. En otras palabras su estatus es por la misericordia y bondad de Dios. Este estatus le ayuda a mantener un carácter humilde, de gratitud, y manso. Todo lo contrario al estatus que nuestra sociedad nos invita continuamente a tener, un estatus de posición, orgullo, autosuficiencia. En otras palabras el estatus del cristiano tiene en balanza que sus capacidades logros y demás están respaldados por la realidad de una intervención divina por esto la gloria no es para él cristiano sino para Dios. La pregunta que nos surge en este punto es realmente que determina nuestro estatus, esta determinado por nuestra nacionalidad, raza, poder económico, educación, dones ministeriales o en la preciosa gracia de Dios? Que carácter reflejamos a otros cuando presentamos nuestro estatus.

4. Finalmente Una vida que da en el blanco tiene una labor, un propósito, un trabajo, una misión

El verso 10 nos describe de manera preciosa que el cristiano tiene una comprensión de que es un poema de Dios, es una obra de arte, una hermosa escultura viviente, que ha sido creada para buenas obras, buenas tareas, oficios, que le dan la oportunidad de crear, de gozar, de servir, obras que han sido preparadas de antemano de acuerdo a sus talentos, dones, capacidades, virtudes. Tareas que no deben producir comparaciones, competencias, ni descalificaciones pues cada uno ha sido equipado con el perfecto diseño para desarrollarlas. En cualquier contexto donde se encuentre.

En una sociedad como la nuestra donde el trabajo, se desarrolla con base a la competencia en la cualificación y la descalificación este concepto es revolucionario y refrescante revolucionario porque si estamos viviendo para su gloria la competencia pierde su poder, no hay que competir delante de Dios con nadie sencillamente hay que dejar que su poder cree nuevas realidades en nosotros y alrededor de nosotros! El trabajo es sencillamente el poder que Dios nos entrega para extender su don creador de nuevas y buenas realidades. El salir de esto libera para crear y glorificar a Dios por el contrario el reducir dar en el blanco en la vida a la profesión o trabajo que desarrollo me esclaviza de la competitividad, comparación, y lucro. Es nuestro trabajo un medio para nuestro sustento, para servir a otros o es nuestro fin para alcanzar reconocimiento, familiar o social?

En conclusión y llamado Dar en el blanco en la vida desde la perspectiva del apóstol Pablo en la epístola de efesios es asumir la identidad nueva que Cristo nos ofrece a través de su muerte y resurrección. Dar en el Blanco en la vida es tener la capacidad de vivir en los lugares celestiales y en este mundo espacial y temporal teniendo con un vista panorámica y una vista detallada del mundo en que Dios nos ha puesto. Teniendo además una visión real y una visión transcendente de nuestra eternidad, y con un discernimiento espiritual en un contexto espacial-temporal.

Dar en el blanco es tener el estatus que Cristo nos ha dado, un estatus que se basa en la gracia no en los meritos y por consiguiente un estatus cuya fachada son las virtudes de la humildad y mansedumbre en donde la arrogancia y la autosuficiencia no tienen lugar. Finalmente dar en el blanco en la vida es tener una misión un trabajo cuyo énfasis no es la competencia, ni el lucro sino por el contrario el servicio y la expresión de la gloria de Dios. La combinación de estos cuatro puntos en la vida a través del tiempo muestra y mostrara a las generaciones venideras la hermosura de la misericordia y la abundancia de la gracia de Dios (ver7)

Nuestro Reto es dar en el blanco en la vida no dejemos que los deseos de la carne, la corriente del mundo y el príncipe de los aires nos desvíen, confundan y nos lleven a errar en nuestro propósito de dar en el blanco en la vida. Por el contrario vivamos una vida con identidad, compartiendo el lugar con Cristo, rebosando en la gracia y cumpliendo la misión como su poema que somos para que de generación a generación su nombre sea Glorificado!!

Arise, Shine![13]

Lisa Scott

(Isaiah 60:1-2)

"Arise, shine; for your light has come! And the glory of the Lord is risen upon you. For behold, the darkness shall cover the earth, and the deep darkness the people; but the Lord will arise over you, and His glory will be seen upon you." Isaiah 60:1-2 (New King James Version).

When asked to speak on these verses of Scripture I was wondering, "What do I do with a passage most often associated with Epiphany and what does it have to do with the conference theme, Koinonia?" Usually, I see these words used as a reading connected with the arrival of the wise men in Bethlehem. I had to think about this passage and its implication for a Saturday in July. But you all know that the Word of God is not limited to a season or holiday. In particular the message of Isaiah 60:1-2 is really one for any day of the week, any year and always to God's people.

According to commentaries I consulted the first hearers of this message were probably Jews who lived in Jerusalem after the Babylonian Captivity. No longer an independent nation, the people are poor, beat down in spirit and in desperate need of God's loving presence. We can hear their cry in the words of an unknown psalmist: "God be merciful to us and bless us, and cause His face to shine upon us. That Your way may be known on earth, Your salvation among all nations," Psalm 67:1. The writer of Isaiah records a possible answer to that petition (Isaiah 60:1-2). God is going to give the people an epiphany, self-manifestation. God will reveal Himself and enlist the people in addressing the human condition, the plight of people who want to know God more fully and those who don't know God at all.

---

[13] A sermon/teaching presented at Koinonia, an inter-denominational church conference on July 27, 2013, in Poplar Bluff, Missouri.

In Isaiah 60:1-2, the Holy Spirit is communicating "Your prayers are being answered; you are part of that answer. Arise, shine! God is with you with power."

"Arise" means to get up, stand up, change position.

It was God's command to Abram when he and his nephew came to a parting of the ways. Lot chose the fertile and well-watered plains of Sodom and Gomorrah. Abram was told to look in another direction and heard "Arise, walk in the land through its length and its width, for I give it to you" (Genesis 13:17).

To Joshua and Jacob's descendants, wanderers in the wilderness for 40 years God would say, "Moses My servant is dead. Now therefore, arise, go over this Jordan, you and all this people, to the land which I am giving them — the children of Israel," Joshua 1:2

God directs the Prophet Samuel to get over his sadness over the disobedience of King Saul (1 Samuel 16:1), to choose from among Jesse's sons a future king of Israel. God's choice is David and so God commands the prophet to "Arise, anoint him; for this is the one!" 1 Samuel 16:12.

In the Gospels we find the Lord Jesus commanding people who were afflicted with sickness or disease to get up.

Matthew 9:1-8, to the paralytic, "Arise, take up your bed, and go to your house," verse 6. Jesus makes a correlation between being forgiven and healing. When we are unencumbered by sin, we are able to get up, change our outlook, our attitude.

You know from the New Testament Jesus raises the dead.

Mark 5:41, the Lord raised a little girl from the dead. He said, "She is sleeping." Then He took the child by the hand, and said to her, "Talitha, cumi, "which is translated, "Little girl, I say to you, arise."

On the outskirts of the village called Nain, Jesus and His disciples meet a funeral procession. Jesus comforts a widow whose only son is dead. He tells her in Luke 7:13 "Do not weep." Then He shows her why she shouldn't be weeping,

> Then He came and touched the open coffin, and those who carried him stood still. And He said, "Young man, I say to you, arise." So he that was dead sat up and began to speak. And He presented him to his mother. Then fear came upon all and they glorified God, saying, "A great prophet has risen up among us" and "God has visited His people." Luke 7:14-16.

When the Lord says, "arise" it should produce an expectation of something good. Don't stay sleeping, burying your head in your pillow, walking around depressed or down cast. A better day is coming! After all, because we have redemption through Christ's blood, the forgiveness of sins, our station has been elevated. Ephesians 2:4-7 gives us this promise,

> But God, who is rich in mercy, because of His great love with which He loved us, even when we were dead in trespasses, made us alive together with Christ (by grace you have been saved), and raised us up together, and made us sit together in heavenly places in Christ Jesus, that in the ages to come He might show the exceeding riches of His grace in His kindness toward us in Christ Jesus.

Forgiven and in relationship with God our Father, we arise. The words to an old hymn carry this theme forward.

"Arise, My Soul, Arise," Charles Wesley.

Rise, my soul, arise; shake of thy guilty fears; the bleeding sacrifice in my behalf appears: before the throne my surety stands, before the throne my surety stands, my name is written on His hands.

He ever lives above, for me to intercede; His all-redeeming love, His precious blood, to plead; His blood atoned for all our race; His blood atoned for all our race, and sprinkles now the throne of grace.

Five bleeding wounds He bears, received on Calvary; they pour effectual prayers; they strongly plead for me: "Forgive him, O forgive," they cry, "Forgive him, O forgive," they cry, "Nor let the ransomed sinner die!"

The Father hears Him pray, His dear Anointed One; He cannot turn away the presence of His Son; His Spirit answers to the blood, His Spirit answers to the blood, and tells me I am born of God.

My God is reconciled; His pardoning voice I hear; He owns me for His child; I can no longer fear; with confidence I now draw nigh, with confidence I now draw nigh, and "Father, Abba, Father," cry.

Forgiven and in relationship with God our Father, we arise. Then we shine!

What does it mean to shine? Roget's Thesaurus offers several options: to shine in a crowd, to standout, be outstanding, be conspicuous, be preeminent, excel, dominate, star. We contrast to shine with dull, lusterless, nondescript, average or below average. On a bell curve to shine would be the highest score. There is nothing obscure, mediocre, sub-par or cloaked about a Christian who is shining for God.

You may recall from your study of the Old Testament the story of one man who really stood out for God, who literally was shining, radiating the presence of God. That man was Moses. After the incident with the Golden Calf God had instructed Moses to return to the mountain and receive the tablets of the law.

Moses spent 40 days and 40 nights with the Lord on the mountain receiving the law. After Moses left the presence of God, people knew that he had been with the Lord (Exodus 34:29-35). The people couldn't handle the sight of such glory. Consequently, Moses wore a veil after being with the Lord. The radiance of God's presence was too much a reminder of holiness and divine power. Because of the cross of Calvary we are unveiled to reflect

God's glory and in that process we "are being transformed into the same image from glory to glory, just as by the Spirit of the Lord," 2 Corinthians 3:18. Veiling our faces, dumbing down our witness so that we blend in with the prevailing culture should never be our aim. The world needs to see our lives are intertwined with the Almighty.

We can be people who shine, stand out, not as arrogant or self-conceited, but those who relish the presence of God, who hear and obey the voice of a good God. We can forgive others because we have been forgiven and are loved. And as we seek Him we will reflect the qualities of God that strengthen each believer and edify the Body of Christ.

Furthermore, "Arise, shine" is a command to get up and let the Light of God become a beacon in you to those who need the Savior. What was it Jesus said? "You are the light of the world. A city that is set on a hill cannot be hidden. Nor do they light a lamp and put it under a basket, but on a lamp stand, and it gives light to all who are in the house," Matthew 5:14-16. The light doesn't originate in us, but is reflected from the Jesus, the Savior and the Light of World.

Think back to the story of Transfiguration in which Jesus takes Peter, James and John up on a high mountain. In Matthew 17:2 "And He was transfigured before them. His face shone like the sun, and His clothes became as white as the light. "In Mark 9:2, "His clothes become shining, exceedingly white, like snow, such as no launderer on earth can whiten them." That which is in Jesus is coming out. When He comes down from the mountain, people are greatly amazed and run to Him (verse 15).

Meanwhile the disciples have been disputing with the scribes. On this occasion the disciples apart from Jesus were thoroughly in the flesh, unable to do the miraculous, to cast out a demon. But there would come a time when the Holy Spirit's would empower the disciples to cast out demons in Jesus' name, to speak with new tongues, to take up serpents, to survive poisonous drink and to lay hands on the sick and to see them recover. Such acts of faith, demonstrations of God's power shine in a dark world.

Koinonia — fellowship, participation — is the theme of our meetings today. We are believers from different denominational backgrounds but find common ground in the Savior. Koinonia in Greek or fellowship in English is described in 1 John 1:3, 6 and is a vital component of the faith community. Fellowship with others begins with loving God and embracing the liberty we have in God's Holy Spirit. Let's consider a practical application drawn from Philippians. Paul encourages the church at Philippi to actively engage in their faith, and to exemplify what it means to stand out for God — to shine for God.

When we read Philippians 2:12-15 we discover the power of fellowship and the call to shine for God. No complaining and no disputing — this should be the witness of every Christian — "shining as lights in the world." We live in a world where complaining and disputing are the norm even among Christians. But if we allow God's Holy Spirit to lead us, our conduct as children of God will prompt a question among family, friends, enemies, brothers and sisters in Christ, "Why aren't you complaining?" "Don't you have a dog in this fight?" Our response, can give further honor to God, "for it is Christ in you, the hope of glory." Arise, shine! We as a people need the Church to do it.

In closing, may this blessing be realized in your life: "The Lord bless you and keep you; the Lord make His face shine upon you, and be gracious to you; the Lord lift up His countenance upon you, and give you peace," (Numbers 6:24-26) Amen.

Invitation to the Kingdom of God　　Nobuko Seki

主日共同の夕礼拝説教　　　　　　　　　　　　　　　２０１４．３．９（主日）

神の国への招き

（イザヤ書６３章１５節～１９節、マルコによる福音書１章１２節～１５節）

I.　　荒れ野の誘惑

今日は受難節第一主日です。受難節は、別名「四旬節」（４０日間という意味）と言います。イースター一前の日曜日を除く４０日間だから、「四旬節」です。日曜日を含めると、実際は４６日の期間ですが、毎年、水曜日から始まってイースターの前日まで、教会はこの期間を大事にします。この期間は、言ってみればキリスト者の「修行」の期間と言えるのかもしれません。

今日の福音は、とても短いのですが主イエスが誘惑にさらされて、それと戦って打ち勝つ場面のと、最初の宣教活動の様子が生き生きと描かれています。荒れ野は生命を寄せつけない場所であり、イスラエルの民も水や食べ物を求めてつぶやいた場所ですから、イエスを誘惑し、神から切り離そうとするサタンにとって絶好の場所です。しかし、イエスを荒れ野に送り出したのは、ヨルダン川で洗礼を受けた際に天から降った「霊」であり、しかも４０日間、「天使」が仕えていた、と記しています。

この時代の終末観によれば、終末の時には天使が人間に仕えるとされ、獣も人間に害を加えることができなくなるとされていますから、マルコの関心は、イエスがどのようにして試練を克服したかにはなく、イエスとともに終末の時が到来していると説くことにあります。

「誘惑」と「試練」は聖書では同じ言葉で表します。誘惑といえば「心を迷わせて、悪いほうに誘い込むこと」ですが、試練といえば「信仰の程度を試して人を鍛えること」を指します。サタンはイエスを誘惑しますが、イエスはそれを試練に変え、私たちに進むべき道を示しました。神に信頼することだけが、誘惑に打ち勝つ方法です。聖書において荒れ野は、試練の場であると同時に、神との出会いの場です。このような厳しい状況のもとでは、いのちのために必死の戦いがなされます。意志は弱まり、楽な手段に容易に屈してしまいがちになります。しかし、荒れ野とその深い静けさは、同時に、神と出会うという供えられた場です。そこで、私たちは孤独を経験しますが、この孤独は私たちの中に交わりへの渇望を生み出します。

II.　　福音を伝える

主イエスはサタンから誘惑を受けた直後に、宣教を開始されます。「宣べ伝える」と訳されている言葉は、布告をするとも訳せます。布告すると言っても、ただ単に王の命令を伝えるということだけではなくて、同時にそれは、国の大きな出来事を告げることでもありました。たとえば、王子が生まれたとか、その王子が結婚するとか、位に就くとか、戦争に勝ったとか、

あるいは悲しい知らせでも、王が死んだとか、あるいは戦争に負けたとか、そのように実際に起こった出来事を伝えます。その意味が聖書のなかで、はっきり受け継がれていると考えることができます。この「宣べ伝える」という言葉は、後に教会の歴史の中でも受け継がれました。たとえば日本語では、これが名詞になりますと、宣教師などというときの〈宣教〉という言葉になります。この宣教という言葉を使うときには、ここで用いられているギリシア語との結び付きで理解出来るのです。

そこで宣べ伝えられた出来事とは何であったでしょうか。ここでは宣べ伝えたのが何であったかということを、まずマルコ福音書は「神の福音」と呼びました。〈福音〉とは、私たちが絶えず聞いているように、それを聞いたら喜べるような言葉、それを聞いたら嬉しくなるような言葉ということです。ただ、ここでのマルコ福音書の表現で、たいへん重要なことでありながら、私たちが読み落とすのは「神の」福音と書いていることです。この「神の福音」という言葉は、聖書のなかにしばしば登場します。おそらく、こうした最古の福音書であるマルコ福音書が、「神の福音」という言葉を使ったときには、そういう特別な教会の信仰のこころが、それに込められていると思います。

どういう意味でここに特別の「神の」という言葉が付けくわえられたのか。こういうふうに考えていいと思います。〈福音〉というのは、その言葉を聞くと、こちらの心が躍ってくるような言葉です。喜びをもたらす知らせということです。そういう喜びをもたらすような知らせとして、神について語る言葉が語られるようになったということです。

III. 時は満ち、神の国は近づいた

ヨハネが捕らえられた後、主イエスはガリラヤにおいて伝道活動を始められました。その説教の初めに「時は満ち、神の国は近づいた。悔い改めて福音を信じなさい」という言葉を、お語りになりました。この三つの言葉で言い表されていることが、主イエスのお言葉のいつも中心にあったということです。

これから後、主イエスは病気を治されたり、あるいは時には、波立つ湖の水をなだめておしまいになったり、いろいろなことをなさいます。それらの主イエスのなさったことも皆、この「時は満ち、神の国は近づいた。悔い改めて福音を信じなさい」という言葉に尽きるのです。

2月に2回続けて週末に大雪が降りました。雪がしんしんと降り続けるのを見ているのは好きです。電車に乗って教会と家を行き来をしている私には大雪は辛いものがありますが、見ていて美しい。晴佐久神父が中学生の頃に書いた短い詩に次のようなものがあります。「雪やこんこん、あられやこんこん。神の国は近づいた」。まさに、神の国の本質をよく表している詩です。一方的で、圧倒的で、誰も止められない。今目の前で現実に、すべておかまいなしに天

から降っていて、どんどん積もっていく。もはや人間のわざを超えて、今、ここに神の国は来た。そのような感じがします。

「時は満ち、神の国は近づいた。福音を信じなさい」。この主イエスの宣言で、世界はまったく変わってしまいました。それは誰も止められない。圧倒的に天から来る力、現実にもう来ている新しい時代。この「神の国は近づいた」という訳ですが、これは「もう神の国は来た」と読んでいただいてけっこうです。たとえば、聖餐式で牧師が「キリストの体」と宣言してパンをいただきます。確かにまだ食べてはいないけれど、もうここに来ている。だから私たちは、喜んで「アーメン」と答えて、それを食べる。「神の国はここに来た。だから心配ない。大丈夫。安心しなさい」。これが主イエスのメッセージです。それを聞いた人たちの喜びが、キリスト教を今日までずっと伝え続けてきたのです。

IV.　悔い改めて福音を信じる

先程、イザヤ書第６３章を読みました。このイザヤ書の言葉は、私たちの心を打ちますが、どこか哀しい響きがあります。１５節にこうあります。「どこにあるのですか　あなたの熱情と力強い御業は。あなたのたぎる思いと憐れみは　抑えられていて、わたしには示されません」。この預言者は、神様のことについて考え、神さまについて思いを巡らし、神さまについて語ろうとすると、かえって暗い思いになる。神について語るということは辛いことでもあります。言い換えれば、神さまが不在なのです。どうも神さまはお留守のようだ、だからこんな目に遭っているのだ。神さま、帰ってきてください。神の福音というのは、このイザヤの祈りが満たされたということを告げることです。神さまが帰ってきてくださった。

このイザヤ書には、しかし、こういう言葉も記されているのです。「あなたはわたしたちの父です。アブラハムがわたしたちを見知らず　イスラエルがわたしたちを認めなくても　主よ、あなたはわたしたちの父です」。暗い思いに立ち向かい、疑いを振り払うように、こう言えるのです。祈りのなかで、神を父と呼び始めているのです。そうだ、神さまが帰ってきてくださる。主イエスが伝道をお始めになって、まずそこで語られたのは、まさにこのイザヤの祈りがここに成就するということです。だから「時は満ちた」のです。ついにその時が来たのです。この神についての喜びの知らせを聞く、自分の心まで躍るようになるというのは、それはまさにそれがこの私に、喜び、救いをもたらすからです。だから、神についての喜びを語るということは、私たちについても今までとは違った喜びの響きをたたえた言葉をもって語ることができるようになるということです。

「神の国は近づいた」。これはどういうことか。言葉は非常にはっきりしています。元のギリシア語も、辞書をひいて、文法を学べば、「神の国は近づいた」としか訳しようがないものでもあることを、すぐに私たちは知ることができます。英語で「ハズ・カム」となります。私

たちが英語を習い始めて、まず「スプリング・ハズ・カム」という表現を覚えます。「春が来た」のです。もうここへ来たのです。

　あるカトリックの司祭の方が、言葉について大変興味のある考察をしている本を読んだことがあります。私たちが駅のプラットフォームで電車が来るのを待っている。そうすると、スピーカーが知らせる。「電車が来ますから、白線のうしろへさがってください」と言う。それは間違いだ、と言うのです。「電車が来ますから」というのでは、まだ電車が来ていないということが言われています。ヨーロッパの言語の細かい文法で言うと、これは、いろいろ電車がここに来たら、「来た」と言う。入ってくるときには、来るという現在形で、となると、来たになる。それが完了形です。しかし、その方の意見によれば、日本語で正しく言うならば、「電車が来ましたから、うしろへさがってください」と言うべきだと言うのです。なぜかというと、電車がもうすぐそこまで近づいたと言ったら、私たちひとつの関係が生まれたことで、今もさがらないと危険だということなのです。そして、その司祭は、そこで既に電車の話ではなくて、私たちと神との関係を語っているのです。「目と鼻の先まで近づいてしまった」というニュアンス。それは、まさしく、ここにおける神の国の接近を告げる言葉が持つ意味でもあるのです。

　主イエスがここで、「神の国は近づいた」とおっしゃったのも、この司祭の言葉でいえば、まさに電車が来たのと同じです。神の国が近づいた。もうあなたがたと関係が出来た。だからこそ、悔い改めなさいという切実な求めが続くのです。そうでなければ、悔い改めるということは起こりません。ちょうど電車が近づいてきた、危険だからうしろへさがらなければいけない、そして、電車が来るのを待たなければいけないように、神さまが今あなたがたと新しい関わりを持ち始めている。その神さまのご支配をあなたがたは受け入れなければならない。そのために大事なことは、うしろへさがって逃げるのではない。前へ出て行くのです。あるいは、向きを変えるのです。悔い改めるのです。今までの考え方を、もう捨てるのです。そうして、この福音を受け容れるのです。「福音を信じなさい」。神についてのよきことを信じなさい。あなたがたについて、すばらしいことが語り始められた、いや、すばらしいことがもう起こったということを受け入れなさい、と主イエスは言われるのです。こういうふうに考えてくると、神の支配が始まった、神の国は来てしまった、と訳す方が正しいのだと考えることさえできるのです。

　時は満ちた。今わたしたちが告げられているのは、イザヤが待ちこがれていた神の救い到来の時だ。神の計画が今ここに成就する。それが第一部です。第三部は、悔い改めて、私たちが語っている福音を信じなさい。教会の仲間に入りなさい。だから洗礼を受けなさい、という勧めになります。中核の第二部、そこで、主イエスご自身は神の国についてお語りになりました。

　先ほど、イザヤ書の第６３章を読みました。そして、神についての福音、喜びとは何かとい

284

いうことを考えてみました。それは神さまが帰ってきてくださることだと言いました。神さまが帰ってきてくださるだけで、私たちは立ちつくしているのではない。私たちも神さまのところへ帰っていかざるを得ない。神さまが戻ってきてくださるときに、私たちは子として神さまのところへ戻っていくのです。これが、悔い改めるということです。なぜかというと、いつも神さまの子らしくなく生きているからです。宗教改革者ルターは、キリスト者の全生活が日々、悔い改めだということを言いました。これが、彼の起こした宗教改革の出発点になった大きな真理の発見です。それはどういうことかというと、毎日毎日、あるいは毎夕毎夕、私たちが自分の向きはどこを向いているか、ということを点検するということです。神さまのほうを向いていなかったならば、主の十字架のほうを向いていなかったならば、甦りのほうを向いていなかったならば、舵をとり直さなければいけない。ぐっと向きを変えて、神さまのほうに向き、主イエスの言葉、喜びの言葉を聞ける耳にしなかればならない。そうしないと、聞こえて来なくなる。聞こえて来なくなったら、私たちの生活から喜びは消えていきます。その意味でも、この主のお言葉は、心にしみ通るように、日々口にすべき言葉です。「時は満ち、神の国は近づいた。悔い改めて、福音を信じなさい」。この御言葉が私たちにとって日々、喜びの響きをたてるものとなりますように、霊の導きを願いたいと思います。

　祈り：　主イエス・キリストがその全存在をかけて私たちに告げてくださいました、あなたのみむねを、あなたがしてくださったことを、いつも新たな喜びをもって思い起こすことができますように。私たちに、いつもこのみ言葉を思い起こさせてくださるみ霊を豊に注いでください。そのみ言葉が聞こえなくなっていると思い込み、自分の信仰すら疑っている者があるとすれば、まさにその人のために、あなたのみ霊が注がれますように。日々この言葉を聞きつつ、日々あなたのみもとに帰って行く、望みある生活をひとりびとりに与えてくださいますように。主イエス・キリストのみ名によって祈ります。アーメン

Untie Me and Let Me Go

Teresa K. Shauf

(Luke 19 : 28-31)

Have you ever thought about the donkey that carried Jesus into Jerusalem?

There is a book that was written by the name of ***The Donkey That No One Could Ride***.[14] It is a story of a lonely, weak donkey that no one wanted because he was too weak for anyone to ride him. He was probably ridiculed because of that and he just believed he had no purpose in life....

Does that sound familiar?

Don't we sometimes feel that way....

Weak....lonely.....having no real purpose in life....

The good news is.....

When Jesus touches our lives......we are changed....

After Jesus touches this donkey........

His life is changed....

.he has the privileged to carry the weight of our lord on his back......down the road to Jerusalem....

The scripture tells us this donkey had never been ridden before.

---

[14] Anthony DeStefano and Richard Cowdrey, **The Donkey That No One Could Ride** (Harvest House Publishers, 2012).

Have you ever ridden an animal that had never had anyone on his back.....

I haven't but I can only imagine what this animal would do ....

But this little donkey took the challenge willingly.

He yielded its back to the creator of the world.

This is exactly what we need to do when we come in contact with the lord....

We need to yield ourselves and our life to him....

What an honor to be of use to the to the almighty god.........

What an honor to have been the donkey that Jesus picked for this special occasion.....

It was special alright....because

We are still reading about him some 2000 years later......

I hope when I'm finished with this message that we shout aloud.......untie me lord and let me go!!!

Do we ever feel like our hands are tied?

You really want to do something for god but something is always stopping you.

Maybe it is fear......maybe it is a lack of confidence....

Maybe it is not the right time for god to use you and you just have to wait......

When we come to god and accept his mercy and grace and commit our lives over to him....

Then he is in control....

Let him use you in the manner he so chooses...

Who are we to think that we have all the answers....

And we know what god wants for our lives...

Just like the donkey.....he was available....and willing....it doesn't say he put up a fight....

So why do we ....

We must be available and willing and trust god in all things.....

There are miracles and opportunities.....out there everyday that god would like to use us ......

But we are not listening and looking for them.....

We need to be....

Meeting people where they are......

Wherever we go....there is someone waiting for us to share this great love of Jesus with them....

I read this story in the daily bread:

A young friend ask his neighbor if he could borrow their car. The neighbor was very hesitant at first. He thought to himself....this is my car and I need it to go to work tomorrow .....and what if he wreaks it .....I will not have transportation back and forth to work...

But he soon felt convicted of his feelings because he was reminded that god wanted us to care for others.

So he handed the keys over to the young man. This young man traveled about 30 miles away to a church service to conduct a youth rally. During this rally many teenagers gave their heart to the lord.

What an opportunity........the neighbor almost persuaded himself not to do this act of kindness....

And look what happened.....hearts were touched and changed by this one act...

Obviously the "lord had need of the vehicle"....because it carried a man to do god's work"

Jesus instructed the disciples to take another man's donkey. Jesus told his men to untie him and bring the donkey to him. And if someone objected....tell them...."the lord has need of it".....and the disciples did as the lord ask

And

The owner let him go......

I think the owner of the donkey had great faith...

He demonstrated what a true follower should do:

Be willing to give what he has unto the lord....

Some may think ......it is just a donkey....why are you making such a big fuss over a donkey...

This was no little thing....because it was something that the "master" needed.....

God doesn't usually ask for big things....

God will not ask us to give what we don't have....

We may feel like we don't have anything significant to give....;

But god takes the simple things and uses them in great ways...

Moses was asked to give his walking stick....

Rahab gave a corner of her roof to hide the spies...;

David gave his sling shot...

The widow at Zarephath gave the last of her oil and flour to make a meal for Elijah...

The Shummanite woman gave a room of her home to Elisha.....

The widow that Jesus praised gave her two mites...

The young boy gave his five loaves and two fish....

So we have no excuse to say to the lord ......I only have a little....talent....a little money.....or a small home......or a little food.....

Because he can use ....what we have.....and make it abundant for his ministry...

Everything we have belongs to god......he has given it to us as a gift from him....we are only the trustees ....and he can ask for it back if he so chooses....

You and I each have something in our lives, which, if given back to god, could like the donkey. Move Jesus and his story further down the road....

What we have is never more valuable than when it is put back into the hands of god....

So here is my question....what is god asking of you...what does he want you to give...

There were two groups of people on that palm Sunday as he rode down that rode to Jerusalem....

It was the enthusiastic people....screaming "hosanna"......at the beginning of the week and at the end of the week were screaming "crucify him"...

Then there were the committed....these were the ones who trust Christ as their lord and savior....he is the lord of their lives....what he commands...they will do...where he sends them...they will go....what he asks for...they will give...

So which group are you this morning....

You see, the issue this palm Sunday is the same as the first palm Sunday.....

Jesus declares himself to be the long awaited king that will redeem those who trust....

The declaration is the same...and so is the choice...

Will you receive him as king and savior and be willing for him to "untie your hands and let you go and do a work for him"

Or will you simply stand on the sidelines...

Let us pray....

The Children's Table

Sandra Shepherd

(Mark 10:13-16)

Last Sunday we celebrated Easter!
    I heard about lots of families gathering:
        grandparents, grandchildren,
  aunts, uncles, brothers, sisters,
        moms, dads, in-laws of all sorts,
  step-folks, dear friends…
      …all sorts of families, kin or not.

When families gather for Easter, Christmas, Thanksgiving,
      or other big family celebrations,
  there's always food…lots of it…
      and everyone crowds around the biggest table available…
        well, almost everyone!

There is often a special table reserved *for the children.*
    In many families,
      getting to sit at "the big table"
        is a rite of passage.
    I have a friend who complains
      that she had to sit at the children's table
        until she was married!

But the children's table can be the fun spot!

No boring report
    of Uncle Whozit's most recent trip to the grocery store
      where "the prices just keep going up and up and up

and these days you can't even get one sack full of groceries
for what used to fill up the back of the station wagon
when Mildred and I lived out on the farm back in the day"

And no suffering through constant cheek-pinching
from Great Aunt Prissy.

And no "wipe your chin"
or "don't talk with your mouth full"
or "be sure to eat those vegetables"
from your momma.

Just kids being kids:
elbows on the table,
napkins ignored,
the really good food being thoroughly enjoyed,
a little conversation about what truly interests them
(not just something to fill the silence).

Ah…the children's table!
Even the reduced height of the table
subliminally sets the expectations at a "lower plane."
The décor is usually more light-hearted.
No one expects the world's problems to be solved
at the children's table.

But sometimes they are…
Well, at least an *example*, which if *followed*,
could solve *some* of the world's problems.

Ever notice how kids left to their own devices
may fuss over insignificant stuff…
but then work it out with compromise
(better known to kids as "sharing" or "taking turns")?

Ever see kids who don't know
  the new "in-law children" or "step-kids" or whatever,
   but accept one another at the table
    as equal partners,
   focusing on what they have in common
    rather than what their differences might be?

…and a little child shall lead them…

Hear now today's gospel lesson--
  Mark 10:13-16.
   I'm reading from *The Message*.

The people brought children to Jesus,
 hoping he might touch them.
The disciples shooed them off.
 But Jesus was irate and let them know it:
  "Don't push these children away.
Don't ever get between them and me.
  These children are at the very center
   of life in the kingdom.
Mark this:
  Unless you accept God's kingdom
   in the simplicity of a child,
    you'll never get in."
Then, gathering the children up in his arms,
 he laid his hands of blessing on them.

The Word of God for the people of God. [thanks be to God]

Jesus said we must receive the kingdom of God
  "like a child."

It is true that Paul said he "gave up childish ways"

when he grew up (I Corinthians 13:11).
>   But ***childishness*** is not what Jesus is talking about
>   in today's passage.   Childishness is irresponsibility, frivolity,
>   capriciousness, pettiness, and petulance.
Childish people imagine the whole world revolves around them
>   and if they cry loudly enough they will be served.
We all know some childish children…
>   and some childish adults.

Jesus, on the other hand, asks us to be *child**like***.
>   He is talking about that open, trusting, responsive part of us—
>   that part that laughs and cries
>   and is willing to dream and to risk.

Listen to the child…
>   and not just the person who is young chronologically.
>   There is a child inside us,
>   no matter how old we are,
>   who needs to be listened to.

Who knows, when we start listening more to the child within us,
>   we may learn to be more joyful,
>   less weighed down with worries and anxieties,
>   able to enjoy the wonder, beauty and mystery of life all the more.
The child in us can show us the giftedness of life
>   and help us live it to the fullest.
The child in us will cherish and share the gift
>   of imagination and creativity.
The child in us can reveal the grace of God all around us
>   and help us speak more intimately
>   in the Parent-child conversation
>   in which we are engaged with our holy parent.

Let's remember that children
>   may fuss over insignificant stuff…

but then decide to share or take turns.

Let's remember that children who don't know each other
    still accept one another as equal partners at the table,
        focusing on what they have in common
            rather than what their differences might be.

Let's remember to listen.
    Let's remember what we learn from the children's table.
        And let's incorporate a childlike wisdom into our lives.

Let us pray:

Holy parent, help us approach you with childlike awe and innocence. Help us be confident in your love for us, so that we may share it with others. Amen.

There's Just Something About This Jesus

Terra Sisco

(Matthew 9:9-13)

"As Jesus went on from there, he saw a man named Matthew sitting at the tax collector's booth. 'Follow me,' he told him, and Matthew got up and followed him. While Jesus was having dinner at Matthew's house, many tax collectors and 'sinners' came and ate with him and his disciples. When the Pharisees saw this, they asked his disciples, 'Why does your teacher eat with tax collectors and 'sinners'? On hearing this, Jesus said, 'It is not the healthy who need a doctor, but the sick. But go and learn what this means: 'I desire mercy, not sacrifice.' For I have not come to call the righteous, but sinners." (NIV)

Jesus is a very popular man. As He was walking the earth, people were flocking to Him. He had just served over 5000 people with 5 loaves of bread and 2 fishes as well as He had done many miraculous healings. The word spread fast through the region, and people wanted to see this man named Jesus.

In the gospel of Matthew, Matthew is called Matthew, but in the gospels of Mark and Luke, he is called Levi. The Lord is in the business of changing names and Levi was one of those blessed ones. The name Matthew means "gift from God".

Matthew is a tax collector, and tax collectors were not very popular men. Even today, tax collectors are not popular people. They have been known to cheat people out of money in order to make themselves rich. Being a tax collector was his job and many people despised him because of his job.

God was doing an amazing, amazing work in him so much that he left his job to follow Him. He touched his heart in a mighty, mighty way that he abandoned his position in order to follow Jesus.

Peter and all the fisherman, when they answered the call, they were not taking as big of a risk as Matthew did. They could always go back to their job, but Matthew could not.

This was a HUGE risk for Matthew, because once he left his tax booth, that was it, he could not go back. Just think about this for a minute, once he left his profession, he could never return to it. So, Matthew did a great sacrifice when he followed Jesus. Not only did he abandon his job, but he also abandoned his life as he knew it for this man named Jesus. There's just something about this Jesus that was drawing him to where he wanted to get up, leave his security to follow this man named Jesus. Praise God!

God was doing a work in Matthew and what is so awesome about this too is that Matthew was a tax collector in which tax collectors had to be good at record keeping. God had gifted Matthew in record keeping, and because He had, Matthew was an excellent record keeper. And Matthew's name means "a gift from God' so what did he do for Jesus? He kept excellent records. What do we have today because of record keeping? The Bible, because people kept records.

So we have this man named Matthew who was secured in his job because he was a good record keeper, and the result of that was a good paying job. But when Jesus said to him, "Follow me" that meant for him to abandon his old life as he knew it, take up his cross and this man named Jesus.

When Jesus says follow me, He is saying to us, "Deny yourselves, take up your cross and follow me. Denying ourselves means abandoning the life that we know, and taking on the new life; taking on what God has called us to do. This calling is a hard thing to do. It is a hard thing to leave your secured place and say, "God, here I am, use me! I might be despised by people. I might be rejected by people. I might be spit on." When we follow Jesus, that is the reality. We will be despised, rejected, and spit on…..we will be persecuted! Why? Because He was persecuted so why would it be any different for us?

So, Matthew follows this man named Jesus when Jesus tells him too. Here's another awesome thing about Matthew's calling is that he uses his gift of record keeping to further the Kingdom of God! We all have gifts folks! Don't you think for a minute that what you have is for nothing! God uses your gifts and talents to further His Kingdom work! Matthew's gift furthers the Kingdom of God today, it did yesterday, and it will tomorrow, because we have his records right here in the palm of our hands! How AWESOME is that? When he was writing his gospel, he wasn't thinking that he would have a HUGE impact on future generations to come! By his gift of record keeping, the world is changed! The world is changed by his gift, his talent that God had given him. People know the Gospel message, because Matthew used the gift that God had given him. Instead of using it for the world, he used it for the glory of God!!! Praise God!!! Praise God for Matthew!!! Praise God that Matthew was willing to abandon all of his life as he knew it in order to follow this man named Jesus!!!

Not only did Matthew have the willingness to abandon his job and obtain the passion to follow Jesus, but he also went and got his friends so they could meet Jesus. In Terra Sisco's mind, "Matthew said, Hey, come to my house! I am going to have dinner and I am going to invite this man named Jesus who has changed my life. I want you to meet Him! I want you to meet this Jesus! He is intriguing! He is awesome! You know if I left my job that was security for me that there's just something about this Jesus!"

Can you imagine this conversation taking place with his friends? "Matthew is great at record keeping, he's rolling in the dough and he left all of this for this man named Jesus?! He left his wealth to follow this man named Jesus! I've got to meet this man! What is it about this man that caused my friend to leave his life of sin, to leave his life as he knew it, to leave his position as tax collector to follow this man named Jesus? And hey you know what; we get a free meal out of this too, so let's go!" What we need to remember, Brothers and Sisters, is that they don't know Jesus as the Son of God yet. All they know is the buzz going on about his teachings, healings, and miracles.

So, his friends come because they had to meet this guy that changed their friend, Matthew's life. So, here they are at the banquet. Jesus is having dinner with them, having a good time along with his disciples being there too, and here comes the Pharisees. The Pharisees are always trying to find ways to trip up Jesus. And when they saw what was taking place, they asked His disciples, "Why does your teacher eat with the tax collectors and sinners?" In my mind, "Why does your teacher lower His standards to hang out with the tax collectors and sinners, because they are not righteous? They have a lot of junk in their lives. They are not who we are."

Pharisees, the religious leaders, had been really good at looking good on the outside, but they didn't get it on the inside! Jesus had said to them at another time in Mark 7 that they had honor God with their lips, but their heart is far from Him. And Jesus called them hypocrites. He also told them in that very same scripture that they had a fine way of setting aside the commands of God to uphold man's traditions! Jesus laid it down on them and did not hesitate! In other words, "You sure talk a good talk and strive to look good on the outside, but you don't walk the walk and the inside is ugly! You don't have grace for My people!" But Jesus changed that for us! In verses 12 & 13, Jesus said that He came for whom? "Not the righteous but the sinners!" He hangs out with the sinners! Praise God!!!

Jesus doesn't compromise His morals and values for the sinners, but He hangs out with the sinners!!! I don't know about you, but I have sinned in my life and Jesus still hangs out with me!!! Praise God!!! Glory to God that He desires to hang out with me thought I have sinned against Him!!! Because of the blood of the Lamb of God that took away my sin and made me a saint, I get to hang out with Jesus!!! Praise be to God that He chose me, He knocked on my heart's door, and He said, "Terra, here it is! I've got a gift for you! Without Me, you are nothing, but with Me, you can do ALL things! Without Me, you are not going to go to Heaven, but with Me, you will go to Heaven, because I am the Way! And let Me explain to you how that way happens. You see a long time ago when I walked the Earth, I took a journey. I was bruised, beaten, spit on, and mocked as I walked up this hill called Calvary. And when I got up on top of this hill called Calvary, I was carrying this tree. I actually carried it a mile out of the city onto this hill and I was beaten, bruised, mocked, and had spit coming down my face. I had people hurling insults at me, but you were on my mind. And I kept thinking, if I don't go, if I don't go up this hill and be crucified, you can't go to Heaven. And as they were nailing Me to the old rugged cross, they had to dislocate my shoulders so I could hang on the cross, and while all of this was happening, you were on my mind. I kept thinking, just a little longer. I've got to endure this pain a little longer. Once I've endured this pain, the sinners will become the righteousness of God!!" When He was getting close to the end, He prayed for those who don't know any better! He prayed for those who had hit Him, spit on Him, mocked Him, dislocated His shoulders and nailed Him to the cross, who didn't believe Him!!! He prayed, "Father, forgive them for they know not what they do." He cried out to God, "Why have You forsaken me?" In other words, "Why have You abandoned me?" He was by Himself, and in His mind, all He was thinking about was all of you, me, and everyone who has ever been born and will be born!!! He was thinking about what this great sacrifice would do for mankind...eternal life!!! Without this great sacrifice, without this bloodshed, we couldn't go to Heaven or into the very presence of God!!! So when He gave up His Spirit, the earth shook, the curtain was torn into two, the veil was removed, and His Holy Presence became accessible to all of us through His bloodshed!!! The Holy of Holies, the very presence of God, is accessible to all of us!!!

Jesus said to me, "Terra, you will have eternal life if you will only receive it. You will have life in abundance. You will have freedom. Every chain that every held you back, I have broken and removed from you. If only you will receive my gift." Brothers and Sisters, this is what Jesus is saying to us today! You may have already made the decision to receive God's gift of salvation a long time ago and I praise God for that, but there are many in our community that have not. Crittenden County, Kentucky, is full of people who have not made that decision, that do not have a home to come to and hang out with Jesus, and feel safe. I don't know about you, but I sin and praise God for His grace!!! I am not any different than that person out there that has issues because I have issues too except I have salvation and they may not! We need to have a great compassion that will move our hearts and because of that, it will move our hands and feet to reach the lost! We need to have a great compassion that will endure just like Jesus did for the cause of those knowing Him and having eternal life! We don't have to endure the cross, because He already did that for us, and it is finished! Every sin that has been committed, is being committed and will be committed has been nailed to the cross! If even one of mine or any of those who have received the gift of salvation sins were left, we would not be able to enter Heaven! Why? Because the wages of sin equals death, so just one sin could stop us from going to Heaven if Jesus didn't take it away.

Jesus loves hanging out with the sinners! He loves healing the sick! The healthy ones don't need the doctor; the sick do! So, we've got to get that mind set, Folks, that we have to go after the people who are sick, and we've got to be willing to do whatever it takes in order to get this mission accomplished!

We have to realize that eternal destinations are at stake! We talk about everything else like weather, sports, jobs, etc. very easily, but we find it hard to talk about the most important decision ever....eternal destination, Heaven or Hell! I know that there is fear involved...fear of rejection, fear of persecution, but we have to get over that and realize that lives are at stake! I, myself, would rather be rejected and/or judged, then to think that I could have shared the most important thing in my life, God with someone else and they may receive this precious gift and change for eternity then to sit back and not say a word! The thought of that someone else may be going to hell motivates me to share with them who

Jesus is and what He did for us! We have got to be like Matthew and invite people to hang out with Jesus and us!

You will hear all kinds of excuses like "If I walk into the church, the walls will cave in or lightning will strike." Well you can answer them this way, "I am a sinner just like you and it hasn't happened yet. I may have made some better choices in my life and had Jesus straightening out my issues, but it doesn't mean that I am better than you!"

Folks, I have a feeling that if we would only go after the mission, we will be amazed at what God is going to do! But that's the decision that we all are going to have to make. We're going to have to decide if we are going to be like the friends in the Word that carried their friends on mats to Jesus to be healed. We are going to have to decide if we are willing to do whatever it takes for the sake of they being introduced, set free, and healed by Jesus or are we just going to sit back and watch the world die and souls be destroyed? I don't know about you, but I am ready to move my feet; I'm ready to see God move in our region and I believe He will do it. I believe there is a whole mission field right where we are. Just take off and watch God move! He has placed you where you are to use your gifts, your talents on the mission field where He has placed you! Use your gifts and talents for His glory just like Matthew did! Let's not just go through life everyday, but let's change the world through the power of Jesus Christ, one person at a time!!!

What Cha Talking About?

Cassandra O. Thomas

Will you pray with me please? Almighty and gracious Lord, we come to a time to be still and know You. A time to open our hearts and our ears and our minds to receive a word from You. Holy Spirit, teach us what You would have us to learn, and use me as You will. For we seek to resonate with people in the world, sharing the good news of a risen Lord and Savior Jesus Christ. Amen.

Well I appreciate the invitation. Thank you for the marquee. I appreciate the opportunity to speak on a very tough topic for us as Christians. I would say the majority of Christians. Some of this is going to be participatory. You haven't seen me in a while so I get to have a little license then if you don't like it, you won't invite me back. But if you do, it's because the Lord has put it in your heart, okay?

What does evangelism mean to you? This is participatory. Somebody tell me. Share it out loud. What does evangelism mean to you? (Response, "Spreading the Word of God.") There is no right or wrong answer. This is what you believe. What does evangelism mean to you? Honestly from the heart. (Response, "Spreading the Love of God.") More responses such as "Sharing and witnessing to the good news.") What does it really mean to you as a Christian here at College Heights? What does evangelism really mean to you? Thank you young people for participating. What does it really mean to you? (Silence then response, "Singing, preaching, listening to the Word of God. Renewing ourselves.") What does evangelism really me to you? Be honest. Somebody tell me the truth about how you really feel about evangelism. (Response, "Spreading the Good News.") Okay, spreading the Good News; that's what evangelism means in the Greek—sharing or witnessing to the Good News.

Most Christians say "that's not my job." Most Christians say "I don't know how to do it so I'm not going to do it." "I don't want to get it wrong." Most people are out there saying evangelism is for an evangelist like in the Bible. I can point you to that. Some were "evangelists, some were apostles, some were teachers..." (Ephesians 4:11). Most of us in the pews say "I don't want to open my mouth out there in public, because I might get rejected, and I'm afraid of what will happen."

Does anybody resonate with that kind of feeling about evangelism? If so would you say an amen? (No amens heard.) So nobody feels that way. Well, I'm glad. I'm glad; that means everything I'm going to share here today you all don't really need to hear. (Audience chuckles.) Because you are already evangelizing. But if you are not already evangelizing, sharing the good news, then maybe there is something here the Lord is going to touch your heart so it is warm and burning and you will respond in Jesus' name. For you see there are scriptures that a lot of churches model and use that say specifically that Jesus did and therefore we should do. And the most popular one, the most familiar one is actually, and again all the gospels have this scenario, of when Jesus draws and calls the first disciples.

The first disciples were doing what? (Wait for response.) Fishing. That was their occupation. Okay think about this for a minute. That was their occupation so that is where Jesus found them. That's where Jesus went. And so He uses an analogy that they could relate to. He says drop your nets and I will make you ... (wait for response) ... fishers of men. We all know that.

So we have this image of if we just cast out our nets. If we just throw out that line, if we would just have the right bait, people will come to church. If we have enough programs with the children, if we have marriage counseling, if we have divorce recovery, if we have youth and singles and choir and all these programs, if they're just good enough. Hey we just have to put our sign out on the door and they will come. Because we are going to become fishers of men and women and children.

Okay so that's a model that a lot of people take. In fact one model that I want to share with you all is one that I got when I went to Leadership School and it was a joy to see all of you who came. Presbytery supported and sponsored (Presbytery of Coastal Carolina PCUSA). And I pray that again as you hear about these opportunities for growth and for learning that you will avail yourselves of it. But one program is called *Catch*.[15] *Catch* is a four week bible study for small groups. It has a DVD. It has a little study guide. It has a way

---

[15]Catch: A Church-wide Program for Invitational Evangelism. Debi Nixon and Adam Hamilton. Nashville: Abingdon Press. 2012.

of helping churches, church leaders, and church members, evaluate what they can do to have invitational evangelism.

Again invitational evangelism meaning we invite you into our church. And there's nothing wrong with that. In fact one author is Debi Nixon and then Adam Hamilton. Adam Hamilton founded United Methodist Church of the Resurrection. I was able to go to that church in Kansas when I was in the military. I was in Kansas at a (military) chaplain workshop. In fact it was on contemporary worship. And we visited and we saw and we heard from him. We saw this great big church. But he started with nothing. With a grassroots commission by his denomination to go out into Kansas to reach out to the unchurched, to the marginally churched, to reach out to them. His church and his group blossomed to hundreds of thousands of people now. And they publish lots of material about how they did it. And one way they did it that [the book] shares...I'm going to talk about these four things briefly. I would encourage you to do as a bible study.

But these are some of the things. He [Hamilton] said [First] becoming relentlessly forwardly focused, not inwardly focused but outwardly focused. [Second] Answering three important questions. Why do people need Jesus? Why do people need the church? And why do people need your church? Third he said making visitors feel welcome. And four inviting others to grow in faith. Now that's another bible study and sermon all in itself.

But I want you to listen to those three questions. Why do people need Jesus? Can you answer that in your good news? Why do people need the Church, the Body of Christ? Can you answer that in your good news? Why do people need College Heights or Mars Hill or wherever your church is that you are attending? Why would they need your particular church? What's special or unique or great about your church? And so these are the kinds of things fishing...what can we do to reel them in?

But there's another book that I got that I actually have more color codes to that is also not heavy reading, but is powerful reading of thinking about this generation, this young generation. And again younger generation is relative for those born in the past 20 years. Okay so for those of us who have been around for longer than 20 years, we have come through different generations. We have an agrarian generation. We've come through an industrial age generation. We've come through the information age generation.

And now we have what Doug Pagitt in his book *Evangelism in the Inventive Age*[16], with cyberspace, with internet, with the fast paceness of this world, with a generation which he describes that is not looking to be told what to do, but is looking to have an equal [say] of their ideas, of their willingness to serve, but in their own way, not in the traditional ways that you and I are very comfortable with and very complacent with and that we can spout this is what you do. They want something more. They want something different. But their spirituality is no less than ours. It's different.

And so Doug Pagitt, (he's a little controversial because of some of his thinking), he's out of Minnesota. He's the founder of Solomon's Porch. And he is reaching out to this generation that is not here in our churches. He's reaching them where they are. And then when he invites them, they meet and feel comfortable, because what he is doing and what they do at his setting resonates with them. And so he talks about his guiding idea of evangelism is not changing somebody.

You know again our evangelism concept is everybody who is not in our church or in church is unsaved. That was our motto. They're unsaved. They have no sense of God. They have no sense of holiness. They have no sense of spirituality. But if you talk to a young person, they do have a sense of the spiritual. It's just articulated differently than ours. They have a sense of God and they are searching. They're seeking Him in their own way. And sometimes our words, our theology language is not reaching them, because it doesn't resonate with them.

So he [Pagitt] talks about it's not about changes. It's not about conversion and trying to get somebody to change their belief system. What it is, he believes and he believes it's scriptural, is that it is a resonance, what is ringing true. Each of us has a core passion. And we have core passions and fears and when our core passions are met by God's actions, we resonate with good news. Hear this again; when our core passions are met by God's actions, when our core fears are calmed by God's actions, it resonates with good news. It resonates with good feelings within us. It's a warm burning in our hearts.

---

[16]*Evangelism in the Inventive Age*. Doug Pagitt. Minneapolis: Sparkhouse Press. 2012.

He [Pagitt] says "evangelism in the inventive age demands that we deliver the good news of God by finding the resonance between God's story and the story that is played out in each of us." It's unique. It's special. It's not a generic message. That's why it's so hard to evangelize. Because we can't teach four spiritual laws and say if you just do that, and teach it to them to just do that, you'll get them to come. It does not work that way. And we know in our hearts it doesn't resonate with us. We're not faithful to that model, because it doesn't ring true to how we received God and how it can be received by others.

And so we let the model go by the wayside and we do nothing. Instead of exploring where
God is leading us. It's going to be about relationships. It's going to be about personal ties. It's going to be about connectivity. And so the problem becomes time for us, doesn't it? We're so busy. We're so busy with life and doing things and doing for other people and all the ministries that we do in our church, and our social organizations, and our family, and at work, and going to school, if we're going to school. We're so busy. And we don't really want to talk strangers that much anyway. It's more comfortable to talk to people like us. And so it becomes a problem when first the model doesn't resonate, because it doesn't give us the amount energy we need to actually use it. Then we don't want to use it, because we have a lot of good excuses and reasons and rationalizations. And yet I have to caution us about that and I'm talking to me too. I have to caution us about this, because that's exactly what Satan wants from us. He wants us to be so busy. He wants us to be so inwardly focused. He wants us to be so tired and worn out and weary. He wants us to be afraid so that we won't go out and share the good news of Jesus Christ. So we won't speak up and speak out about what God has done in our lives. So that we won't go left when everybody else is going right. We want to conform and be complacent.

And so this is the model. No disrespect to either one of these two that I've just shared with you, there is something that we can learn from each of them. But when I read the scripture today, this scripture, not about the fishers of men. But when I read this scripture from Luke, it resonated with me. And here are some things about this scripture that I would like us to consider as doable for reaching [out] and sharing the good news of Jesus Christ.

You've heard the story. You've read the story. You've heard it preached before, some of us. You wonder and I think we understand what this story is all about. We thing it is really about Jesus appearing to the disciples on that day of Easter Sunday and appearing to them to remind them of His promises. And that true. But it's more than that. Because remember this is Luke writing to a community most of whom were not there, did not have the opportunity to see Jesus, and didn't know anything about Jesus except for what they heard from others, right? Luke is writing predominately to a Gentile community, to someone not raised in the Jewish community, not raised with the scriptures of the Old Testament, not raised with the traditions of the Jewish people. He's reaching to those in the world. And so his story is reflecting on something more than just the "in crowd".

So here is Jesus, resurrected from the dead, having gone through all of the horrors of the cross. This is the background of the story. The horrors of the cross, dying on the cross for your and my sins. Giving us a way to renew our relationship with God Almighty so we can be in His kingdom as His children forever. So that when Jesus comes again, and He will come again, we will be ready for Him to call us home.

But as these disciples are going along, and I'm so glad they weren't one of the eleven, one of the twelve. I'm so glad it wasn't Simon or Andrew or John or James. I'm glad it was two of the followers of Jesus. You know why? Because Jesus comes to all of His people. Not just to those in charge. He calls to all of us to hear the good news and speak the good news. So it's not just the pastor. It's not just the moderator. It's not just the Session. It's not just the deacons. It's each one of us who calls Jesus our Lord and our Savior. He comes to us.

And so they're walking along now again they've left Jerusalem. They're going home. And what are they doing? They're talking about something near and dear to their hearts. They are in mourning. And they are talking about Jesus' death. They're talking about what happened to Him. They are emotional. You get where I'm going with this? You cannot rote something. You cannot speak something by rote in monotone and expect people to get excited about it. You cannot. You cannot tell somebody "oh, you know you need to be saved." Or "You're a sinner and going to hell." They're saying "Who are you? You don't know me. What are you judging me? You don't know a thing about me."

We're so quick to have those catch phrases that we were taught, that we hear, that we think are acceptable holy phrases. Y'all need to kick that to the curb. Because it does not resonate with people these days.

But see Jesus just walked along side [of them]. When you are walking these journeys…they walked back then okay? We don't know what that means these days. We drive everywhere, don't we? But as they were walking and talking, as they were living their lives, Jesus walked alongside them. Now again people would start walking in groups for safety, because there would be thieves and robbers along the way. So they ... so just picture this will you? Jesus just casually starts walking alongside them. And He's listening to them. They're talking about Jesus. They're talking about what happened to Him.

You know when you get excited about something. You know when you get excited about your children, your grandchildren, your great-grandchildren. You talk about the raise you got. You talk about the A you got in class, the B you got. Or even that you failed the class. (Laughter) I talk about that one. You talk about how the Lord saved your life from an accident. You were this close to a car accident and it didn't happen. And you go and you what?! You tell somebody you know. You get on the phone or you get on the Facebook, some of y'all, and you start. You start thanking God on the internet for saving your life. You start witnessing because you're so happy. And then when you're sad and when you're grieving and you've lost someone you loved and you know people say "you'll get over it; you'll get over it". I think you need to talk about it. You know people get tired of you talking about it. Find someone new who hasn't heard it. But talk about it. It's a catharsis. These two disciples, that was a catharsis process of getting that emotion out. But saying what was on their hearts and on their minds.

And the irony ... you read the irony in the story don't you? For some reason their eyes were blinded and shielded. The One who they were talking about was the One walking alongside them. And someone would say how, how could that happen? How in the world could somebody not recognize Jesus?

Well I want to share one thing with you real quick. It can happen. There's an example in the *Evangelism in the Inventive Age* (Pagitt, 2012). It talks about how we can see and not see. There was an experiment that was done where this group of people were shown two [basketballs]. Six people, three were in white shirts and three were in black shirts. There were two basketballs. They were in this group. And they were told now count how many times the white shirts catch the ball. So this begins, this experiment begins. Then all of the sudden the gorilla comes in the room. Somebody's heard this story before? (parishioner shares she heard story at a conference.)

So for the rest of you who didn't go to the conference...The gorilla was around there. But these people, all their eyes were focused on what? Counting the balls for the white shirts. Afterwards when they were asked how many balls were counted, they were basically correct about getting the count. But when they were asked did you see anything in the room, nobody saw the gorilla, because they were so focused on counting.

We get so focused sometimes on that one mission and that one purpose. No matter how much we multitask. We women, you know, because we have to multitask quite a bit. We're not focused on any of it. We just try to get it all done and we don't remember a thing about what happened but that it's done. You know a lot of us are like that. We think our memories are gone, but it's because we're not focused. So it can happen.

Jesus is in the midst of us, and we don't even know it. But Jesus was in their midst, and here is the irony, so He goes up to them and asks them "what cha talking about?" So I paraphrased it. He says so what are you all talking about. And they stopped, and they looked at Him, and they're sad, and they're grieving, and they're talking to one another. And so Cleopas says "And are you the only one in all of Jerusalem who doesn't know what's going on? Are you the only one who doesn't know what traumatic things have been going on today? And so Jesus says "Well tell me." And so Cleopas begins to tell the story.

At what point ... not when we go up to someone and say are you saved? There's still people out there that do that. Because they've been taught a model that says you need to save somebody from their sins and this is how you do it. Can I recommend you kick that to the curb too? That's just my opinion, okay? Some of this is my opinion and some of this is God's Word. Let the Lord help you figure this out and I'll try to tell you when it's my opinion.

He only comes and says tell me after He's listened to them share from their heart. Only after He's seen their authentic emotions is He willing to engage to hear what's gotten them so excited. What's got them ... so sad, what's got them so engaged in their conversation.

Now some of us we just hate people interrupting our conversations. We don't want to be bothered, do we? We really don't. Especially if they are strangers. "I don't have time. Lord please don't let them look at me. Please Lord don't let them come over here. Please

Lord I don't have enough time. Don't, don't." And so God won't. Because that's what you prayed. You might not have thought it was a prayer, but that was your prayer. And so you don't engage in conversation. But the step is they are drawn to you because of what you are saying and doing. And if you aren't authentically real, if you aren't resonating with the love of Christ which is in you, then they're not gonna come.

But just on the outside that they do come, okay? Just on the outside that there is something about you …this is the other thing I like. They were two together. Okay, now, in this day and age, I think it could be you and someone on your phone. You could be in the store waiting in line, waiting, waiting, waiting. They can't see you texting okay. But they can hear you [saying] "…and you know the Lord did this….and I'm so happy because…". People are overhearing that conversation. And when you hang up they just might say "hey, I'm a Christian too" or "amen."

You know evangelizing does not mean that you are necessarily out trying to convert or change or transform somebody. It means that you are resonating with them in their souls about a spiritual matter, of sharing the good news. So when they're resonating with you because you are sharing the good news, that's evangelism! Do you see how this model is different than fishing for men? You see how it's different because now you're living your life authentically because you're walking in Christ daily? And you're not ashamed to speak about it. And you're not ashamed to show it. So people in this day and age are going to look for authenticity, realness. And then they're gonna ask you some questions. And then they want real answers. They don't want spiritually high theological responses. They want what you did, what you believe, what are you concerned about, what are your fears. How can you have faith in the midst of this, this, and this? How can you have hope in this and this? You know I can't answer that except by faith I believe and He gives me the peace that passes all understanding. And that's scripture but that's my heart. You see how that's different than quoting scripture? For God so loved the world that He gave...

And so when they are asking questions, the next thing that you need to do after your sharing is exactly what happened in the story. You need to listen to them. See too often we think it is a one way street of just talking, talking, talking, talking, talking. No. Jesus said "what are y'all talking about". He [Cleopas] told [him] then He [Jesus] said "y'all are so foolish; didn't you know?" He began to talk and they listened.

So now that teaches us we need to shut up and we need to listen to them. We have to listen to what they believe without judging them or trying to correct them. This is a problem for me sometimes. Sometimes I say "No you mean ..., you really mean this ..., or no that's not right...". No, no, no! Sandy! Listen to them. Shut up and listen. Hear them. Hear their spirituality. Hear their beliefs. Hear their background. Look at where they've come from. They're no less than me. They're no greater than me. And I'm no greater than them. I'm not better than them. But we Christians think we've got it. We've got Jesus and so we're better than the unsaved. And yet aren't we sinners saved by grace? Not of ourselves.

And so we miss this next step. We don't listen to them as equals. But Jesus He listened to them. They listened to Him. And then here is another step we don't want to do. When the day was going, they reached their village, they reached their home, and He was going to walk on. He acted like He was gonna walk on. In the Near Eastern culture, you invite someone in. And the courtesy thing is "oh no, I don't want to bother you." But the custom, the etiquette, the protocol is you keep inviting them in. You say "no, come, rest with us, the day is going, take a break, rest your feet." So He accepts their invitation into their home.

We wanna say "hey come join our church." And we want to throw them into programs right off. Then when we get them involved, they'll stay. No they won't. They'll come for a time maybe two. But they won't come back. You didn't make them feel welcome. You just wanted to use them. You invited them to church but you didn't invite them to your home. You didn't invite them out for coffee or tea. You didn't have time for them. I didn't have time for them 'cause I was too busy trying to do what the Lord wanted.

But Jesus accepted their invitation into their home. We need to invite personally. We're too busy. We need to look at what we're busy about. Because if we're truly going to follow that Great Commission which again everyone throws out...you know...Jerusalem, Samaria, uttermost parts of the world..., there's no time unless you make the time. And so Jesus sat with them and this is a reverse of the process, the guest takes the bread. He took it, He blessed it, and He broke it, and then He gave it to them, and their eyes were opened.

Communion with the Lord, that revealed Him, in the sharing at the table. Does not that remind us of our relationship with Jesus? And doesn't that remind us of how it was always not about a church structure but a communal setting and relationship? Isn't that what God wants us to do as the children of God is to be in relationship with people? Not just like us. But as He calls them and draws them to us that what we do is authentic and real and exciting.

And so my question to you is how is your relationship with Jesus? How is your love life? Is it boring? Is it complacent? Is it "oh He knows I love Him; I'm so busy and tired"? What is your relationship with Jesus? Is it exciting? If it is not exciting, what's happened to you? Where's the honeymoon period? You've gotta keep the honeymoon period for your whole life long. But we don't, do we? We say if we've gotten through all the steps, of baptism, in the church, and we do these programs in the church, hey I can coast the rest of my life.

Not if you're in relationship with Jesus. 'Cause you know what? Jesus is going to keep growing you, keep maturing you until you come to the fullness of who you should be in Him. And He's gonna keep on changing you, transforming you, and helping you to grow beyond who you think you are. You're not settled; whatever your age is right this moment, you're not done yet! However you are feeling health-wise, God is still working. He's not through with you. And you should be excited. You shouldn't be tired and worn out. You should be excited saying "Lord You're still using me. Lord still using me. Lord You're still showing me. Lord You still have a need for me to reach out in Your name and share Your good news". And if you can't speak it, if you can't sing it, then write it. If you can't write it then draw it. If you can't draw it then, God's given you some kind of gift to use, cook it (chuckles).

God has given you some kind of gift. He's given it to you. Yours is not mine and mine is not yours. That's why you can't have one model of evangelism. What will work for one group of people "oh I can do that." Three other groups say "I can't relate to that" so they don't do anything. No, we give those models that work for different groups and personalities.

So okay, in the end their hearts burned while He was talking. They felt something. And in the end because of what He did with them, their eyes were opened. They got up, they ran back to Jerusalem and shared the good news. No matter that it was late, the path was dangerous, they got up excited sharing the good news. This is the message for the community of believers and this is the message for us today. What cha talking about?

Rock-Faces and Trust

Micaiah Thomas

(Numbers 20: 1-13)

Read Numbers 20: 1-13

Would you join me in prayer:

> *Heavenly Father,*
>
> > *Would your Spirit rest in this place and drench these words with life that comes only from You. Speak Lord, and open our hearts to hear You. Amen.*

Beginning:

When my siblings and I were young, my father decided that we needed to have a 'family adventure.' Some sort of challenge that we would go on together. He ran through several ideas and landed on rock-climbing. As a family, we would go rock-climbing. At the time my siblings and I were ages 7, 9, 11, and 13.

We got to the cliffs, 30 feet of vertical adventure, and picked out what rock face we were going to climb. Now as the four of us took our turns climbing, we found that the beginning part of the climb was pretty easy- what's 6 or 10 feet off the ground? It was fun. No worries, pretty smooth-sailing.

But, the higher we went, slippery rocks, few hand-holds, 20 feet off the gournd, that was when the challenge kicked in. And as each one of us met this challenge in the rock it was evident that we began to feel the feelings of stress and worry and uncertainty. Interestingly, we all reacted differently to the stressful situation we found ourselves in.

- When hanging by his fingers, my older brother became very quiet and began to mumble under his breath.
- When standing on a half inch rock ripple, my sister laughingly screamed in exasperation.

- With his fist jammed in a hole, my younger brother burrowed down into his determination and tried endlessly to scamper up the rock.
- And I, 20 feet up with my foot stretched out as far as I could stretch it looking for a ledge to support my weight, well I, got angry. I began to say things I didn't really mean. Like, "If we were a normal family, we wouldn't be rock-climbing for our family event. We could have just gone to see a movie or stayed home!"

Transition: Like the Israelites, I was exhausted and found things to be hard and found that things weren't going exactly my way, I reacted with mumbling and screaming and frustration.

The Excitement Wears off

God had thrown the Israelites into risk and adventure-it was like their rock-climbing, family event-but, after so many years of wandering in the desert, the novelty and excitement of the big move into the Promised Land had worn off. Twenty feet up with no hand holds is a different perspective. This wandering had stopped being fun a long time ago. Now it was just exhausting, muscles were cramping and hand-holds were uncertain.

Like the adventure of that new job that seemed so promising. A desk, an office, new co-workers…Even the off-brand coffee in the break room is full of excitement. Yet, within months, 20 feet off the ground, the excitement wears off and the deadlines add stress to your life.

Like the adventure of that new house you just moved into. It's exciting as fresh coats of paint go on the walls. It's exciting to hop in the car and figure out all the ways around town. The neighbors bring pies and fruit baskets to welcome you in. But soon, the adventure wears off, 20 feet off the ground and now you are challenged by loving these new neighbors and missing old ones.

Like the adventure of that new relationship. Where everything that person does is gold. They can do no wrong. But with trembling arms and no foot hold to support your weight, you realize that the adventure of this new relationship also brings differing opinions and opposing desires.

When the adventure wears off, all we can feel is exhaustion and all we want to do is complain about the frustrations of life. And often, the complaints are valid. The feelings of frustration are real. The doubts and uncertainties are not to be downplayed.

"Why did you bring us out of Egypt to this terrible place?" That's a fair question. The Israelites are, after all, still roaming around the desert. The Israelites are tired of this adventure that they're on.

Transition: And, then, there's Moses.

Moses-who is called to lead this exhausted and frustrated group.
Moses-who upon hearing the complaints of the Israelites and their need for water,
  falls facedown before God
Moses-who hears God tell him to go and speak to a rock, and the rock will then pour
  out water.

Moses' Reaction

Really?!

Does God not see everything that's going on here? The Israelites are absolutely fed up. And in need of water. Water in order to live. Not to mention, Moses is probably pretty fed up, too. He's got to be exhausted by this point, as well. And his sister Miriam has just died. Moses, along with the Israelites are now 20 feet up the rock, trembling and tired.

And God tells him to go and speak to a rock.

It is here that Moses disconnects from his safety anchor, goes out on his own, and takes it upon himself to fix the problem. Moses is going to free-style this climb.

Out of desperation, in frustration, and with a lack of patience, Moses stands before the disgruntled Israelites, and strikes the rock with his staff, twice.

Transition: Moses fixes the problem himself.

Fixers

We have created a culture of fixing things. We all like to be fixers.

The problem is that there are people in our lives whose hearts have been hardened over like rocks. And instead of speaking to these people, we try to fix the problem, instead.

- There are people whose hearts are like stone because they've poured out so much that they are left poor in Spirit.
- Or because life has handed them unfair expectations and they have failed to meet all of them.
- Their hearts are like stone because they have lost a loved one.
- Or received a scary diagnosis.
- Or because they feel under-appreciated and under-valued.

So, these are the rock-faces that we are called to see and speak to.

These are the people that cannot find living water. And our 'we can fix it attitude' is not good enough. Hitting these rocks with our staffs of holiness is not what brings life.

Yet, we do it anyway. Because fixing the problem is easier.

It's easier to hit the poor with the stick of health care than to speak to the poverty in their souls.

It's easier to hit the angry with a stick of anger management than to speak to the frustration that they've build up in their hearts.

It's easier to hit the bitter with a stick of a 'can-do' attitude than to speak to the pain that has caused their calloused hearts.

It's easier to hit the ill with the line that 'they will get better' than to speak to the reality that this is hard and scary.

It's easier to hit these rocks with our staffs than it is to speak to these rock-faces with the belief that God will do something.

Instead of trusting that God will do something, we free style the climb and take over. We even try to fix ourselves as we try to beat the bitterness, anger, and pain out of our own lives.

If I can just control the problem, if I can just fix it, then I'll find water and, ultimately, life.

There is water in those rocks. You can trust in God, in a God to bring life out of the rocky places.

God isn't asking us to draw living water out of those rocks. God is simply asking that we trust in God.

Transition: And the beauty of trusting in God is this:

- There's more security in who God is than in the water coming from the rock.
- There's more security in a relationship with God than there is in Moses' ability to fix the problem.
- There's more security in a relationship with God than in our own abilities to fix the problem.
- There's more security in who God is.

Ending:

This first time that we all went rock-climbing together as a family, my father did something that has always stuck with me. As each one of us began to climb, maybe 10 feet in the air, he made us stop.

"Let go," he said. "Let go of the rock and fall."

Each one of us looked back at him with a bit of uncertainty. What?! That seemed like the exact opposite thing that we should do.

You see, we were attached to the safety system and our father was the anchor as we climbed. We were tied to him. He was our support.

In an act of showing us that we could trust him, he asked us to let go of the rock. "I just want you to see that if you fall, you're not going to fall very far." He said. "I've got you. You can let go because I've got you."

The God who can break open our calloused, hardened, rocky hearts can be trusted. Our God who brings water out of rocks, who brings life out of death-this is the God that tells us: "I've got you." God says: Trust in me. I've got you.

Whom Will You Serve?

Laura Narowetz Todd

(Joshua 24: 14-27)

This past Summer and Fall was blessed to visit five major league baseball parks. One of those parks was the famous stadium for the New York Yankees where Derek Jeter has played as a short stop for the New York Yankees for 18 years. This weekend I got to visit Tuner Filed to watch one of my favorite baseball players of all time play in person Chipper Jones. Chipper Jones has played for the Atlanta Braves for 19 years. He has played 3rd base and in the outfield for this team. For both of theses players to play for the same major league ball team is a great commitment. Compared to other players in the league they have done an amazing thing by playing for the same team for so many years.

At one time or another though, Chipper Jones and Derek Jeter, had to say to themselves or someone else that I will serve the Atlanta Braves team or New York Yankees team. I will give my blood, sweet, and tears to this team. When I was younger my family would go on vacation for about 2 weeks at a time and we would be able to watch the Atlanta Braves play on the Turner Broadcasting Station. During that time the Braves had some amazing players even some of the best pitchers in the history of baseball including Greg Maddox, Tom Glavin, and John Smoltz. They even won a world series in 1995 and during this time Chipper Jones has served the Atlanta Braves to his best ability. Other players and coaches have come and gone but Chipper Jones has been there through all of the ups and downs of the team. He has given us an example of what it means to serve on a team and give it your all.

At the end of this season Chipper Jones is retiring and as a result throughout this season Chipper Jones is taking in the moments and realizing how important his career has been. He gave his last speech at the Major League All-Start game this year and at many other places because he realizes this will be the last time to play baseball in those ball parks. He will one day be a Hall of Fame member of Major League Baseball. So I wonder what has made him different from all of the other players and I wonder why he decided to stay in Atlanta for 19 years to play baseball.

He did this because he had dedication and he knew who he was serving. Now I am not saying Chipper Jones is perfect, he has made some mistakes on the field and in his life. Chipper Jones has served the baseball fans of the Atlanta Braves those 19 years. He made a choice about who he would serve. Please do not get me wrong I am not equating Chipper Jones with the Israelites or God I am just using him as an example of someone who had to decided which baseball team he will serve and has served the Atlanta Braves for 19 years and will go down in history as one of their greatest players in history to play for the Braves.

How does this connect to the scripture, you must be asking yourself? Like Chipper Jones who is giving his going away speeches because this is his last year to play major league baseball, Joshua is now giving his going away speech. Joshua is speaking at Shechem because it is the place where the Israelites have many memories. For example, God spoke to Abraham there in Genesis 12:6-7. It is the place near Mount Ebal where the Israelites had renewed their covenant with God after they had entered the land. Joshua is at a special place with the Israelites and a special place can sometimes make it easier for us to deal with God.

The people in this story had just been reminded of their history and deliverance. Joshua is now providing them with a challenge to remember who has blessed them and be there for them. Because of this gift that they have received from God Joshua tells the people that they should, "Fear or revere the Lord and serve God faithfully." Joshua wants them to throw away the gods of their past that their families had served and choose now to serve the Lord. He wants them to take action and serve the Lord with their whole hearts. He does not want them to say one thing and then do another. If you notice he did not tell them that they had a few weeks to decide what they wanted to do. He just tells them to put away the old gods and serve the Lord.

My coworker at the Church Health Center that teaches our Commit to Quit class experiences something very similar to this when she talks to people that want to quit smoking. People will come in a say next week or in a month I want to quit smoking. Most of the time she will ask them why wait. What will be different in a week from now or a month and most of the time nothing will really be different. They want to spend their time thinking about it too much instead of making changes. Of course making changes in our lives will not be easy and maybe that is what Joshua is trying to get the Israelites to understand. There are a lot of things in this world that are easier said than done.

Joshua is trying to get them to understand how important this decision is for them. He reminds them of this by saying, "Now if you are unwilling to serve the LORD, choose this day whom you will serve, whether the gods your ancestors served in the region beyond the River or the gods of the Amorites in whose land you are living; but as for me and my household, we will serve the LORD." "The verb to serve occurs 7 times in vv. 14-15 and 15 times in the chapter. It can mean the response to the act of worship (Ps 100:2; Is 29:2; Ezek 20:40), or exclusive and wholehearted loyalty to God (Deut 10:12, 20; 11:13; 1 Sam 12:20)" (The Wesley Study Bible 293-4). Through this question God is giving them the choice to decide whom on this day they will serve. This is a challenge for them because Joshua wants them to trust in the God who has always been there for them over the gods of their past. The gods of their past were just idols but the Lord is not an idol and has been there with them through the good times and the bad times. God has given them the land in which they live on and has protected them from their enemies. The time has come from them to choose who they will be loyal to and trust.

Of course the people quickly respond to Joshua's challenge by saying, "we will not forsake the Lord to serve other gods." But, we must wonder will they really keep that promise. The Israelites respond by saying that God has brought us out of the land of Egypt, God brought us out of slavery. God protected us every where we went. Therefore we will serve God. I wonder if they realize what they are saying and what Joshua is trying to get them to understand.

As we all know talk is cheap. People tell us they will do things and we wait and wait and it never happens. It is easy to say I want this church to grow and I think when people come visit we feel like a welcoming group but in reality is that true? Do we really want our church to grow? Do we really want to be open and welcoming? Are we really serving the Lord or are we serving the idols that are in ours lives and we do not even notice it?

Then Joshua said to the people that they could not serve the Lord because the Lord is Holy and a jealous God. God will not excuse your wrongdoing or sins. God does not want us serving other gods.

Joshua is reminding them that the God they now believe in is a jealous God and does not want them serving other gods. They must now be loyal and show respect to God because if they do not serve God then the Lord will not be happy. The people responded to what Joshua said by saying, "No, we will serve the Lord!" Even after Joshua has told the people that they serve a jealous God they were willing to serve the Lord. In their mind they had committed to serving God with the body, soul, and mind.

Because they said they would serve the Lord Joshua asked them to put away their idols so that they would not be tempted to worship them. Joshua challenged them to take action to do whatever it is they need to do so that they can follow God. If you notice something here the people do not take action to get rid of their old gods. They just say that they will serve God but the do not saying anything about putting those foreign gods away as Joshua mentions. The people just say we will serve and obey the Lord.

After hearing this story I started to wonder: What are ways that we can obey and serve the Lord? What are the idols in our life today that are preventing us from serving the Lord with are whole body, mind, and soul? After we do identify those idols in our lives how do we over come them? How can we as a church and presbytery serve the Lord? The answers to these questions are not easy. In our world today it is not easy to just say I will serve the Lord. We have idols in our lives every where we look. We are reminded of these idols every time we turn on the television, walk out our doors to go shopping, or when we trust in money instead of God. So to end today I will give you a story about a church that had to decide how to give up their idols and serve the Lord.

The church I serve was established sometime in 1950 as a mission project and a few years ago the church had to ask themselves, "Who will we serve?" Will we serve God or will we serve the idols of our time. The church has this huge building with space that can be used to do one of two things. It can be used for nothing or it can be used to serve God and provide love and support to the children of God that are in need.

Then after a time of prayer, bible study, and revitalization the church members decided that they wanted to continue serving the Lord. The church now averages 20-30 people in worship on Sunday morning and the average age of the church members is over the age of 70. But now the church is serving the Lord in mores ways than they were in the past.

We can do this now because of all of the help that we received from the presbytery and from the other Cumberland Presbyterian churches in West TN. With every ministry that we have we have received support, love, and prayers from all of you in the church today.

For the last 6 years this church has run a summer camp for the community and it has only charges $40 a week for per child, we now have a Wednesday program for children and youth that has prevented some teens from joining gangs and has helped one former youth that has lupus stay alive and recover from a heart attack. In fact, this week I was representing the Church Health Center at a Health Fair on campus at the University of Memphis. I was walking around the campus and I came across one of our former youth group members that graduated from high school 3 years ago. I am pretty sure when he was in high school he was a member of the local gang. Jonathan came up to me and was so excited to see me because we had not seen each other in a while. He told me that he was working in the landscaping department at the University of Memphis and wanted to open up his own landscaping business after getting a degree in business management. I walked away from my conversation with him speechless, shocked, and amazed because of what God has done in Jonathan's life. I think Jonathan attended summer camp at Camp Clark Williamson and was a part of this church. This was made possible because of all of the support that he received from others and as well as the support that Colonial has received from the presbytery. Because of our ability to work together and serve the Lord Jonathan's life has been saved in more ways than one.

We also have a clothes closet that provides clothes for people in the area. In fact, I received a thank you note two weeks ago from a mother that has three kids ages (6 year old boy, 3 year old girl, and 3 month old baby girl) that was left by her husband. She thanked us for the love, support, and care that we provided for her and prayed for us. We only gave her a handful of clothes but because of that small gift her life was changed and she was so thankful. To be honest I have no idea where 80-90% of the clothes that we receive come from but I do know that they have come from other Cumberland Presbyterian churches in the area and because of your generous gifts and willingness to serve the Lord lives are changed every time some receives a pair of shoes and or a shirt to wear on their back.
We also work with other churches in the area to feed the homeless, give them clothes, let them shower, and sleep in our building once a week. Our goal this year is hopefully to be able to increase our homeless outreach ministry but this could not be done without the help, love, support, and prayers of other Cumberland Presbyterian Churches in the West Tennessee Presbytery.

The examples that I have provided are what happens when the church decides to be missional and work together to serve the Lord. It will not been easy and it will more than likely continue to get harder. But, if we as a presbytery remember to take action and serve the Lord our God with our whole heart, body, mind, and soul we will be able to meet people where they are and make a difference in the lives of some many people because we answered the God's call to serve the Lord. Amen.

Bibliography

Life Application Study Bible. Grand Rapids: Zondervan, 2005. Print.

The Wesley Study Bible. Nashville: Abingdon Press, 2009. Print.

Normas Celestiales Para No Olvidar
Heavenly Rules You Shouldn't Forget

Diana María Valdez

(Deuteronomy 8)

INTRODUCCIÓN:

Reglas familiares: los padres, casi siempre pedimos una sola cosa de los hijos "OBEDIENCIA A LAS NORMAS FAMILIARES". De no ser cumplidas habrán consecuencias, que a los hijos generalmente no nos agradan, por ejemplo Juanmi TV. Pero cuando Juanmy cumple las reglas estoy segura que no se ha olvidado de nosotros sus padres.

Nosotros somos hijos de Dios, él tiene una regla para nosotros: "OBEDIENCIA A LAS NORMAS CELESTIALES", esta es la mejor forma de no olvidarnos de nuestro Padre Dios

TEXTO: Dt 8

NORMAS CELESTIALES PARA NO OLVIDAR

CONTEXTO:

1- NORMA CELESTIAL PARA NO OLVIDAR ES RECORDAR EL PASADO Y PENSAR EN EL FUTURO CUANDO ANDAMOS CON DIOS

   Vr. 1- 10 Obediencia de los mandamientos y su consecuencia vivir, multiplicarse y tomar posesión de la tierra prometida.

   2-5 EL PASADO: el desierto donde Dios nos ha disciplinado para pulirnos, para conocer nuestros corazones y lo fuertes que nos haríamos para guardar los mandamientos del Señor. Donde nos faltó algo material pero que en últimas Dios

327

suplió para que reconozcamos que Él es el proveedor y que lo material no es suficiente para vivir.

6-19 EL FUTURO: una tierra donde no habrá escases, todo será abundante, la disciplina de aprendizaje ya pasó ahora es tiempo de disfrutar las bondades del Padre. Pero hay que tener cuidado de al momento de disfrutar agradecer a Dios el proveedor.

2-   NORMA CELESTIAL PARA NO OLVIDAR ES SER AGRADECIDO CON DIOS :

Vr.11-16Recordar a Dios es guardar y cumplir sus mandamientos, ordenanzas y estatutos que están en la Biblia.   La expresión "no olvidarse" se refiere a: Dt 4:9…olvidar algo que se vio. Dt 6:12… a olvidar lo que ha hecho Jah. por nosotros, está en contraposición con la el temor de Jah.

¿Cuándo ud se siente satisfecho se olvida de Dios?
¿Es ud de los que busca a Dios solamente cuando tiene necesidad?
¿Se acerca a Dios cuando todo va bien, o sólo cuando las cosas van mal?

Pr 30:8-9
"Y no me des pobreza ni riqueza. Sólo dame mi pan cotidiano; no sea que me sacie y te niegue, o diga: "¿Quién es Jehovah?" No sea que me empobrezca y robe, y profane el nombre de mi Dios."

Vr. 14 Saciedad en la alimentación, tener buena casa en que habitar.
13: Aumento de las posesiones.
14ª: Es una cadena, estando saciado puede llegar a enaltecerse de corazón olvidándose de Jehovah.
14ᵇ-16: Olvidarse de lo que Jehovah Dios ha hecho con nosotros, menospreciar las bendiciones.
8:4… Las bendiciones de Jehovah.

3. NORMA CELESTIAL PARA NO OLVIDAR ES EL RECONOCIMIENTO:

Vr. 17: Todo esto es por mí mismo. "Fui yo" ESTO ES FALSO
Vr. 18   ACUERDATE DEL SEÑOR TU DIOS QUE EL ES EL QUE TE DA FUERZAS PARA TENER RIQUEZAS

Is 10:12-13… una profecía de Isaías contra Asiria.
"El Señor… castigará también el fruto del corazón soberbio del rey de Asiria y la gloria de sus ojos altivos. Porque ha dicho: -Con el poder de mi mano y con mi sabiduría lo he hecho, porque soy inteligente. He eliminado las fronteras de los pueblos, he saqueado sus tesoros y he derribado como hombre fuerte a sus habitantes. Mi mano halló como en un nido las riquezas de los pueblos; y como se juntan los huevos abandonados, así junté yo a toda la tierra. No hubo quien moviese un ala o abriese el pico para chirriar."

¿Reconoce que lo que tiene es dado por Dios? o ¿Cree que es por su sabiduría?
El no reconocerlo es olvidarse de Dios.

Sal 103:2
"Bendice, oh alma mía, a Jehovah, y no olvides ninguno de sus beneficios."

18: En vez de pensar en que es por mi capacidad debo recordar quien es la fuente de todo.
Otra vez no olvidarse de Jehovah está en contra posición a reconocer lo que él nos ha dado.

4.   NORMA CELESTIAL PARA NO OLVIDAR ES SER FIELES:

19ª: Implica: NO
> Caminar en pos de otros dioses.
> Rendirles culto postrándose ante ellos.
> Ir tras otros dioses: Apartarse de lo que Jah manda (Dt 11:28). Abandonar a Jah y su ley (Jer 16:11). Provocar a ira a Jah (Jer 25:6).
> Dioses falsos: compiten por la adoración a Jah (Ge 35:2). Comparado a Jah (Ex 15:11). Está prohibido en la ley (Ex 20:3).
> Ídolo..... ¡Cualquier cosa que para nosotros sea más importante que Dios!

19^b-20: Dios castiga la idolatría.

¿Tiene ud. cosas más importantes que Dios? Su trabajo, su familia, su novio, el estudio, el deporte,   la televisión, o alguna otra cosa. Esto puede ser muestra de olvido al Señor. Estas sin ser malas en sí mismas pueden llegar a ocupar el lugar de Dios.

CONCLUSIÓN:

LAS NORMAS CELESTIALES PARA NO OLVIDAR A DIOS QUE NOS PRESENTA DT. SON:

1-   RECORDAR EL PASADO Y PENSAR EN EL FUTURO CUANDO ANDAMOS CON DIOS
2-   SER AGRADECIDO CON DIOS.
3-   EL RECONOCIMIENTO
4-   SER FIELES

REFLEXION:

"El pobre Juan vivía en una pequeña y destartalada casa, comía a penas lo necesario y nunca tenía dinero para disfrutar de algunas cosas de la vida. Sin embargo, hasta ese momento Juan era un fiel hijo de Dios, dedicaba buen tiempo a estudio de la Biblia, a la oración y al trabajo en la iglesia. Juan siempre le pedía a Dios para que mejorara su situación, él no entendía cómo un hijo de Dios viviera así. Un día Dios le dio un empleo y Juan comenzó a ganar buen dinero y se compró un televisor, pero de tanto ver la tele dejó de leer la Palabra de Dios; después se compró un buen equipo de sonido, pero de tanto escuchar radio dejó de orar; Finalmente compró un hermoso carro, pero por salir cada fin de semana con mujeres no volvió a la iglesia. Juan se había olvidado de Dios, lo que él pensó que le traería felicidad lo hizo alejarse del Señor. Con su vida desordenada Juan terminó muy mal y su estado postrer vino a ser peor que el primero."

Get Up!

Fran Vickers

(Matthew 2:13-23)

December 29, 2013

Get Up! It is time to go to church! Did any of you hear that this morning? Get up it is time to go to school! Get up and answer the phone! Get up and take the trash out! It is time to... get... up! Do you ever hear these kinds of statements?

Even when I lived alone, I could be sitting in my recliner with my feet up, and I would hear, "get up and make sure the door is locked". "Get up and take the clothes out of the dryer before they wrinkle again." "It is Thursday, get up and take the trash out". "Get up, you have to go to work today". I hear these kinds of reminders from within my own self. Get up!

Perhaps Mary and Joseph had these familiar commands in their world also. They had already experienced the Angel of the Lord's voice to them as they prepared and experienced the birth of the Christ Child. In today's story, Joseph hears anew; Get up and take the child and his mother to Egypt. Matthews concludes his infant birth story with the Holy family escaping to Egypt. Get up and take the child and his mother! And Joseph got up and took!

We began the season of Advent with two Sunday's about John the Baptist. The first experience of John the Baptist was his message of repentance: turn away from your old ways and prepare for the One who is to come. John's words challenged us to look at our lives and be open to the newness that Christ brings to us.

The next Sunday we were challenged to look at our expectation of Jesus: Have we, like John, expected Jesus, the Christ, to be who we need him to be instead of receiving him as God sends him to us? I have been challenged to make some changes in my life this Advent season and perhaps you have also.

331

We finally were able to experience the joy and sweetness of the birth of Christ on the third Sunday of Advent as our choir led us in worship with their annual cantata. We ended the season of Advent with our Christmas Eve Communion Service. The baby is born! Glory in the highest and peace on earth goodwill toward all people!

Now that is Christmas! Isn't that what we felt when we left here on Christmas Eve? Now, this is Christmas! Surely when we came to church this morning we were expecting to continue to bask in the glory and joy of this Holy night.

But, here we are again beginning the season of Christmas much like we did the season of Advent with gloom and doom, darkness instead of Light. There is no "Glory in the Highest and peace on earth to all people!" in our text today. Instead we are hearing the Angel of the Lord tell the Holy family to "Get up and take the baby and escape to Egypt." Joseph is told to take his family to a new place.

Herod had heard of the birth of this baby and his power was threatened. He was filled with fear. Instead of continuing with these wonderful Holy night images, we hear of babies being killed. We hear of a mother grieving over the loss of her children. We see the Holy family having to leave the place Jesus was born, Bethlehem and going to a new place. Matthew reminds us that all of this had been prophesied and now it was being fulfilled.

The Angel of the Lord spoke, "Get up and take the child to a safe place. Babies are being killed. Mothers are grieving. Why do we have to deal with this as we bask in the joy of the season? Why did I not choose to skip over the last part of Matthew's story and let us talk about peace, love and joy this morning? We have covered the important parts of the story, haven't we? And it has all been good. Why do we have to hear this today?

Why choose this to talk about today? We do have choices within the lectionary readying. I choose this to share with you today because it spoke to me! And just perhaps it may speak to some of you today.

To me this story is not only about Herod and his fears that caused him to order babies killed or the sadness of the image of a mother grieving for her children. Nor is it about the Holy family who had to leave a special place and bring up their child in a new and strange place.

This story is about what God did in the lives of God's people, and it is about what God is doing today in our lives.

We know the incarnation is about God coming to live and dwell among us in his Son, Jesus. Today in our story we hear the good news for us. Not just the traditions and the wonderful experiences of the Holy Season, but how this effects our lives and why it makes a difference for us that Jesus Christ live and that God lives and dwells among us.

Our story today gives us a picture of the world that Jesus Christ was born into, a world of darkness, fears, pain, grief, and difficult times. Our Old Testament text tells us that there were many dark years when all the people had to hang on to were the words of the prophets proclaiming the hope of the coming Messiah. It was into a dark world that Jesus Christ was born. Matthew gives us a picture of this world.

Can you image moving around from place to place as we understand life to have been in Jesus' world? It was no simple thing to get up and take the child to another place. There was government oppression and control. The people had no power or resources. Matthews gives us a glimpse of this world. When we look around us this Christmas season, we also see a world with much darkness, grief and pain.

So, this morning we are jerked from our traditions and joys of the Christmas season and set down in the middle of the world in which we live. The world we hear about on the news, the world we experience with our outreach here at the church, the world filled with hurting, grieving people who have lost loved ones, and lost jobs. Yes, and those who are facing the loss of their own lives.

To fully look at our world we have to see it from not only our lives, our safe, secure, world, but from other people's lives. We have to see it from the hungry, the homeless, and all the hurting people we know. Matthew shares with us a picture of the Holy Family's world so we can hear the good news that God brings to us. Let us look at our world. I mean really look at our world as we hear the good news Matthew brings us today.

Are you ready for it? Do we really want to be reminded this morning of all the violence, all the unrest, all the weather disasters, homes burning while people sleep, all the deaths we hear about on the news? Are we ready to look around us and really see what our world actually looks like?

Let me give you an example of my day on Monday, December 23. I was so excited. My two sons and their four children were coming up to spend the day with Anna and me. I was treasuring this day and this moment with my family. We had not been able to gather last year and had not seen each other in several months, so this was very special to me.

I told the Senior Pastor that I did not know what they were going to do at the office on Monday, but I was not going to be there. It was my family time. A day off from work!

I was told me no cooking that we would go out to eat. I learned about the time they arrived that an elder's dad was in Physical Regional Medical Center and seriously ill. I called her to tell her it was my family gathering for Christmas and I would see him when I could. Not feeling real good about this, but really wanting to make the world go away if for only a few hours.

Family arrives and the day is filled with peace, love, joy and laughter! We were in the middle of our meal at Gondelars when another elder called to tell me he was at a homebound member's home to deliver the DVD, and this member was really sick but refused to come out of the bathroom. This elder worked with me in seeing to the needs of this homebound member, but he could not get him to come out of the bathroom and go to the hospital. For the rest of the meal, I was talking back and forth telling the elder what to say to the homebound member to get him to go to the hospital and it finally worked. I told the elder if he could get him to the Emergency room, I could take it from there.

After our meal, the cousins all went back to our house for their own laughter and games and my sons and I went to see a friend of mine who had been diagnosed with terminal cancer and wanted to talk with my sons. We had visited a while when I left them to go to the hospital to see patient. When he was aware I knew he was sick and I read scripture and had a prayer, I could go finish my visit with my family. Later that evening, I went back to spend time with him.

Was my day ruined by the invasion of the outside world? It could have been if I had let it, but as a family we had a wonderful, joyful day. The world around us is real. People are hurting, dying, and grieving. There are times when we are called to "get up and take".

I told the elder that he had been a God sent for me that day. He said, "Well, I may have been! I had originally planned to take the DVD on Tuesday when I finished my work, but had the thought that I might need to do it on Monday and I did". He was "nudged" to get up and go. You know, it really didn't make any difference in the elder's life if he went on Monday or Tuesday. But it made a lot of difference in this homebound member's life and my life. I know many of you have had such experiences because you have shared some of them with me. Our devotion for Triple L Club this last month was someone sharing his experiences of God nudging him to get up and go and it made a difference in other people's lives.

The Angel of the Lord spoke to Mary and Joseph to get up and take Jesus to another place. They hear again and yet again, "Get up and take the child". God was working in their lives keeping Jesus safe so he could grow and become who God created him to be and accomplish the purpose he was created to do. That is the good news for us today. God is still active in our lives and continues to guide us, lead us into places where we can grow in grace and love for our God.

So, are we ready to get up and follow where God calls us to go? Do you need to get up and move to another place in the sanctuary because there may be someone who needs you to sit by them? Are you ready to get up and become part of a Sunday school class where you just may grow in your faith and love for our God? Are you ready to get serious about your health, exercise, or healthy eating? We were challenged in Advent to turn around and see life from a new perspective and to look at our hidden expectations of Jesus Christ in our lives. Now in the season of Christmas, are we ready to get up and move into the unknown where God is calling us and leading us? Perhaps leading us to the places we need to be to be safe in God's love and grace, a place where we can grow in our faith and be nurtured to become who God created us to be.

In dark times we have a tendency to withdraw back into ourselves, to hold on tightly to what we can hold on to. Our fears take over. We get into our "I can do it mode". Matthew's good news for us to day is to remember in the darkest times of our lives, God's Light shines for us but we have to hear the call to get up and move with this light to be brought down the path of grace that will lead us though the darkness.

I think most of you know why Matthew's words spoke to me today. It has been a dark year for me since my daughter Mitzi's death. But, in that darkness? But, in that darkness? Well, the Light has guided me. The grace sustained me. The love of God and community calmed my fears and took me out of the "I can do this" mode and brought me into the "I can't do this, but God through me can." There were times this past year when I had to "get up" and do something differently. I had to "get up" and try just one more time. And when I did that, I found myself being lead down the path of grace.

I know many of you have had darkness enter into your lives this past year and I pray you, too, have experienced Matthew's good news for us today. God is working in our lives. Let us get up and be willing to work with God in bringing about goodness and joy for us.

Yes. Jesus was born into a world of darkness! Many had heard of the coming Messiah who would bring hope to this world. But this hope did not happen for them. A question I have often asked when reading this text is, why did God not intervene and save of the babies that Herod killed? I have no magic answer to that, but I believe God did not impose his will onto this world that was rejecting him but he saved the One who could save the world. When darkness comes into our lives, we have that Savior to lead, guide, and bring us to the places we need to be. That is what we celebrate this Christmas season and that is the good news for us today.

Reign of the Shepherd

Joy Warren

(Ezekiel 34:11-16, 20-24)

For thus says the Lord GOD: I myself will search for my sheep, and will seek them out. As shepherds seek out their flocks when they are among their scattered sheep, so I will seek out my sheep. I will rescue them from all the places to which they have been scattered on a day of clouds and thick darkness.

I will bring them out from the peoples and gather them from the countries, and will bring them into their own land; and I will feed them on the mountains of Israel, by the watercourses, and in all the inhabited parts of the land.

I will feed them with good pasture, and the mountain heights of Israel shall be their pasture; there they shall lie down in good grazing land, and they shall feed on rich pasture on the mountains of Israel.

I myself will be the shepherd of my sheep, and I will make them lie down, says the Lord GOD.

I will seek the lost, and I will bring back the strayed, and I will bind up the injured, and I will strengthen the weak, but the fat and the strong I will destroy. I will feed them with justice.

Therefore, thus says the Lord GOD to them: I myself will judge between the fat sheep and the lean sheep.

Because you pushed with flank and shoulder, and butted at all the weak animals with your horns until you scattered them far and wide,

I will save my flock, and they shall no longer be ravaged; and I will judge between sheep and sheep.

I will set up over them one shepherd, my servant David, and he shall feed them: he shall feed them and be their shepherd.

And I, the LORD, will be their God, and my servant David shall be prince among them; I, the LORD, have spoken.

(Ephesians 1:15-23)

I have heard of your faith in the Lord Jesus and your love toward all the saints, and for this reason

I do not cease to give thanks for you as I remember you in my prayers.

I pray that the God of our Lord Jesus Christ, the Father of glory, may give you a spirit of wisdom and revelation as you come to know him,

so that, with the eyes of your heart enlightened, you may know what is the hope to which he has called you, what are the riches of his glorious inheritance among the saints,

and what is the immeasurable greatness of his power for us who believe, according to the working of his great power.

God put this power to work in Christ when God raised him from the dead and seated him at God's right hand in the heavenly places,

far above all rule and authority and power and dominion, and above every name that is named, not only in this age but also in the age to come.

And God has put all things under his feet and has made him the head over all things for the church,

which is his body, the fullness of him who fills all in all.

"When the Son of Man comes in his glory, and all the angels with him, then he will sit on the throne of his glory.

All the nations will be gathered before him, and he will separate people one from another as a shepherd separates the sheep from the goats,

and he will put the sheep at his right hand and the goats at the left.

Then the king will say to those at his right hand, 'Come, you that are blessed by my Father, inherit the kingdom prepared for you from the foundation of the world;

for I was hungry and you gave me food, I was thirsty and you gave me something to drink, I was a stranger and you welcomed me,

I was naked and you gave me clothing, I was sick and you took care of me, I was in prison and you visited me.'

Then the righteous will answer him, 'Lord, when was it that we saw you hungry and gave you food, or thirsty and gave you something to drink?

And when was it that we saw you a stranger and welcomed you, or naked and gave you clothing?

And when was it that we saw you sick or in prison and visited you?'

And the king will answer them, 'Truly I tell you, just as you did it to one of the least of these who are members of my family, you did it to me.'

Then he will say to those at his left hand, 'You that are accursed, depart from me into the eternal fire prepared for the devil and his angels;

for I was hungry and you gave me no food, I was thirsty and you gave me nothing to drink,

I was a stranger and you did not welcome me, naked and you did not give me clothing, sick and in prison and you did not visit me.'

Then they also will answer, 'Lord, when was it that we saw you hungry or thirsty or a stranger or naked or sick or in prison, and did not take care of you?'

Then he will answer them, 'Truly I tell you, just as you did not do it to one of the least of these, you did not do it to me.' And these will go away into eternal punishment, but the righteous into eternal life."

Reign of the Shepherd

I've had kind of a little private joke going on for the past few weeks. I have been battling sickness and travelling and working and doing family things, and I guess I've found that I'm not sleeping as well as I should. The joke is really ironic, because they tell you, in order to go to sleep you should think about sheep, right? Well, part of the reason I **don't** sleep is that I'm thinking about sheep. I've been thinking about the scripture in the lectionary for today and trying to fit it together with Reign of Christ Sunday. I wasn't trying to force them together; it was more like something was speaking to me about how they complemented each other and I needed to search more carefully to see the connections.

Why does Jesus appear as a shepherd in so many places? On the surface, I understand the metaphor describing a protector and guide for a multitude of helpless creatures. But on the day when we celebrate the **reign** of Christ, why are we still talking about a shepherd? A first century audience knew what shepherds were: these were people who were outcasts from society, people who dealt with dirty animals, who had their hands in muck and yuck and the blood of the wounded, people who had charge of a bunch of animals who did not belong to them, and the loss of one meant the loss of a job that paid precious little but might mean the difference between life and death. These are NOT people you invite to dinner or fellowship with in any sort of way. And this is who Jesus claims as a metaphor for his vocation?

The scripture in Matthew 25 tells us Jesus will be working like a shepherd, separating sheep and goats. This follows the parable of the talents and before that the parable of the ten brides. These stories indicate a certain action on our part in order to be ready for favorable judgment when Christ comes again. The passage from Ezekiel furthers the pastoral picture I have in my mind of a beautiful pasture, full of all manner of sheep and goats. I imagine being one of these animals, and you are all there, too. All of us and many others in the pasture together. Some of us are aware of the divine judge at the far side of the field, separating sheep and goats. The problem is that since there are no mirrors, we don't know what we are. We think we know, to be sure, but we don't have complete knowledge. We know what we see around us, we're sure of what others appear to be: sheep, sheep, goat, GOAT, goat, sheep, etc. And so what do we do? Some rush up to Jesus, bleating an earnest question: am I a sheep??? Some hang back, thinking maybe Jesus will find he hasn't sorted as many as he'd like to the right and his judgment will get a little more merciful toward the end of the crowd. Some are completely oblivious, thinking, "oh my! This is the most fabulous grass I've ever tasted, and the weather, how nice! The temperature is so comfortable and I'm surrounded by so many friends, new and old, what a wonderful shepherd I have to lead me here to this place!"

Maybe it's like that…maybe there's a goat in the crowd, a particular goat who is in line to see Jesus. As she moves up the line, she notices a small sheep, skinny and ragged, who is trying to eat some grass and a big fat sheep pushes the little one out of the way. The goat puts her head down and head butts the fat sheep, knocking it away from the hungry one. Another goat, in line with this goat, is worried. "I don't know what's going to happen to me; I've been a bad, bad animal. I always thought of myself and my own desires; I got kicked out of my community; I've been alone on a steep and rocky mountainside, and now here I stand, awaiting judgment." The first goat talks with him and calms him. "Look around," she says, "isn't this the most beautiful place you've ever seen? I have made my share of mistakes, too, brother. Let's be grateful to be in the presence of the good shepherd, grazing from this field more wonderful than any in our best dreams, if only for a little while." Another small sheep, shivering in the shadows, cannot stand. The goat helps nudge him into the sunlight. She enlists the help of others to get him up on her back. When she reaches Jesus, she says, "Shepherd, I know I am a goat. I have made many mistakes in my life. Please care for this little one who could not come to you on his own." Jesus takes the little sheep and puts him down gently. He takes the front hooves of the goat and puts them on his lap, looking into her eyes. "Sister, Come, you that are blessed by my Father, inherit the kingdom prepared for you from the foundation of the world; for I was hungry and you gave me food, I was thirsty and you gave me something to drink, I was a stranger and you welcomed me, I was naked and you gave me clothing, I was sick and you took care of me,

I was in prison and you visited me." The goat, confused, says, "Lord, I do not understand." Jesus places his hand on the face of the goat. He strokes her head and side and as he does so, the goat's coarse fur becomes soft and fluffy, her horns disappear. And Jesus says, "'Truly I tell you, just as you did it to one of the least of these who are members of my family, you did it to me." The goat, now transformed to a sheep, steps to Jesus' right, into the Kingdom of God.

Maybe it's like this…maybe. Maybe the field is full of dirty, lame, hungry animals. Maybe these animals roll around and moan in squalor, unable to help themselves, unable to pick themselves up and feed themselves. Maybe they yearn for someone to come and care for them, someone to lead them, some kind of powerful ruler. As animals, maybe they dream of a great, ruling lion who will care for them rather than destroy them. When they see Jesus performing the act of shepherd, they don't recognize him as their king; they ignore him and look around in vain for signs of a powerful, familiar looking lord with a scepter and crown. But then, this sounds familiar. We're about to celebrate the season of advent, when the Church celebrates the birth of a baby in mean circumstances. We celebrate our God, who came to the world to teach it, save it, redeem it, not as a powerful king, but as a helpless baby. Well, if we know Jesus as a helpless baby, why are we still confused at the sight of a shepherd? Why do we still expect an earthly king?

For some reason, we think Jesus is sitting on top of the pyramid, on top of the social and economic structure we know and in which we participate. Because that's where the king is, right? Right up above the 1%. And surely that's where any judge worth its gavel would sit, right? At the top. But throughout scripture, we find this image of shepherd, a person who doesn't even rank high enough to be on the bottom of the pyramid because it's such a lowly position. And this shepherd, this person who struggles to have enough food and shelter to survive, is a leader of many, a protector of many, a comforter of many. When we hear these verses wherein Jesus tells the righteous "when you did it to the least of these, you did it to me" and to the accursed he says, "when you did not do it to one of the least of these, you did not do it to me," we tend to have kind of a "we-know-the-whole-story" kind of perspective. We know the punch line already, don't we? We know the good ones, the bad ones. Jesus is among the poor, we know that. We hear that over and over in scripture. Care for the poor, feed the hungry, visit the sick and those in prison. Right. Right.

So are you a sheep, headed for the right hand of the Lord, our good shepherd? After all, if we know all this…surely we know the answer to this question. We're here in church after all. Surely we're all sheep. I mean, we know what a goat looks like, don't we? The Reformed Tradition, of which our church is a part, speaks of something called the visible and the invisible church. The visible church is the one we see: the one with buildings and members and clergy worshipping together and carrying out the mission of the church in the world. The invisible church is the one we can't see: the one that contains the sheep, who could be anywhere. God knows who the sheep are, the ones whose hearts belong to God. We have some discipline rules in the visible church for those who are living with gross indifference to the commandments to love God and neighbor, but for the most part we leave judgment to God. God knows our hearts. **This is why Christ will have to do the work of the shepherd, separating the goats from the sheep, because we do not have the proper knowledge to do it ourselves.**

And we must submit ourselves to the reign of this kind of king. The king who sits outside of the structures built by the world, who lives and dwells and suffers among us. The king who is our brother. And the way we serve this type of king is by caring for those on the margins, those who also live outside of the hierarchy of the world. We come and worship God in community, and maybe some of those within our community have known, do know, real need. We certainly know there are people like this, people who are hungry and thirsty, strangers, those who need clothes, people who are sick, others who are in prison, certainly we know in our minds that people like this exist in the immediate area outside our church. Jesus says when we care for them, we care for him. When we come to church, proclaiming that we yearn for Christ to rule our lives, and we hear these words, what stands in the way of doing what Christ says? What stands in your way? We come to church, hoping to meet Christ here. When we hear the Word of God proclaimed, Christ tells us he's also in the streets, in the gutters, in the hospital, in the prison, in the line at the food pantry. Why don't we rush to meet him there?

And this is how, I think, something we thought we knew surprises us again and again. We go about our lives, all year, thinking about how sheep-like we are. We're just good folks, good church folks, aren't we? And then the good shepherd comes and stands in the middle of the pasture and shows us how goat-like we are. But before our final judgment, he puts his hand to our face and looks us in the eyes and transforms us. This is what our king does for us. Our sovereign transforms us, renews us, if we let him. He fits us for the kin-dom of God. We are broken and helpless; we are hungry and thirsty for things other than food and water. From time to time some of us have the means to help provide things for those who have little or nothing, but we often don't do all we could. Often without realizing it, we push the scrawny and hungry sheep out of the way while we get more for ourselves. But the good shepherd provides what we need to satisfy our hunger, our thirst. We must not reject the riches of the kin-dom of God instead yearning for the riches of this world. God chose David, a shepherd, to be an earthly king. And when Christ the king returns, he will judge us like a shepherd. From shepherd to shepherd. What a surprise!

As we look forward to the season of Advent, I hope the surprise of a baby, the song of a young girl, the message of good news to the shepherds…I hope all of this will remind us of the ways we deceive ourselves. I hope it will remind us not to pursue the rewards of this world, for our sovereign lord does not sit atop our earthly power structures in judgment; our ruler dwells among us and knows our hearts. Our good shepherd cares for us, even when we disobey. Let us respond in gratitude by renewing our efforts. Let us seek out and serve Christ with humble hearts. Amen.

The Storms in Life

Gloria Washburn

(Matthew 8:23-27 and Mark 4:39)

The Storms in Life... How many times have we; seen a storm, quickly approaching? Watched storm clouds form and start moving towards us. A few rain drops may begin to fall... until the sky lets loose with an initial down pour. The sky grows dark, the thunder sounds and the lightening strikes.... making that crackling sound along the way. Depending on how close it is; we may feel the ground shake beneath our feet.

Whether it be a physical storm; or a storm of a different kind.
We may or may not see it coming....

Other times; it is the little things in life, that may gently rock our sense of calm. A flat tire comes to mind; it may impact our life with a big bang kind of surprise! Other times, these flat tires, they sneak up on us, real quiet like...... and when we are ready to go some place.... we discover the tire is flat. That we are not going anywhere, anytime soon. We may catch the tire half flat; and are able to get the tire aired up, before we do much damage. The tire problems for some of us, may come as a nuisance, for others it may be annoying, and yet for others it is a serious problem or a road block.

Depending on what we have going on in our lives; it may have compounding effects and cause ripples in our lives; like the wind moving across the water, causes it to ripple and spread outward.

From a flat tire, to late to work or to an important meeting, to loosing a job, to other issues..... it was something that was so small an issue and the effects from that situation grew.

For some of us, a test in school may be a subtle storm. We need to study and prepare for our tests and they may not be easy. A sibling taking our favorite toy; as we are being asked to share... may not be easy. The pressure of life is on us; no matter what age we are.

We sometimes encounter rough waves, rough times, and tough situations in our lives. From accidents to illness—from financial storms to physical storms, from bullies in school, and the storms in our lives, take on so many different forms and shapes.

In the past couple of weeks; we have had several events take place globally and nationally possibly even locally that caused us concern or even despair.

When these storms in life come upon us, these storm waves can overlap in our lives. It seems like we are facing one problem after another, after another. There are times; when we may have multiple issues and problems to deal with, all at the same time.

While the disciples encountered a physical storm, it is a wonderful example of the storms in our lives.

This storm in particular, caught the disciples by surprise. They saw it coming, they were not prepared for it. Even if, they could have prepared for it; they were in the water. Far away from land and there was not much, they could do. Trying to maneuver a boat, in a storm, is sometimes difficult, or next to impossible. Fighting the wind and the waves, is hard and tiresome work.

It was bad enough that the storm came suddenly; but to complicate the situation the waves and the water was sweeping up and over the sides of the boat. The unsteadiness and the rocking of the boat, due to the pounding of the waves; tossed it's passengers around. We may not like to be in a boat like that. There was a risk for life and for death; the boat could take on only so much water and then possibly capsize. The situation was perilous.

What will we face, before there is to much water in our boat? Wave after wave of problems; unsteadiness, and complications. The more problems we have, the harder it is to keep them balanced and under control. We only have two hands and two feet to juggle multiple problems with.

How many times in our lives; have the storms of life, taken us by surprise?
How many of us, have been in that boat?; or are still in that boat??
How will we deal with the problems of life; as the waves crash and fill our boats
    with water?

It makes me wonder—How many of the disciples were good swimmers? Or were the waves so big, that even the strongest swimmer would drown?

The disciples faith was shaken due to the situation.

Which is comforting; because at times; our faith may be shaken and we too, may loose sight of our faith and Jesus.

We too may be caught up in the moment of the storm. We may panic in a moment, when the waves of life are rocking our boat, and the waves are crashing in on us.

The waves tossed the boat that the disciples were in, from side to side; upward and suddenly dropping it, with the rise and fall of each passing wave. Some of the disciples may have gotten wet; and with the wind blowing; they may have gotten cold.—Cold and wet..... and uncomfortable. The disciples were faced with circumstances beyond their control... it was then they called on Jesus.

Who will we call out to; in the midst of our storm?—Jesus, we call out to Jesus, in our times of need!

What would have happened, if Jesus did not wake up and calm the seas?
We may not have had, this wonderful example, of how God works in our lives....

Jesus could have woken up—the way many of us do. We consider the thought of waking up, but we roll over and go back to sleep, thinking—just for five more minutes. As we are hitting the snooze alarm as we lay our heads back down. But Jesus didn't do that; and he doesn't do that.

Jesus could have also said. "Let me sleep"—and not have gotten up at all... but this was not the example he was teaching us.

Jesus, was teaching us, to get up in the storms of life, and turn to Him. To have faith; even if we think we have lost our faith.... along the way.

Jesus, was not afraid in the midst of the storm. In fact; when Jesus was shaken out of his slumber, our Lord heard the panic in the disciples voices and the words. "Lord, save us; we are going to drown!!"

The Lord our God, Jesus was there with them. He might have been asleep, but when he was called upon, Jesus was awake in the storm.

How many times in our life, when we are being pounded by the waves of problems, do we cry out, with our voice—Lord, help us.... we are drowning in our sea of problems! Do we take the time to talk to Jesus and share our hearts and thoughts with him?

To which Jesus responded; "You of little faith, Why are you so afraid"? Why are we so afraid? We are not alone... Jesus is with us!

The smaller the boat or our faith, the more it seems to rock; the larger the ship or faith, especially when connected to the faith of others, the body of believers; the less seems to pitch and lean.

What is nipping at our heals; making us afraid or worry this day? The possibilities are so many.

How many times; when we are going through the trials and storms in life; do we throw ourselves into a pity party? Not a little pity party; but a BIG pity party!....You know the kind; where the miry clay mud pit, is optional—we all do it. At some point and time in our lives we all get to asking the famous question, "Lord, Why Me?" Lord, why are we in the particular tempest? How long we stay there, is up to us. It depends on how long, we take to call on our Savior, Jesus to lift us out of the miry pit. To follow His ways step out, in and on faith.

I saw a movie recently called, "Last Holiday. —Has anyone else seen it?"

The main actress, is named Georgia, and she was going through a series of problems. She bumped her head, became ill, was told that she was terminally ill. To complicate matters, she was told that her health insurance would not pay for her treatment. On top of that she was told that she only had a few weeks to live. She was going through some storms in life... So, in church.... She asked God; "Why me?"

Georgia could not find the long term relationship that she hoped for; but kept the hope alive, for that and for many other things; in her book of possibilities. Again, she asked God "Why me?"

Faced with the fact that she was dying;—Georgia decided to take a vacation. She was staying at a big fancy and very expensive hotel. It was in these moments she learned how to embrace life, how to find the courage to take chances, she learned to find her voice, to speak her mind. But she never stopped talking to God. She didn't stop acknowledging His presence and she didn't stop working on her relationship with God. For those of you who have not seen this movie; I will not tell you the ending...

Our lives are not always, as simple as a one or two hour movie, with all of the loose ends tied up; with a happily ever after, ending on top... sometimes... our lives are more complex.

But had it not been for the storms in our lives; we would not see the sky, change from the dark to .... eventually clear...... to a beautiful shade of blue. Then see the beautiful multicolored rainbow that comes out after the storm. We would not look back and see the changes that God is working, in our very own lives. Sometimes, after the storms, we see life, with a new set of eyes. A new perspective, new insight or understanding.

We may desire to reflect, on how this or these particular storms in life—in fact changed us, for the better. Making us stronger in faith, stronger in our prayer life, drawing us closer yet, to our Lord, Jesus Christ.

There was a man who didn't like to fly and low and behold, he ended up on an airplane. The trip was anything but smooth... he clutched anything firm that he could hold onto, with the strongest grip he could muster. His knuckles soon turned white, as the air plane gently bounced on the air currents. His stomach churned and the color in his face began to fade and change colors. When the plane safely landed, he got off that plane as fast as he could. As soon as his feet hit the pavement, he moved over to let the other passengers go by and he kissed the ground feeling "Thankful" for being still being in one piece and arriving safe at last. But my question is this; did he Thank Jesus?

I recently read an internet article which can be found at [(www.airliners.net/aviation-forums/non-aviation humor. The original author of this article is unknown, but was posted by Boeing 787 from India in May of 2004.)] Here are a few excerpts from the article:

After every airline flight the Captain of the plane, fills out a gripe sheet. It is a form for problems that need to be addressed and fixed. The pilot fills out the concerns and the Mechanics read them and they are to correct the problems and respond to the complaint on the form.

Pilot: Left main inside tire almost needs replaced
Mechanic: Almost replaced main inside tire

Pilot: Something loose in cockpit
Mechanic: Tightened something in cockpit

Pilot: Number three engine is missing
Mechanic: Engine found on right wing after a brief search

Pilot: Aircraft handles funny
Mechanic: Aircraft warned to straighten up and fly right, and to be serious

Pilot: Target radar hums
Mechanic: Reprogrammed target radar with lyrics

Pilot: Mouse in cockpit
Mechanic: Cat installed.

While they have their sense of humor.... I think the man on the plane, who was holding on for dear life—may have been one of those mechanics.... I wonder if he counted all of his blessings after that flight? Many of us are so very "thankful" that we made it through storms and trials along the way. Are we remembering to thank Jesus, for his help?

What a wonderful Savior we have, who is awake with us during these storms of our lives. Who can calm the waters and the wind, in our lives. Who provides the strength and faith to ride out the storms of life.

In Mark chapter 4 verse 39... Jesus, rebuked the wind and the waves... and said, "Peace, be still" and the waters calmed.

The storms in our lives, may make us uncomfortable too, but hopefully we grow from them. We learn from them and the storms are only for a season or a time in our lives..... because Jesus says to them; "Peace, be still" and our problems calm. May we embrace, the love of our Savior and focus on him.

May the Peace of Jesus, enter our lives and calm the storms in our lives... and may our problems be made, still. May our faith and trust in Jesus grow, as we encounter and deal with the storms of life.

Blinded by the Light

Diann White

(John 3:14-21)

What an odd image the scripture gives us in comparing Jesus to a snake! Let's look at the story of Moses lifting up the snake, which comes from Numbers 21. Probably none of us are surprised to hear that Israel had become "impatient" and "spoke against God and against Moses [saying], 'Why have you brought us up out of Egypt to die in the wilderness? For there is no food and no water, and we detest this miserable food'" (Numbers 21:4-5). God responded to their complaints by sending poisonous snakes which bit and killed many people. Needless to say, the people repented and asked Moses to intervene so that God would remove the snakes. When Moses prayed, God told him to make a replica of a poisonous snake and mount it on top of a pole so that everyone could see it. Anyone bitten by a snake (essentially condemned to death) could look at the snake and live. Moses constructed the snake on stick (that sounds like something we'd fry and eat in Louisiana where I'm from) and instead of dying, people were healed when they looked at it. Interestingly, the image of a snake curled around a pole is still used today by doctors as a symbol of healing. It's called a caduceus. The author of John compares Jesus' crucifixion, his body on the cross, to the snake on a stick, because it gives life to believers who otherwise will die of sin. Not only do we receive healing but also a new life. Jesus' last breath became for us the breath of a new life that far surpasses the original life.

In giving Jesus, God acted out of love for us, not to condemn us – our sin has already condemned us. It's like throwing a life jacket to someone who is drowning. The life jacket offers life. If the person dies because he didn't grab the life jacket, it doesn't mean that the jacket condemned him to die. Dying is the natural consequence of rejecting the life jacket. In the same way, the natural consequence of rejecting God's gift of salvation is judgment. It's pretty straightforward: believe and live or fail to believe and die. The choice is ours.

This text discusses darkness: "And this is the judgment, that the light has come into the world, and people loved darkness rather than light because their deeds were evil" (John 3:19). When I think about total darkness, I think about my trip last summer when I went to a coal mine in England. I know there are more conventional tourist attractions but actually the mine was in Beamish, a simulation of village life in the late 1800s. A miner led our group into a very poorly lit tunnel that twisted and turned in the darkness. We walked hunched over to keep our hard hats from bumping the top of the tunnel. When we reached the furthest point in the mine, our guide extinguished the few lights. I don't remember ever experiencing such total and complete darkness. I had no idea that the feeble lights made such a difference until they were off. Even more shocking was how bright they seemed when they were turned back on.

My experience was thankfully short and not at all like what happened to the miners in Chile. Do you remember that? On August 5, 2010, 33 miners were trapped about 2000 feet below the surface when part of the mine collapsed. Imagine how terrified they were as they tried to get out of the mine and not be buried alive. At first, they probably felt some relief that they had survived the initial crisis as they gathered in an area that had first aid kits and some food. Then someone did the math and worked out the food rations: 1 cracker topped with canned fish and equally frugal portions of milk and peaches. And these weren't daily rations, they were every other day rations. For 17 days, they tried to believe that people were searching for them and dared to hope that they would be rescued. Not only were they in darkness, they were separated from their families and friends, and the world. As they faced the very real possibility that they would die of starvation, they must have been incredibly aware of the mortality of their fragile bodies. On August 22, a drill bit penetrated the area of the mine where the men were. These grown men were so thrilled that some of them actually hugged the drill! At long last, they were able to communicate to the searchers that they were alive. But rescue was not guaranteed, and if it was possible, it would happen only after the men had spent a lot more time in the dark.

Now let's return to the light and darkness imagery in the text: "And this is the judgment, that the light has come into the world, and people loved darkness rather than light because their deeds were evil. For all who do evil hate the light and do not come to the light, so that their deeds may not be exposed. But those who do what is true come to the light, so that it may be clearly seen that their deeds have been done in God." When this text was written in the 1st C, light and darkness meant more than what happens when we flip a light switch. Darkness represented the old reality of life without Jesus while light represented the new reality introduced by Jesus. In those days, keeping secrets and telling lies were common ways to protect against public shame. People would keep their doors and windows open to show that they had nothing to hide. Obviously, they didn't have air conditioning! Today, we know that a lot of things that we'd rather not see or hear about happen at night under the cover of darkness - drug deals, muggings, home invasions and drive by shootings to name a few. And we know that we often close our blinds so our neighbors can't see us yelling at our spouse and children, draining a six pack of beer or a bottle of wine, or watching trash on TV.

Another thing that was different about the 1ˢᵗ C society is that peoples' identity and sense of right and wrong came from whatever group they belonged to which was usually their extended family. And words like love and hate didn't really refer to feelings but instead how you acted. If you think about it, loving your children is more than having a warm fuzzy feeling about them, it involves actions like feeding them, teaching them and taking care of them. To love the darkness means to be attached to the old way of living without Jesus. Also, people in the 1ˢᵗ C didn't have to worry about who they were or how they were supposed to act. All of that was determined by who their family was. Sometimes, we think that way too. You know, "Bless his heart, Bobby can't help being dumb – all the Johnson men are slow." Also, in those days, if you did good deeds, that was a sign that you were born from above and you were a member of God's family.

Do you remember that we left the Chilean miners still trapped under 2000 feet of dirt and rock? Let me tell you what happened to them. While the rescue efforts were underway, limited supplies were lowered to the men to help them cope with life underground. In the meantime, the drills kept breaking and the mining company was running out of money. Finally, after 69 long days of darkness, separation and facing death, the miners were transported to the surface and safety. They must have been excited beyond words at the thought of being reunited with their loved ones, having access to basic comforts and to finally have light, as much as they wanted – daylight, moonlight, starlight, spotlights, headlights, overhead lights, desk lamps, night lights – are you getting the picture? But first they faced reentry problems. These were not the same men who had entered the mine almost 70 days earlier. They had lost weight and some were sick. They were psychologically impaired and were going to be inundated with media attention. And there was a real concern that their retinas would be damaged by the bright lights when they came out of the mine. Each miner was given wrap-around sunglasses, and even the ones who emerged during the night wore them to protect their eyes from the powerful artificial lights.

Like the miners, when we come from the darkness into the light, we face great risks – the bright light can disintegrate our pride as we publically acknowledge that our old path was wrong, it can expose us to legal consequences if we have committed crimes, it can cut us loose from our job if we try to stop unethical or immoral actions, and it can sever friendships if we take a stand against destructive behaviors. Like those in our text, coming out of the dark is often much easier if you have nothing to lose. Sadly, the more you think you have to lose, the harder it is to move into the light. I have some personal experience with this issue. I've spent many years in a secular profession and have attained a level of expertise as a result of my experience. With that comes a level of income that allows me to live comfortably. Sounds good, right? And it was, till I began to suspect that God was calling me to ordained ministry. I felt woefully inadequate. I was sure that I would be laughed out of my church if anyone found out that I thought that God might be calling me to ordained ministry. I literally spent years "exploring a call." For a long time, I was very careful to keep people I worked with from finding out that I attended seminary. I couldn't let myself believe that God really wanted me and was skeptical of the signs God gave me. And complicating the situation was my reluctance to consider starting over as a rookie. Talk about pride rearing its ugly head. I was too old to have to make all of the mistakes that come with inexperience. I felt like I had earned my professional status and paycheck - believe me, I have had some very demanding and difficult jobs – and I stubbornly fought against giving them up. I had too much to lose to acknowledge God's call. I was too attached to the darkness of my old life. But God loved me through my resistance and I finally mustered the trust and courage to let myself step into the light of God's call. The truth is that, like the miners, we all have everything to lose. If we stay in the darkness, our sins will kill us as surely as a poisonous snakebite will. But the God who loves us unconditionally has provided the remedy. By looking at Jesus on the cross and believing that he died for each of us, his light cures us of our life-threatening condition. No matter where our sin has taken us, God's Holy Spirit illuminates our path out of the darkness of sin and into the light of forgiveness and new life.

Belief is more than an intellectual action. Like "love" and "hate," belief was understood by 1st C people to include action. When we truly believe something, we are changed, and our actions change to be in accordance with what we believe. As God's children, we have nothing to hide. We begin to act in plain view in broad daylight. Our focus is on pleasing God rather than worrying about whether others think we are naïve, stupid or crazy. Our acts of love are a direct result of our encounter with Jesus.

The rescue plan for the miners was risky – they could have died before or during the trip to the surface. But like all of us, they had nothing to lose. To remain in the dark was a certain death sentence. In spite of all of the dangers and problems associated with their return to the light, it was their only chance for life and they gladly seized it. Miraculously, all 33 were successfully rescued. One of the miners, Mario Sepulveda, said of his ordeal in the mine, "I was with God, and I was with the devil. They fought, and God won." The God of light always triumphs over darkness. Thanks be to God!

Let Your Light Shine in the Darkest Places

Virginia Washington

(Matthew 5:16)

Let your light so shine before men, that they may see your good works, and glorify your Father which is in Heaven. **Matthew 5:16**

Introduction: Darkness is the absence of light and light illuminate. Darkness appears black and light appears bright. Darkness comes and darkness goes. The sun comes up and the sun goes down. Good things happen to and not so good things. Today we are well and the next day we are sick. Today we have money in our pocket and the next day we are broke. Today we are happy and tomorrow we are sad. Today we are praising God and tomorrow we are acting as if we don't know him. There are dark times in our life when we allow our light to get dim or go out. But with God on our side we can see the light at the end of the tunnel! Amen! How can you be that light in the darkest places if your light is out? There many dark places in the known and unknown. No matter what comes your way kept your light shining bright! Why?

We should be a Mirror Image of Jesus Christ, no matter our situations or our circumstances. *God is still good and He is worthy to be praised! Let this mind be in you, which was also in Christ Jesus.* **Philippians 2:5 KJV**

What Image do you see or portray? (Outward & Inward)

But the LORD said unto Samuel, Look not on his countenance, or on the height of his stature; because I have refused him: for the LORD seeth not as man seeth; for man looketh on the outward appearance, but the LORD looketh on the heart. **1 Samuel 16:7**

Genesis 1:27 *So God created man in his own image, in the image of God created he him; male and female created he them. We are the clay and thou art the potter, we are work of thy hand.* **Isaiah 64:8**

Think about it?   We must be like Christ. Why? Only the pure and heart shall see God!

Are You Who God says you Are? Ephesians 2: 10 For we are his workmanship, created in Christ Jesus unto good works, which God hath before ordained that we should walk in them.

Do You Manage Conflict God's Way? **Eph 4:1-5** *¹ I therefore, the prisoner of the Lord, beseech you that ye walk worthy of the vocation wherewith ye are called, ² With all lowliness and meekness, with longsuffering, forbearing one another in love; ³ Endeavoring to keep the unity of the Spirit in the bond of peace. ⁴ There is one body, and one Spirit, even as ye are called in one hope of your calling; ⁵ One Lord, one faith, one baptism.*

Are You Fulfilling Your Purpose, Spiritual Gifts & Talents?

Proverb 3:6: In all thy ways acknowledge him, and he shall direct thy paths.

Is your light shining in the Darkest Places? Are mixing in with the unsaved world?

We are to be different from the unsaved world no matter if the situation or circumstance we are to let us light shine. The light in us is Jesus! Jesus is the light of the world.

Roman12:1-2 *¹ I beseech you therefore, brethren, by the mercies of God, that ye present your bodies a living sacrifice, holy, acceptable unto God, which is your reasonable service. ² And be not conformed to this world: but be ye transformed by the renewing of your mind, that ye may prove what is that good, and acceptable, and perfect, will of God.* **1 John 2:6** *He that saith he abideth in him ought himself also so to walk, even as he walked.* Walk in the light, the beautiful light, isn't it glorious, isn't it beautiful..

God made you beautiful! **Genesis 1:31** *And God saw everything that he had made, and, behold, it was very good.* The key to better understanding yourself and your destiny lies in appreciating how God created us individually and uniquely. We should understand our spiritual gifts, talents and stressors to build self-esteem, reduce conflict which will prepare our ministry.

We're Christ's representatives. God uses us to persuade men and women to drop their differences and enter into God's work of making things right between them. We're speaking for Christ himself now: Become friends with God; he's already a friend with you. **2 Corinthians 5:20** (Message translation)

But the fruit of the Spirit is love, joy, peace, longsuffering, gentleness, goodness, faith, Meekness, temperance: against such there is no law. **Galatians 5:22-23**

No matter the place you should demonstrate the Fruit of the Spirit. We should walk the walk as well talk the talk on our Christian journey if we are a follower of Jesus Christ. The Bible tells us that when we do that, the Holy Spirit fills us with God's love and produces some good fruit in our life. If you see an apple tree, what do you expect to find on that tree? Apples! Well, when you see someone who is filled with the Holy Spirit, you expect to see what the Bible calls the fruit of the Spirit. What is that? It is love, joy, peace, patience, kindness, goodness, faithfulness, gentleness, and self-control. Oh my, that is some good fruit, isn't it? Are you always patient? Are you always gentle and kind? No, there will be times when you fail. When you fail, ask God to forgive you and fill you with his Spirit so that you will produce the kind of fruit that he wants to see in your life. Our light as Christian should be as an A "never go out" candle. When you blow them out, they keep re-lighting. Jesus is our light. Lift him up and let him shine through you!

Scripture: Matthew 5:13 -16 *[13] Ye are the salt of the earth: but if the salt have lost his savour, wherewith shall it be salted? It is thenceforth good for nothing, but to be cast out, and to be trodden under foot of men. [14] Ye are the light of the world. A city that is set on a hill cannot be hid. [15] Neither do men light a candle, and put it under a bushel, but on a candlestick; and it giveth light unto all that are in the house. [16] Let your light so shine before men, that they may see your good works, and glorify your Father which is in heaven.*

The Bible tells us that we should let our light shine so that people will see our good works and praise our heavenly Father. I'm sure all of you know the song, "This Little Light of Mine." Hey! It's like those candles you can't blow out! I tried, but it just kept shining. Does Satan ever blow your light out? If you make up your mind to let your light shine for

Jesus, there is no way that Satan can blow it out because the Bible says, "Greater is he that is in you than he that is in the world?" Jesus is your light. Lift him up high because Jesus said, "If I be lifted up, I will draw all men to me."

Michael Jackson recorded a song "The Man in the Mirror" I say if you wanna make the world a better place take a look at yourself and make a change, take a look at yourself and make a change. ***"Starting with the man [or Woman] in the mirror."*** So if your light is out or your light is dim, you can get it right today. Why don't you make a change? If you have lost your savors and your spiritual life is no longer effective, you can make it right today. Give God your heart, he is waiting. He will never leave you nor forsake you! **John 3:17** *For God sent not His son into the world to condemn the world but that the world through Him might be saved.*

Don't be left with your work undone? Jesus is coming back and it want be long.

The Ten Virgins- Matthew 5:1-13

[1] Then shall the kingdom of heaven be likened unto ten virgins, which took their lamps, and went forth to meet the bridegroom. [2] And five of them were wise, and five were foolish. [3] They that were foolish took their lamps, and took no oil with them: [4] But the wise took oil in their vessels with their lamps. [5] While the bridegroom tarried, they all slumbered and slept. [6] And at midnight there was a cry made, Behold, the bridegroom cometh; go ye out to meet him. [7] Then all those virgins arose, and trimmed their lamps. [8] And the foolish said unto the wise, Give us of your oil; for our lamps are gone out. [9] But the wise answered, saying, Not so; lest there be not enough for us and you: but go ye rather to them that sell, and buy for yourselves. [10] And while they went to buy, the bridegroom came; and they that were ready went in with him to the marriage: and the door was shut. [11] Afterward came also the other virgins, saying, Lord, Lord, open to us. [12] But he answered and said, Verily I say unto you, I know you not. [13] Watch therefore, for ye know neither the day nor the hour wherein the Son of man cometh.

Don't be like the five foolish virgins and let your light go out! The bible says Jesus will return as a thief in the night, be ye ready for no one know the day not the hour when He shall return. Keep light shining in all places no matter where or when. You will not have worry about your light shining when things are going well but watch out and pray because your midnight will come.

Conclusion:

No matter your dark place let your light so shine before other naturally that they may see your good works and glorify your Father who is in heaven. It must shine in the darkness places so that it does not win praise for itself but for Him who kindled it. We do not praise the street lights which provide light for us to help keep us safe but we praise the Municipal administration for furnishing the light. We thank God today for Jesus, our light, our bright and morning star! He is everything we need in any darkness that may occur in our lives. Christ is the light; we will shine reflected light if we walk in His light. If we give forth light in the darkest places it will honor God! Honoring God is our Christian due every day for He loved us first.

For God so loved the world that He gave His only begotten son that who so every believeth in Him shall have everlasting life. John 3:16 *Jesus our Lord and savior is the light that shined in us! He paid the price on Calvary, he was crucified, buried but God raised Jesus up from the grave with all power in His hand.* Amen!

The Father's Heart

Eliza Yau

(Luke15:11-24)

Introduction

In many religious the position of "God" is very supernatural, highest… People can't understand, nor touch nor see Him.

For Christian, the people who believe in Jesus Christ: their God is supernatural, glorious, powerful to control everything…etc, but these descriptions are not enough to explain our God, because the Bible said, God is also full of love, His tender love is shown in His willingness to walk with humans, stay with them, forgive them. His greatest love is fully shown, when He sent His begotten son Jesus Christ to the world to save all the sinful people.

Today, I will tell you a story which was taught by Jesus Christ. Through the story, He wants to say, God so love the world, His beloved people.

Story

Luke15:11-24, there was a father who had two sons, the younger son was eager to inherit half of his father's wealth. So, his father divided his wealth and gave him his share according to his request. After that, he packed his bag and took all his money and left his father for a distant country. Then he wasted everything he had. Desperately, he asked to slop the pigs for his living, he was so hungry that he would rather have eaten the corncobs in the pig slop. In such a hopeless situation, it brought him to his senses, "I could get up and go back to my father, I will beg for his pardon because I have sinned against God and against him, and say to him that I don't deserve to be his son, just make me as a hired servant."

While he was still a long way off, his father saw him, his heart was pounding, he ran out, embraced him and kissed him. Once again, his father made him as his precious son, not the hired servant.

In this story, Jesus wants to let you know some important messages:

1.   You are the children of God

Many people take themselves as creatures. Yes! We all are created by God, but we are not the creatures like animals. The Bible told us that God created us in His image. Only mankind is made in His image, and has His glory in the image.

In the story, the lost son thought that he had sinned against the father, he did not deserve the identity of son, he just wanted himself be as a hired servant. However, it's not the same in his father's thought. Once you are a son of your father, you are the son forever. It's not the title only, it's a relationship. The father still takes him as his precious son.

2.   You are very precious in the eyes of the Heavenly Father

Jesus used five actions to describe the father, when he met his son again:

Saw him

This father longs for his son to be back home. The Bible said, when the son was still a long way off, the father saw him. The long distance didn't block the eyes of this father, he always watched over us.

Our experience may be telling us that no one sees us, no one recognizes us, no one cares about us...

There was an old couple, they were weak and not in good health, they were living a painful life. One day, they planned to commit suicide. By the time they started to execute their plan, the phone rang. They were then saved by this call. After that, they shared with others this testimony that God is watching over them and saved them. God cared for them!

Although we are forsaken by the world, God meets us. We may be neglected, betrayed, or forgotten by our friends, family or whole world, but God—our Heavenly Father watches us from heaven.

His heart pounding

The father was touched by the return of his son.

Let us put ourselves into the role of the father. Your son took half of your wealth and left you without saying goodbye. How do you feel when you see him again? I would be very angry and he must beg my forgiveness. Otherwise, I can't calm down my temper.

But in opposite, the father felt passion when this lost son returned and fell into his sight.

Can you imagine a circumstance in which a handicapped child made a great effort to use her hand to draw a picture and give it to her mother on her mother's birthday? How touched is that mother?

Our Heavenly Father was touched because you are willing to come back to Him. Have you experienced how important you are that someone's heart was pounding because you came back. It is because you are so precious in His eyes!

Running

This father was not young. He was an old man. He wanted to meet his son as early as possible, so he used his effort to run. How eager to meet his son he was! Maybe he feared that his son would be lost again.

In our life, who will be willing to run for us? I can tell you that the one who is willing to run for you must be in love with you. Parents will run for their children. This is like the heart of Heavenly Father. He wants to run for you in order to get closer to you!

Embracing

The attitude of people meeting each other shows the relationship between them. Bend the head, shake hands, hold hands, embrace…

Here embracing means I hold the whole of you, you belong to me, I belong to you. This is a kind of link. This is a real form of two people linking together.

The Heavenly Father, the highest God in heaven, he is not the One you can't touch, you can't feel or experience. And in reality, He is the one who wants to link with you again just like in the beginning of Creation before the fall of Adam.

Jesus Christ is the only way to link God with men, by receiving Him as savior through your belief.

He shall hug you and tell you that you belong to Him!

Kissing

The last but not the least action is kissing. This is an expression of love. Even though the son was so dirty, poor, bad smelling, sweeping… but the love inside the father overcame all these negative things, worst situation, bad relationship…the father just wanted to show his love, he forgave all his son's sins. The son's return made the father very excited. Love is the only thing left between them and "kissing" is the expression of this great love.

Conclusion

Our God is the Heavenly Father, He is watching you, His heart is touching you, running for you, embracing and kissing you. It is because you are so precious to Him, you are His children.

On earth, our parents may, or may not, love us, but the Bible said, "can a mother forget the infant at her breast…, but even if mothers forget, I'd never forget you." Today, Heavenly Father still waits for your return, you are beloved! Come and enjoy the love of your Father through Jesus Christ!

Strangers in a Strange Land

Betty Youngman

(Ephesians 3:1-10)

So there we were—45 Cumberland Presbyterians, set down on Chinese soil…35 Anglo Americans who spoke nary a word of Chinese—couldn't read it, write it, understand it…much less imitate it. We included 15 San Francisco Chinese Cumberlands who were bouncing in anticipation of seeing lands of their heritage, of making contact with relatives in Hong Kong, and glorying in this opportunity to try to teach the rest of us about their culture, their foods, and their language.

Some of us came to see the mission work of their church; some—like Judy Burroughs Keith director of the Childrens' Home in Denton and Olive Estes Boston, an elder of the St. Luke church—had grown up in homes where the plight of the Chinese Christian churches had been a primary focus of prayer and concern during the Japanese occupation and the subsequent Cultural Revolution and the terror filled reign of Chairman Mao. Some came simply to explore the culture, see the sights, and to climb the Great Wall.

We were all strangers in a strange land. All of us. We struggled to learn the currency; of necessity we valiantly learned to use chop sticks in a method that got the food to our mouths rather than in our laps. The sky was filled with smog, the streets were filled with people, the contrast between our four star hotels and the tenements where the citizens lived was confounding. We knew we were not in Kansas…or Texas, or Tennessee or Alabama. Our light skin, our weight, our curly hair, straight teeth and the style of our eyeglasses marked us as strangers.

I had been studying the book of Ruth in the weeks prior to this journey, so it wasn't surprising that I was identifying with Ruth and Naomi in their experience as strangers in a strange land. You remember the story…or at least you're familiar with Ruth's famous vow of commitment when she said to her mother-in-law "Entreat me not to leave you or to stop following you; for where you go, I will go; and where you lodge, I will lodge; your people shall be my people, and your God, my God."

The title and much of the focus of the biblical story are on Ruth, for, after all, she did finally marry Boaz, have a son, and thus became the great grandmother of King David, in the line of Jesse…and thus a direct ancestor to Jesus of Nazareth.

But the person I was pondering over was Naomi. You may recall, a famine had fallen upon the land of Judah, and so Naomi left her home, friends, and country; she went with her husband and two sons to live in the strange land of Moab, a strange place with strange customs. They lived there a long time, it seems, for first her husband died and she was left to raise the sons; and then those sons became adults, married, and they too died, leaving her with daughters-in-law who were natives of that strange land of Moab. Having no way of caring for them or for herself, Naomi decided to return to Judah…and told her daughters-in-law to leave her. Thus, we have Ruth's promise of faithfulness.

What I wondered, was this: what was it about Naomi—Hebrew wife, mother, mother-in-law, that so inspired such devotion and commitment in Ruth? After all, the sane and sensible thing to do was what the other daughter-in-law— Orpah was her name…the culturally acceptable thing to do was what she did…return to the house of her parents. And Naomi accepted Orpah's decision by hugging and kissing her and sending her on her way. She certainly did not encourage either of the women to return to Judah with her.

So what was there about Naomi, AND her religion that spoke so clearly to Ruth? Think about it. When Naomi moved to Moab, she didn't find the comfort of a community of people who worshiped Yahweh, the God of the Israelites. There was no neighborhood synagogue, no congregation, no place for her to connect or continue with her pattern of worship. She was a stranger, in a strange land, with strange customs, and strange ideas about her God. How did this decision by Ruth come about? Why was she so impressed with what she saw in Naomi?

I pondered this question, as Naomi and I watched the Chinese people worship in their temples, as they prayed devoutly at the altars in the lamaseries, or lit their incense sticks so the smoke would waft to the gods in the skies. I questioned what it could be that any of us strangers could say or do that would make real to them the God revealed through Jesus Christ. How could we possibly be true to that mission expounded in Ephesians, that of sharing with all the world—at least this particular part of the world—how could we share what Paul called "the news of the boundless riches of Christ?" How could we dare to call ourselves stewards of God's grace when we knew so little about the people we encountered? We know, deep in our hearts that the Wisdom of God is that a welcome table has been spread for all the nations…that Jew and gentile are united in the mystery of God's love. Did not Paul write of the inclusion of all peoples when he wrote "there is no longer Jew or Greek, there is no longer slave or free, there is no longer male and female: for ALL of you are one in Christ Jesus." (Gal. 3:28) So, how do we—how could we—share God's love incarnate in Jesus Christ?

What would Naomi have done?

There's more, you see…I struggled with another problem, there as a stranger in China. Far too often, the history of white, Western Christian expansion, has been one of subjugation. I fear that the gospel message for all the peoples of the earth has been portrayed as one of self-designation of privilege by those telling the story. And thus, the good news of Jesus Christ has been experienced more as cultural domination than as good news. And I saw, both in mainland China and even more in Hong Kong, that things western were considered to be a "good", to be valued as a way to obtain a materialistic way of life—a consumer product easily acquired. I fear that the Christian faith becomes confused—equated even—with a western consumer oriented culture in the minds of many—in China as well as here at home.

So I pondered, and I prayed, and I reflected…and then this wondrous God of ours, this mysterious , surprising, God, this amazing totally other who knows the ways of humans…this God gave us American Cumberland Presbyterian strangers a gift.

Actually, it was two gifts, maybe more, but I want to share the experience of one with you this morning…from this pulpit.

It happened this way: We were on our tour buses, and for the first time, more than a week into our trip, we were actually out in the country. It was rice planting time, and we chaffed at wanting to stop and watch the farmers, trudging through the knee high mud behind a primitive plow drawn by a single ox. We stopped to visit the farm where Chairman Mao had been born and raised, and marveled at the ability of the Chinese to simultaneously revere and to dismiss the man who had caused such turmoil in their history for 50 plus years. Then it seemed as if we were lost, wandering through the countryside on dirt roads that got narrower and narrower…often no more than paths barely wide enough to allow the bus to pass through. At last we halted, and our guide told us to climb on foot to the top of the hill since the bus could go no further.

There was a church…a building that appeared to be nearly new. We must have been expected, for women and small children were gathered around awaiting our arrival…one of them apparently was the leader…an elderly wisp of a person…who chattered earnestly with Rev. Larry Fung of the San Francisco C.P. Church. Her Chinese and his Chinese were totally different dialects…(Cantonese vs. Mandarin) but he managed to get the gist of her speech. We learned that this congregation that had met in the homes of "the sisters" during the Cultural Revolution; remaining in hiding. But they have completed this cinder block building within the last few years and now the congregation numbers several hundred. People must have come from miles around because we could see no near-by dwelling places. And then, bouncing like a wren on a high wire, she waved her hands in the air, and chatted on and on…Larry didn't have to translate…we knew she was saying "Just Praise the Lord!" and when she stopped, we knew to chime in..."Amen."

Then some of the sisters of the village carried in some elderly well-used water thermoses—and we were told they wanted to share refreshments with us. They must have borrowed tea bowls from every home in the village to serve us…a very pale, lukewarm green tea. When the serving began, I could see many of my companions mentally gulping and calculating…let's see, we're not supposed to drink the water unless it's bottled or boiled…yet when we were served, with such grace and sincerity, with such open hospitality…we drank that pale lukewarm tea—every drop—and we knew that we had shared in the body of Christ.

As we left, the women gathered around us, showing off their children, shaking our hands, grinning from ear to ear…and we were no longer strangers…and the land was no longer strange.

The writer of the story of Naomi and Ruth doesn't tell us much about what Naomi said and did during her years in the strange land of Moab…but there is a hint…for we are told that Naomi's sons married Moabite women…those good Jewish boys married outside the faith. But it would seem that Naomi received those young women with love and acceptance…that she exhibited to them the ultimate in inclusion and hospitality.

Make no mistake about it. As much talk as there is in the world today about what is and what isn't a sin…to the God of our Bible, to the God of the Hebrew people of the Old Testament, and to the God of the gentiles in the New Testament…the sin of failing to show hospitality to the stranger ranks high above all else. In fact, showing hospitality is so important that John Wesley listed it— first—when he drew up his "Six Ordinary Means of Grace," a document that resulted in the establishment of the Methodist church. For Wesley, showing hospitality meant welcoming each and every person in all of their diversity…What's more—grace-filled hospitality mean—and means—being constantly aware of the ways in which hospitality is and is not present, in our homes, our communities, as well as in our churches.

Now, Texans are rightfully known for their hospitality, but biblical hospitality goes further than "have a nice day, now" or "you all come back, hear". Biblical hospitality means welcoming all of God's children into your homes, your churches and your hearts. I had to travel to the other side of the world to witness this fruit of God's grace in action.

It was through her hospitality and acceptance that Naomi revealed to Ruth a God worth worshiping and changing her life for…

It was through the hospitality and acceptance of those people in Hunan Province, in the heart of China, that God's love was revealed as being beyond western ways, beyond proper utensils, and beyond even words . As we were leaving, our hostess told us that people around the area would know that Americans had visited that little church, and would come to ask what they were doing there. And they would be told about the God who is a loving, accepting God, who is God to all peoples.

Now, isn't that a gift to be cherished?

My friends, we are all sojourners on this land…strangers in a pretty strange place when you think about it…and yet God has called us, the very least of all the saints, commissioned us to go forth and to preach the unsearchable riches of Christ. We do this…first and foremost by showing acceptance and hospitality to other strangers, not only welcoming them in the name of Christ…but because of Christ…because we are brothers and sisters together. Our messages, our Christian message, is not one of saying "Come, join us…" but rather it is one that says "We are one…through Christ, we proclaim that none of us are strangers to God's encompassing love."

That is the good news of the gospel. Amen.

Do Not Be Afraid[17]

Grace Yu

(Matthew 10:1-31)

1. Sending out of the twelve—who were these people? 10 : 1-4

"Jesus called his twelve disciples," when we go over the names, we find out that Jesus chose His disciples from a variety of backgrounds and life experiences. Only in Matthew's record, he added "Matthew the tax collector," Matthew was saying, yes, though a sinner, I was called by Jesus! Ordinary people, fishermen, sinners were called and used by God!

Only in Matthew, the twelve are called apostles. The word apostle literally means one who is sent out; it is the word for an ambassador. They are God's ambassador, God's messenger, sent forth by Jesus to proclaim the message of God's kingdom!

Jesus also gave them power. When God calls, he also equips!

We are called to do God's work, men and women, young and old, well educated and the lowly, never look down on you! We are given the authority and empowered by the Spirit to serve God.

2. Commissioning and Equipping the disciples 10 : 5-15

vv.5-8 The disciples were sent out to a specific place—to the lost sheep of Israel, and the message was clear : the kingdom of God is near, and they were empowered by God to heal the sick, raise the dead, cleanse those who have leprosy and drive out demons, these are the signs of God's kingdom on earth. Their ministry was the continuity of the ministry of Jesus Christ.

---

[17]Preached in 2011 in Nepal when Grace Yu was leading a camp for ministers and church leaders.

A disciple is a person who follows the footsteps of his master, Jesus said ''where I am, my servants also will be '' John 12:26. We are called to do His work, we are called to proclaim the gospel of Jesus Christ. We must focus on what God calls us to do!

Jesus Christ also taught them how they should go forth to preach the gospel Vv.9-15, they had to learn to depend totally on God's providence. But on the other hand, Jesus Christ also reminded us that God's people should also take care of the needs of God's servant! As church leaders, does it remind us that we must be the co-workers of those who are sent out into the mission field, spiritual support and material support are both important.

Vv. 11-14 had its eastern cultural background that was if the house/family was unworthy to receive blessing, the messenger could take it back. V.14 was also a common practice of the Jews, the dust of a gentile city was dirty, and so they had to shake it off after crossing over a gentile city. Jesus was not saying that some people were outside God's salvation, but time is short, go to those people who are willing to listen!

3. The three-fold challenges   10: 16-22

Jesus stated clearly to His disciples that there were three kinds of trials. The Jewish people would persecute them v. 17 . The state would persecute them v. 18 and even the family would stand against them v. 21. Jesus warned them, the day would come! When we go through the book of Acts, we see how the disciples were brought before the high priest, rulers, elders and teachers of the law in Jerusalem, and even to Rome. The persecution was severe, yet ''they were all filled with the Holy Spirit and spoke the word of God boldly''. Acts 4:31

Jesus Christ called His disciples, commissioned them with a clear task, stated clearly how to go forth with the mission, and also warned them of the persecution that was to come. Does it sound somehow like our situation, we received the calling from God, sent to a specific place or position to serve, but we also face with lots of challenges. Are we able to accomplish the mission for which we are called?

4. Do not be afraid!   10 : 26-31

Jesus said tenderly and firmly to His disciples, ''Do not be afraid'', three times in six verses he reminded His disciples ''do not be afraid''.

a.   Speak boldly what you have heard from Jesus, truth will prevail! 10: 26-27
Jesus said, "What I tell you in the dark, whisper in your ears, proclaim the truth!" What makes us boldly proclaim the message is that we preach what we have heard from the Bible, and we know that it is the truth! Paul said, 2 Cor. 4: 5, and he encouraged Timothy, 2 Tim. 2:15 . So, do not fear them even when trials come, we know that truth will prevail!

If we preach ourselves, if we seek personal satisfaction, if our ministry focuses on personal success, when trials come, we will protect ourselves and run away from difficulties. But if we are the faithful servant of God, we preach Jesus Christ is Lord, when trials come, we will never be afraid. So, speak boldly and speak with wisdom, if God is with us, who can against us!

b.   Know what we need to fear—the fear of God   10: 28
What the most Satan could do is killing of the body, persecution might be severe to the point of losing one's life, so, do not be afraid of them. The fear of the Lord should be always in the minds of God's servant, when the day comes, we shall see Him face to face, we want to hear God saying, good and faithful servant!

Know what we need to fear!

c.   We are precious in God's eyes   10: 29-31
In Luke 12: 6 "five sparrow sold for two pennies," here is "two sparrows sold for a penny" (NIV), that is, the fifth sparrow is free, anything you do not have to pay for usually is something unworthy. Jesus is saying, even this unworthy sparrow is so dear to God, it is precious in God's eyes.

What Jesus said is so comforting, He calls us, equips us and sends us out to face challenges and persecutions, and He also holds us in His loving and tender care, not because of any achievements we have done, even if I serve

Him in a lonely concern of the city, no one seems to care, and my service is not so successful. Jesus said, I know you, you are so precious to me, so, do not be afraid of the challenges and problems you are facing, don't let the dangers frighten you, I am the One who sent you, I will give you power, authority and wisdom. So, do not be afraid, go on!

題目：耶和華的膀臂　　　　　　　　　**The Arm of the Lord**
經文：賽 53:1-12
講員：阮莎燕宣教師
大綱：　　　　　　　　　　　　　　　**Susanna Yuen**
1. 祂-被鄙視（1-3 節）
2. 祂-替罪人受苦受死（4-9 節）
3. 祂-復活得勝（10-12 節）

　　這段經文加上 52 章 13-15 節傳統被稱為第 4 首僕人之歌，教會傳統指這位義僕是彌賽亞，預表耶穌基督。

　　這段經文是舊約其中一段好重要的經文，是最多新約直接引用或間接提及的舊約經文，大家可以參考講道筆記的列表。

　　列表除了想大家掌握聖經的內證怎樣證明耶穌基督是的彌賽亞外，亦想大家留意新約時代初期還未有新約聖經，使徒是一手拿著舊約聖經來驗證他們見證的耶穌是否彌賽亞，然後寫成新約，舊約是幫助我們掌握新約。新舊約聖經是一本書，需要整體來看。

賽 53:1　　我們所傳的有誰信呢？耶和華的膀臂向誰顯露呢？

　　耶和華用「指頭」創造天地：詩 8:3　我觀看你指頭所造的天

　　耶和華用「手」拯救以色列人出埃及：出 13:3　摩西對百姓說：「你們要記念從埃及為奴之家出來的這日，因為耶和華用大能的手將你們從這地方領出來。」

現在，耶和華用「膀臂」拯救人類：那膀臂、即經文中那個「他」，預表耶穌基督。（表：1 節）

1. 祂被鄙視（1-3 節）

這膀臂是怎樣的呢？

賽 53:2 上　　他在耶和華面前生長如嫩芽，像根出於乾地。

　　「嫩芽」、「根」指農夫想拔除的雜草/很脆弱的小樹苗，與詩篇第 1 篇那棵「栽在溪水旁，按時候結果子，葉子也不枯乾」的茂盛大樹有很大的對比。（投影片 1）

賽 53:2 下　　他無佳形美容；我們看見他的時候，也無美貌使我們羨慕他。

　　當我們以為耶穌像大衛王「容貌俊美」（撒上 16:18），祂卻「無佳形美容」、「無美貌」。

賽 53:3　他被藐視，被人厭棄；多受痛苦，常經憂患。他被藐視，好像被人掩面不看的一樣；我們也不尊重他。

　　主耶穌以嬰孩而不是君王姿態出現；祂降生馬槽而不是皇宮；祂是木匠的兒子。

當時的人怎會想這樣普通的人會是耶和華救贖的膀臂？無可能，諗都唔洗諗啦。

一位母親從沒有想過患有痙攣的兒子長大後會有甚麼成就，因為對她來說，個仔識自己照顧自己已經好好。電視廣告裡呢位母親的讀白係咁既：「我以為，他以後都要行得比人慢。最後，他跑得比人快。」這個廣告所說的人就是在傷殘人士奧運會田徑項目取得多個金牌的蘇樺偉先生。（投影片 2）

沒有人會相信一個被社會殘疾歧視、因病飽受痛苦憂患的痙攣人士，有天能成為家傳戶曉的運動員，連他母親亦不曾想過。

同樣，主耶穌也是這樣被人掩面不看、不被尊重。當世的人沒人想過他是彌賽亞，是耶和華救贖的膀臂。（表：3 節）

---

2. 祂-替罪人受苦受死（4-9 節）

賽 53:4　他誠然擔當我們的憂患，背負我們的痛苦；我們卻以為他受責罰，被神擊打苦待了。

賽 53:5　哪知他為我們的過犯受害，為我們的罪孽壓傷。因他受的刑罰，我們得平安；因他受的鞭傷，我們得醫治。

賽 53:6　我們都如羊走迷；各人偏行己路；耶和華使我們眾人的罪孽都歸在他身上。

當世的人更以為耶穌基督是因自己的過犯接受應得的責罰。將苦難、天災、疾病看為**必定**是神懲罰的想法，是一個幾普遍的謬誤，也是約伯朋友的錯誤想法。事實卻是耶穌基督替代世人受肉體的苦與心靈與天父隔絕的苦，去潔淨世人的罪。主耶穌為你為我成為了贖罪祭的祭牲。

世人就如第 6 節的羊一樣。（投影片 3）羊係短視的，掛住望草，喜歡跟住前面行，帶頭個隻行錯路，全群跟住錯，就好似以色列人的領袖和君王叛逆神，百姓亦跟住叛逆神。

主耶穌不單受苦，而且受死：

賽 53:7　他被欺壓，在受苦的時候卻不開口；他像羊羔被牽到宰殺之地，又像羊在剪毛的人手下無聲，他也是這樣不開口。

賽 53:8　因受欺壓和審判，他被奪去，至於他同世的人，誰想他受鞭打、從活人之地被剪除，是因我百姓的罪過呢？

賽 53:9　他雖然未行強暴，口中也沒有詭詐，人還使他與惡人同埋；誰知死的時候與財主同葬。

以賽亞先知繼續用羊作比喻（投影片 4），不過今次是用羊無保護自己、羊的無聲來形容主耶穌默然受死，沒有抗辯。（表：7 節）

第 8 節的「百姓」不單指以色列人，也指全人類。因為約翰壹書 2:2：「他為我們的罪作了挽回祭，不是單為我們的罪，也是為普天下人的罪。」

第 9 節（表：9 節），順理成章，主耶穌原本會同與祂同釘的囚犯同埋；但無人想到財主約瑟會不怕受牽連，竟主動向猶太巡撫彼拉多求取主耶穌的身體，安放在自己的新墳墓裡。經文看似唔知講緊乜，到新約應驗在主耶穌身上時，我們才明白經文描述緊乜嘢。

1941 年，納粹奧斯威辛集中營少了一個囚犯，司令官想餓死 10 個囚犯來殺一儆佰，以防再有人逃走。

當加法蘭聽到自己被選中時（投影片 5），他大聲喊叫：「可憐我還有妻子兒女！」當時 47 歲、因在修道院藏匿 2,000 位猶太人而遭納粹德軍逮捕的麥斯米林神父站出來，說：「我是神父，願意代替他死，他有妻有兒，我卻沒有。」集中營司令官答應神父的要求。

慢慢等餓死其間，神父帶領 9 個囚犯禱告唱詩，有士兵說囚室竟像教堂般詳和安靜。2 週後他們竟仍未死，最終改為注射毒藥致死。

幾十年後，1982 年 10 月 10 日，聖彼得廣場上有 15 萬人聚集，在羅馬教廷帶領下紀念麥斯米林神父的死，參加者包括被神父拯救的加法蘭和他的妻子兒孫。教宗形容麥斯米林神父的偉大犧牲，就像主耶穌基督：因一人頂替捨命，許多人得救。

加法蘭於 1995 年去世，享年 93 歲，訃(音負)文這樣寫：「為答謝麥斯米林神父，加法蘭一生不斷地述說他救命之恩。」

我們如果真的明白我們的生命是重價救贖回來，我們就能活出不一樣的生命，更能體會每年聖誕節述說耶穌基督救贖大愛的真正意義。

3. 祂復活得勝（10-12 節）

賽 53:10　耶和華卻定意將他壓傷，使他受痛苦。耶和華以他為贖罪祭。他必看見後裔，並且延長年日。耶和華所喜悅的事必在他手中亨通。

「他必看見後裔，並且延長年日」暗示祂從死裡復活，祂的犧牲將人由罪的奴隸變為神的子民。

11 節有許多人因認識我的義僕得稱為義；並且他要擔當他們的罪孽。

「有許多人」是指歷世歷代的信徒，包括今天的我同大家都是因信主耶穌而得稱為義。

賽 53:12 上　所以，我要使他與位大的同分，與強盛的均分擄物。

現今，主耶穌正坐在父上帝的右邊，正如啟示錄第 6 章描繪曾被殺的羔羊配受一切所造之物的敬拜。

再看 12 節下　因為他將命傾倒，以致於死；他也被列在罪犯之中。他卻擔當多人的罪，又為罪犯代求。（表：12 節）

神在第 10 節「定意」或「喜悅」主耶穌受苦，不是指天父好開心主耶穌受苦受死，而是指天父為著主耶穌能成就救贖人的旨意而喜悅。同樣，當主耶穌回望受死復活帶來的救贖，便「心滿意足」（11 節）。

話說哥哥和弟弟都熱愛繪畫，可是家境清貧，只好由弟弟先當礦工供哥哥學畫，打算四年後再由哥哥賺錢供弟弟學畫。

哥哥學畫表現優秀，衣錦榮歸，家人為他設宴慶祝。在歡宴中哥哥向弟弟敬酒，多謝弟弟對他的支持，說：「弟弟，現在輪到你了，你可以去讀書，實現夢想。」想不到弟弟只低頭垂淚，搖著頭說：「不需要……不需要啦……。」

原來4年礦工生涯已令弟弟的手關節嚴重受損，連舉杯祝賀也不行，又怎能繪畫？一切已經太遲了！

有一天，哥哥去探望弟弟，看見他正合上粗糙的雙手，為自己祈禱。哥哥深深感受弟弟的愛，便把這合起來的雙手畫了下來，成為家傳戶曉的作品「祈禱的手」（投影片6）。

這位哥哥就是德國文藝復興大師丟勒。「祈禱的手」之所以感動人不是因為我們見到那雙傷殘的手，而是因為它代表著愛與犧牲的精神；同樣，耶和華的膀臂之（投影片7）所以感動我們，令我們「心滿意足」，不是因為我們見到那雙被釘痕刺穿的手，而是因為它代表著上帝犧牲的愛。

結語

「我們所傳的有誰信呢？耶和華的膀臂向誰顯露呢？」

今天耶和華的膀臂已藉著主耶穌基督向我們親自顯明。我們對耶和華的膀臂或許有不同的期望，但我想我們真係無諗過這膀臂會是一雙有釘痕的手，更沒想過是為了我們的罪。

要信靠一雙力大無窮或者戴滿金銀寶石飾物的手可能好容易，但誰願意信靠一雙以釘痕為受苦受死記號的手呢？

請大家靜默觀看（投影片7），再一次思想這雙膀臂、這雙手，思想耶穌基督為我們所作的犧牲。

我們同心禱告：

主耶穌基督，踏入12月，當我們再次記念主祢的降生，當我們再次領主祢的餅主的杯時，求主讓我們一同思想祢這雙以釘痕為受苦受死記號的手。禱告奉受苦受死最終復活得勝的主耶穌基督的名求，阿們。

賽 53 章	新約引用/提及、應驗在耶穌基督身上的部份經文
1 節	（約 12:38）這是要應驗先知以賽亞的話，說：主啊，我們所傳的有誰信呢？主的膀臂向誰顯露呢？
3 節	（可 9:12） 耶穌說：「以利亞固然先來復興萬事；經上不是指著人子說，他要*受許多的苦被人輕慢*呢？ （路 23:11）希律和他的兵丁就*藐視*耶穌，戲弄他，給他穿上華麗衣服，把他送回彼拉多那裡去。
4 節	（太 8:17） 這是要應驗先知以賽亞的話，說：*他代替我們的軟弱，擔當我們的疾病。*
5 節	（彼前 2:24） 他被掛在木頭上，親身擔當了我們的罪，使我們既然在罪上死，就得以在義上活。*因他受的鞭傷，你們便得了醫治。*
7 節	（太 27:12-14） 他被祭司長和長老控告的時候，*什麼都不回答*。彼拉多就對他說：「他們作見證告你這麼多的事，你沒有聽見嗎？」耶穌仍不回答，*連一句話也不說*，以致巡撫甚覺希奇。 （徒 8:32-33）他所念的那段經，說：*他像羊被牽到宰殺之地，又像羊羔在剪毛的人手下無聲；他也是這樣不開口。*他卑微的時候，人不按公義審判他；誰能述說他的世代，因為他的生命從地上奪去。』 （彼前 2:23） *他被罵不還口；受害不說威嚇的話*，只將自己交託那按公義審判人的主。
9 節	（彼前 2:22）*他並沒有犯罪，口裡也沒有詭詐。* （太 27:57-60）到了晚上，有一個*財主*，名叫約瑟，是亞利馬太來的，他也是耶穌的門徒。這人去見彼拉多，求耶穌的身體；彼拉多就吩咐給他。約瑟取了身體，用乾淨細麻布裹好，*安放在自己的新墳墓裡*，就是他鑿在磐石裡的。他又把大石頭輥到墓門口，就去了。
10 節	（約 1:29）次日，約翰看見耶穌來到他那裡，就說：「*看哪，神的羔羊，除去世人罪孽的！*
11 節	（羅 5:18-19）如此說來，因一次的過犯，眾人都被定罪；照樣，因一次的義行，*眾人也就被稱義得生命了*。因一人的悖逆，眾人成為罪人；照樣，因一人的順從，*眾人也成為義了*。
12 節	（路 22:37）我告訴你們，經上寫著說：『*他被列在罪犯之中。*』這話必應驗在我身上；因為那關係我的事必然成就。」 （林後 5:21）*神使那無罪的，替我們成為罪*，好叫我們在他裡面成為神的義。 （路 23:34）*當下耶穌說：「父啊！赦免他們；因為他們所做的，他們不曉得。」*兵丁就拈鬮分他的衣服。 （來 7:25）凡靠著他進到神面前的人，他都能拯救到底；因為他是長遠活著，*替他們祈求*。

The Contributors

Mindy Acton
Minister, Grace Presbytery
Faith: Dead or Alive?

Marty Aden
Minister, Red River Presbytery
Find Your Passion

Lisa Anderson
Minister, West Tennessee Presbytery
The Space Between Us

Mary McCaskey Benedict
Minister, Murfreesboro Presbytery
Blessed Be the Tie That Binds

Elizabeth Karen Brasher
Minister, *in transitu* (Grace Presbytery to
Trinity Presbytery)
The Walk of Love

Elinor Swindle Brown
Minister, West Tennessee Presbytery
The Holy Spirit Is Coming

Whitney Brown
Candidate, Presbytery of East Tennessee
Does Prayer Make a Difference?

Jill Davis Carr
Candidate, Missouri Presbytery
Ditching Jesus

Amber Clark
Minister, Murfreesboro Presbytery
180 Degrees: Jacob

Marcia Compton
Minister, North Central Presbytery
Getting Rid of Our Excess Baggage

Lisa Cook
Minister, Nashville Presbytery
What Is Your Name?

María del Socorro Delgado
Minister, Cauca Valley Presbytery
Missionary in Guatemala
Un Llamado a Romper Paradigmas
A Call to Break Paradigms

Esperanza Díaz
Minister, Andes Presbytery
El Amor Que Transforma Vidas
The Transforming Love

Gloria Villa Diaz
Minister, Trinity Presbytery
Misses To Be Avoided

Virginia Espinoza
Minister, Choctaw Presbytery
The Hem of Jesus' Robe

Nancy J. Fuqua
Minister, Florence Presbytery
Cumberland Presbyterian Church in America
If Walls Could Talk

Michele Gentry
Minister, Andes Presbytery
Nueva Vida En Cristo
New Life in Christ

Linda Glenn
Minister, West Tennessee Presbytery
Putting our Baskets in the Water

Melissa Goodloe
Minister, West Tennessee Presbytery
God is in Control: Easter Sunday

Susan Carole Guin Groce
Candidate, West Tennessee Presbytery
Witness

Luz Dary Guerrero
Minister, Andes Presbytery
La Adoración o Servicio del Creyente, Ha de
Ser en Obediencia Respetuosa, Pues
Dios es Soberano Señor
The Responsibility of the Believer is to Be
Respectfully Obedient to God, Our
Sovereign Lord

Donna Stockberger Heflin
Minister, West Tennessee Presbytery
The Call

Luz María Heilbron
Minister, Andes Presbytery
¿Por Qué Nosotros No Podemos Dejar De
Decir Lo Que Hemos Visto Y Oído?
For We Cannot But Speak the Things Which
We Have Seen and Heard

Donna Lee Hollingshed
Candidate, Tennessee-Georgia Presbytery
Nothing is Trivial to God

Linda Smith Howell
Minister, Grace Presbytery
The Present of Christ's Presence in the
Present

Cardelia Howell-Diamond
Minister, Robert Donnell Presbytery
Ms Helen's Funeral Service

Ella Hung
Licentiate, Hong Kong Presbytery
Hero of the Era

Versey Jones
Minister, Huntsville Presbytery
Cumberland Presbyterian Church in America
Women are Always Starting "Stuff"

Abby Cole Keller
Minister, East Tennessee Presbytery
The Difference a Dollar Can Make

Mary Kathryn Kirkpatrick
Minister, Trinity Presbytery
I Am Calling You

Sherry Whitaker Ladd
Minister, Columbia Presbytery
Baptism of Christ

Jenny Lam
Candidate, Hong Kong Presbytery
God's Refination

Paula Shepard Louder
Minister, Nashville Presbytery
Step out and Follow the Leader

Tiffany Hall McClung
Minister, West Tennessee Presbytery
Wake Up!

Rhonda McGowan
Minister, Tennessee-Georgia Presbytery
The Price for the Book

Judy Madden
Minister, Red River Presbytery
Sheep or Goat? Trouble Everywhere!

Melissa Malinoski
Minister, West Tennessee Presbytery
Earthly Treasures

Theresa Martin
Minister, Tennessee-Georgia Presbytery
What Happens When Jesus Comes to Town?

Brittany P. Meeks
Minister, West Tennessee Presbytery
Bridges

Luciria Aguirre Naranjo
Minister, Cauca Valley Presbytery
Una Madre Sobreprotectora
An Overprotective Mother

Jennifer Newell
Minister, Tennessee -Georgia Presbytery
With God on the Mountain

Sharon Notley
Minister, Presbytery del Cristo
Waiting on God

Lisa Oliver
Minister, Nashville Presbytery
Not What But Who

Susan Parker
Minister, Hope Presbytery
Doubt

Lisa Peterson
Minister, West Tennessee Presbytery
Hunger Pangs

Pam Phillips-Burk
Minister, West Tennessee Presbytery
The Towel of Jesus

Patricia J. Pickett
Minister, Nashville Presbytery
Gone Fishing

Zenobia Rivera
Minister, Andes Presbytery
Padre Perdónalos
Father Forgive Them

Linda Rodden
Minister, Missouri Presbytery
Love—the Most Excellent Way

Missy Rose
Minister, West Tennessee Presbytery
In the Garden

Josefina Sanchez
Minister, East Tennessee Presbytery
Una Vida Que Da En El Blanco
A Life That Hits the Bullseye

Lisa Scott
Minister, Missouri Presbytery
Arise, Shine!

Nobuko Seki
Minister, Japan Presbytery
Invitation to the Kingdom of God

Teresa Hyams Shauf
Minister, Covenant Presbytery
Untie Me and Let Me Go

Sandra Shepherd
Minister, Robert Donnell Presbytery
The Children's Table

Terra Sisco
Minister, Covenant Presbytery
There's Just Something About This Jesus

Cassandra Thomas
Minister, Red River Presbytery
What Cha Talking About?

Micaiah Thomas
Licentiate, Grace Presbytery
Rock-Faces and Trust

Laura Narowetz Todd
Candidate, West Tennessee Presbytery
Whom Will You Serve?

Diana María Valdez
Minister, Andes Presbytery
Normas Celestiales Para no Olvidar
Heavenly Rules You Shouldn't Forget

Fran Vickers
Minister, East Tennessee Presbytery
Get Up!

Joy Warren
Minister, Murfreesboro Presbytery
Reign of the Shepherd

Gloria Washburn
Candidate, Arkansas Presbytery
The Storms in Life

Virginia Washington
Minister, Huntsville Presbytery
Cumberland Presbyterian Church in America
Let Your Light Shine in the Darkest Places

Diann White
Minister, West Tennessee Presbytery
Blinded by the Light

Eliza Yau
Licentiate, Hong Kong Presbytery
The Father's Heart

Betty Youngman
Minister, Red River Presbytery
Strangers in a Strange Land

Grace Yu
Minister, Hong Kong Presbytery
Do Not Be Afraid

Susanna Yuen

Licentiate, Hong Kong Presbytery

The Arm of the Lord

Printed in Great Britain
by Amazon

18792339R00228